The North American Fourth Edition

Cambridge Latin Course

Unit 3

REVISION TEAM

Stephanie M. Pope, Chair
Norfolk Academy, Norfolk, Virginia

Patricia E. Bell
formerly of Centennial Collegiate and Vocational Institute,
Guelph, Ontario, Canada

Stan Farrow
formerly of the David and Mary Thomson Collegiate Institute,
Scarborough, Ontario, Canada

Richard M. Popeck
Stuarts Draft High School and Stuarts Draft Middle School,
Stuarts Draft, Virginia

Anne Shaw
Lawrence High School and Lawrence Free State High School,
Lawrence, Kansas

CAMBRIDGE
UNIVERSITY PRESS

CAMBRIDGE UNIVERSITY PRESS
Cambridge, New York, Melbourne, Madrid, Cape Town, Singapore, São Paulo

Cambridge University Press
40 West 20th Street, New York, NY 10011–4211, USA

www.cambridge.org
Information on this title: www.cambridge.org/9780521894708

The *Cambridge Latin Course* is an outcome of work jointly commissioned by
the Schools Council before its closure and the Cambridge School Classics Project,
and is published under the aegis of the University of Cambridge School Classics
Project in the United Kingdom and the North American Cambridge Classics Project.

First published 1971
Second edition 1983
Third edition 1989
Fourth edition 2002
5th printing 2005

Printed in the United States of America

Library of Congress cataloging in publication data

Cambridge Latin Course. Unit 3 / revision team, Stephanie Pope ... [et al.].-- North
American 4th ed.
     p. cm.
   Includes bibliographical references and indexes.
   ISBN-13   978-0-521-89470-8 paperback
   ISBN-10   0-521-89470-0 paperback
   1. Latin language--Grammar.   I. Pope, Stephanie.
  PA2087.5.C335 2002
  478.2'421--dc21   2002067313

ISBN-13   978-0-521-78230-2 hardback
ISBN-10   0-521-78230-9 hardback
ISBN-13   978-0-521-89470-8 paperback
ISBN-10   0-521-89470-0 paperback

Layout by Newton Harris Design Partnership
Cover photographs: *front* head of Sulis Minerva, Roman Baths Museum, Bath, Ara Pacis,
Roger Dalladay; *back* Kunsthistorisches Museum, Vienna.
Maps and plans by Robert Calow / Eikon
Illustrations by Peter Kesteven, Joy Mellor, Leslie Jones, and Neil Sutton

Contents

Stage 21   Aquae Sūlis   page   1
Stage 22   dēfīxiō   27
Stage 23   haruspex   45
Stage 24   fuga   65
Stage 25   mīlitēs   85
Stage 26   Agricola   105
Stage 27   in castrīs   123
Stage 28   imperium   141
Stage 29   Rōma   165
Stage 30   Haterius   191
Stage 31   in urbe   211
Stage 32   Euphrosynē   235
Stage 33   pantomīmus   256
Stage 34   lībertus   273

Language Information   293
                About the Language   296
                Complete Vocabulary   340
Index of Cultural Topics   370
Index of Grammatical Topics   374
Time Chart   376

IN MEMORIAM

Ed Phinney

1935–1996

AQUAE SULIS

Stage 21

Britain in the Later First Century A.D.

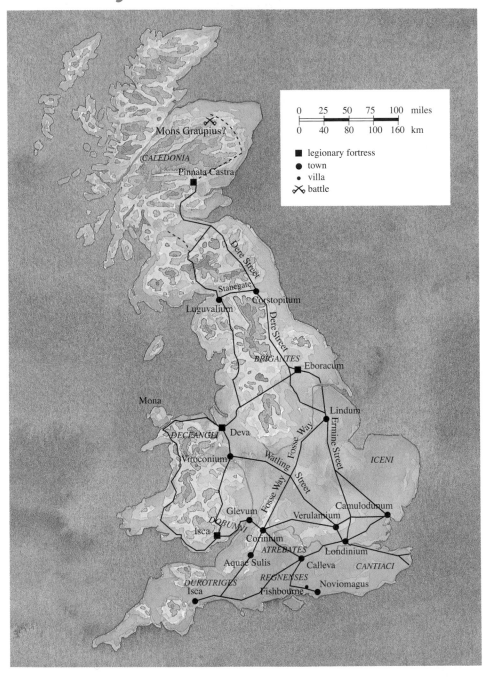

1 in oppidō Aquīs Sūlis labōrābant multī fabrī, quī thermās maximās
exstruēbant. architectus Rōmānus fabrōs īnspiciēbat.

2 faber prīmus statuam deae Sūlis sculpēbat. architectus fabrum
laudāvit, quod perītus erat et dīligenter labōrābat. faber, ab architectō
laudātus, laetissimus erat.

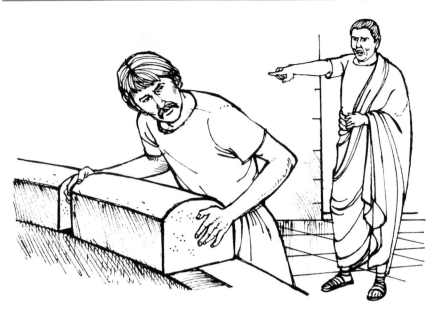

3 faber secundus mūrum circum fontem pōnēbat. architectus fabrum incitāvit, quod fessus erat et lentē labōrābat. faber, ab architectō incitātus, rem graviter ferēbat. nihil tamen dīxit, quod architectum timēbat.

4 faber tertius aquam ad balneum ē fonte sacrō portābat. architectus fabrum vituperāvit, quod ignāvus erat et minimē labōrābat. faber, ab architectō vituperātus, īnsolenter respondit.

5 architectus, ubi verba īnsolentia fabrī audīvit, servōs suōs arcessīvit. servī, ab architectō arcessītī, fabrum comprehendērunt et in balneum dēiēcērunt.

6 "linguam sordidam habēs," inquit architectus cachinnāns. "melius est tibi aquam sacram bibere."

fōns sacer

Quīntus apud Salvium manēbat per tōtam hiemem. saepe ad aulam Cogidubnī ībat, ā rēge invītātus. Quīntus eī multa dē vītā suā nārrābat, quod rēx aliquid novī audīre semper volēbat.

ubi vēr appropinquābat, Cogidubnus in morbum gravem incidit. multī medicī, ad aulam arcessītī, remedium morbī 5 quaesīvērunt. ingravēscēbat tamen morbus. rēx Quīntum et Salvium dē remediō anxius cōnsuluit.

"mī Quīnte," inquit, "tū es vir magnae prūdentiae. volō tē mihi cōnsilium dare. ad fontem sacrum īre dēbeō?"

"ubi est iste fōns?" rogāvit Quīntus. 10

"est in oppidō Aquīs Sūlis," respondit Cogidubnus. "multī aegrōtī, quī ex illō fonte aquam bibērunt, posteā convaluērunt. architectus, ā Rōmānīs missus, thermās maximās ibi exstrūxit. prope thermās stat templum deae Sūlis, ā meīs fabrīs aedificātum. ego deam saepe honōrāvī; nunc fortasse dea mē sānāre potest. 15 Salvī, tū es vir magnae calliditātis; volō tē mihi cōnsilium dare. quid facere dēbeō?"

"tū es vir sapiēns," respondit ille. "melius est tibi testāmentum facere."

fōns	*fountain, spring*
aliquid novī	*something new*
morbum: morbus	*illness*
gravem: gravis	*serious*
cōnsuluit: cōnsulere	*consult*
vir magnae prūdentiae	*a man of great prudence, a man of good sense*
cōnsilium: cōnsilium	*advice*
oppidō: oppidum	*town*
Aquīs Sūlis: Aquae Sūlis	*Aquae Sulis (Roman name of modern Bath)*
aegrōtī: aegrōtus	*invalid*
convaluērunt: convalēscere	*get better, recover*
exstrūxit: exstruere	*build*
deae Sūlis: dea Sūlis	*the goddess Sulis (a Celtic deity)*
calliditātis: calliditās	*cleverness, shrewdness*

Lūcius Marcius Memor

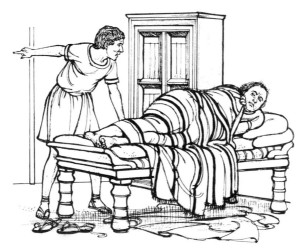

When you have read this story, answer the questions at the end.

oppidum Aquae Sūlis parvum erat, thermae maximae. prōcūrātor thermārum erat Lūcius Marcius Memor, nōtissimus haruspex, homō obēsus et ignāvus. quamquam iam tertia hōra erat, Memor in cubiculō ēbrius dormiēbat. Cephalus, haruspicis lībertus, Memorem excitāre temptābat.   5

prōcūrātor	*manager*
haruspex	*diviner (who reads the future by inspecting the livers and other organs of animals), soothsayer*
obēsus	*fat*

"domine! domine!" clāmābat.

haruspex, graviter dormiēns, nihil respondit.

"dominus nimium vīnī rūrsus bibit," sibi dīxit lībertus. "domine! surge! hōra tertia est."

Memor, ā lībertō tandem excitātus, ūnum oculum aperuit.   *10*

"fer mihi plūs vīnī!" inquit. "tum abī!"

"domine! domine! necesse est tibi surgere," inquit Cephalus.

"cūr mē vexās, Cephale?" respondit Memor. "cūr tū rem administrāre ipse nōn potes?"

"rem huius modī administrāre nōn possum," respondit   *15* lībertus. "sunt multī servī, multī fabrī, quī mandāta prōcūrātōris exspectant. tē exspectat architectus ipse, vir magnae dignitātis. tē exspectant aegrōtī. adsunt sacerdōtēs parātī. adsunt mīlitēs, ab hostibus vulnerātī. adsunt nōnnūllī mercātōrēs, quōs arcessīvistī. tū rem ipse administrāre dēbēs."   *20*

"numquam dēsinit labor," clāmāvit Memor. "quam fessus sum! cūr ad hunc populum barbarum umquam vēnī?"

Cephalus, quī rīsum cēlāre temptābat, Memorī respondit,

"haruspex callidissimus es. nōnne aegrōtīs remedia praebēre vīs? nōnne Britannīs mōrēs Rōmānōs impōnere vīs?"   *25*

"es homō magnae stultitiae," respondit Memor. "aegrōtōs floccī nōn faciō. Britannōs etiam minōris pretiī habeō. officia mea molestissima sunt. ego ad maiōrēs honōrēs ascendere velim. ego virōs potentēs colere velim. ēheu! in hāc īnsulā sunt paucī virī potentēs, paucī clārī."   *30*

"quid vīs mē facere, Memor?" inquit lībertus.

"iubeō tē omnēs dīmittere," clāmāvit Memor. "nōlī mē iterum vexāre!"

Memor, postquam haec verba dīxit, statim obdormīvit. Cephalus, ā dominō īrātō territus, invītus exiit. in thermīs   *35* multitūdinem aegrōtōrum vehementer clāmantium fabrōrumque Memorem absentem vituperantium invēnit. eōs omnēs Cephalus dīmīsit.

graviter	*heavily, soundly*	**dignitātis: dignitās**	*importance, prestige*
nimium vīnī	*too much wine*		
rūrsus	*again*	**hostibus: hostis**	*enemy*
fer!	*bring!*	**dēsinit: dēsinere**	*end, cease*
plūs vīnī	*more wine*	**labor**	*work*
huius modī	*of this kind*	**populum: populus**	*people*
mandāta:		**umquam**	*ever*
mandātum	*instruction, order*	**rīsum: rīsus**	*smile*

praebēre	*provide*	colere	*seek favor of,*
mōrēs: mōs	*custom*		*make friends*
impōnere	*impose*		*with*
stultitiae: stultitia	*stupidity*	clārī: clārus	*famous,*
etiam minōris	*I care even*		*distinguished*
pretiī habeō	*less about*	verba: verbum	*word*
officia: officium	*duty*	territus: terrēre	*frighten*
honōrēs: honor	*honor*	absentem: absēns	*absent*
velim	*I would like*		
potentēs: potēns	*powerful*		

Questions

1 **oppidum … maximae**. Why might a visitor to Aquae Sulis have been surprised on seeing the town and its baths?

2 **prōcūrātor … ignāvus** (lines 1–3). Read this sentence and look at the picture. Which two Latin adjectives describe Memor as he appears in the picture? Translate them.

3 What was the time of day at the start of this story? What was Memor's freedman trying to do?

4 What does the word **rūrsus** (line 8) suggest about Memor's habits?

5 After Memor was awake, what two orders did he give to Cephalus? What did he think Cephalus should do (lines 13–14)?

6 Why did Cephalus say **mandāta prōcūrātōris** (line 16) rather than **mandāta tua**?

7 How many different groups and individuals were waiting to see Memor, according to Cephalus (lines 16–19)?

8 What do you think made Cephalus smile (line 23)? Why did he try to hide the smile?

9 According to Cephalus (lines 24–25), what were Memor's reasons for coming to work at Bath? Did Cephalus mean this seriously?

10 According to Memor himself (lines 28–29), what were his real goals? Why had he found it hard to achieve them?

11 Which two Latin words show how Cephalus was feeling when he left Memor's bedroom?

12 What did he find when he arrived in the baths (lines 35–37)?

13 In line 32, Memor said **iubeō tē omnēs dīmittere**. Which words in the last paragraph tell you that this order was obeyed?

senātor advenit

mox tamen, Cephalus cubiculum rūrsus intrāvit Memoremque
dormientem excitāvit. Memor, simulac Cephalum vīdit, īrātus
clāmāvit,

"cūr prohibēs mē dormīre? cūr mihi nōn pārēs? stultior es quam
asinus."   5

"sed domine," inquit Cephalus, "aliquid novī nūntiāre volō.
postquam hinc discessī, mandāta, quae mihi dedistī, effēcī. ubi
tamen aegrōtōs fabrōsque dīmittēbam, senātōrem thermīs
appropinquantem cōnspexī."

Memor, valdē vexātus, "quis est ille senātor?" inquit. "unde   10
vēnit? senātōrem vidēre nōlō."

"melius est tibi hunc senātōrem vidēre," inquit Cephalus. "nam
Gāius Salvius est."

"num Gāius Salvius Līberālis?" exclāmāvit Memor. "tibi nōn
crēdō."   15

Cephalus tamen facile eī persuāsit, quod Salvius iam in āream
thermārum equitābat.

Memor perterritus statim clāmāvit,

"fer mihi togam! fer calceōs! ōrnāmenta mea ubi sunt? vocā
servōs! quam īnfēlīx sum! Salvius hūc venit, vir summae   20
auctōritātis, quem colere maximē volō."

Memor celerrimē togam calceōsque induit. Cephalus eī
ōrnāmenta trādidit, ex armāriō raptim extracta. haruspex lībertum
innocentem vituperābat, lībertus Salvium.

prohibēs: prohibēre	*prevent*
hinc	*from here*
effēcī: efficere	*carry out, accomplish*
calceōs: calceus	*shoe*
ōrnāmenta	*badges of office*
auctōritātis: auctōritās	*authority*
raptim	*hastily, quickly*

About the Language: Perfect Passive Participles

A In Stage 20, you met sentences like these, containing present participles:

> servī per vīllam contendērunt, arāneās **quaerentēs**.
> *The slaves hurried through the house, **looking for** spiders' webs.*

> puella mātrem in hortō **sedentem** vīdit.
> *The girl saw her mother **sitting** in the garden.*

B In Stage 21, you have met sentences like these:

> Memor, ā lībertō **excitātus**, īrātissimus erat.
> *Memor, **having been awakened** by the freedman, was very angry.*

> thermae, ā Rōmānīs **aedificātae**, maximae erant.
> *The baths, **having been built** by the Romans, were very big.*

The words in boldface are perfect participles.

C All participles are part verb and part adjective. **excitātus** above is from the verb **excitō, excitāre, excitāvī** and, as an adjective, describes the noun **Memor**. Like all adjectives, participles change their endings to agree with the nouns they describe. Compare the following pairs of sentences:

singular   faber, ab architectō **laudātus**, rīsit.
           *The craftsman, **having been praised** by the architect, smiled.*

plural   fabrī, ab architectō **laudātī**, rīsērunt.
           *The craftsmen, **having been praised** by the architect, smiled.*

However, these perfect participles differ in two ways from present participles:

1 While present participles indicate an action happening at the same time as another ("hurrying" and "looking for"), perfect participles indicate an action happening before another (being awakened, then being angry).

2 Present participles are active, i.e. the slaves are doing the "looking for." These new perfect participles are passive, i.e. Memor is receiving the "awakening."

D Notice that the perfect passive participle can be translated in a number of ways:

> architectus, ā Rōmānīs **missus**, thermās exstrūxit.
> *The architect, **having been sent** by the Romans, built the baths.*
> Or, in more natural English:
> *The architect **sent** by the Romans built the baths.*

> servī, ā dominō **accessītī**, statim ad tablīnum festīnāvērunt.
> *The slaves, **having been summoned** by their master, hurried at once to the study.*
> Or, in more natural English:
> ***When** the slaves **had been summoned** by their master, they hurried at once to the study.*
> *The slaves, **who had been summoned** by their master, hurried at once to the study.*

E Translate the following examples:

1 servus, ā dominō verberātus, ex oppidō fūgit.
2 nūntiī, ā rēge arcessītī, rem terribilem nārrāvērunt.
3 ancillae, ā Quīntō laudātae, laetissimae erant.
4 templa, ā fabrīs perītīs aedificāta, erant splendida.
5 mīlitēs, ab hostibus vulnerātī, thermās vīsitāre voluērunt.
6 uxor, ā marītō vexāta, ē vīllā discessit.

In each sentence, write down the perfect passive participle and the noun it describes. State whether each pair is masculine, feminine, or neuter, singular or plural.

Memor set up a statue near the altar of the goddess Sulis. The statue has disappeared, but this is the statue base with his name on it. The altar is in the background.

Memor rem suscipit

I

Salvius et Memor, in hortō sōlī ambulantēs, sermōnem gravem habent.

Salvius: Lūcī Marcī Memor, vir summae prūdentiae es. volō tē rem magnam suscipere.

Memor: tālem rem suscipere velim, sed occupātissimus sum. exspectant mē aegrōtī et sacerdōtēs. vexant mē 5 architectus et fabrī. sed quid vīs mē facere?

Salvius: Tiberius Claudius Cogidubnus, rēx Rēgnēnsium, hūc nūper advēnit. Cogidubnus, quī in morbum gravem incidit, aquam ē fonte sacrō bibere vult.

Memor: difficile est mihi tē adiuvāre, mī senātor. Cogidubnus est 10 vir octōgintā annōrum. difficile est deae Sūlī Cogidubnum sānāre.

Salvius: nōlō tē reddere Cogidubnum sānum. volō tē rem contrāriam efficere.

Memor: quid dīcis? num mortem Cogidubnī cupis? 15

Salvius: ita vērō! porrō, quamquam tam occupātus es, volō tē ipsum hanc rem efficere.

Memor: vīsne mē rēgem interficere? rem huius modī facere nōn ausim. Cogidubnus enim est vir clārissimus, ā populō Rōmānō honōrātus. 20

Salvius: es vir summae callidiātis. hanc rem efficere potes. nōn sōlum ego, sed etiam Imperātor hoc cupit. Cogidubnus enim Rōmānōs saepe vexāvit. Imperātor mihi, nōn Cogidubnō, cōnfīdit. Imperātor tibi praemium dignum prōmittit. num praemium recūsāre vīs, tibi ab 25 Imperātōre prōmissum?

tālem: tālis	*such*	**porrō**	*what's more, furthermore*
octōgintā	*eighty*	**nōn ausim**	*I wouldn't dare*
reddere	*make*	**nōn sōlum …**	
sānum: sānus	*well, healthy*	**sed etiam**	*not only … but also*
rem contrāriam:		**dignum: dignus**	*worthy, appropriate*
rēs contrāria	*the opposite*		

Memor:	quō modō id facere possum?
Salvius:	nescio. hoc tantum tibi dīcō: Imperātor mortem Cogidubnī exspectat.
Memor:	ō mē miserum! rem difficiliōrem numquam fēcī. _30_
Salvius:	vīta, mī Memor, est plēna rērum difficilium.

exit Salvius.

nescio: nescīre   *not know*

II

Memor:	Cephale! Cephale! (*lībertus, ā Memore vocātus, celeriter intrat. pōculum vīnī fert.*) cūr mihi vīnum offers? nōn vīnum, sed cōnsilium quaerō. iubeō tē mihi cōnsilium quam celerrimē dare. rēx Cogidubnus hūc venit, remedium morbī petēns. Imperātor, ā Cogidubnō _5_ saepe vexātus, iam mortem eius cupit. Imperātor ipse iubet mē hoc efficere. quam difficile est!
Cephalus:	minimē, facile est! pōculum venēnātum habeō, mihi ā latrōne Aegyptiō ōlim datum. venēnum, in pōculō cēlātum, vītam celerrimē exstinguere potest. _10_
Memor:	cōnsilium, quod mihi prōpōnis, perīculōsum est. Cogidubnō venēnum dare timeō.
Cephalus:	nihil perīculī est. rēx, quotiēns ē balneō exiit, ad fontem deae īre solet. tum necesse est servō prope fontem deae stāre et pōculum rēgī offerre. _15_
Memor:	(*dēlectātus*) cōnsilium optimum est. nūllīs tamen servīs cōnfīdere ausim. sed tibi cōnfīdō, Cephale. iubeō tē ipsum Cogidubnō pōculum offerre.
Cephalus:	ēheu! mihi rem difficillimam impōnis.
Memor:	vīta, mī Cephale, est plēna rērum difficilium. _20_

venēnātum: venēnātus	*poisoned*
datum: dare	*give*
venēnum	*poison*
exstinguere	*extinguish, destroy*
prōpōnis: prōpōnere	*propose, put forward*
nihil perīculī	*no danger*
quotiēns	*whenever*
balneō: balneum	*bath*
difficillimam: difficillimus	*very difficult*

Word Patterns: Adjectives and Adverbs

A Study the form and meaning of the following words:

laet**us**	*happy*	laet**ē**	*happily*
perīt**us**	*skillful*	perīt**ē**	*skillfully*
ferōcissim**us**	*very fierce*	ferōcissim**ē**	*very fiercely*

B As you already know, the words in the left-hand column are adjectives. The words on the right are known as **adverbs**.

C Using the pattern in Section A as a guide, complete the following table:

ADJECTIVES		ADVERBS	
cautus	*cautious*	cautē	. . . . .
superbus	*proud*	. . . . .	*proudly*
crūdēlissimus	*very cruel*	. . . . .	. . . . .

How do you recognize all the adverbs?

D Divide the following words into two lists, one of adjectives and one of adverbs. Then give the meaning of each word.

intentē, gravissimus, callidus, tacitē, ignāvus, miserrimē, dīligentissimus, firmē, saevissimē.

E Choose the correct Latin words to translate the words in boldface in the following sentences:

1 Memor was a **very hard** (dūrissimus, dūrissimē) master.
2 The merchant always treated his customers **honestly** (probus, probē).
3 The senator **very generously** (līberālissimus, līberālissimē) promised a large donation.
4 A **cautious** (cautus, cautē) man proceeds **slowly** (lentus, lentē).

Practicing the Language

A Complete each sentence with the correct case of the noun. Then translate the sentence.

1 omnēs aegrōtī (fōns, fontem, fontis) vīsitāre volēbant.
2 plūrimī servī in fundō (dominus, dominum, dominī) labōrābant.
3 "fortasse (dea, deam, deae) morbum meum sānāre potest," inquit rēx.
4 (prīncipēs, prīncipum) Cogidubnum laudāvērunt, quod līberālis et sapiēns erat.
5 mercātor, postquam (dēnāriī, dēnāriōs, dēnāriōrum) in saccō posuit, ē forō discessit.
6 senex, quī in Arabiā diū habitāverat, magnum numerum (statuae, statuās, statuārum) comparāverat.

B Translate each English sentence into Latin by selecting correctly from the pairs of Latin words.

For example: *The messenger heard the voice of the old man.*
  nūntius   vōcem   senem   audīvī
  nūntium   vōcī   senis   audīvit
Answer: nūntius vōcem senis audīvit.

1 *The priests showed the statue to the architect.*
  sacerdōtēs   statuam   architectum   ostendit
  sacerdōtibus   statuās   architectō   ostendērunt
2 *The king praised the skillful doctor.*
  rēx   medicus   perītum   laudāvit
  rēgēs   medicum   perītī   laudāvērunt
3 *A friend of the soldiers was visiting the temple.*
  amīcus   mīlitis   templum   vīsitābat
  amīcō   mīlitum   templī   vīsitāvit
4 *The shouts of the invalids had annoyed the soothsayer.*
  clāmōrem   aegrōtī   haruspicem   vexāverant
  clāmōrēs   aegrōtōrum   haruspicēs   vexāvērunt
5 *We handed over the master's money to the farmers.*
  pecūnia   dominum   agricolās   trādidimus
  pecūniam   dominī   agricolīs   trādidērunt

C Complete each sentence with the correct word from the list below and then translate.

parāvī, rapuērunt, amīcōrum, hastam, nūntius, hospitibus

1 puer, in cubiculō dormiēns, vōcēs . . . . . nōn audīvit.
2 "optimam cēnam tibi . . . . ., domine," inquit coquus.
3 senex, quī avārus erat, ... vīnum offerre nōlēbat.
4 in rīpā flūminis stābat servus, quī . . . . . in manibus tenēbat.
5 subitō latrōnēs irrūpērunt et pecūniam . . . . . .
6 . . . . ., quem rēx mīserat, epistulam in itinere āmīsit.

D Complete each sentence with the correct word from the list below, and then translate.

honōrāta, prōpositum, iussus, exstructīs, petentēs, prōmissum, cōnfīdēns, rogātus

1 Quīntus dē thermīs ā Rōmānīs . . . . . audīvit.
2 rēx Cogidubnus ā Quīntō . . . . ., "aegrōtī," inquit, "remedium . . . . . ad hās thermās veniunt."
3 fōns sacer est prope thermās. dea Sūlis ā Britannīs Rōmānīsque . . . . . multōs aegrōtōs sānat.
4 Salvius, tamen, ab Imperātōre . . . . ., Cogidubnum nōn sānum sed mortuum voluit.
5 Memor, quod praemium ā Salviō . . . . . cupīvit, cōnsilium quaesīvit.
6 cōnsilium ā Cephalō . . . . . Memorem dēlectāvit.
7 haruspex, tamen, nūllīs servīs . . . . . Cephalum rēgī venēnum dare iussit.

Aquae Sulis and its Baths

The Roman town of Aquae Sulis lies beneath the modern city of Bath in the valley of the River Avon. In a small area, enclosed by a bend in the river, mineral springs of hot water emerge from underground at the rate of over a quarter of a million gallons (a million liters) a day, and at a temperature of between 104 and 121 degrees Fahrenheit (40 and 49 degrees Celsius). The water we see today fell as rain 10,000 years ago and then percolated two miles down into the earth before rising to the surface as hot springs. These have a low mineral content, consisting mainly of calcium, magnesium, and sodium.

Long before the Romans came, the springs were regarded as a sacred place. Since these hot springs are unique in Britain, it is not surprising that the Celts worshiped the place as the home of their goddess Sulis and believed in the goddess' power to cure their illnesses through immersion in the hot spring waters.

When the Romans arrived they were quick to recognize the importance and potential of the springs as a place of pilgrimage. They erected a set of huge public baths so that visitors could enjoy their experience of the hot springs in comfort.

The largest of the three plunge baths at Bath: it is now called the Great Bath. Notice the steam rising from the naturally hot water.

Some of the objects people threw into the spring.

The Sacred Spring

The most important part of the bath complex was the sacred spring. The Romans enclosed it in a large reservoir wall of massive stone blocks, lined with lead sheets nearly one half inch (one centimeter) thick, and surrounded by a simple stone balustrade. Because of the skill of the Roman engineers, water still flows into the baths through a lead-lined channel from an opening provided in the very top of the reservoir. The hot spring with its bubbling waters overhung with clouds of steam presented an awesome and mysterious sight to the many visitors to the baths. Excavation has revealed thousands of items – coins, jewelry, and silver and pewter cups – thrown into the spring as offerings by worshipers.

Plan of the baths

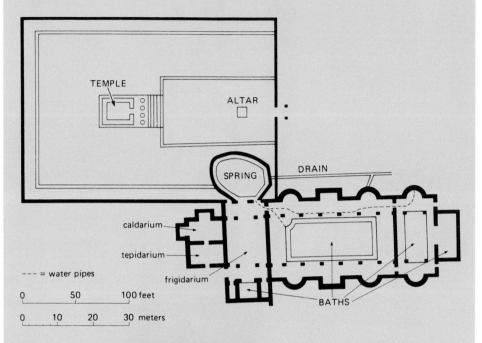

TEMPLE

ALTAR

SPRING

DRAIN

caldarium

tepidarium

--- = water pipes

frigidarium

BATHS

0   50   100 feet

0   10   20   30 meters

In addition to the pools of natural hot water, there was a set of baths heated by a hypocaust in the Roman manner, with a caldarium, tepidarium, and frigidarium. Part of the hypocaust is seen below.

Water ran from the spring to the baths through lead pipes.

The Baths

The main building was a long, rectangular structure, possibly the largest and most magnificent set of baths west of Rome at this date. It contained three main plunge baths filled with a constant supply of mineral water at a pleasant temperature. The water was carried by lead pipes which still work today. The pool nearest the spring naturally contained the hottest water, whereas the furthest pool was the coolest, since the water lost much of its heat on the way to it. There was also a suite of warm and hot baths heated by a hypocaust. The bath complex at Aquae Sulis is one of the wonders of Roman Britain. The knowledge and planning of the hydraulic engineers, who were probably assigned from the army, and the skill and quality of the plumbers' work are impressive reminders of the high standards of Roman engineering.

How the Great Bath probably looked around the time of our stories, late first century A.D.

Some people traveled long distances to Aquae Sulis, attracted by the fame of its spring and its healing powers. No doubt the heat of the water relieved conditions such as rheumatism and arthritis, but many people must have visited the spring in the hope of miraculous cures for all kinds of diseases. One elderly woman, Rusonia Aventina, came from Metz in eastern Gaul. Her tombstone shows that she died at Aquae Sulis at the age of fifty-eight, perhaps from the illness which she had hoped the spring would cure. Julius Vitalis was a soldier serving as armorer to the Twentieth Legion, based at Deva (Chester). His tombstone records that he had served for just nine years when he died at the age of twenty-nine; possibly his commanding officer had sent him to Aquae Sulis on sick leave.

The Temple

Many visitors seeing the mysterious steaming waters would feel that they were in a holy place. They would believe that a cure for their ailments depended as much on divine favor as on the medicinal powers of the water. Therefore, a temple was constructed next to the bath buildings, with the sacred spring enclosed within the temple precinct. In front of the temple stood an altar. The temple itself was built in the

This sculpture was placed over the entrance to the Temple of Sulis Minerva.

Roman style with a **cella**, a porch with Corinthian columns, and a richly decorated pediment. The life-sized gilded bronze head of Sulis Minerva (see illustration, page 60) was possibly from the cult statue in the cella. The pediment of the temple was remarkable for its roundel (see illustration, page 22) depicting a Celtic male with a long mustache, fierce brow, and long flowing hair. Below the roundel are Minerva's owl and helmet. By linking the name and attributes of Minerva to those of Sulis, the Romans encouraged the Britons to recognize the power of the Roman goddess of wisdom and the arts and to associate her with the Sulis they already knew.

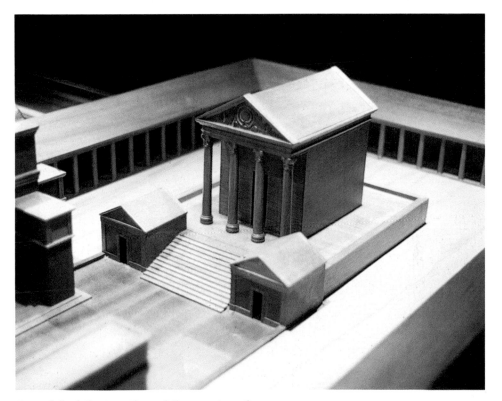

A model of the temple and the courtyard.

When the temple precinct was excavated the stone base of a statue was found. The inscription records that the statue was dedicated to the goddess Sulis by a Roman official, Lucius Marcius Memor, an **haruspex**. Nothing more is known about him, but his presence attests to the reputation of the complex at Aquae Sulis, which was famous enough to bring him there. Many such officials must have contributed to the policy of Romanization in this way.

The City

At the time of our stories (c. A.D. 83), Aquae Sulis was a small but growing community. The complex of bath buildings and temple was the most impressive feature of the town. There were probably a few other public buildings, such as a basilica for the administration of law and local government, and possibly a theater, but most of the other buildings would have been houses for those who were already living there and inns for the town's many visitors. Aquae Sulis lay within tribal territory over which Cogidubnus may have had control. In our stories we imagine that he was involved in the development of the baths.

Aquae Sulis was, of course, a tourist center as well as a place of religious pilgrimage, and one can imagine the entrance to the baths crowded with souvenir stalls, much as it is today. Visitors would buy such things as good luck charms and offerings to throw into the sacred spring with a prayer for future good health. These offerings were sometimes expensive; they included beautifully carved gemstones and items of jewelry.

Aerial view of the city of Bath (Aquae Sulis) in southwestern England. The Roman Baths can be seen just below the Abbey Church.

Word Study

A Complete the following analogies with words from the Stage 21 Vocabulary Checklist:

1 oculus : caput : : ___ : diēs
2 diēs : nox : : vacuus : ___
3 ad : ab : : ōlim : ___
4 puella : fēmina : : ___ : urbs
5 flōs : hortus : : diēs : ___
6 vir : homō : : callidus : ___

B Match the definition to the derivative of **ā, ab**.

1 abduct   **a** to abolish, cancel
2 abstract   **b** to shrink from in fear
3 abdicate   **c** the earliest known inhabitant
4 abhor   **d** to take away unlawfully
5 aborigine   **e** a washing away of, a cleansing
6 ablution   **f** theoretical, intangible
7 abscond   **g** to run away and hide
8 abrogate   **h** to give up formally

C Answer the following questions:

1 What is the difference between biennial and biannual?
2 What is the difference between confidant and confident?
3 What is the Latin root word for both efficient and effective? Explain why one word is spelled effic- and the other effec-.

Stage 21 Vocabulary Checklist

From now on, most verbs in the Checklists are listed as in the Language Information (i.e. perfect passive participles are usually included).

ā, ab (+ ABL)	by
adiuvō, adiuvāre, adiūvī	help
annus, annī, m.	year
ascendō, ascendere, ascendī	climb, rise
barbarus, barbarī, m.	barbarian
cēlō, cēlāre, cēlāvī, cēlātus	hide
circum (+ ACC)	around
cōnfīdō, cōnfīdere (+ DAT)	trust
dēiciō, dēicere, dēiēcī, dēiectus	throw down
dūrus, dūra, dūrum	harsh, hard
efficiō, efficere, effēcī, effectus	carry out, accomplish
extrahō, extrahere, extrāxī, extractus	drag out, pull out
fōns, fontis, m.	fountain, spring
gravis, gravis, grave	heavy, serious
haruspex, haruspicis, m.	diviner, soothsayer
hōra, hōrae, f.	hour
īnfēlīx, īnfēlīx, īnfēlīx, *gen.* īnfēlīcis	unlucky
iubeō, iubēre, iussī, iussus	order
morbus, morbī, m.	illness
nōnnūllī, nōnnūllae, nōnnūlla	some, several
nūper	recently
occupātus, occupāta, occupātum	busy
oppidum, oppidī, n.	town
perītus, perīta, perītum	skillful
plēnus, plēna, plēnum	full
plūs, plūris, n.	more
pretium, pretiī, n.	price
sapiēns, sapiēns, sapiēns, *gen.* sapientis	wise
suscipiō, suscipere, suscēpī, susceptus	undertake, take on
unde	from where

An earring found in the spring.

DEFIXIO

Stage 22

1 fūr thermīs cautē
   appropinquāvit. fūr, thermās
   ingressus, ad fontem sacrum
   festīnāvit.

their *bathhouse* *cautiously*
having entered *to* *fountain* *sacred*

2 fūr, prope fontem stāns,
   circumspectāvit. fūr, senem
   cōnspicātus, post columnam sē
   cēlāvit.

3 senex, amulētum aureum
   tenēns, ad fontem prōcessit.
   senex manūs ad caelum
   sustulit et deae Sūlī precēs
   adhibuit.

4 senex, deam precātus,
  amulētum in fontem iniēcit
  et exiit.

5 fūr, quī amulētum aureum
  vīderat, ad fontem revēnit.
  fūr, ad fontem regressus,
  amulētum in aquā quaesīvit.

6 fūr, amulētum adeptus, attonitus lēgit:

fūr amulētum dēiēcit et ē
thermīs perterritus fūgit.

Vilbia

translate

Vilbia et Rubria, pōcula sordida lavantēs, in culīnā tabernae
garriēbant. hae puellae erant fīliae Latrōnis. Latrō, quī tabernam
tenēbat, erat vir magnae dīligentiae sed minimae prūdentiae.
Latrō, culīnam ingressus, puellās castīgābat.

"multa sunt pōcula sordida. iubeō vōs pōcula quam celerrimē   5
lavāre. labōrāte! nōlīte garrīre! loquāciōrēs estis quam psittacī."

Latrō, haec verba locūtus, exiit.

Vilbia, tamen, quae pulchra et obstināta erat, patrem floccī nōn
faciēbat. pōcula nōn lāvit, sed Rubriae fībulam ostendit. Rubria
fībulam, quam soror tenēbat, avidē spectāvit.   10

Rubria: quam pulchra, quam pretiōsa est haec fībula, mea Vilbia!
               eam īnspicere velim. quis tibi dedit? num argentea est?

Vilbia: sānē argentea est. Modestus, mīles Rōmānus, eam mihi
               dedit.

Rubria: quālis est hic mīles? estne homō mendāx, sīcut cēterī   15
               mīlitēs Rōmānī? multī mīlitēs vulnera fingunt, quod
               perīcula bellī vītāre volunt. Modestus quoque ignāvus
               est?

Vilbia: minimē! est vir maximae virtūtis. ōlim tria mīlia hostium
               occīdit. nunc lēgātum ipsum custōdit.   20

Rubria: Herculēs alter est! ego autem tālēs fābulās saepe ex aliīs
               mīlitibus audīvī.

Vilbia: cēterī mīlitēs mendācēs sunt, Modestus probus.
               Modestus hūc vēnit aeger. Modestus, in thermās
               ingressus, aquam sacram bibit. Modestus, deam Sūlem   25
               precātus, statim convaluit.

Rubria: dissentīre nōn ausim. quō modō huic tam mīrābilī mīlitī
               occurristī?

Vilbia: simulac tabernam nostram intrāvit Modestus, eum
               statim amāvī. quantī erant lacertī eius! quanta bracchia!   30

Rubria: tibi favet fortūna, mea Vilbia. quid autem dē Bulbō dīcis,
               quem ōlim amābās? tibi perīculōsum est Bulbum
               contemnere, quod rēs magicās intellegit.

Vilbia: nōlī illam pestem commemorāre! Bulbus, saepe dē
               mātrimōniō locūtus, nihil umquam effēcit. sed   35
               Modestus, quī fortissimus et audācissimus est, mē
               cūrāre potest. Modestus nunc est suspīrium meum.

Latrōnis: Latrō	*Latro (What does his name mean?)*	**virtūtis: virtūs**	*courage*
dīligentiae: dīligentia	*industry, hard work*	**tria mīlia**	*three thousand*
		occīdit: occīdere	*kill*
minimae: minimus	*very little*	**lēgātum: lēgātus**	*commander*
		alter	*another, a second*
ingressus	*having entered*	**autem**	*but*
locūtus	*having spoken*	**precātus**	*having prayed to*
fībulam: fībula	*brooch*	**huic**	*this (dative of **hic**)*
avidē	*eagerly*	**occurristī:**	
Modestus	*Modestus (a soldier in the Second Legion. What does his name mean?)*	**occurrere**	*meet*
		quantī: quantus	*how big*
		lacertī: lacertus	*muscle*
		bracchia:	
		bracchium	*arm*
quālis?	*what sort of man?*	**Bulbō: Bulbus**	*Bulbus (His name means "onion.")*
vulnera fingunt	*pretend to be wounded, invent wounds*	**contemnere**	*reject, despise*
		mātrimōniō:	
		mātrimōnium	*marriage*
bellī: bellum	*war*	**suspīrium**	*heart-throb*

Modestus

Modestus et Strȳthiō ad tabernam Latrōnis ambulant. Strȳthiō, quamquam amīcus Modestī est, eum dērīdet.

Modestus: ubi es, Strȳthiō? iubeō tē prope mē stāre.

Strȳthiō: adsum. hercle! quam fortūnātus sum! prope virum summae virtūtis stō. tū enim fortior es quam Mārs ipse.   5

Modestus: vērum dīcis. Martem saepe in proeliō servāvī.

Strȳthiō: omnēs victōriās tuās numerāre nōn possum, sed illum elephantum commemorāre velim. tū, elephantum aggressus, bracchium eius facile frēgistī.   10

Modestus: bracchium elephantī dīcis?

Strȳthiō: ēheu! femur elephantī dīcere voluī.

Strȳthiō	*Strythio (His name means "ostrich.")*
Mārs	*Mars (Roman god of war)*
vērum: vērum	*the truth*
proeliō: proelium	*battle*
aggressus	*having attacked*
femur: femur	*thigh*

Modestus:	eum vix tetigī. habēsne cērās in quibus victōriās meās nōtāvistī?
Strȳthiō:	cērās habeō. ecce! tū, centum Brigantēs aggressus, _15_ omnēs occīdistī. centum et quīnquāgintā Calēdoniōs, trīgintā Damnoniōs, sexāgintā Votadinōs in ūnō proeliō occīdistī.
Modestus:	quanta est summa illōrum? volō tē summam facere.
Strȳthiō:	tria mīlia. _20_
Modestus:	ratiōnem rēctē reddidistī.
Strȳthiō:	nōn necesse est mihi nārrāre id quod omnēs sciunt. tū es vir summae virtūtis summīque cōnsiliī. omnēs puellae tē amant, quod tam pulcher es. illa Vilbia, heri tē cōnspicāta, statim adamāvit. multa dē tē rogāvit. _25_
Modestus:	quid dīxit?
Strȳthiō:	mē avidē rogāvit, "estne Herculēs?" "minimē! est frāter eius," respondī. tum fībulam, quam puella alia tibi dederat, Vilbiae trādidī. "Modestus, vir benignus et nōbilis," inquam, "tibi hanc fībulam grātīs dat." _30_ Vilbia, fībulam adepta, mihi respondit, "quam pulcher Modestus est! quam līberālis! velim cum eō colloquium habēre."
Modestus:	ēheu! nōnne molestae sunt puellae? mihi difficile est puellās vītāre. nimis pulcher sum. _35_
Strȳthiō:	ecce! ad tabernam Latrōnis advēnimus. fortasse inest Vilbia, quae tē tamquam deum adōrat.

tabernam intrant.

tetigī: tangere	*touch*
nōtāvistī: nōtāre	*jot down*
sexāgintā	*sixty*
summa	*total*
ratiōnem: ratiō	*sum, addition*
rēctē	*correctly*
cōnspicāta: cōnspicātus	*having caught sight of*
inquam	*I said*
grātīs	*free*
adepta: adeptus	*having received, having obtained*
colloquium: colloquium	*talk, chat*
nimis	*too*
inest: inesse	*be inside*
tamquam	*as, like*

About the Language I: Perfect Active Participles

A In Stage 21, you met sentences containing perfect passive participles:

> rēx, ā Rōmānīs **honōrātus**, semper fidēlis manēbat.
> *The king, **having been honored** by the Romans, always remained loyal.*

> puellae, ā patre **vituperātae**, nōn respondērunt.
> *The girls, **having been blamed** by their father, did not reply.*

B In Stage 22, you have met another kind of perfect participle. Study the way it is translated in the following examples:

> Vilbia, culīnam **ingressa**, sorōrī fībulam ostendit.
> *Vilbia, **having entered** the kitchen, showed the brooch to her sister.*

> senex, deam **precātus**, abiit.
> *The old man, **having prayed** to the goddess, went away.*

The words in boldface are perfect active participles. Like other participles they change their endings to agree with the nouns they describe. Compare the following pair of sentences:

singular puer, mīlitēs **cōnspicātus**, valdē timēbat.
plural   puerī, mīlitēs **cōnspicātī**, valdē timēbant.

C Translate the following examples:
1 Modestus, tabernam ingressus, Vilbiam cōnspexit.
2 Vilbia, multa verba locūta, tandem tacuit.
3 mercātōrēs, pecūniam adeptī, ad nāvēs contendērunt.
4 fēmina, deam Sūlem precāta, amulētum in fontem iniēcit.
5 ancillae, ānulum cōnspicātae, eum īnspicere volēbant.

In each sentence, pick out the perfect active participle and the noun which it describes. State whether each pair is singular or plural.

D Only a small group of verbs have a perfect active participle. Most verbs have only a perfect passive participle.

amor omnia vincit

scaena prīma

Bulbus et Gutta, amīcus eius, in tabernā Latrōnis sunt. vīnum bibunt āleamque lūdunt. Bulbus amīcō multam pecūniam dēbet.

Gutta: quam īnfēlīx es! nōn sōlum puellam, sed etiam pecūniam āmīsistī.

Bulbus: pecūniam floccī nōn faciō, sed puellam, quam maximē   5
amō, āmittere nōlō.

Gutta: quō modō eam retinēre potes? mīles Rōmānus, vir summae virtūtis, eam petit. heus! Venerem iactāvī! caupō! iubeō tē plūs vīnī ferre.

Bulbus: mīles, quī eam dēcēpit, homō mendāx, prāvus, ignāvus   10
est. Vilbia, ab eō dēcepta, nunc mē contemnit. eam saepe monuī, "nōlī mīlitibus crēdere, praesertim Rōmānīs." Vilbia tamen, hunc Modestum cōnspicāta, statim eum amāvit.

Gutta: puellīs nōn tūtum est per viās huius oppidī īre. tanta est   15
arrogantia hōrum mīlitum. hercle! tū etiam īnfēlīcior es. canem iterum iactāvistī. alium dēnārium mihi dēbēs.

Bulbus: dēnārium libenter trādō, nōn puellam. ōdī istum mīlitem. Modestus tamen puellam retinēre nōn potest, quod auxilium ā deā petīvī. thermās ingressus, tabulam   20
in fontem sacrum iniēcī. dīra imprecātiō, in tabulā scrīpta, iam in fonte deae iacet. (*intrant Modestus et Strȳthiō.*) exitium Modestī laetus exspectō. nihil mihi obstāre potest.

Gutta: hercle! īnfēlīcissimus es. ecce! nōbīs appropinquat ipse   25
Modestus. necesse est mihi quam celerrimē exīre.

exit currēns.

amor	*love*	**arrogantia**	*arrogance, excessive pride*
omnia: omnia	*all, everything*		
scaena	*scene*	**canem: canis**	*dog (lowest throw at dice)*
Gutta: Gutta	*Gutta (His name means "drop" or "droplet.")*		
		ōdī	*I hate*
eius	*his*	**tabulam: tabula**	*tablet, writing-tablet*
āleam … lūdunt	*are playing dice*		
Venerem: Venus	*Venus (highest throw at dice)*	**imprecātiō**	*curse*
		scrīpta: scrībere	*write*
iactāvī: iactāre	*throw*	**exitium: exitium**	*ruin, destruction*
praesertim	*especially*		

scaena secunda

The Romans were very fond of games involving dice, both the kind we are used to (left), and more novel varieties like the little man (right), who can fall six ways up; here he scores 2. The larger of the cubic dice has a hollow in it, possibly for loading the dice.

Modestus īrātus Bulbum vituperat, quod verba eius audīvit.

Modestus: quid dīcēbās, homuncule? exitium meum exspectās? asine! tū, quod mīlitem Rōmānum vituperavistī, in magnō perīculō es. mihi facile est tē, tamquam hostem, dīlaniāre. Strȳthiō! tē iubeō hanc pestem 5 verberāre. postquam eum verberāvistī, ē tabernā ēice!

Strȳthiō invītus Bulbum verberāre incipit. Bulbus, fortiter sē dēfendēns, vīnum in caput Strȳthiōnis fundit. Modestus Bulbum, simulac tergum vertit, ferōciter pulsat. Bulbus exanimātus prōcumbit. Vilbia clāmōrēs audit. ingressa, Bulbum humī iacentem videt et Modestum mollīre 10 incipit.

Vilbia: dēsine, mī Modeste. iste Bulbus, ā tē verberātus, iterum mē vexāre nōn potest. tū es leō, iste rīdiculus mūs. volō tē clēmentem esse et Bulbō parcere. placetne tibi? 15

Modestus: mihi placet. victōribus decōrum est victīs parcere. tē, nōn istum, quaerō.

Vilbia: ō Modeste, quam laeta sum! cūr mē ex omnibus puellīs ēlēgistī?

Modestus: necesse est nōbīs in locō sēcrētō noctū convenīre. 20

Vilbia: id facere nōn ausim. pater mē sōlam exīre nōn vult. ubi est hic locus?

dīlaniāre	*tear to pieces*	**parcere**	*spare*
ēice: ēicere	*throw out*	**victīs: victī**	*the conquered*
humī	*on the ground*	**sēcrētō: sēcrētus**	*secret*
mollīre	*soothe*	**noctū**	*by night*
clēmentem: clēmēns	*merciful*		

Modestus:	prope fontem deae Sūlis. nōnne tibi persuādēre possum?
Vilbia:	mihi difficile est iussa patris neglegere, sed tibi resistere nōn possum.
Modestus:	dā mihi ōsculum.
Vilbia:	ēheu! ō suspīrium meum! mihi necesse est ad culīnam redīre, tibi noctem exspectāre.

25

exeunt. Bulbus, quī magnam partem huius colloquiī audīvit, surgit. 30
quam celerrimē ēgressus, Guttam petit, cui cōnsilium callidum prōpōnit.

iussa: iussum	*order, instruction*
neglegere	*neglect*
ēgressus	*having gone out*
cui	*to whom (dative of* **quī***)*

scaena tertia

per silentium noctis thermās intrant Bulbus et Gutta. prope fontem
sacrum sē cēlant. Bulbus Guttae stolam et pallium, quod sēcum tulit,
ostendit.

Bulbus:	Gutta, volō tē haec vestīmenta induere. volō tē persōnam Vilbiae agere. nōbīs necesse est dēcipere Modestum, quem brevī exspectō.
Gutta:	vah! virō nōn decōrum est stolam gerere. praetereā barbam habeō.
Bulbus:	id minimī mōmentī est, quod in tenebrīs sumus. nōnne tibi persuādēre possum? ecce! decem dēnāriōs tibi dō. nunc tacē! indue stolam palliumque! stā prope fontem deae! ubi Modestus fontī appropinquat, dīc eī verba suāvissima!

5

10

Gutta, postquam stolam invītus induit, prope fontem stat. Modestus,
sōlus thermās ingressus, fontī appropinquat. 15

Modestus:	Vilbia, mea Vilbia! Modestus, fortissimus mīlitum, adest.
Gutta:	ō dēliciae meae! venī ad mē.
Modestus:	quam rauca est vōx tua! num lacrimās, quod tardus adveniō?

20

pallium: pallium	*cloak*	**vah!**	*ugh!*
vestīmenta: vestīmenta	*clothes*	**praetereā**	*besides*
persōnam Vilbiae agere	*play the part of Vilbia*	**mōmentī: mōmentum**	*importance*
brevī	*in a short time*	**tenebrīs: tenebrae**	*darkness*

| Gutta: | ita vērō! tam sollicita eram. |
| Modestus: | lacrimās tuās siccāre possum. (*Modestus ad Guttam advenit.*) dī immortālēs! Vilbia! barbam habēs? quid tibi accidit? ō! |

tum Bulbus Modestum in fontem dēicit. Vilbia, thermās ingressa, ubi 25
clāmōrēs audīvit, prope iānuam perterrita manet.

Modestus:	pereō! pereō! parce! parce!
Bulbus:	furcifer! Vilbiam meam, quam valdē amō, auferre audēs? nunc mihi facile est tē interficere.
Modestus:	reddō tibi Vilbiam. nōn amō Vilbiam. eam ā tē auferre 30 nōn ausim. nōlī mē innocentem interficere. Vilbiam floccī nōn faciō.

Vilbia, simulatque haec audīvit, īrāta fontī appropinquat. Modestum vituperāre incipit.

Vilbia:	mē floccī nōn facis? ō hominem ignāvum! ego ipsa tē 35 dīlaniāre velim.
Bulbus:	mea Vilbia, victōribus decōrum est victīs parcere.
Vilbia:	mī Bulbe, dēliciae meae, miserrima sum! longē errāvī.
Bulbus:	nōlī lacrimāre! ego tē cūrāre possum.
Vilbia:	ō Bulbe! ō suspīrium meum! 40

Bulbus et Vilbia domum redeunt. Gutta stolam palliumque exuit.
dēnāriōs laetē numerat. Modestus ē fonte sē extrahit et madidus abit.

siccāre	*dry*
auferre	*take away, steal*
longē errāvī: longē errāre	*make a big mistake*
exuit: exuere	*take off*

The sacred spring as it is today.

About the Language II: More About the Genitive

A In Unit 2 you met examples of the genitive case like these:

> marītus **Galatēae** erat Aristō.
> *Galatea's husband was Aristo.*

> prō templō **Caesaris** stat āra.
> *In front of the temple of Caesar stands an altar.*

B In recent stories you have met another use of the genitive. Study the following examples:

satis pecūniae	*enough money*, literally, *enough of money*
nimium vīnī	*too much wine*
plūs sanguinis	*more blood*

Each phrase is made up of two words:

1 A word like **plūs** or **nimium** indicating an amount or quantity.
2 A noun in the genitive case.

C Further examples:

1 nimium pecūniae   3 plūs labōris
2 nihil perīculī   4 multum cibī

D You have also met examples like these:

> homō ingeniī prāvī   fēmina magnae dignitātis
> *a man of evil character*   *a woman of great prestige*

In both examples, a noun (**homō**, **fēmina**) is described by another noun and an adjective both in the genitive case. Such phrases can be translated in different ways. For example:

> puella magnae prūdentiae   vir summae virtūtis
> *a girl of great sense*   *a man of the utmost courage*
> Or, in more natural English: Or, in more natural English:
> *a very sensible girl*   *a very courageous man*

E Further examples:

1 homō minimae prūdentiae   4 fābula huius modī
2 iuvenis vīgintī annōrum   5 puella maximae calliditātis
3 fēmina magnae sapientiae   6 vir optimī ingeniī

Word Patterns: More Adjectives and Adverbs

In Stage 21 you met the following pattern:

A ADJECTIVES   ADVERBS

 laetus *happy* laetē *happily*
 perītus *skillful* perītē *skillfully*

How do you recognize the adverbs? To what declension do the adjectives belong?

B Study another common pattern of adjectives and adverbs:

 ADJECTIVES   ADVERBS
 brevis *short* **breviter** *shortly*
 ferōx *fierce* **ferōciter** *fiercely*

How do you recognize the adverbs? To what declension do the adjectives belong?

C Using this pattern as a guide, complete the following table:

 suāvis *sweet* suāviter .....
 neglegēns ..... neglegenter *carelessly*
 audāx ..... audācter .....

D Divide the following words into two lists, one of adjectives and one of adverbs. Then give the meaning of each word:

 fortis, fidēliter, īnsolēns, fortiter, sapienter, īnsolenter, fidēlis, sapiēns.

E Choose the correct Latin word to translate the word in boldface in the following sentences:
1 Quintus was a **sensible** (prūdēns, prūdenter) young man.
2 Salvius rode **quickly** (celer, celeriter) into the courtyard.
3 The soldier was **happy** (laetus, laetē) because the goddess had cured him.
4 Vilbia worked **diligently** (dīligēns, dīligenter) only when her father was watching.
5 Salvius sometimes acted very **cruelly** (crūdēlissimus, crūdēlissimē) to his slaves.

Practicing the Language

A Complete each sentence with the correct form of the noun. Then translate the sentence.

1 Modestus per viās (oppidī, oppidō) ambulābat, puellās quaerēns.
2 Gutta, vir benignus, auxilium (amīcī, amīcō) saepe dabat.
3 Rubria, quae in tabernā labōrābat, (iuvenis, iuvenī) vīnum obtulit.
4 prope vīllam (haruspicis, haruspicī), turba ingēns conveniēbat.
5 tabernārius (ancillārum, ancillīs) multās rēs pretiōsās ostendit.
6 clāmōrēs (fabrōrum, fabrīs) architectum vexāvērunt.
7 centuriō gladiōs hastāsque (mīlitum, mīlitibus) īnspicere coepit.
8 caupō vīnum pessimum (hospitum, hospitibus) offerēbat.

B Complete each sentence with the correct form of the adjective. Then translate the sentence.

1 subitō ancilla (perterrita, perterritae) in ātrium irrūpit.
2 rēx, postquam hoc audīvit, fabrōs (fessum, fessōs) dīmīsit.
3 senātor quī aderat iuvenēs (callidum, callidōs) laudāvit.
4 omnēs cīvēs nāvem (sacram, sacrās) spectābant.
5 ubi in magnō perīculō eram, amīcus (fidēlis, fidēlēs) mē servāvit.
6 "in illā īnsulā," inquit senex, "habitant multī virī (ferōx, ferōcēs)."
7 fēmina (fortis, fortem, fortēs), quae in vīllā manēbat, fūrem superāvit.
8 cīvēs in viīs oppidī (multus, multī, multōs) mīlitēs vidēre solēbant.

C Look back over **scaena prīma** and **scaena secunda** of **amor omnia vincit**, and make three lists: one for present participles (three examples), one for perfect passive participles (four examples), and one for perfect active participles (four examples). Translate each participle.

Magic, Curses, and Superstitions

Many thousands of offerings have been recovered from the spring at Aquae Sulis. Some of the finds indicate that there were people anxious to use the powers of the gods for unpleasant purposes, believing it was possible to "dedicate" an enemy to the gods of the Underworld.

When Roman religious sites are excavated, archaeologists sometimes find small sheets of lead or pewter inscribed with curses. These are known as **dēfīxiōnēs**, or curse tablets, which call for the punishment of an enemy. Over three hundred have been found in Britain alone.

The method of putting a curse on someone followed a general formula. The name of the offender, if known, was written on a tablet, with details of the crime. The offender was then dedicated to a god, who was called on to punish the offender, usually in a very unpleasant way. If the offender was unknown, the tablet would provide a list of suspects. The completed tablet was rolled or folded up and then fastened to a tomb with a long nail or thrown into a well or spring.

About ninety curse tablets were found in the sacred spring at Aquae Sulis. One such defixio reads:

> **Basilia gives to the Temple of Mars her silver ring, that so long as someone, slave or free, keeps silent or knows anything about it, he may be accursed in his blood and eyes and every limb, or even have all his intestines entirely eaten away, if he has stolen the ring or been an accomplice.**

A jealous lover wrote one of the most famous tablets of Aquae Sulis, a tablet that inspired the stories about Vilbia and Modestus in this Stage:

Many curses were written backwards to increase the mystery of the process. Magical and apparently meaningless words like **bescu**, **berebescu**, **bazagra** were sometimes added to increase the effect, rather like the use of "abracadabra" in spells. Sometimes we find a figure roughly drawn on the tablet, as in the illustration below. It depicts a bearded demon, carrying an urn and a torch, which were symbols of death. The boat in which he stands may represent the boat of Charon, the ferryman of the Underworld, who took the souls of the dead across the River Styx.

The wording of the curse can be very simple, just "I dedicate" followed by the intended victim's name. But sometimes it can be ferociously eloquent, as in the following example:

> **May burning fever seize all her limbs, kill her soul and her heart. O Gods of the Underworld, break and smash her bones, choke her, let her body be twisted and shattered – phrix, phrox.**

It may seem strange that religion should be used to bring harm to people in this very direct and spiteful way, but the Romans tended to see their gods as possible allies in the struggles of life. When they wished to injure an enemy, they thought it natural and proper to seek the gods' powerful help.

Some Romans also considered it natural that the gods might give ōmina, omens or warnings, of impending danger and that proper action could avert a misfortune. It was safer to stay at home after stumbling on the threshold, hearing the hooting of an owl, or having a bad dream. Many people would take care to marry only on certain days and in certain months, to cross the threshold with the right foot, and to wear an amulet to ward off the evil eye. Carefully observing the signs sent by the gods and taking appropriate precautions could turn aside some of the perils of life.

Word Study

A Match the following Latin words to their antonyms:

1 minimus c   **a** cōnsentiō
2 hostis d   **b** terra
3 caelum b   **c** maximus
4 tūtus e   **d** amīcus
5 dissentiō a **e** perīculōsus

B Match the appropriate definition to each word.

1 deception c   **a** the act of putting into words
2 quantification f **b** the act of warning
3 verbalization a **c** the act of deceiving
4 imprecation d   **d** the act of cursing
5 retardation e   **e** the act of slowing down
6 admonition b   **f** the act of counting

C Give the Latin root for each of the following English words. Give a meaning for the English words.

1 parsimonious   5 dire   9 hostility
2 minimize   6 ingress   10 adept
3 inevitability   7 tutelary
4 amorous   8 celestial

D From the following list of verbs, give one English derivative from the first principal part and one English derivative from the last principal part given. Write the meaning for each derivative.

e.g. efficere: efficient – producing results at minimum cost
              effective – producing desired results

dissentīre   ēligere   incipere

Stage 22 Vocabulary Checklist

adeptus, adepta, adeptum	having received, having obtained
amor, amōris, m.	love
aureus, aurea, aureum	golden, made of gold
avidē	eagerly
caelum, caelī, n.	sky
dēcipiō, dēcipere, dēcēpī, dēceptus	deceive, trick
dīrus, dīra, dīrum	dreadful, awful
dissentiō, dissentīre, dissēnsī	disagree
ēligō, ēligere, ēlēgī, ēlēctus	choose
exitium, exitiī, n.	ruin, destruction
fundō, fundere, fūdī, fūsus	pour
hostis, hostis, m.	enemy
iactō, iactāre, iactāvī, iactātus	throw
incipiō, incipere, incēpī, inceptus	begin
ingressus, ingressa, ingressum	having entered
iniciō, inicere, iniēcī, iniectus	throw in
lacrima, lacrimae, f.	tear
minimus, minima, minimum	very little, least
molestus, molesta, molestum	troublesome
moneō, monēre, monuī, monitus	warn, advise
parcō, parcere, pepercī (+ DAT)	spare
precātus, precāta, precātum	having prayed (to)
prūdentia, prūdentiae, f.	prudence, good sense
quantus, quanta, quantum	how big
quō modō?	how?
tardus, tarda, tardum	late
tūtus, tūta, tūtum	safe
verbum, verbī, n.	word
virtūs, virtūtis, f.	courage
vītō, vītāre, vītāvī, vītātus	avoid

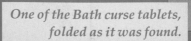

One of the Bath curse tablets, folded as it was found.

HARUSPEX

Stage 23

in thermīs

I

prope thermās erat templum, ā fabrīs Rōmānīs aedificātum. rēx
Cogidubnus cum multīs prīncipibus servīsque prō templō
sedēbat. Quīntus prope sellam rēgis stābat. rēgem prīncipēsque
manus armātōrum custōdiēbat. prō templō erat āra ingēns, quam
omnēs aspiciēbant. Memor, togam praetextam gerēns, prope āram   5
stābat.

　　duo sacerdōtēs, agnam nigram dūcentēs, ad āram lentē
prōcessērunt. postquam rēx signum dedit, ūnus sacerdōs agnam
sacrificāvit. deinde Memor, quī iam tremēbat sūdābatque, alterī
sacerdōtī,   10
　　"iubeō tē," inquit, "ōmina īnspicere. dīc mihi: quid vidēs?"
sacerdōs, postquam iecur agnae īnspexit, anxius,
　　"iecur est līvidum," inquit. "nōnne hoc mortem significat?
nōnne mortem virī clārī significat?"
　　Memor, quī perterritus pallēscēbat, sacerdōtī respondit,   15
　　"minimē. dea Sūlis, quae precēs aegrōtōrum audīre solet, nōbīs
ōmina optima mīsit."
　　haec verba locūtus, ad Cogidubnum sē vertit et clāmāvit,
　　"ōmina sunt optima! ōmina tibi remedium mīrābile significant,
quod dea Sūlis Minerva tibi favet."   20
　　tum rēgem ac prīncipēs Memor in apodytērium dūxit.

manus armātōrum	*a band of soldiers*	iecur	*liver*
aspiciēbant:		līvidum: līvidus	*lead-colored*
aspicere	*look towards*	significat:	
praetextam:		significāre	*mean, indicate*
praetextus	*with a purple border*	pallēscēbat:	
agnam: agna	*lamb*	pallēscere	*grow pale*
ōmina: ōmen	*omen*	ac	*and*

The altar at Bath. The base and the sculptured corner blocks are original; the rest of the Roman stone must have been re-used elsewhere during the Middle Ages. At the top left of the photograph can be seen the stone statue base which is inscribed with Memor's name.

II

deinde omnēs in eam partem thermārum intrāvērunt, ubi balneum maximum erat. Quīntus, prīncipēs secūtus, circumspectāvit et attonitus,

"hae thermae," inquit, "maiōrēs sunt quam thermae Pompēiānae!"   5

servī magnā cum difficultāte Cogidubnum in balneum dēmittere coepērunt. maximus clāmor erat. rēx prīncipibus mandāta dabat. prīncipēs lībertōs suōs vituperābant, lībertī servōs.

tandem rēx, ē balneō ēgressus, vestīmenta, quae servī tulerant, induit. tum omnēs fontī sacrō appropinquāvērunt.   10

Cephalus, quī anxius tremēbat, prope fontem stābat, pōculum ōrnātissimum tenēns.

"domine," inquit, "pōculum aquae sacrae tibi offerō. aqua est amāra, sed remedium potentissimum."

secūtus	*having followed*	**dēmittere**	*let down, lower*
difficultāte: difficultās	*difficulty*	**amāra: amārus**	*bitter*

haec verba locūtus, rēgī pōculum obtulit. rēx pōculum ad labra 15
sustulit.

subitō Quīntus, pōculum cōnspicātus, manum rēgis prēnsāvit
et clāmāvit,

"nōlī bibere! hoc est pōculum venēnātum. pōculum huius modī
in urbe Alexandrīā vīdī." 20

"longē errās," respondit rēx. "nēmō mihi nocēre vult. nēmō
umquam mortem mihi parāre temptāvit."

"rēx summae virtūtis es," respondit Quīntus. "sed, quamquam
nūllum perīculum timēs, tūtius est tibi vērum scīre. pōculum
īnspicere velim. dā mihi!" 25

tum pōculum Quīntus īnspicere coepit. Cephalus tamen
pōculum ē manibus Quīntī rapere temptābat. maxima pars
spectātōrum stābat immōta. sed Dumnorix, prīnceps Rēgnēnsium,
saeviēbat tamquam leō furēns. pōculum rapuit et Cephalō obtulit.

"facile est nōbīs vērum cognōscere," clāmāvit. "iubeō tē 30
pōculum haurīre. num aquam bibere timēs?"

Cephalus pōculum haurīre nōluit, et ad genua rēgis prōcubuit.
rēx immōtus stābat. cēterī prīncipēs lībertum frūstrā resistentem
prēnsāvērunt. Cephalus, ā prīncipibus coāctus, venēnum hausit.
deinde, vehementer tremēns, gemitum ingentem dedit et mortuus 35
prōcubuit.

| labra: labrum | *lip* | genua: genū | *knee* |
| prēnsāvit: prēnsāre | *take hold of, clutch* | coāctus: cōgere | *force, compel* |

About the Language I: More About Participles

A In Stage 20 you met the present participle:

lībertus dominum **intrantem** vīdit.
The freedman saw his master entering.

B In Stage 21 you met the perfect passive participle:

fabrī, ab architectō **laudātī**, dīligenter labōrābant.
The craftsmen, (having been) praised by the architect, were working hard.

C In Stage 22 you met the perfect active participle:

Vilbia, thermās **ingressa**, clāmōrem audīvit.
Vilbia, having entered the baths, heard a noise.

D Translate the following examples:

1 rēx, in mediā turbā sedēns, prīncipēs salūtāvit.
2 lībertus, in cubiculum regressus, Memorem excitāre temptāvit.
3 Vilbia fībulam, ā Modestō datam, Rubriae ostendit.
4 sacerdōtēs, deam precātī, agnam sacrificāvērunt.
5 templum, ā Rōmānīs aedificātum, prope fontem sacrum erat.
6 sorōrēs, in tabernā labōrantēs, mīlitem cōnspexērunt.
7 fūr rēs, in fontem iniectās, quaesīvit.
8 nōnnūllae ancillae, ā dominā incitātae, cubiculum parāvērunt.

Pick out the noun and participle pair in each sentence and state whether the participle is present, perfect passive, or perfect active.

E Give the case, number, and gender of each noun and participle pair in Section D.

epistula Cephalī

postquam Cephalus periit, servus eius rēgī epistulam trādidit, ā
Cephalō ipsō scrīptam:

"rēx Cogidubne, in maximō perīculō es. Memor īnsānit. mortem
tuam cupit. iussit mē rem efficere. invītus Memorī pāruī. fortasse
mihi nōn crēdis. sed tōtam rem tibi nārrāre velim.   *5*

"ubi tū ad hās thermās advēnistī, remedium quaerēns, Memor
mē ad vīllam suam quam celerrimē arcessīvit. vīllam ingressus,
Memorem perterritum invēnī. attonitus eram. numquam
Memorem adeō perterritum vīderam. Memor mihi,

"'Imperātor mortem Cogidubnī cupit,' inquit. 'iubeō tē hanc   *10*
rem administrāre. iubeō tē venēnum parāre. tibi necesse est eum
interficere. Cogidubnus enim est homō ingeniī prāvī.'

"Memorī respondī,

"'longē errās. Cogidubnus est vir ingeniī optimī. tālem rem
facere nōlō.'   *15*

"Memor īrātus,

"'sceleste!' inquit, 'lībertus meus es, et servus meus erās. tē
līberāvī et tibi multam pecūniam dedī. mandāta mea facere dēbēs.
cūr mihi obstās?'

"rēx Cogidubne, diū recūsāvī obstinātus. diū beneficia tua   *20*
commemorāvī. Memor tamen custōdem arcessīvit, quī mē
verberāvit. ā custōde paene interfectus, Memorī tandem cessī.

"ad casam meam regressus, venēnum invītus parāvī. scrīpsī
tamen hanc epistulam et servō fidēlī trādidī. iussī servum tibi
epistulam trādere. veniam petō, quamquam facinus scelestum   *25*
parāvī. Memor nocēns est. Memor coēgit mē hanc rem efficere.
Memorem, nōn mē, pūnīre dēbēs."

īnsānit: īnsānīre	*be crazy, be insane*
beneficia: beneficium	*act of kindness, favor*
facinus: facinus	*crime*
coēgit: cōgere	*force, compel*

About the Language II: Comparison of Adverbs

A Study the following sentences:

1 Loquāx vōcem suāvem habet; **suāviter** cantāre potest.
*Loquax has a sweet voice; he can sing **sweetly**.*
2 Melissa vōcem suāviōrem habet; **suāvius** cantāre potest.
*Melissa has a sweeter voice; she can sing **more sweetly**.*
3 Helena vōcem suāvissimam habet; **suāvissimē** cantāre potest.
*Helena has a very sweet voice; she can sing **very sweetly**.*

The words in boldface above are adverbs. An adverb describes a verb, adjective, or other adverb.

Study the following patterns:

Comparative

ADJECTIVE: suāvior, suāvior, suāvius   ADVERB: suāvius
tardior, tardior, tardius   tardius
celerior, celerior, celerius   celerius

Superlative

ADJECTIVE: suāvissimus   ADVERB: suāvissimē
tardissimus   tardissimē
celerrimus   celerrimē

B Study the following sentences:

1 balneum Pompēiānum erat magnum; Quīntum **magnopere** dēlectāvit.
*The bath at Pompeii was large; it pleased Quintus **a lot**.*
2 balneum Alexandrīnum erat maius; Quīntum **magis** dēlectāvit.
*The bath at Alexandria was larger; it pleased Quintus **more**.*
3 balneum Britannicum erat maximum; Quīntum **maximē** dēlectāvit.
*The bath in Britain was the largest; it pleased Quintus **the most**.*

Some adverbs, like their corresponding adjectives, are compared irregularly.

POSITIVE	COMPARATIVE	SUPERLATIVE
bene	melius	optimē
well	*better*	*best, very well*
male	peius	pessimē
badly	*worse*	*worst, very badly*
magnopere	magis	maximē
greatly	*more*	*most, very greatly*
paulum	minus	minimē
little	*less*	*least, very little*
multum	plūs	plūrimum
much	*more*	*most, very much*

For the adjectives corresponding to these adverbs, see page 301 in the Language Information.

C Notice a special meaning for the comparative:

> medicus **tardius** advēnit.
> *The doctor arrived **too late** (i.e. later than necessary).*

D Notice the idiomatic use of the superlative with **quam**:

> medicus **quam celerrimē** advēnit.
> *The doctor arrived **as quickly as possible**.*

E Translate the following examples:

1 āthlēta Cantiacus celerius quam cēterī cucurrit.
2 fūrēs senem facillimē superāvērunt.
3 ubi hoc audīvī, magis timēbam.
4 mīlitēs, quam fortissimē pugnāte!
5 medicus tē melius quam astrologus sānāre potest.
6 illī iuvenēs fīliam nostram avidius spectant.
7 canis dominum mortuum fidēliter custōdiēbat.
8 eī, quī male vīxērunt, male pereunt.

Britannia perdomita

When you have read this story, answer the questions at the end.

Salvius cum Memore anxius colloquium habet. servus ingressus ad Memorem currit.

servus: domine, rēx Cogidubnus hūc venit. rēx togam praetextam ōrnāmentaque gerit. magnum numerum armātōrum sēcum dūcit.   *5*

Memor: rēx armātōs hūc dūcit? togam praetextam gerit?

Salvius: Cogidubnus, nōs suspicātus, ultiōnem petit. Memor, tibi necesse est mē adiuvāre. nōs enim Rōmānī sumus, Cogidubnus barbarus.

intrat Cogidubnus. in manibus epistulam tenet, ā Cephalō scrīptam.   *10*

Cogidubnus: Memor, tū illās īnsidiās parāvistī. tū iussistī Cephalum venēnum comparāre et mē necāre. sed Cephalus, lībertus tuus, mihi omnia patefēcit.

Memor: Cogidubne, id quod dīcis, absurdum est. mortuus est Cephalus.   *15*

Cogidubnus: Cephalus homō magnae prūdentiae erat. tibi nōn crēdidit. invītus tibi pāruit. simulac mandāta ista dedistī, scrīpsit Cephalus epistulam in quā omnia patefēcit. servus, ā Cephalō missus, epistulam mihi tulit.   *20*

Memor: epistula falsa est, servus mendācissimus.

Cogidubnus: tū, nōn servus, es mendāx. servus enim, multa tormenta passus, in eādem sententiā mānsit.

Salvius: Cogidubne, cūr armātōs hūc dūxistī?

Cogidubnus: Memorem ē cūrā thermārum iam dēmōvī.   *25*

Memor: quid dīcis? tū mē dēmōvistī? ego innocēns sum. Salv …

perdomita: perdomitus	*conquered*
armātōrum: armātī	*armed men*
suspicātus	*having suspected*
ultiōnem: ultiō	*revenge*
patefēcit: patefacere	*reveal*
absurdum: absurdus	*absurd*
falsa: falsus	*false, untrue*
tormenta: tormentum	*torture*
passus	*having suffered*
eādem: īdem	*the same*
dēmōvī: dēmovēre	*dismiss*

Salvius:	rēx Cogidubne, quid fēcistī? tū, quī barbarus es, haruspicem Rōmānum dēmovēre audēs? nimium audēs! tū, summōs honōrēs ā nōbīs adeptus, *30* numquam contentus fuistī. nōs diū vexāvistī. nunc dēnique, cum armātīs hūc ingressus, perfidiam apertē ostendis. Imperātor Domitiānus, arrogantiam tuam diū passus, ad mē epistulam nūper mīsit. in hāc epistulā iussit mē rēgnum tuum *35* occupāre. iubeō tē igitur ad aulam statim redīre.
Cogidubnus:	ēn iūstitia Rōmāna! ēn fidēs! nūllī perfidiōrēs sunt quam Rōmānī. stultissimus fuī, quod Rōmānīs adhūc crēdidī. amīcōs meōs prōdidī; rēgnum meum āmīsī. ōlim, ā Rōmānīs dēceptus, ōrnāmenta *40* honōrēsque Rōmānōs accēpī. hodiē ista ōrnāmenta, mihi ā Rōmānīs data, humī iaciō. Salvī, mitte nūntium ad istum Imperātōrem, "nōs Cogidubnum tandem vīcimus. Britannia perdomita est." *45*

senex, haec locūtus, lentē per iānuam exit.

perfidiam:		fidēs	loyalty,
perfidia	treachery		trustworthiness
apertē	openly	perfidiōrēs:	treacherous,
rēgnum: rēgnum	kingdom	perfidus	untrustworthy
occupāre	seize, take over	adhūc	until now
ēn iūstitia!	so this is justice!	prōdidī: prōdere	betray
		vīcimus: vincere	conquer

Questions

1 Who is described as **anxius**?
2 From the slave's words (lines 3–5), how do Memor and Salvius know that Cogidubnus' visit is not an ordinary one (two reasons)?
3 What is Salvius' explanation for Cogidubnus' visit (line 7)?
4 Why does he think Memor should help him?
5 What accusation does Cogidubnus make against Memor (lines 11–12)?
6 Why is Memor certain that Cogidubnus is unable to prove his accusation (lines 14–15)?
7 What proof does Cogidubnus have? How did it come into his possession (lines 17–20)?
8 Why is Cogidubnus convinced that the slave is trustworthy?
9 What question does Salvius ask Cogidubnus?
10 Why do you think that he has remained silent up to this point?

11 What answer does Cogidubnus give to Salvius' question?

12 Why does Salvius interrupt Memor's response to that answer?

13 Salvius tells Cogidubnus: **nimium audēs** (lines 29–30). How has he explained that comment in the words he says immediately before it?

14 What two other accusations does he make?

15 What order does Salvius say he has received? Who has sent it (lines 33–36)?

16 **ista ōrnāmenta ... humī iaciō** (lines 41–42). What is Cogidubnus doing when he says these words? Why do you think he does this?

17 How are the attitudes or situations of Memor, Salvius, and Cogidubnus different at the end of this story from what they were at the beginning? Make one point about each character.

Word Patterns: Verbs and Nouns

A Study the form and meaning of the following verbs and nouns:

INFINITIVE		PERFECT PASSIVE PARTICIPLE	NOUN	
pingere	*to paint*	pictus	pictor	*painter*
vincere	*to win*	victus	victor	*winner, victor*
līberāre	*to set free*	līberātus	līberātor	*liberator*

B Using the pattern in Section A as a guide, complete the table below:

emere	*to buy*	emptus	emptor	.....
legere	.....	lēctus	.....	*reader*
spectāre	.....	spectātus	.....	.....

C What do the following nouns mean:

dēfēnsor, vēnditor, prōditor, amātor, praecursor, arātor, gubernātor, saltātor

D Many English nouns ending in -or are derived from Latin verbs. Which verbs do the following English nouns come from? Use the Complete Vocabulary to help you if necessary.

demonstrator, curator, navigator, narrator, tractor, doctor

E Suggest what the ending -or indicates in Latin and English.

Practicing the Language

A Complete each sentence with the correct word. Then translate.

1 nōs ancillae fessae sumus; semper in vīllā (labōrāmus, labōrātis, labōrant).

2 "quid faciunt illī servī?" "saxa ad plaustrum (ferimus, fertis, ferunt)."

3 quamquam prope āram (stābāmus, stābātis, stābant), sacrificium vidēre nōn poterāmus.

4 ubi prīncipēs fontī (appropinquābāmus, appropinquābātis, appropinquābant), Cephalus prōcessit, pōculum tenēns.

5 in maximō perīculō estis, quod fīlium rēgis (interfēcimus, interfēcistis, interfēcērunt).

6 nōs, quī fontem sacrum numquam (vīderāmus, vīderātis, vīderant), ad thermās cum rēge īre cupiēbāmus.

7 dominī nostrī sunt benignī; nōbīs semper satis cibī (praebēmus, praebētis, praebent).

B Translate the verbs in the left-hand column. Then, keeping the person and number unchanged, use the verb in parentheses to form a phrase with the infinitive and translate again. For example:

festīnat.   (dēbeō)   This becomes: festīnāre dēbet.
He hurries.   *He ought to hurry.*

1 incipitis.   (dēbeō)   4 reveniunt.   (dēbeō)
2 pārēmus.   (volō)   5 ēligimus.   (possum)
3 adiuvat.   (possum)   6 num dissentīs? (volō)

C Complete each sentence with the most suitable participle from the list below and then translate.

adeptus, locūtus, ingressus, missus, excitātus, superātus

1 Cogidubnus, haec verba . . . . . , ab aulā discessit.
2 nūntius, ab amīcīs meīs . . . . . , epistulam mihi trādidit.
3 fūr, vīllam . . . . . , cautē circumspectāvit.
4 Bulbus, ā Modestō . . . . . , sub mēnsā iacēbat.
5 haruspex, ā Cephalō . . . . . , invītus ē lectō surrēxit.
6 mīles, amulētum . . . . . , in fontem iniēcit.

Roman Religious Beliefs

Sacrifices and Presents to the Gods

In our stories Cogidubnus sacrificed a lamb to Sulis Minerva in the hope that the goddess would be pleased with his gift and would restore him to health. This was regarded as the right and proper thing to do in such circumstances. From earliest times the Romans had believed that all things were controlled by **nūmina** (spirits or divinities). The power of numina was seen, for example, in fire or in the changing of the seasons. To ensure that the numina used their power for good rather than harm, the early Romans presented them with offerings of food and wine. After the third century B.C., when Roman spirits and agricultural deities were incorporated into the Greek pantheon (system of gods), this idea of a contract between mortals and the gods persisted.

To communicate their wishes to the gods, many Romans presented an animal sacrifice, gave a gift, or accompanied their prayers with promises of offerings if the favors were granted. These promises were known as **vōta**. In this way, they thought, they could keep on good terms with the gods and stand a better chance of having their prayers answered. This was true at all levels of society. For example, if a general was going off to war, there would be a solemn public ceremony at which prayers and expensive sacrifices would be offered to the gods. Ordinary citizens would also offer sacrifices, hoping for a successful business deal, a safe voyage, or the birth of a child; and in many Roman homes, to ensure the family's prosperity, offerings of food would be made to Vesta, the spirit of the hearth, and to the **larēs** and **penātēs**, the spirits of the household and food cupboard.

People also offered sacrifices and presents to the gods to honor them at their festivals, to thank them for some success or an escape from danger,

An emperor, as Chief Priest, leads a solemn procession. He covers his head with a fold of his toga. A bull, a sheep, and a pig are to be sacrificed.

or to keep a promise. For example, a cavalry officer stationed in the north of England set up an altar to the god Silvanus with this inscription:

> **C. Tetius Veturius Micianus, captain of the Sebosian cavalry squadron, set this up as he promised to Silvanus the unconquered, in thanks for capturing a beautiful boar, which many people before him tried to do but failed.**

Another inscription from a grateful woman in north Italy reads:

> **Tullia Superiana takes pleasure in keeping her promise to Minerva the unforgetting for giving her her hair back.**

Often people promised to give something to the gods if they answered their prayers. Thus, Censorinus dedicated this thin silver plaque to Mars-Alator, in order to fulfill a vow.

A model liver. Significant areas are labeled to help haruspices interpret any markings.

Divination

An haruspex, like Memor, would be present at important sacrifices. He and his assistants would watch the way in which the victim fell; they would observe the smoke and flames when parts of the victim were placed on the altar fire; and, above all, they would cut the victim open and examine its entrails, especially the liver. They would look for anything unusual about the liver's size or shape, observe its color and texture, and note whether it had spots on its surface. They would then interpret what they saw and announce to the sacrificer whether the **ōmina** from the gods were favorable or not.

Such attempts to discover the future were known as divination. Another type of divination was performed by priests known as **augurēs** (augurs), who based their predictions on observations of the flight of birds. They would note the direction of flight and observe whether the birds flew together or separately, what kind of birds they were, and what noises they made.

The Roman State Religion

Religion in Rome and Italy included a bewildering variety of gods, demigods, spirits, rituals and ceremonies, whose origin and meaning was often a mystery to the worshipers themselves. The Roman state respected this variety but particularly promoted the worship of Jupiter and his family of gods and goddesses, especially Juno, Minerva, Ceres, Apollo, Diana, Mars, and Venus. They were closely linked with their equivalent Greek deities, whose characteristics and colorful mythology were readily taken over by the Romans.

The rituals and ceremonies were organized by colleges of priests and other religious officials, many of whom were senators, and the festivals and sacrifices were carried out by them on behalf of the state. Salvius, for

In this sculpture of a sacrifice, notice the pipe-player, and the attendants with the decorated victim.

example, was a member of the Arval Brotherhood, whose religious duties included praying for the emperor and his family. The emperor always held the position of Pontifex Maximus or Chief Priest. Great attention was paid to the details of worship. Everyone who watched the ceremonies had to stand quite still and silent, like Plancus in Stage 17. Every word had to be pronounced correctly; otherwise the whole ceremony had to be restarted. A pipe-player was employed to drown out noises and cries, which were thought to be unlucky for the ritual.

A priest's ritual headdress, from Roman Britain.

Three sculptures from Bath illustrate the mixture of British and Roman religion there.
Above: *a gilded bronze head of Sulis Minerva, presumably from her statue in the temple, shows the goddess as the Romans pictured her.*
Top right: *three Celtic mother-goddesses.*
Right: *Nemetona and the horned Loucetius Mars.*

Religion and Romanization

The Roman state religion played an important part in the Romanization of the provinces of the empire. The Romans generally tolerated the religious beliefs and practices of their subject peoples unless they were thought to threaten their rule or their relationship with the gods, which was so carefully fostered by sacrifices and correct rituals. They encouraged their subjects to identify their own gods with Roman gods who shared some of the same characteristics. We have seen at Aquae Sulis how the Celtic Sulis and the Roman Minerva were merged into one goddess, Sulis Minerva, and how a temple in the Roman style was built in her honor.

Emperor Augustus as Pontifex Maximus.

Another feature of Roman religion which was intended to encourage acceptance of Roman rule was the worship of the emperor. In Rome itself, emperor worship was generally discouraged, while the emperor was alive. However, the peoples of the eastern provinces of the Roman empire had always regarded their kings and rulers as divine and were equally ready to pay divine honors to the Roman emperors. Gradually the Romans introduced this idea in the west as well. The Britons and other western peoples were encouraged to worship the **genius** (protecting spirit) of the emperor, linked with the goddess Roma. Altars were erected in honor of "Rome and the emperor." When an emperor died, it was usual to deify him (make him a god), and temples were often built to honor the deified emperor. One such temple, that of Claudius in Camulodunum (Colchester), was destroyed, before it was even finished, during the revolt led by Queen Boudica in A.D. 60. The historian Tacitus tells us that this temple was a blatant stronghold of alien rule, and its observances were a pretext to make the natives appointed as its priests drain the whole country dry.

In general, however, the policy of promoting Roman religion and emperor worship proved successful in the provinces. Like other forms of Romanization it became popular with the upper and middle classes, who looked to Rome to promote their careers; it helped to make Roman rule acceptable, reduced the chance of uprisings, and gave many people in the provinces a sense that they belonged to one great empire.

Astrology

Many Romans were content with the official state religion but some found greater satisfaction in other forms of belief. Many took part in both the state religion and some other kind of worship without feeling any conflict between the two. One very popular form of belief was astrology. Astrologers, like the one in Barbillus' household in Unit 2, claimed that the events in a person's life were controlled by the stars and that it was possible to forecast the future by studying the positions and movements of stars and planets. The position of the stars at the time of a person's birth was known as an **hōroscopos** (horoscope) and regarded as particularly important. Astrology was officially disapproved of, especially if people used it to try to determine when their relatives or acquaintances were going to die, and from time to time all astrologers were banished from Rome. It was a particularly serious offense to inquire about the horoscope of the emperor. Several emperors, however, were themselves firm believers in astrology and, like Barbillus, kept astrologers of their own.

Atlas holding the globe inscribed with constellations.

Word Study

A Complete the following analogies with words from the Stage 23 Vocabulary Checklist:

   1 venīre : īre : : ___ : resistere
   2 fortis : ignāvus : : ___ : benignus
   3 verbum : dīcere : : ___ : iubēre
   4 exitium : dēlēre : : ___ : parcere
   5 ingressus : intrāre : : ___ : dīcere
   6 pecūnia : numerāre : : discus : ___
   7 sānāre : interficere : : remedium : ___

B Give a definition for each of the following derivatives of **cēdō, cēdere, cessī**:

   1 precedent   **6** secede
   2 recession   **7** intercession
   3 cessation   **8** incessant
   4 antecedent   **9** predecessor
   5 necessary

C Copy the following words. Then put parentheses around the Latin root from this Stage contained inside these derivatives; give the Latin word and its meaning from which the derivative comes.

   For example: conservation   con(serva)tion   servāre – to save

   1 declaration   **6** potentate
   2 depraved   **7** retaliate
   3 elocution   **8** science
   4 errant   **9** venial
   5 mandate   **10** regression

Stage 23 Vocabulary Checklist

administrō, administrāre,
  administrāvī   *manage*
cēdō, cēdere, cessī   *give in, give way*
clārus, clāra, clārum   *famous*
commemorō, commemorāre,
  commemorāvī, commemorātus   *mention, recall*
cōnspicātus, cōnspicāta, cōnspicātum   *having caught sight of*
cūra, cūrae, f.   *care*
enim   *for*
errō, errāre, errāvī   *make a mistake*
gerō, gerere, gessī, gestus   *wear*
honor, honōris, m.   *honor*
iaciō, iacere, iēcī, iactus   *throw*
immōtus, immōta, immōtum   *still, motionless*
ingenium, ingeniī, n.   *character*
locūtus, locūta, locūtum   *having spoken*
magnopere   *greatly*
  magis   *more, rather*
  maximē   *very greatly, most of all*
mandātum, mandātī, n.   *instruction, order*
modus, modī, m.   *manner, way, kind*
  rēs huius modī   *a thing of this kind*
nimium, nimiī, n.   *too much*
ōrnō, ōrnāre, ōrnāvī, ōrnātus   *decorate*
pāreō, pārēre, pāruī (+ DAT)   *obey*
potēns, potēns, potēns,
  gen. potentis   *powerful*
prāvus, prāva, prāvum   *evil*
regressus, regressa, regressum   *having returned*
scio, scīre, scīvī   *know*
tālis, tālis, tāle   *such*
tamquam   *as, like*
umquam   *ever*
venēnum, venēnī, n.   *poison*
venia, veniae, f.   *mercy*

This bronze statuette represents a Romano-British
worshiper bringing offerings to a god.

FUGA

Stage 24

in itinere

Modestus et Strȳthiō, ex oppidō Aquīs Sūlis ēgressī, Dēvam
equitābant. in itinere ad flūmen altum vēnērunt, ubi erat pōns
sēmirutus. cum ad pontem vēnissent, equus trānsīre nōluit.

"equus trānsīre timet," inquit Modestus. "Strȳthiō, tū prior
trānsī!"   5

cum Strȳthiō trānsiisset, equus trānsīre etiam tum nōlēbat.
Modestus igitur ex equō dēscendit. cum dēscendisset, equus
statim trānsiit.

"caballe! redī!" inquit Modestus. "mē dēseruistī."

equus tamen in alterā rīpā immōtus stetit. Modestus cautissimē   10
trānsīre coepit. cum ad medium pontem vēnisset, dēcidit pōns,
dēcidit Modestus. mediīs ex undīs clāmāvit,

"caudicēs, vōs pontem labefēcistis."

Dēvam	*to Deva (Chester, modern town in western England)*
altum: altus	*deep*
sēmirutus	*rickety*
cum	*when*
caballe: caballus	*nag, horse*
labefēcistis: labefacere	*weaken*

Peutinger Table, showing Roman Britain.

Quīntus cōnsilium capit

When you have read this story, answer the questions at the end.

cum Cogidubnus trīstis īrātusque ē vīllā Memoris exiisset, Salvius
quīnquāgintā mīlitēs arcessīvit. eōs iussit rēgem prīncipēsque
Rēgnēnsium comprehendere et in carcere retinēre. hī mīlitēs,
tōtum per oppidum missī, mox rēgem cum prīncipibus
invēnērunt. eōs statim comprehendērunt. Dumnorix tamen, ē   5
manibus mīlitum ēlāpsus, per viās oppidī noctū prōcessit et
Quīntum quaesīvit. Quīntō enim crēdēbat.

cubiculum Quīntī ingressus, haec dīxit:
"amīce, tibi crēdere possum. adiuvā mē, adiuvā Cogidubnum.
paucīs Rōmānīs crēdō; plūrimī sunt perfidī. nēmō quidem   10
perfidior est quam iste Salvius quī Cogidubnum interficere nūper
temptāvit. nunc Cogidubnus, ā mīlitibus Salviī comprehēnsus, in
carcere iacet. Salvius crīmen maiestātis in eum īnferre cupit. rēx, in
carcere inclūsus, omnīnō dē vītā suā dēspērat.

"tū tamen es vir summae virtūtis magnaeque prūdentiae.   15
quamquam Salvius potentissimus est, nōlī rēgem, amīcum tuum,
dēserere. nōlī eum, ab homine scelestō oppugnātum, relinquere. tū
anteā eum servāvistī. nōnne iterum servāre potes?"

cum Dumnorix haec dīxisset, Quīntus rem sēcum anxius
cōgitābat. auxilium Cogidubnō ferre volēbat, quod eum valdē   20
dīligēbat; sed rēs difficillima erat. subitō cōnsilium cēpit.

"nōlī dēspērāre!" inquit. "rēgī auxilium ferre possumus. hanc
rem ad lēgātum Gnaeum Iūlium Agricolam clam referre dēbēmus.
itaque nōbīs festīnandum est ad ultimās partēs Britanniae ubi
Agricola bellum gerit. eī vēra patefacere possumus. Agricola sōlus   25
Salviō obstāre potest, quod summam potestātem in Britanniā
habet. nunc nōbīs hinc effugiendum est."

Dumnorix, cum haec audīvisset, cōnsilium audāx magnopere
laudāvit. tum Quīntus servum fīdissimum arcessīvit, cui mandāta
dedit. servus exiit. mox regressus, cibum sex diērum Quīntō et   30
Dumnorigī trādidit. illī, ē vīllā ēlāpsī, per viās dēsertās cautē
prōcessērunt.

vīllam Memoris praetereuntēs, Quīntus et Dumnorix duōs
equōs cōnspexērunt, ad pālum dēligātōs. Quīntus, quī fūrtum
committere nōlēbat, haesitāvit.   35

Dumnorix rīdēns "nōlī haesitāre," inquit. "hī sunt equī Salviī."

Quīntus et Dumnorix equōs cōnscendērunt et ad ultimās partēs
īnsulae abiērunt.

carcere: carcer	*prison*
ēlāpsus	*having escaped*
quidem	*indeed*
crīmen maiestātis	*charge of treason*
īnferre	*bring against*
inclūsus	*shut up, imprisoned*
omnīnō	*completely*
sēcum … cōgitābat	*considered … to himself*
dīligēbat: dīligere	*be fond of*
Agricolam: Agricola	*Agricola (Roman governor of Britain)*
nōbīs festīnandum est	*we must hurry*
ultimās: ultimus	*furthest*
bellum gerit: bellum gerere	*wage war, campaign*
potestātem: potestās	*power*
fīdissimum: fīdus	*trustworthy*
praetereuntēs: praeterīre	*pass by, go past*
pālum: pālus	*stake, post*
fūrtum: fūrtum	*theft, robbery*
committere	*commit*
haesitāvit: haesitāre	*hesitate*
cōnscendērunt: cōnscendere	*mount, climb on*

Questions

1 How many soldiers did Salvius send for? What did he tell them to do?
2 Which British chieftain escaped? Whose help did he seek? Why?
3 What was Dumnorix's opinion of the Romans (line 10)?
4 **nēmō quidem perfidior est quam iste Salvius** (lines 10–11). Why did Dumnorix think this?
5 What further action did Salvius intend to take against Cogidubnus?
6 What event was Dumnorix referring to when he said **tū anteā eum servāvistī** (lines 17–18)?
7 Whom did Quintus suggest he and Dumnorix should visit? Where was this man? Why was he the only one who could help Cogidubnus?
8 How much food did Quintus obtain? How did he obtain it?
9 How did the two men obtain horses?
10 Why did Quintus support a British king and a British chieftain, instead of supporting his fellow-Roman, Salvius?

About the Language I: cum + Pluperfect Subjunctive

A Study the following sentences:

> cum Modestus ad pontem **advēnisset**, equus cōnstitit.
> *When Modestus **had arrived** at the bridge, the horse stopped.*

> cum servī omnia **parāvissent**, mercātor amīcōs in triclīnium dūxit.
> *When the slaves **had prepared** everything, the merchant led his friends into the dining-room.*

The form of the verb in boldface is known as the subjunctive.

B The subjunctive is often used with the word **cum** meaning *when*, as in the examples above.

C Further examples:

1 cum rēx exiisset, Salvius mīlitēs ad sē vocāvit.
2 cum gladiātōrēs leōnem interfēcissent, spectātōrēs plausērunt.
3 cum dominus haec mandāta dedisset, fabrī ad aulam rediērunt.
4 sorōrēs, cum culīnam intrāvissent, pōcula sordida lavāre coepērunt.

D The examples of the subjunctive in Sections A and C are all in the same tense: the pluperfect subjunctive. Compare the 3rd person of the pluperfect subjunctive with the ordinary form (called the **indicative**) of the pluperfect:

	PLUPERFECT INDICATIVE		PLUPERFECT SUBJUNCTIVE	
	singular	*plural*	*singular*	*plural*
first conjugation	portāverat	portāverant	portāvisset	portāvissent
second conjugation	docuerat	docuerant	docuisset	docuissent
third conjugation	trāxerat	trāxerant	trāxisset	trāxissent
fourth conjugation	dormīverat	dormīverant	dormīvisset	dormīvissent
irregular verbs				
esse (*to be*)	fuerat	fuerant	fuisset	fuissent
velle (*to want*)	voluerat	voluerant	voluisset	voluissent

Salvius cōnsilium cognōscit

postrīdiē, cum Quīntus et Dumnorix ad ultimās partēs īnsulae contenderent, mīlitēs Dumnorigem per oppidum frūstrā quaerēbant. rem dēnique Salviō nūntiāvērunt. ille, cum dē fugā Dumnorigis cognōvisset, vehementer saeviēbat; omnēs mīlitēs, quī Dumnorigem custōdīverant, poenās dare iussit. Quīntum 5 quaesīvit; cum eum quoque nusquam invenīre potuisset, Belimicum, prīncipem Cantiacōrum, arcessīvit.

"Belimice," inquit, "iste Dumnorix ē manibus meīs effūgit; abest quoque Quīntus Caecilius. neque Dumnorigī neque Quīntō crēdō. Quīntus enim saepe Dumnorigī favēbat, saepe cum eō 10 colloquium habēbat. ī nunc; dūc mīlitēs tēcum; illōs quaere in omnibus partibus oppidī. quaere servōs quoque eōrum. facile est nōbīs servōs torquēre et vērum ita cognōscere."

Belimicus, multīs cum mīlitibus ēgressus, per oppidum dīligenter quaerēbat. intereā Salvius anxius reditum eius 15 exspectābat. cum Salvius rem sēcum cōgitāret, Belimicus subitō rediit exsultāns. servum Quīntī in medium ātrium trāxit.

"fūgērunt illī scelestī," inquit, "sed hic servus, captus et interrogātus, vērum patefēcit."

Salvius ad servum trementem conversus, 20

"ubi est Quīntus Caecilius?" inquit. "quō fūgit Dumnorix?"

"nescio," inquit servus quī, multa tormenta passus, iam vix quicquam dīcere poterat. "nihil scio."

fugā: fuga	*escape*
nusquam	*nowhere*
ī: īre	*go*
torquēre	*torture*
reditum:	
reditus	*return*
exsultāns:	*exult,*
exsultāre	*be triumphant*
conversus	*having turned*
quicquam	*anything*

Belimicus, cum haec audīvisset, gladium dēstrictum ad iugulum servī tenuit. 25

"melius est tibi," inquit, "vērum Salviō dīcere."

servus quī iam dē vītā suā dēspērābat,

"cibum sex diērum tantum parāvī," inquit susurrāns. "nihil aliud fēcī. dominus meus cum Dumnorige in ultimās partēs Britanniae discessit." 30

Salvius "hercle!" inquit. "ad Agricolam iērunt. Quīntus, ā Dumnorige incitātus, mihi obstāre temptat; homō tamen magnae stultitiae est; mihi resistere nōn potest, quod ego maiōrem auctōritātem habeō quam ille."

Salvius, cum haec dīxisset, Belimicō mandāta dedit. eum iussit 35 cum trīgintā equitibus exīre et fugitīvōs comprehendere. servum carnificibus trādidit. deinde scrībam arcessīvit cui epistulam dictāvit. ūnum ē servīs suīs iussit hanc epistulam quam celerrimē ad Agricolam ferre.

intereā Belimicus, Quīntum et Dumnorigem per trēs diēs 40 secūtus, eōs tandem in silvā invēnit. equitēs statim impetum in eōs fēcērunt. amīcī, ab equitibus circumventī, fortiter resistēbant. dēnique Dumnorix humī cecidit mortuus. cum equitēs corpus Dumnorigis īnspicerent, Quīntus, graviter vulnerātus, magnā cum difficultāte effūgit. 45

dēstrictum: dēstringere	*draw*	**scrībam: scrība**	*secretary*
iugulum: iugulum	*throat*	**corpus: corpus**	*body*
fugitīvōs: fugitīvus	*fugitive*		

Aerial view of Roman road followed by Quintus and Dumnorix to Deva.

About the Language II: cum + Imperfect Subjunctive

A At the beginning of this Stage, you met sentences with **cum** and the pluperfect subjunctive:

> senex, cum pecūniam **invēnisset**, ad vīllam rediit.
> *When the old man **had found** the money, he returned to the villa.*

> cum rem **cōnfēcissent**, abiērunt.
> *When they **had finished** the job, they went away.*

B Now study the following examples:

> cum custōdēs **dormīrent**, captīvī ē carcere effūgērunt.
> *When the guards **were sleeping**, the prisoners escaped from the prison.*

> Modestus, cum in Britanniā **mīlitāret**, multās puellās amābat.
> *When Modestus **was serving in the army** in Britain, he loved many girls.*

In these sentences, **cum** is being used with a different tense of the subjunctive: the imperfect subjunctive.

C Further examples:

1. cum hospitēs cēnam cōnsūmerent, fūr cubiculum intrāvit.
2. cum prīnceps rem cōgitāret, nūntiī subitō revēnērunt.
3. iuvenēs, cum bēstiās agitārent, mīlitem vulnerātum cōnspexērunt.
4. puella, cum epistulam scrīberet, sonitum mīrābilem audīvit.

D Compare the 3rd person of the imperfect subjunctive with the infinitive:

	INFINITIVE	IMPERFECT SUBJUNCTIVE	
		singular	*plural*
first conjugation	portāre	portāret	portārent
second conjugation	docēre	docēret	docērent
third conjugation	trahere	traheret	traherent
fourth conjugation	audīre	audīret	audīrent
irregular verbs	esse	esset	essent
	velle	vellet	vellent

Word Patterns: Antonyms

A You have already met the following antonyms:

volō	*I want*	nōlō	*I do not want*
scio	*I know*	nescio	*I do not know*

Study the words in the left column and find their antonyms on the right. Then fill in their meanings.

1	umquam	*ever*	nefās	. . . . .
2	homō	*man*	nusquam	. . . . .
3	usquam	*anywhere*	negōtium	. . . . .
4	ōtium	*leisure*	numquam	. . . . .
5	fās	*morally right*	nēmō	. . . . .

B Study these further ways of forming antonyms and give the meanings of the words on the right:

1	patiēns	*patient*	impatiēns	. . . . .
2	ūtilis	*useful*	inūtilis	. . . . .
3	nocēns	*guilty*	innocēns	. . . . .
4	cōnsentīre	*to agree*	dissentīre	. . . . .
5	facilis	*easy*	difficilis	. . . . .
6	similis	*similar*	dissimilis	. . . . .

C From the box choose the correct Latin words to translate the words in boldface in the following sentences:

sānus	fēlīx	indignus	inimīcus
dignus	īnsānus	amīcus	īnfēlīx

1 Entering a room right foot first was thought to be **lucky** but a stumble was **unlucky**.
2 Bulbus must be **mad** to love Vilbia.
3 Strythio is the **friend** of Modestus, but Bulbus is his **enemy**.
4 I am **worthy** of Vilbia's love; Modestus is **unworthy**.

D Work out the meanings of the following words:

immōtus, incertus, dissuādeō, incrēdibilis, inīquus, ignōtus, neglegō, ingrātus

Practicing the Language

A Complete each sentence with the correct form of the adjective. Then translate the sentence.

1 medicus puellae (aegram, aegrae) pōculum dedit.
2 hospitēs coquum (callidum, callidō) laudāvērunt.
3 faber mercātōrī (īrātum, īrātō) dēnāriōs reddidit.
4 ancillae dominō (crūdēlem, crūdēlī) pārēre nōlēbant.
5 centuriō mīlitēs (ignāvōs, ignāvīs) vituperābat.
6 puer stultus nautīs (mendācēs, mendācibus) crēdidit.
7 stolās (novās, novīs) emēbat fēmina.
8 (omnēs, omnibus) amīcīs pecūniam obtulī.

B With the help of Section C on page 306 of the Language Information, replace the words in boldface with the correct form of the pronoun **is** and then translate. For example:

> Rūfilla in hortō ambulābat. Quīntus **Rūfillam** salūtāvit.
> This becomes:
> Rūfilla in hortō ambulābat. Quīntus **eam** salūtāvit.
> *Rufilla was walking in the garden. Quintus greeted her.*

In sentences 7 and 8, you may need to look up the gender of a noun in the Complete Vocabulary.

1 Quīntus mox ad aulam advēnit. ancilla **Quīntum** in ātrium dūxit.
2 Salvius in lectō recumbēbat. puer **Salviō** plūs cibī obtulit.
3 Rūfilla laetissima erat; marītus **Rūfillae** tamen nōn erat contentus.
4 Britannī ferōciter pugnāvērunt, sed legiōnēs nostrae tandem **Britannōs** vīcērunt.
5 barbarī impetum in nōs fēcērunt. **barbarīs** autem restitimus.
6 multae fēminae prō templō conveniēbant. līberī **fēminārum** quoque aderant.
7 in illō oppidō est fōns sacer; **fontem** saepe vīsitāvī.
8 in Britanniā sunt trēs legiōnēs; imperātor **legiōnēs** iussit barbarōs vincere.

C Select the correct word from the parentheses and then translate.

1 Belimicus, cum servum fīdum (invēnisset, dēseruisset), ātrium intrāvit exsultāns.

2 equitēs, cum fugitīvōs (commemorāvissent, cōnspexissent), impetum quam celerrimē fēcērunt.
3 Modestus, cum equus pontem trānsīre (voluisset, nōluisset), invītus dēscendit.
4 barbarī multās iniūriās passī, cum vērum (ōrnāvissent, cognōvissent), oppidum oppugnāvērunt.
5 mīles perfidus, cum Vilbiam (iniceret, exspectāret), fontī appropinquāvit.
6 Dumnorix, cum Cogidubnus in carcere (iacēret, indueret), auxilium petīvit.
7 Quīntus, cum prope aulam (habitāret, clāmāret), saepius cum Cogidubnō quam cum Salviō colloquium habēbat.

D Make up six Latin sentences using some of the words listed below. Write out each sentence and then translate it. Include two sentences which do not contain nominatives.

NOMINATIVES	DATIVES	ACCUSATIVES	VERBS
senātor	fīliae	flōrēs	emō
centuriōnēs	uxōrī	dōna	emit
prīnceps	mīlitibus	gladiōs	emunt
nūntius	agricolae	fēlem	ostendō
amīcī	dominō	plaustra	ostendit
marītus	hospitibus	vīnum	ostendunt
puella	fēminīs	cibum	dat
iuvenēs	imperātōrī	epistulās	damus
virī	carnificibus	fūrem	dant
ancillae	servīs	cēram	trādit
			trāditis
			trādunt

A stretch of Roman road which survives.

Travel and Communication

Judged by modern standards, traveling in the Roman world was neither easy nor comfortable; nevertheless, people traveled extensively and there was much movement of goods throughout the provinces of the empire. This was made possible by a great network of straight, well-surfaced roads – estimated at 56,000 miles (92,000 kilometers) at the peak of the empire – which covered the Roman world using the shortest possible routes. The roads, with tunnels and bridges as necessary, crossed plains, forests, mountains, rivers, valleys, marshes, and deserts.

A Roman road was laid out by military surveyors who used a **grōma** to achieve a straight line. Where trees or hills were in the way, the surveyors took sightings from high points using smoke from fires to ensure that each section of road took the shortest practical route between the points. River valleys and impassable mountains forced the surveyors to make diversions, but once past the obstructions, the roads usually continued along their original line.

Vitruvius, a Roman architect and engineer, gives us a description of road-building which utilizes local resources and adjusts to local terrain. After the line was chosen, a cut was made the width of the planned road and deep enough to hold the filling. If the earth was soft at that depth, piles were driven in to strengthen it. On this base the road was built up in four layers up to 5 feet (1.5 meters) thick and between 6 to 20 feet (2 to 6 meters) wide. At the bottom was a footing of large stones. This was covered with a layer of smaller stones, concrete, or rubble, and then a layer of rolled sand concrete. The surface or **pavīmentum** was made of local materials, usually large flat paving stones dressed on the top side.

Road surface with large flat stones on the Appian Way in Italy.

Rubble layer and curbstones in Britain.

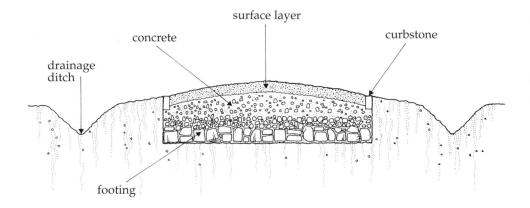

drainage ditch | concrete | surface layer | curbstone | footing

This final surface was curved or "cambered" to provide effective drainage. The Romans liked to raise their roadways on an embankment of earth, called an **agger**, which was raised about 3 feet (1 meter) both to aid drainage and to give marching troops a good view of the territory. Ditches on either side of the agger also provided drainage.

Roman road-building was generally carried out with great skill and thoroughness: a fully paved Roman road lasted 80–100 years before it had to be renewed. The roads were so well made that some are still in use today. Many modern roads in Europe still follow the Roman routes and these can be seen very clearly on maps. Only in the last hundred years, with the advent of heavy vehicle traffic, have nations begun to return to road-building methods like the Romans'.

The roads' original purpose was to allow rapid movement of Roman troops and supplies and so ensure military control of the provinces. However, roads were a vital part of the empire since they extended the civilization as well as the power of Rome. Government correspondence and government officials made use of a system known as the Imperial Post (**cursus pūblicus**). A government warrant (**diplōma**) indicated that the bearer was on official business and was entitled to secure fresh horses at posting stations (**mutātiōnēs**), and to stay at the resthouses (**mansiōnēs**) which were situated at frequent intervals along all main roads. It has been estimated that an official courier could average 50 miles (80 kilometers) a day; in an emergency, by traveling night and day, he could triple this distance. Private letters, either carried by a person's own slave or sent with a traveler, took much longer but even so letters came and went in all directions.

An official world map of the empire, begun by Agrippa and completed by Augustus, was publicly displayed. Copyists made roll maps (**itinerāria**) for travelers. The **itinerārium** showed distances between cities and way stops and marked important buildings as well as

Two forms of transport: a light carriage with two horses, passing a milestone; and a pair of oxen which, harnessed in this way, were used for transporting goods.

rivers, bridges, and mountains. The only surviving itinerarium is the **Tabula Peutingeriana** (the Peutinger Table) which is a twelfth-century copy of a fourth- or fifth-century road guide of the Roman world (see page 67).

Travelers walked, used carriages or carts, or rode, generally on mules or ponies. Horses were ridden mainly by cavalrymen or government officials. Journey times were affected by many factors, such as the freshness of animals and travelers, the time of year, and the gradients of the road.

Relief of light carriage approaching a milestone.

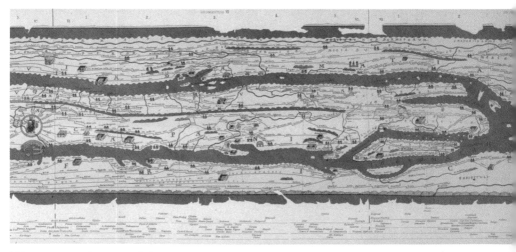

Diagrammatic map of the sort used in the Roman empire. Using standard symbols, it shows travelers the road system and accommodation available.

Wealthy travelers would make arrangements, wherever possible, to break long journeys by staying at their family houses or with friends, acquaintances, even business associates. Ordinary travelers, however, with no estates, wealthy friends, or letters of introduction, would have to stay at roadside inns, where they were at the mercy of the **caupōnēs** (innkeepers), who were often dishonest. The inns were, for the most part, small, dirty, and uncomfortable and were frequented by thieves, prostitutes, and drunks. The Roman poet Horace, traveling on the Appian Way from Rome to Brundisium, writes of the "wicked innkeepers" and Pliny complains of the bedbugs. The graffiti found on the walls also testify to a lower-class clientele: "Innkeeper, I urinated in the bed. Want to know why? There was no mattress!" It is no wonder that respectable travelers tried to avoid such inns.

Travelers, both military and civilian, could also use flat-bottomed river and canal barges for transportation. Some of these barges had oars but most, especially when going upstream, were propelled by men or mules hauling towropes along towpaths. In an effort to avoid the unsavory people and inns one night, Horace and his traveling party boarded a canal barge, arranging to be towed to their next major stop while they slept. Imagine their disgust to awake the next morning at the same dock with the mule unhitched and the shiftless sailors snoring!

Traveling by sea was generally more popular, although it was restricted to the sailing season (March to November) and was subject to danger from pirates, storms, and shipwrecks. Most sea journeys were

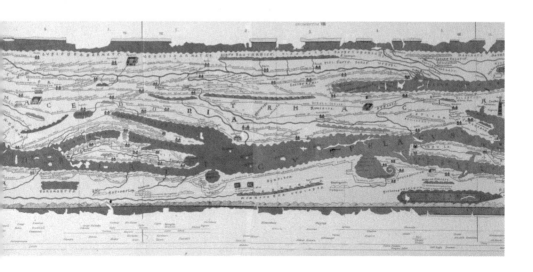

undertaken on merchant ships; passenger shipping as we know it did not exist, except for the occasional ferry. A traveler would have to wait until a merchant ship was about to put to sea and bargain with the captain for an acceptable fare.

The ship would not set sail until the winds were favorable and an animal had been sacrificed to the gods. There were also certain days which were considered unlucky, rather like our Friday the 13th, when no ship would leave port. When at last all was ready, the passenger would come on board with his slaves, bringing enough food and wine to last them until the next port of call. No cabins were provided, except for the very wealthy, and passengers would sleep on deck, perhaps in a small portable shelter, which would be taken down during the day.

When the ship came safely to port, the captain would thank the gods. Then a tugboat, manned by rowers, would tow the ship to her berth at the dockside.

A merchant ship in a harbor. On the left is a lighthouse approached by a causeway. The stern of the ship can be seen, with a carved swan's head, one of the large oars used for steering, and a small shelter to the left of the sail.

A tugboat.

Word Study

A Match the Latin word to its antonym.

1	perfidus	**a**	cēlāre
2	nusquam	**b**	laetus
3	patefacere	**c**	adiuvāre
4	vērum	**d**	timidus
5	dēserere	**e**	līberāre
6	audāx	**f**	amīcus
7	trīstis	**g**	probus
8	īnfestus	**h**	mendācium
9	comprehendere	**i**	ubīque

B Complete the following analogies with words from the Stage 24 Vocabulary Checklist:

1 locūtus : dīcere : : _____ : exīre
2 rēx : aula : : captīvus : _____
3 inimīcus : hostis : : sermō : _____
4 mare : lītus : : flūmen : _____
5 nāvigāre : marī : : ambulāre : _____
6 laetus : rīdēre : : _____ : lacrimāre

C Copy the following words. Then put parentheses around the Latin root from this Stage contained inside these derivatives; give the Latin word and its meaning from which the derivative comes.

For example: conservation   con(serva)tion   servāre – to save

1 colloquial
2 pontoon
3 audacious
4 perfidious
5 transient
6 passive
7 incarceration
8 infestation
9 riparian

Stage 24 Vocabulary Checklist

auctōritās, auctōritātis, f.	*authority*
audāx, audāx, audāx, *gen.* audācis	*bold, daring*
carcer, carceris, m.	*prison*
colloquium, colloquiī, n.	*talk, chat*
comprehendō, comprehendere, comprehendī, comprehēnsus	*arrest*
cōnscendō, cōnscendere, cōnscendī	*climb on, mount*
cum	*when*
dēscendō, dēscendere, dēscendī	*go down, come down*
dēserō, dēserere, dēseruī, dēsertus	*desert*
ēgressus, ēgressa, ēgressum	*having gone out*
eques, equitis, m.	*horseman*
flūmen, flūminis, n.	*river*
humī	*on the ground*
īnfestus, īnfesta, īnfestum	*hostile*
intereā	*meanwhile*
neque … neque	*neither … nor*
nusquam	*nowhere*
oppugnō, oppugnāre, oppugnāvī, oppugnātus	*attack*
passus, passa, passum	*having suffered*
patefaciō, patefacere, patefēcī, patefactus	*reveal*
perfidus, perfida, perfidum	*treacherous, untrustworthy*
pōns, pontis, m.	*bridge*
rīpa, rīpae, f.	*river bank*
tantum	*only*
trānseō, trānsīre, trānsiī	*cross*
trīstis, trīstis, trīste	*sad*
vērum, vērī, n.	*the truth*

A Roman milestone.

MILITES

Stage 25

explōrātor Britannicus

1 mīles legiōnis secundae per castra ambulābat. subitō iuvenem ignōtum
prope horreum latentem cōnspexit.

    "heus tū," clāmāvit mīles, "quis es?"

    iuvenis nihil respondit. mīles iuvenem iterum rogāvit quis esset.
iuvenis fūgit.

2 mīles iuvenem petīvit et facile superāvit. "furcifer!" exclāmāvit. "quid
prope horreum facis?"

    iuvenis dīcere nōlēbat quid prope horreum faceret. mīles eum ad
centuriōnem dūxit.

3 centuriō, iuvenem cōnspicātus, "hunc agnōscō!" inquit. "explōrātor
Britannicus est, quem saepe prope castra cōnspexī. quō modō eum
cēpistī?"
    tum mīles explicāvit quō modō iuvenem cēpisset.

4 centuriō, ad iuvenem conversus, "cūr in castra vēnistī?" rogāvit.
iuvenis tamen tacēbat.
    centuriō, ubi cognōscere nōn poterat cūr iuvenis in castra vēnisset,
mīlitem iussit eum ad carcerem dūcere.

iuvenis, postquam verba centuriōnis audīvit, "ego sum Vercobrix,"
inquit, "fīlius prīncipis Deceanglōrum. vōbīs nōn decōrum est mē in
carcere tenēre."
    "fīlius prīncipis Deceanglōrum?" exclāmāvit centuriō. "libentissimē
tē videō. nōs tē diū quaerimus, cellamque optimam tibi in carcere
parāvimus."

Deceanglōrum: Deceanglī   *the Deceangli (a British tribe)*

Strȳthiō

optiō per castra ambulat. Strȳthiōnem, iam ad castra regressum, cōnspicit.

optiō:	heus Strȳthiō! hūc venī! tibi aliquid dīcere volō.
Strȳthiō:	nōlī mē vexāre! occupātus sum. Modestum quaerō, quod puella eum exspectat. hercle! puellam pulchriōrem numquam vīdī. vōx eius est suāvissima; oculī eius …
optiō:	mī Strȳthiō, quamquam occupātissimus es, dēbēs maximā cum dīligentiā mē audīre. ā centuriōne nostrō missus sum. centuriō tē iubet ad carcerem statim festīnāre.
Strȳthiō:	īnsānit centuriō! innocēns sum.
optiō:	tacē! centuriō Modestum quoque iussit ad carcerem festīnāre.
Strȳthiō:	deōs testēs faciō. innocentēs sumus. nūllum facinus commīsimus.
optiō:	caudex! tacē! difficile est rem tibi explicāre! Valerius, centuriō noster, vōs ambōs carcerem custōdīre iussit.
Strȳthiō:	nōlī mē vituperāre! rem nunc intellegō! Valerius nōs vult custōdēs carceris esse. decōrum est Valeriō nōs ēligere, quod fortissimī sumus, ego et Modestus, cum in Āfricā mīlitārēmus, sōlī tōtam prōvinciam custōdiēbāmus.
optiō:	(*susurrāns*) difficile est mihi hoc crēdere.
Strȳthiō:	quid dīcis?
optiō:	quamquam fortissimī estis, dīligentiam quoque maximam praestāre dēbētis. nam inter captīvōs est Vercobrix, iuvenis magnae dignitātis, cuius pater est prīnceps Deceanglōrum. necesse est vōbīs Vercobrigem dīligentissimē custōdīre.
Strȳthiō:	nōlī anxius esse, mī optiō. nōbīs nihil difficile est, quod fortissimī sumus, ut anteā dīxī. tū redī ad Valerium. dīc Valeriō haec omnia verba. nōlī quicquam omittere! "Strȳthiō, mīles legiōnis secundae, Valeriō, centuriōnī legiōnis secundae, salūtem plūrimam dīcit. optiō, ā tē missus, mandāta tua nōbīs tulit. nōs mandātīs tuīs pārentēs, ad statiōnem prōcēdimus."

exeunt. optiō centuriōnem quaerit, Strȳthiō amīcum.

optiō	*optio (military officer, ranking below centurion)*
castra: castra	*military camp*
ambōs: ambō	*both*
prōvinciam: prōvincia	*province*
praestāre	*show, display*
captīvōs: captīvus	*prisoner, captive*
cuius	*whose (genitive of* **quī***)*
omittere	*leave out, omit*
salūtem plūrimam dīcit	*sends his best wishes*
pārentēs: pārēre	*obey*
statiōnem: statiō	*post*

Modestus custōs

Modestus et Strȳthiō, carcerem ingressī, cellās in quibus captīvī erant īnspiciēbant. habēbat Strȳthiō tabulam in quā nōmina captīvōrum scrīpta erant. Modestus eum rogāvit in quā cellā Vercobrix inclūsus esset. Strȳthiō, tabulam īnspiciēns, cognōvit ubi Vercobrix iacēret, et Modestum ad cellam dūxit. Modestus,   5 cum ad portam cellae advēnisset, haesitāns cōnstitit.

    Strȳthiō "num cellam intrāre timēs?" inquit. "vīnctus est fīlius prīncipis Deceanglōrum. tē laedere nōn potest."

    cum Strȳthiō haec dīxisset, Modestus īrātus exclāmāvit,

    "caudex, prīncipis fīlium nōn timeō! cōnstitī quod tē   10 exspectābam. volō tē mihi portam aperīre!"

    cum portam Strȳthiō aperuisset, Modestus rūrsus haesitāvit.

    "obscūra est cella," inquit Modestus anxius. "fer mihi lucernam."

    Strȳthiō, vir summae patientiae, lucernam tulit amīcōque   15 trādidit. ille, cellam ingressus, ē cōnspectū discessit.

cōnstitit: cōnsistere	*halt, stop*
vīnctus: vincīre	*bind, tie up*
obscūra: obscūrus	*dark, gloomy*
lucernam: lucerna	*lamp*
patientiae: patientia	*patience*
cōnspectū: cōnspectus	*sight*

in angulō cellae iacēbat Vercobrix. Modestus, cum eum vīdisset, gladium dēstrīnxit. tum, ad mediam cellam prōgressus, Vercobrigem vituperāre coepit. Vercobrix tamen contumēliās eius audīre nōn poterat, quod graviter dormiēbat. *20*

subitō arānea, ē tēctō cellae lāpsa, in nāsum Modestī incidit et trāns ōs cucurrit. Modestus, ab arāneā territus, ē cellā fūgit, vehementer clāmāns. Strȳthiō, quī extrā cellam stābat, attonitus erat. nesciēbat enim cūr Modestus clāmāret.

"Strȳthiō! Strȳthiō!" inquit. "claude portam cellae. nōbīs *25* necesse est summā cum dīligentiā Vercobrigem custōdīre. etiam arāneae eum adiuvant!"

Strȳthiō cum portam clausisset, Modestum territum rogāvit quid accidisset.

"Modeste," inquit, "quam pallidus es! num captīvum timēs?" *30*

"minimē! pallidus sum, quod nōn cēnāvī," respondit.

"vīsne mē ad culīnam īre et tibi cēnam ferre?" rogāvit Strȳthiō.

"optimum cōnsilium est!" inquit alter. "tū tamen hīc manē. melius est mihi ipsī ad culīnam īre, quod coquus decem dēnāriōs mihi dēbet." *35*

haec locūtus, ad culīnam statim cucurrit.

angulō: angulus	*corner*
prōgressus	*having advanced*
contumēliās: contumēlia	*insult, abuse*
arānea	*spider*
tēctō: tēctum	*ceiling, roof*
lāpsa: lāpsus	*having fallen*
trāns	*across*
pallidus	*pale*
hīc	*here*

Legionary helmet from the River Thames, with shield boss from VIIIth Legion found in the River Tyne.

About the Language I: Indirect Questions

A In Unit 1, you met sentences like this:

"quis clāmōrem audīvit?"   "ubi est captīvus?"
"Who heard the shout?"   *"Where is the prisoner?"*

In each example, a question is being asked. These examples are known as direct questions.

B In Stage 25, you have met sentences like this:

centuriō nesciēbat **quis clāmōrem audīvisset**.
*The centurion did not know **who had heard the shout**.*

equitēs cognōvērunt **ubi rēx habitāret**.
*The horsemen found out **where the king was living**.*

In each of these examples, the question is referred to, but not asked directly. These examples are known as indirect questions. The verb in an indirect question in Latin is subjunctive.

C Further examples of direct and indirect questions:

1 "quis puerum interfēcit?"
2 nēmō sciēbat quis puerum interfēcisset.
3 "ubi pecūniam invēnērunt?"
4 iūdex mē rogāvit ubi pecūniam invēnissent.
5 Salvius nesciēbat cūr Quīntus rēgem adiuvāret.
6 Cogidubnus cognōvit quō modō Cephalus venēnum comparāvisset.
7 Quīntus scīre voluit quid in templō esset.
8 Salvius tandem intellēxit quō Quīntus et Dumnorix fugerent.

In each of the **indirect** questions state whether the subjunctive is imperfect or pluperfect.

Modestus perfuga

I

Modestus, ēgressus ē culīnā ubi cēnam optimam cōnsūmpserat, ad carcerem lentē redībat. cum ambulāret, sīc cōgitābat,

"numquam cēnam meliōrem gustāvī; numquam vīnum suāvius bibī. sollicitus tamen sum. nam coquus illam cēnam et mihi et Strȳthiōnī parāvit, sed ego sōlus cōnsūmpsī. nunc mihi necesse est 5
hanc rem Strȳthiōnī explicāre. fortūna tamen mihi favet, quod Strȳthiō est vir magnae patientiae, minimīque cibī."

ubi carcerī appropinquāvit, portam apertam vīdit.

"dī immortālēs!" clāmāvit permōtus. "Strȳthiō, num portam carceris apertam relīquistī? nēminem neglegentiōrem quam tē 10
nōvī. "

carcerem ingressus, portās omnium cellārum apertās invēnit. cum hoc vīdisset,

"ēheu!" inquit. "omnēs portae apertae sunt! captīvī, ē cellīs ēlāpsī, omnēs fūgērunt!" 15

Modestus rem anxius cōgitāvit. nesciēbat enim quō captīvī fūgissent; intellegere nōn poterat cūr Strȳthiō abesset.

"quid facere dēbeō? perīculōsum est hīc manēre ubi mē centuriō invenīre potest. ūna est spēs salūtis. mihi fugiendum est. ō Strȳthiō, Strȳthiō! coēgistī mē statiōnem dēserere. mē perfugam 20
fēcistī. sed deōs testēs faciō. invītus statiōnem dēserō, invītus centuriōnis īram fugiō."

perfuga	deserter
sīc	in this way
et ... et	both ... and
permōtus	alarmed, disturbed
nēminem	accusative of nēmō
spēs	hope
īram: īra	anger

II

Modestus, haec locūtus, subitō sonitum audīvit. aliquis portam cellae Vercobrigis aperīre et exīre temptābat!

"mihi ē carcere fugiendum est," aliquis ē cellā clāmāvit.

Modestus, cum haec audīvisset, ad portam cellae cucurrit et clausit.   5

"Vercobrix, tibi in cellā manendum est!" clāmāvit Modestus. "euge! nōn effūgit Vercobrix! eum captīvum habeō! euge! nunc mihi centuriō nocēre nōn potest, quod captīvum summae dignitātis in carcere retinuī."

Modestus autem anxius manēbat; nesciēbat enim quid   *10* Strȳthiōnī accidisset. subitō pugiōnem humī relictum cōnspexit.

"heus, quid est? hunc pugiōnem agnōscō! est pugiō Strȳthiōnis! Strȳthiōnī dedī, ubi diem nātālem celebrābat. ēheu! cruentus est pugiō. ō mī Strȳthiō! nunc rem intellegō. mortuus es! captīvī, ē cellīs ēlāpsī, tē necāvērunt. ēheu! cum ego tuam cēnam in culīnā   *15* cōnsūmerem, illī tē oppugnābant! ō Strȳthiō! nēmō īnfēlīcior est quam ego. nam tē amābam sīcut pater fīlium. tū tamen nōn inultus periistī. Vercobrix, quī in hāc cellā etiam nunc manet, poenās dare dēbet. heus! Vercobrix, mē audī! tibi moriendum est, quod Strȳthiō meus mortuus est."   *20*

haec locūtus, in cellam furēns irrūpit. captīvum, quī intus latēbat, verberāre coepit.

captīvus:	Modeste! mī Modeste! dēsine mē verberāre! nōnne mē agnōscis? Strȳthiō sum, quem tū amās sīcut pater fīlium. *25*
Modestus:	Strȳthiō? Strȳthiō! num vīvus es? cūr vīvus es? sceleste! furcifer! ubi sunt captīvī quōs custōdiēbās?
Strȳthiō:	fūgērunt, Modeste. mē dēcēpērunt. coēgērunt mē portās omnium cellārum aperīre.
Modestus:	ēheu! quid facere dēbēmus? *30*
Strȳthiō:	nōbīs statim ē carcere fugiendum est: centuriōnem appropinquantem audiō.
Modestus:	ō Strȳthiō! ō, quam īnfēlīx sum!
Strȳthiō:	nōlī dēspērāre. cōnsilium habeō. tibi necesse est mihi cōnfīdere. *35*

amīcī ē carcere quam celerrimē fūgērunt.

aliquis	*someone*	**inultus**	*unavenged*
relictum: relinquere	*leave*	**tibi moriendum est**	*you must die*
cruentus	*blood-stained*	**vīvus**	*alive, living*

About the Language II: More About the Subjunctive

A In Stages 24 and 25 you have met the 3rd person singular and plural ("he," "she," "it," and "they") of the imperfect and pluperfect subjunctive. For example:

> nēmō sciēbat ubi Britannī **latērent**.
> *Nobody knew where the Britons were lying hidden.*

> centuriō, cum hoc **audīvisset**, saeviēbat.
> *When the centurion had heard this, he was furious.*

B Now study the forms of the 1st person ("I," "we") and the 2nd person ("you") of the imperfect and pluperfect subjunctive.

SINGULAR	IMPERFECT	PLUPERFECT
1st person	portārem	portāvissem
2nd person	portārēs	portāvissēs
3rd person	portāret	portāvisset

PLURAL		
1st person	portārēmus	portāvissēmus
2nd person	portārētis	portāvissētis
3rd person	portārent	portāvissent

C Translate the following examples:

1 custōdēs nōs rogāvērunt cūr clāmārēmus.
2 nesciēbam quō fūgissēs.
3 cum in Britanniā mīlitārem, oppidum Aquās Sūlis saepe vīsitābam.
4 cum cēnam tuam cōnsūmerēs, centuriō tē quaerēbat.
5 rēx nōbīs explicāvit quō modō vītam suam servāvissētis.
6 cum nōmina recitāvissem, hospitēs ad rēgem dūxī.
7 amīcus meus cognōscere voluit ubi habitārētis.
8 puella nōs rogāvit cūr rem tam difficilem suscēpissēmus.

In each sentence state whether the subjunctive is 1st or 2nd person singular or plural and whether it is imperfect or pluperfect.

Word Patterns: Male and Female

A Study the following nouns:

dominus, rēx, leaena, dea, domina, fīlia, captīvus, fīlius, captīva, leō, deus, rēgīna.

Organize these nouns in pairs and write them out in two columns headed male and female.

B Add the following nouns to your columns. Some meanings are given to help you.

saltātrīx, vēnātor (*hunter*), avus (*grandfather*), vēnātrīx, victor, avia, victrīx, ursus, lupa, lupus, ursa, saltātor.

C Which two endings here indicate the masculine form of a Latin noun? What are the feminine equivalents for those two endings?

Practicing the Language

A Translate each English sentence into Latin by selecting correctly from the list of Latin words.

1 *The kind citizens had provided help.*
| cīvis | benignī | auxilium | praebuērunt |
| cīvēs | benignōs | auxiliī | praebuerant |

2 *They arrested the soldier in the kitchen of an inn.*
| mīlitem | per culīnam | tabernae | comprehendunt |
| mīlitis | in culīnā | tabernārum | comprehendērunt |

3 *Master! Read this letter!*
| domine | haec | epistula | lege |
| dominus | hanc | epistulam | legis |

4 *The old men departed, praising the brave messenger.*
| senēs | discēdunt | fortem | nūntium | laudāns |
| senum | discessērunt | fortī | nūntiōs | laudantēs |

5 *How can we avoid the punishments of the gods?*
| quō modō | poenae | deōrum | vītantēs | possumus |
| quis | poenās | deīs | vītāre | poterāmus |

6 *The words of the soothsayer frightened him.*
| verbum | haruspicis | eam | eum | terruit |
| verba | haruspicī | eōs | terruērunt |

B Complete the sentences of this story with the most suitable word from the list below, and then translate.

clāmāvit, cucurrit, invēnit, coxit, bibit, cōnsūmpsit, exiit

Modestus ad culīnam īrātus . . . . . . culīnam ingressus, coquum occupātum . . . . . . coquus cibum parābat.
  "ubi sunt denāriī quōs mihi dēbēs?" . . . . . Modestus.
  coquus, ubi Modestum īrātum vīdit, eī pōculum vīnī obtulit.
Modestus libenter vīnum . . . . . . deinde coquus cēnam . . . . . et
Modestō obtulit. Modestus, simulac cēnam gustāvit, avidus . . . . . .
  postrēmō Modestus, optimē cēnātus, ē culīnā ēbrius . . . . . ,
immemor pecūniae. coquus in culīnā stābat cachinnāns.

C Complete each sentence with the correct participle from the list below. Then translate the sentence.

missōs, līberātī, territa, regressam, tenentēs, passus

1 captīvī, ē cellīs subitō . . . . . ., ad portam carceris ruērunt.
2 Britannī, hastās in manibus . . . . . ., castra oppugnāvērunt.
3 ancilla, ā dominō īrātō . . . . . ., respondēre nōn audēbat.
4 Cogidubnus, tot iniūriās . . . . . ., Rōmānōs vehementer
   vituperāvit.
5 māter puellam, ē tabernā tandem . . . . . ., pūnīvit.
6 centuriō mīlitēs, ex Ītaliā nūper ab Imperātōre . . . . . ., īnspexit.

D This exercise is based on the story **Modestus custōs** on pages 89–90. Read the story again. Complete each of the sentences below with one of the following groups of words. Then translate the sentence. Use each group of words once only.

a cum Modestus extrā cellam haesitāret
b cum Modestus ad culīnam abiisset
c cum arānea in nāsum dēcidisset
d cum lucernam tulisset
e cum Modestus vehementer clāmāret

1 . . . . ., Strȳthiō eum rogāvit cūr timēret.
2 Strȳthiō, ..., Modestō trādidit.
3 . . . . ., Vercobrix graviter dormiēbat.
4 . . . . ., Modestus fūgit perterritus.
5 . . . . ., Strȳthiō in carcere mānsit.

The Legionary Soldier

The soldiers who served in the legions formed the elite of the Roman army (**exercitus**). Each soldier (**mīles**) was a Roman citizen and full-time professional who had signed on for twenty-five years. Roman soldiers were highly trained in the skills of infantry warfare and were often specialists in other fields as well. In fact a Roman legion, consisting normally of about 5,000 foot soldiers, was a miniature army in itself, capable of constructing forts and camps, manufacturing its weapons and equipment, and building roads. On its staff were engineers, architects, carpenters, smiths, doctors, medical orderlies, clerks, and accountants.

Building camps and erecting bridges were among the skills required of the army. In this picture, auxiliary soldiers stand guard while soldiers from the legions do engineering work.

Recruitment

An investigating board (**inquīsītiō**) would first ensure that a new recruit was a Roman citizen and that he was given a medical examination. Vegetius, who wrote a military manual in the fourth century A.D., laid down guidelines for choosing recruits:

A young soldier should have alert eyes and should hold his head upright. The recruit should be broad-chested with powerful shoulders and brawny arms. His fingers should be long rather than short. He should not be pot-bellied or have a fat bottom. His calves and feet should not be flabby; instead they should be made entirely of tough sinew. The whole well-being of the Roman state depends on the kind of recruits you choose; so you must choose men who are outstanding not only in body but also in mind.

A centurion, a legionary, and the aquilifer (eagle-bearer) of the legion.

Training, Armor, and Weapons

After being accepted and sworn in, the new recruit was sent to his unit to begin training. This was thorough, systematic, and physically hard. First the young soldier had to learn to march at the regulation pace for distances of up to 24 Roman miles (about 22 statute miles or 35 kilometers). Physical fitness was further developed by running, jumping, swimming, and carrying heavy packs. Next came weapons training, starting with a wooden practice-sword, wicker shield, and dummy targets and progressing to actual equipment. Vegetius again:

They are also taught not to cut with their swords but to thrust. The Romans find it so easy to defeat people who use their swords to cut rather than thrust that they laugh in their faces. For a cutting stroke, even when made with full force, rarely kills. The vital organs are protected by the armor as well as by the bones of the body. On the other hand, a stab even two inches deep is usually fatal.

Soldiers marching with their kit slung from stakes.

Besides the short stabbing sword (**gladius**) worn on the right, the legionary was armed with a dagger (**pugiō**) worn on the left, and a javelin (**pīlum**). The legionary shield (**scūtum**) was a three-foot-long (1 meter), curved rectangle made of strips of wood glued together and covered with hide. Soldiers learned to handle their shields correctly and to attack dummy targets with the point of their swords.

Another phase of weapons training was to learn to throw the pilum. This had a wooden shaft 5 feet (1.5 meters) long and a pointed iron head of 2 feet (60 centimeters). The head was cleverly constructed so that the first 10 inches (25 centimeters) of tempered metal penetrated the target, but the rest, untempered, was fairly soft and liable to bend. When the javelin was hurled at an enemy, from a distance of 25–30 yards (23–28 meters), its point penetrated and stuck into his shield, while the neck of the metal head bent and the shaft hung down. This not only made the javelin unusable, so that it could not be thrown back, but also made the encumbered shield so difficult to manage that the enemy might have to abandon it altogether.

By the time of our stories, the legionary soldier was wearing segmented armor of metal strips (**lōrīca segmentāta**) with leather straps and buckle fastenings over a woolen tunic. The military belt (**cingulum**) was worn at all times, even without the armor. At first the Roman soldier did not wear trousers, but short leggings were gradually adopted. The legionary helmet was padded on the inside and designed to protect the head, face, and neck without obstructing hearing or vision. Strong military sandals (**caligae**) with very thick soles and iron hobnails were designed to withstand weight and miles of marching.

When the recruit could handle his weapons competently and was physically fit, he was ready to leave the barracks for training in the open countryside. This began with route marches on which he carried not only his body armor and weapons but also a heavy pack which weighed about 90 pounds (40 kilograms), and which included dishes, water bottle, woolen cloak, several days' ration of food, and equipment for making an overnight camp, such as a saw, an axe, and a basket for moving earth. Much importance was attached to the proper construction of the camp at the end of the day's march, and the young soldier was given careful instruction and practice. Several practice camps and forts have been found in Britain.

Life and Work of a Soldier

The fully trained legionary did not spend all or even much of his time on combat duty. Most of it was spent on peacetime duties, such as building or roadmaking, and he was given free time and leave. During the first century A.D. at least, he had good prospects of surviving until his term of service expired.

Many of the daily duties and activities were the same wherever the soldier was stationed. Inscriptional evidence gives us insights into the everyday life of a soldier. A duty roster, written on papyrus and covering the first ten days in October possibly in the year A.D. 87, lists the names of thirty-six soldiers in the same unit in a legion stationed in Egypt. C. Julius Valens, for example, was to spend October 2nd on guard duty, October 5th and 6th in the armory, and October 7th in the bath house, probably stoking the furnace. Letters and documents on wax and wooden tablets, dating from the late first to the early second century A.D., have been found at the fortress of Vindolanda (modern Chesterholm) in Britain. Duty rosters show men assigned to work in the pottery kilns, the bakery, and the brewery; to build a bath house and a hospital; and to make shields and swords. Other Vindolanda tablets contain an intelligence report, a list of foodstuffs for the fort and their prices, a request for leave, and a complaint for non-delivery of items. From correspondence between officers' wives, we learn that Sulpicia Lepidina received an

Relief of legionary soldiers and cavalry auxiliary.

invitation to a birthday party from the wife of a commander of a neighboring fort. And one fragment offers a very personal glimpse:

> I have sent you ... woolen socks, ... two pairs of sandals and two pairs of underpants ... .

Vindolanda tablets.

Pay and Promotion

In both war and peacetime the soldier received the same rate of pay. In the first century A.D., up to the time of the Emperor Domitian (A.D. 81–96), this amounted to 225 denarii per annum; Domitian improved the rate to 300 denarii. These amounts were gross pay; before any money was handed to the soldier certain deductions were made. Surprising though it may seem, he was obliged to pay for his food, clothing, and equipment. He would also leave some money in the military savings bank. What he actually received in cash may have been only a quarter or a fifth of his gross pay. Whether he felt badly treated is difficult to say. Certainly we know of cases of discontent and – very occasionally – mutiny, but pay

*Centurion in the Ermine Street Guard,
wearing his decorations and his helmet
with transverse plume and leaning on his
vine-wood staff (vītis).*

and conditions of service were apparently not bad enough to discourage recruits. Any soldier could hope for promotion, in which case his life began to change in several ways. He was paid more and he was exempted from many of the duties performed by the ordinary soldier. In addition, any soldier could look forward to an honorable discharge at the end of 20 to 25 years of service with a lump sum of 3,000 denarii or an allocation of land.

The Auxiliaries

The heavily armed legionaries formed the best-trained fighting force in the Roman army but they needed to be supplemented by large numbers of specialized troops. These were provided by men from different parts of the empire who had developed particular skills, for example, archers from Arabia and slingers from Majorca and Minorca. The most important and prestigious were the cavalry, who were regularly used in battle to support the infantry. They were usually positioned on each side of the legionaries from where they could protect the center, launch attacks themselves, or pursue defeated enemy forces.

Auxiliaries were paid less than legionary soldiers. However, when they completed their service, those who were not already Roman citizens were granted citizenship. This was another way of making people in the provinces feel loyalty to Roman rule.

Word Study

A Match the Latin word to its antonym:

1	aperīre	a	nēmō
2	dēsinere	b	praemium
3	nescīre	c	incipere
4	poena	d	scīre
5	scelestus	e	induere
6	aliquis	f	claudere
7	dēpōnere	g	bonus

B Complete the following analogies with words from the Stage 25 Vocabulary Checklist:

1 aedificium : urbs : : mīles : ___
2 vir : homō : : iterum : ___
3 custōs : iubēre : : ___ : pārēre
4 velle : cupere : : dulcis : ___
5 turba : multitūdō : : malus : ___

C Give the Latin root of the following English words. Define the English word, using the meaning of the Latin word in your definition.

1 penal
2 immemorial
3 oral
4 lesion
5 extraterrestrial
6 deposit
7 aperture
8 nomenclature

D Answer the following questions:

1 What do the cities of Lancaster, Rochester, and Worcester have in common?
2 Based on meaning, explain which word does NOT belong.

a	umerus	lītus	oculus	ōs	manus
b	prāvus	scelestus	molestus	benignus	malus
c	saevus	furēns	īrātus	dūrus	tūtus

Stage 25 Vocabulary Checklist

accidō, accidere, accidī — *happen*
aliquis — *someone*
aperiō, aperīre, aperuī, apertus — *open*
autem — *but*
captīvus, captīvī, m. — *prisoner, captive*
castra, castrōrum, n. pl. — *military camp*
cōgō, cōgere, coēgī, coāctus — *force, compel*
dēpōnō, dēpōnere, dēposuī, dēpositus — *put down, take off*
dēsinō, dēsinere — *end, cease*
dignitās, dignitātis, f. — *importance, prestige*
dīligentia, dīligentiae, f. — *industry, hard work*
explicō, explicāre, explicāvī, explicātus — *explain*
extrā (+ ACC) — *outside*
furēns, furēns, furēns, *gen.* furentis — *furious, in a rage*
haesitō, haesitāre, haesitāvī — *hesitate*
immemor, immemor, immemor,
  gen. immemoris — *forgetful*
immortālis, immortālis, immortāle — *immortal*
  dī immortālēs! — *heavens above!*
laedō, laedere, laesī,
  laesus — *harm*
lateō, latēre, latuī — *lie hidden*
legiō, legiōnis, f. — *legion*
nescio, nescīre, nescīvī — *not know*
nōmen, nōminis, n. — *name*
ōs, ōris, n. — *face*
poena, poenae, f. — *punishment*
  poenās dare — *pay the penalty, be punished*

rūrsus — *again*
scelestus, scelesta,
  scelestum — *wicked*
statiō, statiōnis, f. — *post*
suāvis, suāvis, suāve — *sweet*
testis, testis, m. f. — *witness*

A Roman soldier's dagger.

AGRICOLA

Stage 26

adventus Agricolae

mīlitēs legiōnis secundae, quī Devae in castrīs erant, diū et strēnuē labōrābant. nam Gāius Iūlius Sīlānus, lēgātus legiōnis, adventum Agricolae exspectābat. mīlitēs, ā centuriōnibus iussī, multa et varia faciēbant. aliī arma poliēbant; aliī aedificia pūrgābant; aliī plaustra reficiēbant. Sīlānus neque quiētem neque commeātum mīlitibus 5 dedit.

mīlitēs, ignārī adventūs Agricolae, rem graviter ferēbant. trēs continuōs diēs labōrābant; quārtō diē Sīlānus adventum Agricolae nūntiāvit. mīlitēs, cum hoc audīvissent, maximē gaudēbant quod Agricolam dīligēbant. 10

tertiā hōrā Sīlānus mīlitēs in ōrdinēs longōs īnstrūxit, ut Agricolam salūtārent. mīlitēs, cum Agricolam castra intrantem vīdissent, magnum clāmōrem sustulērunt.

"iō, Agricola! iō, iō, Agricola!"

tantus erat clāmor ut nēmō iussa centuriōnum audīret. 15

Agricola ad tribūnal prōcessit ut pauca dīceret. omnēs statim tacuērunt ut contiōnem Agricolae audīrent.

"gaudeō," inquit, "quod hodiē vōs rūrsus videō. nūllam legiōnem fidēliōrem habeō, nūllam fortiōrem. disciplīnam studiumque vestrum valdē laudō." 20

mīlitēs ita hortātus, per ōrdinēs prōcessit ut eōs īnspiceret. deinde prīncipia intrāvit ut colloquium cum Sīlānō habēret.

adventus	arrival	gaudēbant:	be pleased,
Devae	at Deva	gaudēre	rejoice
strēnuē	hard,	tertiā hōrā	at the third hour
	energetically	iō!	hurrah!
aliī ... aliī ... aliī	some ...	tribūnal: tribūnal	platform
	others ...	contiōnem:	
	others	contiō	speech
arma: arma	arms, weapons	disciplīnam:	discipline,
poliēbant: polīre	polish	disciplīna	orderliness
pūrgābant: pūrgāre	clean	studium: studium	enthusiasm,
quiētem: quiēs	rest		zeal
commeātum:		vestrum: vester	your
commeātus	(military) leave	hortātus	having
trēs ... diēs	for three days		encouraged
continuōs: continuus	continuous,	prīncipia:	
	in a row	prīncipia	headquarters
quārtō diē	on the fourth day		

in prīncipiīs

When you have read this story, answer the questions at the end.

Salvius ipse paulō prius ad castra advēnerat. iam in legiōnis secundae prīncipiīs sedēbat, Agricolam anxius exspectāns. sollicitus erat quod in epistulā, quam ad Agricolam mīserat, multa falsa scrīpserat. in prīmīs Cogidubnum sēditiōnis accūsāverat. in animō volvēbat num Agricola sibi crēditūrus esset. Belimicum 5 sēcum dūxerat ut testis esset.

subitō Salvius, Agricolam intrantem cōnspicātus, ad eum festīnāvit ut salūtāret. deinde renovāvit ea quae in epistulā scrīpserat. Agricola, cum haec audīvisset, diū tacēbat. dēnique maximē commōtus, 10

"quanta perfidia!" inquit. "quanta īnsānia! id quod mihi patefēcistī, vix intellegere possum. īnsānīvit Cogidubnus.

paulō prius	a little earlier
in prīmīs	in particular
sēditiōnis: sēditiō	rebellion
in animō volvēbat: in animō volvere	wonder, turn over in the mind
num	whether
crēditūrus	going to believe
renovāvit: renovāre	repeat, renew
īnsānia	insanity, madness

īnsānīvērunt prīncipēs Rēgnēnsium. numquam nōs oportet barbarīs crēdere; tūtius est eōs omnēs prō hostibus habēre. nunc mihi necesse est rēgem opprimere quem quīnque annōs prō amīcō habeō." 15

haec locūtus, ad Sīlānum, lēgātum legiōnis, sē vertit.

"Sīlāne," inquit, "nōs oportet rēgem prīncipēsque Rēgnēnsium quam celerrimē opprimere. tibi statim cum duābus cohortibus proficīscendum est." 20

Sīlānus, ē prīncipiīs ēgressus, centuriōnibus mandāta dedit. eōs iussit cohortēs parāre. intereā Agricola plūra dē rēgis perfidiā rogāre coepit. Salvius eī respondit,

"ecce Belimicus, vir ingeniī optimī summaeque fideī, quem iste Cogidubnus corrumpere temptābat. Belimicus autem, quī 25 blanditiās rēgis spernēbat, omnia mihi patefēcit."

"id quod Salvius dīxit vērum est," inquit Belimicus. "rēx Rōmānōs ōdit. Rōmānōs ē Britanniā expellere tōtamque īnsulam occupāre cupit. nāvēs igitur comparat. mīlitēs exercet. etiam bēstiās saevās colligit. nūper bēstiam in mē impulit ut mē 30 interficeret."

Agricola tamen hīs verbīs diffīsus, Salvium dīligentius rogāvit quae indicia sēditiōnis vīdisset. cognōscere voluit quot essent armātī, num Britannī cīvēs Rōmānōs interfēcissent, quās urbēs dēlēvissent. 35

subitō magnum clāmōrem omnēs audīvērunt. per iānuam prīncipiōrum perrūpit homō squālidus. ad Agricolam praeceps cucurrit genibusque eius haesit.

"cīvis Rōmānus sum," inquit. "Quīntum Caecilium Iūcundum mē vocant. ego multās iniūriās passus hūc tandem advēnī. hoc 40 ūnum dīcere volō. Cogidubnus est innocēns."

haec locūtus humī prōcubuit exanimātus.

nōs oportet	*we must*
prō hostibus habēre	*consider as enemies*
opprimere	*crush*
tibi ... proficīscendum est	*you must set out*
cohortibus: cohors	*cohort*
corrumpere	*corrupt*
blanditiās: blanditiae	*flatteries*
spernēbat: spernere	*despise, reject*
diffīsus	*having distrusted*
indicia: indicium	*sign, evidence*
perrūpit: perrumpere	*burst through, burst in*
squālidus	*covered with dirt, filthy*

Questions

1 Why was Salvius in the headquarters?
2 Why is he described as **sollicitus** (lines 3–4)?
3 What particular accusation had he made?
4 Why had he brought Belimicus with him?
5 **Agricola ... diū tacēbat** (line 9). What is there in his subsequent comments which would explain his hesitation?
6 What conclusion did he come to about the proper treatment for barbarians?
7 What did Agricola tell Silanus they had to do? What order was Silanus given?
8 After Silanus left, what did Agricola try to find out?
9 How did Salvius describe Belimicus' character? According to Salvius, how had Belimicus helped him?
10 From Belimicus' information in lines 27–31, find one thing that Agricola might have believed and one thing about which he might have had doubts.
11 In lines 32–35 Agricola asked Salvius for evidence of the rebellion. What three details did he want to find out? What do you think of Agricola for not asking these questions before sending out the cohorts?
12 What happened before Salvius could answer Agricola?
13 What two things did the **homō squālidus** do (lines 37–38)?
14 What did he say first? Why? What were his final words?
15 **haec locūtus humī prōcubuit exanimātus** (line 42). Which three Latin words in his speech explain why he suddenly collapsed?

About the Language I: Purpose Clauses

A Study the following examples:

> mīlitēs ad prīncipia convēnērunt **ut Agricolam audīrent**.
> *The soldiers gathered at the headquarters **in order that they might hear Agricola**.*

> per tōtam noctem labōrābat medicus **ut vulnera mīlitum sānāret**.
> *The doctor worked all night **in order that he might treat the soldiers' wounds**.*

The groups of words in boldface are known as purpose clauses, because they indicate the purpose for which an action was done. The verb in a purpose clause in Latin is always subjunctive.

B Instead of translating **ut** and the subjunctive as *in order that I (you, s/he, etc.) might ...*, it is often possible to use a simpler form of words:

> mīlitēs ad prīncipia convēnērunt **ut Agricolam audīrent**.
> *The soldiers gathered at the headquarters **in order to hear Agricola**.*

Or, simpler still:
> *The soldiers gathered at the headquarters **to hear Agricola**.*

C Further examples:
1 omnēs cīvēs ad silvam contendērunt ut leōnem mortuum spectārent.
2 dominus stilum et cērās poposcit ut epistulam scrīberet.
3 dēnique ego ad patrem rediī ut rem explicārem.
4 rēx iter ad fontem fēcit ut aquam sacram biberet.
5 equōs celeriter cōnscendimus ut ex oppidō fugerēmus.
6 vīllam intrāvistī ut pecūniam nostram caperēs.

tribūnus

Agricola, ubi hoc vīdit, custōdēs iussit Quīntum auferre medicumque arcessere. tum ad tribūnum mīlitum, quī adstābat, sē vertit.

"mī Rūfe," inquit, "prūdentissimus es omnium tribūnōrum quōs habeō. tē iubeō hunc hominem summā cum cūrā interrogāre." 5

Salvius, cum Rūfus exiisset, valdē commōtus,

"cūr tempus terimus?" inquit. "omnia explicāre possum. nōtus est mihi hic homō. nūper in vīllā mē vīsitāvit, quamquam nōn invītāveram. trēs mēnsēs apud mē manēbat, opēs meās dēvorāns. 10 duōs tripodas argenteōs habēbam, quōs abstulit ut Cogidubnō daret. sed eum nōn accūsāvī, quod hospes erat. ubi tamen Aquās Sūlis mēcum advēnit, facinus scelestum committere temptāvit. venēnum parāvit ut Memorem, haruspicem Rōmānum, necāret. postquam rem nōn effēcit, mē ipsum accūsāvit. nōlī eī crēdere. 15 multō perfidior est quam Britannī."

haec cum audīvisset, Agricola respondit,

"sī tālia fēcit, eī moriendum est."

mox revēnit Rūfus valdē attonitus.

"Quīntus Caecilius," inquit, "est iuvenis summae fideī. patrem 20 meum, quem Alexandrīae relīquī, bene nōverat. hoc prō certō habeō quod Quīntus hanc epistulam mihi ostendit, ā patre ipsō scrīptam."

Agricola statim Quīntum ad sē vocāvit, cēterōsque dīmīsit. Salvius, Quīntum dētestātus, anxius exiit. Agricola cum Quīntō 25 colloquium trēs hōrās habēbat.

tribūnus	tribune (high-ranking officer)
adstābat: adstāre	stand by
prūdentissimus: prūdēns	shrewd, intelligent
tempus terimus:	
tempus terere	waste time
opēs: opēs	money, wealth
dēvorāns: dēvorāre	devour, eat up
multō perfidior	much more
	treacherous
tālia	such things
prō certō habeō:	
prō certō habēre	know for certain
dētestātus	having cursed

contentiō

Agricola, cum Quīntum audīvisset, Salvium furēns arcessīvit. quī, simulatque intrāvit, aliquid dīcere coepit. Agricola tamen, cum silentium iussisset, Salvium vehementer accūsāvit.

"dī immortālēs! Cogidubnus est innocēns, tū perfidus. cūr tam īnsānus eram ut tibi crēderem? quīnque annōs hanc prōvinciam   5
iam administrō. rēgem Cogidubnum bene cognōvī. saepe rēx mihi
auxiliō fuit. neque perfidum neque mendācem umquam sē
praestitit. cūr tū crīmen falsum in eum intulistī? accūsāvistīne eum
ut potentiam tuam augērēs? simulatque ad hanc prōvinciam
vēnistī, amīcī mē monuērunt ut tē cavērem. aliī calliditātem tuam   10
commemorāvērunt, aliī superbiam. nunc rēs ipsa mē docuit. num
Imperātor Domitiānus hanc tantam perfidiam ferre potest? ego
sānē nōn possum. in hāc prōvinciā summam potestātem habeō.
iubeō tē hās inimīcitiās dēpōnere. iubeō tē ad Cogidubnī aulam īre,
veniamque ab eō petere. praetereā tē oportet Imperātōrī ipsī rem   15
explicāre."

haec ubi dīxit Agricola, Salvius respondit īrātus,

"quam caecus es! quam longē errās! tē ipsum oportet Imperātōrī
id quod in Britanniā fēcistī explicāre. quīnque annōs hanc
prōvinciam pessimē administrās. tū enim in ultimīs Britanniae   20
partibus bellum geris et victōriās inānēs ē Calēdoniā refers; sed
Imperātor pecūniās opēsque accipere cupit. itaque rēgnum

Cogidubnī occupāre cōnstituit; Calēdoniam floccī nōn facit. tū
sānē hoc nescīs. in magnō perīculō es, quod cōnsilium meum
spernis. nōn sōlum mihi sed Imperātōrī ipsī obstās."   25
    cum hanc contentiōnem inter sē habērent, subitō nūntius
prīncipia ingressus exclāmāvit,
    "mortuus est Cogidubnus!"

auxiliō fuit	was a help, was helpful	tē oportet	you must
		caecus	blind
potentiam: potentia	power	victōriās: victōria	victory
augērēs: augēre	increase	inānēs: inānis	empty, meaningless
cavērem: cavēre	beware of		
superbiam: superbia	arrogance	Calēdoniā:	
Imperātor Domitiānus	the Emperor Domitian	Calēdonia	Scotland
		cōnstituit:	
inimīcitiās: inimīcitia	feud, dispute	cōnstituere	decide

About the Language II: Gerundives

A From Stage 14 onwards you have met sentences of this kind:

> necesse est mihi ad castra contendere.
> *I must hurry to the camp.*

> necesse est vōbīs labōrāre.
> *You must work.*

B You have now met another way of expressing the same idea:

> necesse est nōbīs currere.   necesse est eī revenīre.
> nōbīs **currendum** est.   eī **reveniendum** est.
> *We must run.*   *He must come back.*

The word in boldface is known as the gerundive.

C Further examples:

1 mihi fugiendum est.
2 nōbīs ambulandum est.
3 tibi hīc manendum est.
4 servīs dīligenter labōrandum est.
5 omnibus cīvibus tacendum est quod sacerdōtēs
   appropinquant.
6 sī Imperātōrem vidēre volunt, eīs festīnandum est.

Word Patterns: Verbs and Nouns

A Some verbs and nouns are closely connected. For example:

VERBS		NOUNS	
amāre	*to love*	amor	*love*
clāmāre	*to shout*	clāmor	*a shout, shouting*
terrēre	*to terrify*	terror	*terror*

B Now complete the table below:

timēre	*to fear*	timor	. . . . .
dolēre	(1) *to hurt, to be in pain*	dolor	(1) . . . . .
dolēre	(2) *to grieve*	dolor	(2) . . . . .
favēre	. . . . .	favor	*favor*
furere	. . . . .	furor	*rage*
labōrāre	. . . . .	. . . . .	. . . . .

C Work out the meanings of the following words:

ardor, error, fulgor, pallor, sudor

Practicing the Language

A Complete each sentence with the most suitable word from the list below, and then translate.

epistulam, audīvisset, ēgressus, invēnērunt, equīs, captī

1 Salvius, ē prīncipiīs . . . . ., Belimicum quaesīvit.
2 Agricola, cum haec verba . . . . ., ad Rūfum sē vertit.
3 dominus . . . . . ē manibus servī impatiēns rapuit.
4 custōdēs nūntium humī iacentem . . . . . .
5 quattuor Britannī, in pugnā . . . . ., vītam miserrimam in carcere agēbant.
6 aliī mīlitēs . . . . . aquam dabant, aliī frūmentum in horrea īnferēbant.

B Complete each sentence with the correct form of the noun and then translate.

[handwritten: when he heard Quintus's words,]

1 Agricola, ubi verba (Quīntum, Quīntī, Quīntō) audīvit, Salvium arcessīvit. *[handwritten: Summoned Salvius.]*
2 omnēs hospitēs (artem, artis, arte) saltātrīcis laudāvērunt.
3 iter nostrum difficile erat, quod tot cīvēs (viās, viārum, viīs) complēbant.
4 post mortem Dumnorigis Quīntus sine (comitem, comitis, comite) prōcessit.
5 prō prīncipiīs stābat magna turba (mīlitēs, mīlitum, mīlitibus).
6 lēgātus, postquam mandāta (centuriōnēs, centuriōnum, centuriōnibus) dedit, legiōnem ad montem proximum dūxit.
7 Quīntus, ab (equitēs, equitum, equitibus) vulnerātus, Agricolam petīvit.
8 iūdex, quī (puerōs, puerōrum, puerīs) nōn crēdēbat, īrātissimus fīēbat.

C Complete each sentence with the right form of the subjunctive. Then translate the sentence.

[handwritten: when Silanus set up the legion,]

1 cum Sīlānus legiōnem (īnstrūxisset, īnstrūxissent), Agricola ē prīncipiīs prōcessit. *[handwritten: Agricola proceeded out of the headquarters]*
2 mīlitēs in flūmen dēsiluērunt ut hostēs (vītāret, vītārent).
3 senātor scīre voluit num pater meus Imperātōrī (fāvisset, fāvissent).
4 cum senex (dormīret, dormīrent), fūrēs per fenestram tacitē intrāvērunt.
5 nōs, cum in Britanniā (essem, essēmus), barbarōs saepe vīcimus.
6 intellegere nōn poteram cūr cīvēs istum hominem (laudāvisset, laudāvissent).
7 latrōnem interfēcī ut īnfantem (servārem, servārēmus).
8 māter tua mē rogāvit quid in tabernā (fēcissēs, fēcissētis).

Diagram of a Legion

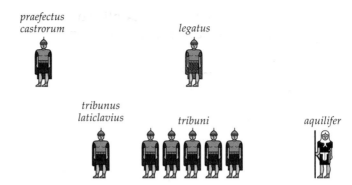

praefectus
castrorum

legatus

tribunus
laticlavius

tribuni

aquilifer

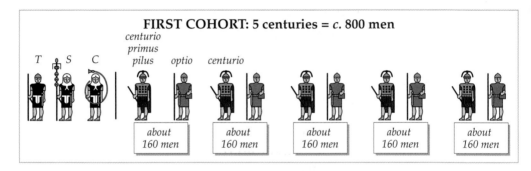

FIRST COHORT: 5 centuries = *c*. 800 men

T S C

centurio
primus
pilus   optio   centurio

| about 160 men | about 160 men | about 160 men | about 160 men | about 160 men |

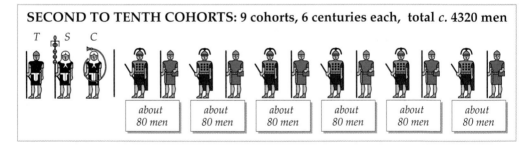

SECOND TO TENTH COHORTS: 9 cohorts, 6 centuries each, total *c*. 4320 men

T S C

| about 80 men | about 80 men | about 80 men | about 80 men | about 80 men | about 80 men |

HORSEMEN: about 120

Key
T = tesserarius
S = signifer
C = cornicen (horn player)
Each cohort had one of each of these.
Each century had a centurion and an optio.

Organization of the Legion

Each legion was made up of ten cohorts. Nine of these, cohorts two to ten, were composed of six centuries, each commanded by a centurion and containing about 80 men. The first cohort was the most prestigious unit and consisted of five double-sized centuries commanded by five senior centurions known as **prīmī ōrdinēs** (first rank).

Each centurion was assisted by an **optiō** or deputy who would take control of the century if the centurion were absent or lost in battle. There was also in each century a **signifer** (standard-bearer) and a **tesserārius**, who organized the guards and distributed the passwords, and one or two clerks. The centurions were the backbone of the legion. Most of them had long experience in the army and had risen from the ranks because of their courage and ability. There were sixty of them, each responsible for the training and discipline of a century. As a symbol of rank, each centurion carried a **vītis** or cane with which he could punish his soldiers. The importance of the centurions was reflected in their pay, which was probably about 1,500 denarii per annum. The most senior centurion of the legion was the **prīmus pīlus**, a highly respected figure; he was at least fifty years old and had worked his way up through the various grades of centurion. He held office for one year, then received a large payment and was allowed to retire; or he might go on still further to become the **praefectus castrōrum** (the commander of the camp), the highest-ranking officer to serve his entire career in the army.

The Senior Officers

The officer commanding a legion was called a **lēgātus**. He was a member of the Senate in Rome and usually in his middle thirties. He was assisted by six military tribunes. Of these, one was the **tribūnus lāticlāvius** (senior tribune with a broad stripe) who was usually a young man of noble birth, serving his military apprenticeship before starting a political career. After holding civilian posts in Rome or one of the provinces, he might be appointed as legatus and spend three or four years commanding his legion. Then he would usually resume his civilian career.

The other five tribunes, the **tribūnī angusticlāviī** (tribunes with the narrow stripe), were members of a slightly lower social class (**equitēs**), and they would also be in their thirties. They were generally able, wealthy, and educated men, often aiming at important posts in the imperial administration. Some of them returned to the army later to command auxiliary cavalry units.

How We Know About Agricola

The two inscriptions below both contain the name of Gnaeus Iulius Agricola. The first is on a lead water pipe found at Chester.

With the abbreviated words written out, this reads:

> **imperatore Vespasiano VIIII Tito imperatore VII consulibus Cnaeo Iulio Agricola legato Augusti propraetore**

This shows that the pipe was made in A.D. 79, when Vespasian and Titus were consuls and Agricola was governor of Britain.

The inscription drawn below was found in the forum of Verulamium (see map page 2). Only fragments have survived, giving us the letters in red. But it is possible to guess at the rest of the first five lines because they contain only the names and titles of the emperor Titus, his brother and successor Domitian, and Agricola. There is not enough left to reconstruct the last line.

```
IMP·TITVS·CAESAR·DIVI·VESPASIANI·F·VESPASIANVS·AVG
P·M·TR·PVIIII·IMPXV·COSVIIDESIG·VIII·CENSOR·PATER·PATRIAE
ET·CAESAR·DIVI·VESPASIANI·F·DOMITIANVS·COS·VI·DESIG·VII
PRINCEPS·IVVENTVTIS·COLLEGIORVM·OMNIVM·SACERDOS
CN·IVLIO·AGRICOLA·LEG·AVG·PRO·PR
            VE                        NATA
```

These inscriptions might have been virtually all that we knew about Agricola if his life-story had not been written by his son-in-law, the historian Tacitus.

The senior officers usually spent only short periods in the army, unlike the centurions and the legionaries who served for the whole of their working lives. They had therefore to rely heavily on the expertise and experience of the centurions for advice. Because the army was highly trained and well organized, the appointment of relatively inexperienced officers rarely affected the success of its operations.

Some officers like Agricola proved themselves to be extremely competent and were promoted to become governors of provinces like Britain where military skill and powers of leadership were required.

Agricola, Governor of Britain

Agricola was born in A.D. 40 in the Roman colony of Forum Iulii (modern Frejus) in southeast Gaul. His father had been made a senator by the Emperor Tiberius, but later fell out of favor with the Emperor Gaius Caligula and was executed shortly after Agricola was born.

Agricola went to school at Massilia (Marseille), which was the cultural and educational center of southern Gaul. He followed the normal curriculum for the young sons of upper-class Roman families: public speaking and philosophy. He enjoyed the latter, but the historian Tacitus, Agricola's son-in-law and biographer, records his mother's reaction:

> I remember that Agricola often told us that in his youth he was more enthusiastic about philosophy than a Roman and a senator was expected to be and that his mother thought it wise to restrain such a passionate interest.

At the age of eighteen, Agricola served in the Roman army in Britain with the rank of **tribūnus**. He used this opportunity to become familiar with the province. The soldiers under his command had a similar opportunity to get to know him. Two years later, during the revolt of Boudica in A.D. 60, he witnessed the grim realities of warfare. Agricola was by now very knowledgeable about the province of Britain and this knowledge was very useful during his governorship some eighteen years later.

Back in Rome, he continued his political career. In A.D. 70, he returned to Britain to take command of the Twentieth Legion which was stationed at Viroconium (Wroxeter) in the west of England and had become undisciplined and troublesome. His success in handling this difficult task was rewarded by promotion to the governorship of Aquitania (the central region in modern France) in Gaul. He then became consul in

Rome and in A.D. 78 returned to Britain for a third time, as propraetor (governor) of the province. The political experience and military skill which he had acquired by then equipped him to face an exciting and demanding situation.

Agricola rose to the challenge in many different ways. He completed the conquest of Wales and then fought a series of successful campaigns in Scotland, culminating in a great victory at Mons Graupius in the north of the Grampian mountains. He extended the network of roads and forts across northern Britain and established the legionary fortress at Deva (Chester).

A triumphant Roman cavalryman.

In addition to his military exploits Agricola carried out an extensive program of Romanization. Tacitus tells us that he "encouraged individuals and helped communities to build temples, fora, and houses in the Roman style" and that he made the people realize that under good laws it was better to live at peace with the Romans than to rebel against them. Tacitus also tells us of his plans to improve the education of the British:

> **Agricola arranged for the sons of British chiefs to receive a broad education. He made it clear that he preferred the natural abilities of the British to the skill and training of the Gauls. As a result, instead of hating the language of the Romans, they became very eager to learn it.**

Agricola was governor of Britain for seven years, an unusual length of time and longer than any other imperial Roman governor. During this time Britain was circumnavigated and the area under direct Roman control was nearly doubled. The rapid expansion of urban life in Britain in the second century may have owed as much to Agricola's civil policies and provincial sympathies as to his military successes. Agricola was recalled from Britain in A.D. 85, possibly because of the jealousy of Domitian. When he returned to Rome, Agricola was given the honors due to a successful general – a statue and a citation; but this was the end of his career. He retired into the safety of private life. Any hopes he may have had of a further governorship were not fulfilled, and he lived in retirement until his death in A.D. 93.

Word Study

A Match the meaning to the following "-tion" words:

1	relation	a	knowledge given or taught
2	occupation	b	disturbance, uproar
3	ablation	c	business, employment; vocation
4	delegation	d	an accumulation; things gathered
5	commotion	e	a group sent to act for others
6	accusation	f	surgical removal of a body part
7	instruction	g	connection of persons by blood or marriage
8	collection	h	a charge of wrongdoing

B Give a derivative from a Vocabulary Checklist word which matches the following definitions:

1 limited in perspective; narrow-minded
2 Latin case expressing direction from
3 a final offer or proposal
4 treacherous
5 crazy
6 an associate or colleague
7 a person who has obtained the highest academic degree in a particular field

C Give a definition for the following English words based on your knowledge of the Stage 26 Vocabulary Checklist:

1 quotient
2 reference
3 belligerence
4 diffidence
5 docent

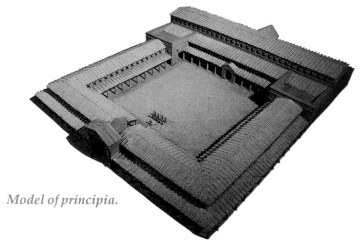

Model of principia.

Stage 26 Vocabulary Checklist

accūsō, accūsāre, accūsāvī, accūsātus — *accuse*
auferō, auferre, abstulī, ablātus — *take away, steal*
bellum, bellī, n. — *war*
  bellum gerere — *wage war, campaign*
cohors, cohortis, f. — *cohort*
colligō, colligere, collēgī, collēctus — *gather, collect*
commōtus, commōta, commōtum — *moved, excited, upset*
doceō, docēre, docuī, doctus — *teach*
facinus, facinoris, n. — *crime*
falsus, falsa, falsum — *false, dishonest*
fidēs, fideī, f. — *loyalty, trustworthiness*
īnsānus, īnsāna, īnsānum — *crazy, insane*
īnstruō, īnstruere, īnstrūxī, īnstrūctus — *draw up*
lēgātus, lēgātī, m. — *commander*
num — *whether*
occupō, occupāre, occupāvī, occupātus — *seize, take over*
oportet — *it is right*
  mē oportet — *I must*
perfidia, perfidiae, f. — *treachery*
praebeō, praebēre, praebuī, praebitus — *provide*
prīncipia, prīncipiōrum, n. pl. — *headquarters*
prōvincia, prōvinciae, f. — *province*
quot? — *how many?*
referō, referre, rettulī, relātus — *bring back, deliver*
rēgnum, rēgnī, n. — *kingdom*
saevus, saeva, saevum — *savage, cruel*
sānē — *obviously*
sī — *if*
tribūnus, tribūnī, m. — *tribune (high-ranking officer)*
ultimus, ultima, ultimum — *furthest*
ut — *that, in order that*

A small figure of a teacher reading from a scroll. Agricola encouraged the British to learn Latin.

IN CASTRIS

Stage 27

Deva/Chester

Artist's reconstruction of Deva.

Aerial view of Chester, showing how the River Dee has altered its course. The main bridge, however, crosses the river at the same point as the Roman one did.

1 "fuge mēcum ad horreum!"

extrā carcerem, Modestus et
Strȳthiō sermōnem anxiī
habēbant.
Modestus Strȳthiōnem
monēbat ut ad horreum sēcum
fugeret.

2 "invenīte Modestum Strȳthiōnemque!"

prō prīncipiīs, centuriō
Valerius mīlitibus mandāta
dabat.
centuriō mīlitibus imperābat ut
Modestum Strȳthiōnemque
invenīrent.

3 "castra Rōmāna oppugnāte! horrea incendite!"

in silvā proximā, Vercobrix
contiōnem apud Britannōs
habēbat.
Vercobrix Britannōs incitābat
ut castra Rōmāna oppugnārent
et horrea incenderent.

sub horreō

When you have read this story, answer the questions at the end.

Modestus et Strȳthiō, ē carcere ēgressī, ad horreum fūgērunt. per
aditum angustum rēpsērunt et sub horreō cēlātī manēbant.
centuriō Valerius, cum portās cellārum apertās carceremque
dēsertum vīdisset, īrātissimus erat. mīlitibus imperāvit ut
Modestum et Strȳthiōnem caperent. mīlitēs tamen, quamquam per   5
tōta castra quaerēbant, eōs invenīre nōn poterant. illī duōs diēs
manēbant cēlātī. tertiō diē Modestus tam miser erat ut rem diūtius
ferre nōn posset.

Modestus:	quam īnfēlīx sum! mālim in illō carcere esse potius
	quam sub hōc horreō latēre. quālis est haec vīta? *10*
	necesse est mihi grāna quae mūrēs relīquērunt
	cōnsūmere. adest Strȳthiō, comes exiliī, sed mē nōn
	adiuvat. nam Strȳthiō est vir maximī silentiī,
	minimīque iocī. ēheu! mē taedet huius vītae.
Strȳthiō:	mī Modeste, difficile est nōbīs hīc diūtius manēre. *15*
	nunc tamen advesperāscit. vīsne mē, ex horreō
	ēgressum, cibum quaerere? hominibus miserrimīs
	cibus sōlācium semper affert.
Modestus:	id est cōnsilium optimum. nōbīs cēnandum est.
	Strȳthiō, tē huic reī praeficiō. ī prīmum ad coquum. *20*
	eum iubē cēnam splendidam coquere et hūc portāre.
	deinde quaere Aulum et Pūblicum, amīcōs nostrōs!
	invītā eōs ad cēnam! iubē Aulum amphoram vīnī
	ferre, Pūblicum lucernam āleāsque. tum curre ad
	vīcum; Nigrīnam quaere! optima est saltātrīcum; *25*
	mihi saltātrīcēs quoque sōlācium afferunt.
Strȳthiō:	quid dīcis? vīsne mē saltātrīcem in castra dūcere?
Modestus:	abī, caudex!

Strȳthiō, ut mandāta Modestī efficeret, invītus discessit. coquō
persuāsit ut cēnam splendidam parāret; Aulō et Pūblicō persuāsit   *30*
ut vīnum et lucernam āleāsque ferrent; Nigrīnam ōrāvit ut ad
horreum venīret, sed eī persuādēre nōn poterat.

aditum: aditus	*entrance*
angustum: angustus	*narrow*
rēpsērunt: rēpere	*crawl*
imperāvit: imperāre	*order, command*
mālim	*I would prefer*

potius	*rather*
grāna: grānum	*grain*
exiliī: exilium	*exile*
mē taedet	*I am tired, I am bored*
advesperāscit: advesperāscere	*get dark, become dark*
sōlācium	*comfort*
affert: afferre	*bring*
praeficiō: praeficere	*put in charge*
prīmum	*first*
vīcum: vīcus	*town, village*
ōrāvit: ōrāre	*beg*

Questions

1 Why was the floor of a horreum raised above ground level? What did this enable Modestus and Strythio to do?
2 After two days, what had Modestus been forced to do?
3 What made Strythio think he could go outside without getting caught?
4 What instructions did Modestus give Strythio about the party?
5 Why was Strythio **invītus** (line 29)? How successful was he in carrying out Modestus' instructions?
6 Which would you expect to be built first, the **castra** or the **vīcus**?

Reconstruction of a granary.

About the Language I: Indirect Commands

A In previous stories, you met sentences like this:

"redīte!"   "pecūniam trāde!"
"Go back!"   "Hand over the money!"

In each example, an order or command is being given. These examples are known as direct commands.

B In Stage 27, you have met sentences like this:

lēgātus mīlitibus imperāvit **ut redīrent**.
*The commander ordered his soldiers **that they should go back**.*
Or, in more natural English:
*The commander ordered his soldiers **to go back**.*

latrōnēs mercātōrī imperāvērunt **ut pecūniam trāderet**.
*The robbers ordered the merchant **that he should hand over the money**.*
Or, in more natural English:
*The robbers ordered the merchant **to hand over the money**.*

In each of these examples, the command is not being given, but is being reported or referred to indirectly. These examples are known as indirect commands. The verb in an indirect command in Latin is usually subjunctive.

C Further examples of direct and indirect commands:

1 "tacē!"
2 centuriō mihi imperāvit ut tacērem.
3 "parcite mihi!"
4 senex nōs ōrābat ut sibi parcerēmus.
5 nēmō ancillae persuādēre poterat ut saltāret.
6 coquus servīs imperāvit ut vīnum in mēnsam pōnerent.
7 vōs saepe monēbam ut dīligenter labōrārētis.
8 comitēs mercātōrem monuērunt ut ab oppidō clam discēderet.

Modestus attonitus

cum Strȳthiō cēnam et amīcōs quaereret, decem Britannī ā Vercobrige ductī, castrīs cautē appropinquābant. Vercobrix enim eīs persuāserat ut castra oppugnārent. Britannī, postquam custōdēs vītāvērunt, vallum tacitē trānscendērunt et castra intrāvērunt. in manibus facēs tenēbant ut horrea incenderent. 5
celeriter processērunt quod prius cognōverant ubi horrea sita essent.

Modestus, ignārus adventūs Britannōrum, sub horreō sedēbat. adeō ēsuriēbat ut dē vītā paene dēspērāret. per rīmam prōspiciēbat, reditum Strȳthiōnis exspectāns. 10

"trēs hōrās Strȳthiōnem iam exspectō. quid eī accidit?"

subitō manum hominum per tenebrās cōnspexit.

"euge! tandem vēnērunt amīcī! heus, amīcī, hūc venīte!"

Britannī, cum Modestī vōcem audīvissent, erant tam attonitī ut immōtī stārent. respondēre nōn audēbant. Vercobrix tamen, quī 15
raucam Modestī vōcem agnōverat, ad comitēs versus,

"nōlīte timēre," inquit susurrāns. "nōtus est mihi hic mīles. stultior est quam asinus. nōbīs nocēre nōn potest."

tum Britannī per aditum tacitī rēpsērunt. simulatque intrāvērunt, Modestus eīs obviam iit, ut salūtāret. 20

"salvēte, amīcī! nunc nōbīs cēnandum ac bibendum est."

tum Britannus quīdam, vir ingēns, in Modestum incurrit.

"ō Nigrīna, dēliciae meae!" clāmāvit Modestus. "tē nōn agnōvī! quam longī sunt capillī tuī! age! cōnsīde prope mē! dā mihi ōsculum! quis lucernam habet?" 25

Vercobrix, cum Modestum lucernam rogantem audīvisset, Britannīs imperāvit ut facēs incenderent. Modestus, Vercobrigem Britannōsque cōnspicātus, palluit.

"dī immortālēs!" inquit. "abiit Nigrīna, appāruērunt Britannī! mihi statim effugiendum est." 30

vallum: vallum	*rampart, earth embankment*
trānscendērunt: trānscendere	*climb over*
facēs: fax	*torch*
ēsuriēbat: ēsurīre	*be hungry*
rīmam: rīma	*crack, chink*
prōspiciēbat: prōspicere	*look out*
versus	*having turned*
obviam iit: obviam īre	*meet, go to meet*
incurrit: incurrere	*bump into*

About the Language II: Result Clauses

A Study the following examples:

> tanta erat multitūdō **ut tōtam aulam complēret.**
> *So great was the crowd **that it filled the whole palace.***

> Modestus erat adeō pulcher **ut paucae puellae eī resistere possent.**
> *Modestus was so handsome **that few girls could resist him.***

The groups of words in boldface are known as result clauses, because they indicate a result. The verb in a result clause in Latin is always subjunctive.

B Further examples:

1 tam stultus erat dominus ut omnēs servī eum dērīdērent.
2 tantus erat clāmor ut nēmō iussa centuriōnum audīret.
3 Agricola tot mīlitēs ēmīsit ut hostēs fugerent.
4 centuriōnem adeō timēbam ut ad castra redīre nōn audērem.
5 tot servōs habēbās ut eōs numerāre nōn possēs.
6 ancillae nostrae tam dīligenter labōrābant ut eās saepe laudārēmus.

C Notice that in the first part of each sentence there is a word that signals that a result clause is coming. For example, study the first sentence in Section A. **tanta**, *so great*, is a signal for the result clause **ut tōtam aulam complēret**. In the last three sentences in Section B, what are the signal words? What do they mean?

Modestus prōmōtus

Vercobrix, cum Modestus effugere temptāret, suīs imperāvit ut eum comprehenderent. ūnus ē Britannīs Modestō appropinquāvit ut dēligāret. fax, tamen, quam tenēbat, tunicam Modestī forte incendit.

"ēheu!" ululāvit ille. "ardeō! mē dēvorant flammae!" 5

tum ē manibus Britannōrum ēlāpsus fūgit praeceps. simulac per aditum ērūpit, Strȳthiōnī amīcīsque occurrit. amphoram vīnī ē manibus Aulī ēripuit et vīnum in tunicam fūdit.

"īnsānit Modestus!" clāmāvit Strȳthiō attonitus.

Modestus tamen, Strȳthiōnis clāmōrum neglegēns, amphoram 10 in aditum impulit. tum in amphoram innīxus, magnōs clāmōrēs sustulit.

"subvenīte! subvenīte! Britannōs cēpī!"

statim manus mīlitum, ā Valeriō ducta, ad horrea contendit. tantī erant clāmōrēs Modestī ut tōta castra complērent. praefectus 15 castrōrum ipse accurrit ut causam strepitūs cognōsceret.

Modestus exsultāns "īnsidiās Britannīs parāvī," inquit. "Vercobrix ipse multīs cum Britannīs sub horreō inclūsus est."

breve erat certāmen. tantus erat numerus mīlitum Rōmānōrum ut Britannōs facile superārent. Rōmānī Britannōs ex horreō 20 extractōs ad carcerem redūxērunt. tum lēgātus legiōnis ipse Modestum arcessītum laudāvit.

"Modeste," inquit, "mīlitem fortiōrem quam tē numquam anteā vīdī. sōlus decem hostibus īnsidiās parāvistī. nōs decet praemium tibi dare." 25

Modestus, ā lēgātō ita laudātus, adeō gaudēbat ut vix sē continēre posset. pecūniam laetus exspectābat.

"carcerī tē praeficiō," inquit lēgātus.

prōmōtus: prōmovēre	*promote*	**nōs decet**	*it is proper for us*
suīs: suī	*his men*	**continēre**	*contain*
ēripuit: ēripere	*snatch, tear*		
innīxus	*having leaned*		
subvenīte: subvenīre	*help, come to help*		
praefectus	*commander*		
causam: causa	*reason, cause*		
strepitūs: strepitus	*noise, din*		
breve: brevis	*short, brief*		
certāmen	*struggle, contest, fight*		
redūxērunt: redūcere	*lead back*		

Word Patterns: Adjectives and Nouns

A Study the form and meaning of the following adjectives and nouns:

ADJECTIVES		NOUNS	
longus	*long*	longitūdō	*length*
sollicitus	*worried*	sollicitūdō	*worry, anxiety*
altus	*deep*	altitūdō	*depth*

B Now complete the table below:

sōlus	*alone, lonely*	solitūdō	.....
magnus	.....	magnitūdō	.....
lātus	*wide*	.....	.....
mānsuētus	*tame*	mānsuētūdō	.....

C Give the meaning of the following nouns:

> fortitūdō, pulchritūdō, multitūdō

D How many of the Latin nouns in Sections A–C can be translated into English by a noun ending in -tude? If you are unsure, use an English dictionary to help you.

E Notice some slightly different examples:

cupere	*to desire*	cupīdō	*desire*
		Cupīdō	*Cupid, the god of desire*
valēre	*to be well*	valētūdō	*health*
			(1) *good health*
			(2) *bad health*

The imperative of **valēre** has a special meaning which you have met before:

valē	*be well*, i.e. *farewell, good-bye*

Practicing the Language

A Translate the following examples:

1 faber, prope iānuam tabernae stāns, pugnam spectābat.
2 Vilbia, ē culīnā ēgressa, sorōrem statim quaesīvit.
3 fūrēs, ad iūdicem ductī, veniam petīvērunt.
4 centuriō, amphoram vīnī optimī adeptus, ad amīcōs celeriter rediit.
5 subitō equōs appropinquantēs audīvimus.
6 puer callidus pecūniam, in terrā cēlātam, invēnit.

Pick out the participle in each sentence and say whether it is present, perfect passive, or perfect active. Then write down the noun described by each participle.

B Change the words in boldface from singular to plural. Then translate the new sentences.

1 Imperātor **īnsulam** vīsitābat.
2 **nauta** pecūniam **poscēbat**.
3 haec verba **senem** terrēbant.
4 iuvenēs **captīvum** custōdiēbant.
5 fūr **pōculum** īnspiciēbat.
6 **lcō** ad pāstōrem **contendēbat**.
7 equī **flūmen** trānsīre nōlēbant.
8 **templum** in forō **erat**.

C Complete each of the sentences below with the correct person of the subjunctive verb. Then translate the sentence. For example:

> tam perterritī erant ut ex urbe fugere… .
> tam perterritī erant ut ex urbe **fugerent**.
> *They were so frightened that they fled from the city.*

1 Quīntus nesciēbat quō modō Cogidubnus periisse… .
2 cīvēs, cum tabernam intrāvisse…, vīnum poposcērunt.
3 Agricola mīlitibus imperāvit ut ad castra redīre… .
4 tantus erat clāmor ut nēmō centuriōnem audīre… .
5 nōs, cum Agricolam vīdisse…, maximē gaudēbāmus.
6 rēxne tibi persuāsit ut sēcum templum vīsitāre…?
7 domum rediī ut parentēs meōs adiuvāre… .
8 cūr dīcere nōlēbātis ubi illō diē mātrem vestram vīdisse…?

The Legionary Fortress

If the legion itself was like a miniature army, the fortress in which it lived when not on campaign could be compared to a fortified town. It covered about 50–60 acres (20–25 hectares), about one third of the area of Pompeii. The design of the fortress was based on a standard pattern (see page 135).

The chief buildings, grouped in the center, were the **prīncipia** (headquarters), the **praetōrium** (the living-quarters of the commanding officer), **valētūdinārium** (the hospital), and the **horrea** (granaries). Numerous streets and alleyways were laid out in an orderly grid pattern throughout the fortress, but there were three main streets: the **via praetōria** ran from the main gate to the front entrance of the principia; the **via prīncipālis** extended across the whole width of the fortress, making a T-junction with the via praetoria just in front of the principia; the **via quīntāna** passed behind the principia and also extended across the width of the fortress. The fortress was surrounded by a ditch, a rampart (**vallum**), which was an earth wall or mound, and battlements, with towers at the corners and at intervals along the sides. Each side had a fortified gateway.

The principia was a large and impressive building at the heart of the fortress. A visitor would first enter a flagstone courtyard surrounded on three sides by a colonnade and storerooms. On the far side of the courtyard was a surprisingly large **basilica** or a great hall, where the commander worked with his officers, interviewed important local people, and administered military justice. The one at Deva, for example, was about 240 feet (73 meters) long; its central nave, bounded by tall columns supporting a vaulted roof, was 40 feet (12 meters) wide and flanked by two aisles each 20 feet (6 meters) wide.

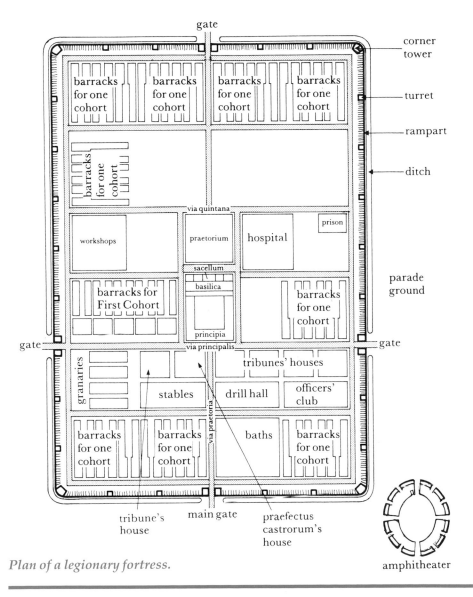

Plan of a legionary fortress.

In the center of the far long wall of the basilica and directly facing the main gate was the most sacred place in the fortress, the **sacellum** or chapel. This housed the standard of the legion, the **aquila**, an image of an eagle perched with outspread wings on the top of a pole. It was made of gold and in its talons it clutched a bundle of golden darts that represented the thunderbolts of Jupiter. The aquila represented the spirit of the legion and aroused feelings of intense loyalty and an almost religious respect. To lose it in battle was the worst possible disgrace and misfortune; this rarely happened. The soldier who looked after the aquila and carried it in battle was called the **aquilifer** (eagle-bearer). He was always a soldier of the first cohort.

aquilifer

On either side of the sacellum were the rooms where the clerks kept the payrolls and attended to all the paperwork that was needed to run a large organization. Close by and usually underground was the legion's strong-room, in which pay and savings were kept safely locked.

The praetorium was situated by the side of or just behind the principia. It was a luxurious house in the style of an Italian **domus urbāna** and it provided the legatus and his family with those comforts which they would expect and regard as necessary for a civilized life: central heating, a garden, and a private suite of baths. The very high standard of the commander's quarters would demonstrate the attractions of Roman civilization to any local civilian leaders entertained in the praetorium. However, whether this display of wealth made them any happier about the taxes which they had to pay to the Romans is another question.

The valetudinarium or hospital contained many small wards which were designed to ensure peace and quiet for the sick and injured. There was also a large reception hall to accommodate an influx of casualties from the battlefield and a small operating theater equipped with running water.

The horrea were skillfully designed to keep grain dry and cool for long periods. In the first century A.D., like many other buildings in the fortress, they were built mainly of wood, but from the second century stone was the regular material. A granary was a long, narrow building; to carry the rain-water away from the walls the roof had wide overhanging eaves; and to prevent damp rising from the ground the floor was supported on small piers or low walls which allowed air to circulate freely underneath. There were several of these granaries in a fortress, often arranged side by side in pairs, and they could contain stocks of grain sufficient for at least one year and possibly two.

The barracks, housing 5,000–6,000 men, occupied the largest area. These long, narrow, rectangular buildings were divided into pairs of rooms, each pair providing accommodation for an eight-man section (**contubernium**). Along the front of each building ran a colonnaded veranda. Each section cooked for itself on a hearth in the front living-room, which was slightly the smaller of the two rooms, and slept in the larger room at the back. Each block housed a century (80 men). At the end of the block a larger suite of rooms was provided for the centurion, who may have shared it with his optio. The blocks themselves were arranged in pairs facing each other across an alleyway.

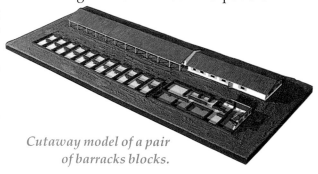

Cutaway model of a pair of barracks blocks.

The bath house was important both for hygienic reasons and because it provided a social center for the troops; every fortress and many smaller forts had one. Like the civilian baths, it consisted of a tepidarium, caldarium, and frigidarium. Sometimes it was outside the fortress, by a nearby stream or river, sometimes inside.

One other building, always outside, should be mentioned: the amphitheater. It had the same shape and layout as the civilian amphitheater and could seat the whole legion. It was used for ceremonial parades, weapon training, and displays of tactics, as well as for occasional gladiatorial shows.

Not surprisingly, civilians also tended to gather around military bases. At first they were traders who set up little bars to sell appetizing food and drink to supplement the plain rations served in the barracks. Naturally, too, these bars gave soldiers opportunities to meet the local girls. Legally soldiers were not allowed to marry, but the army tolerated unofficial unions. While the father lived in barracks, his family grew up just outside, and his sons often followed his profession and enlisted when they were eighteen or nineteen. Many such settlements (**vīcī**) developed gradually into towns. A few became large, self-governing cities, such as Eboracum (York). Thus the military fortress, which had begun as a means of holding down newly conquered territory, ended by playing an important part in the development of civilian town life.

The Roman Fortress

The Romans built their fortresses of wood, for speed, and later rebuilt them in stone. The top picture shows a reconstruction of a wooden gate at a fort in central England (seen from the inside). Below is a stone gateway (seen from the outside) rebuilt at a fortress used as a supply base for Hadrian's Wall.

Word Study

A Match the definition to the English derivative.

1 imperious   a sheer, steep
2 noxious   b domineering
3 precipitous   c tiresome, boring
4 tedious   d harmful, unwholesome
5 insidious   e crafty, wily

B Match the definition to the English derivative.

1 advent   a glowing; passionate
2 apparent   b an arrival
3 ardent   c free from guilt; pure
4 decent   d readily seen or understood, evident
5 innocent   e proper, fitting, respectable

C Complete the following analogies with words from the Stage 27 Vocabulary Checklist:

1 īrātus : saevīre : : laetus : _____
2 coepī : incēpī : : conveniō : _____
3 cupere : velle : : iubēre : _____
4 contendere : festīnāre : : laedere : _____
5 laetus : trīstis : : clāmor : _____
6 virtūs : fortitūdō : : mandātum : _____

A stone-built granary at a camp near Hadrian's Wall.

Stage 27 Vocabulary Checklist

adeō — *so much, so greatly*
adventus, adventūs, m. — *arrival*
anteā — *before*
appāreō, appārēre, appāruī — *appear*
ardeō, ardēre, arsī — *burn, be on fire*
certāmen, certāminis, n. — *struggle, contest, fight*
comes, comitis, m. f. — *comrade, companion*
decet — *it is proper*
  mē decet — *I ought*
fax, facis, f. — *torch*
gaudeō, gaudēre — *be pleased, rejoice*
ignārus, ignāra, ignārum — *not knowing, unaware*
imperō, imperāre, imperāvī (+ DAT) — *order, command*
incendō, incendere, incendī, incēnsus — *burn, set fire to*
īnsidiae, īnsidiārum, f. pl. — *trap, ambush*
iocus, iocī, m. — *joke*
iussum, iussī, n. — *order*
manus, manūs, f. — *band (of men)*
noceō, nocēre, nocuī (+ DAT) — *hurt*
occurrō, occurrere, occurrī (+ DAT) — *meet*
ōsculum, ōsculī, n. — *kiss*
praeceps, praeceps, praeceps,
  gen. praecipitis — *headlong*
praemium, praemiī, n. — *prize, reward*
proximus, proxima,
  proximum — *nearest*
quālis, quālis, quāle — *what sort of*
silentium, silentiī, n. — *silence*
sub (+ ABL or ACC) — *under, beneath*

tacitus, tacita, tacitum — *silent*
taedet — *it is tiring*
  mē taedet — *I am tired, I am bored*

tantus, tanta, tantum — *so great, such a great*

An eagle and other standards.

IMPERIUM

ultiō Rōmāna

post mortem Cogidubnī, Salvius rēgnum eius occupāvit. pecūniam ā Britannīs extorquēre statim coepit. Salvium adiuvābat Belimicus, prīnceps Cantiacōrum.

    prope aulam habitābat agricola Britannicus, quī Salviō pecūniam trādere nōluit. Salvius igitur mīlitibus imperāvit ut casam agricolae dīriperent. centuriōnem mīlitibus praefēcit.

1 mīlitēs, gladiīs hastīsque armātī, casam agricolae oppugnāvērunt.

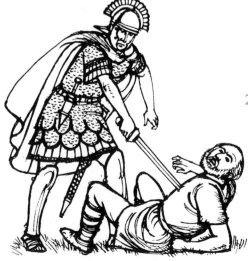

2 agricola, gladiō centuriōnis vulnerātus, exanimātus dēcidit.

3 servī, clāmōribus territī,
fūgērunt.

4 fīlius agricolae, fūste armātus,
frūstrā restitit.

5 Belimicus, spē praemiī adductus,
mīlitēs Rōmānōs adiuvābat et
incitābat.

6 mīlitēs casam intrāvērunt et
arcam, pecūniā complētam,
extulērunt.

7 deinde mīlitēs fēminās,
catēnīs vīnctās, abdūxērunt.

8 postrēmō mīlitēs casam
incendērunt. flammae, ventō
auctae, casam celeriter
cōnsūmpsērunt.

9 pāstōrēs, quī prope casam habitābant, immōtī stābant, spectāculō
attonitī.
casam vīdērunt, flammīs cōnsūmptam.
fīlium agricolae vīdērunt, hastā graviter vulnerātum.
agricolam ipsum vīdērunt, gladiō centuriōnis interfectum.
tandem abiērunt, timōre īrāque commōtī, Belimicum Rōmānōsque
vituperantēs.

testāmentum

ego, Tiberius Claudius Cogidubnus, rēx magnus Britannōrum, morbō gravī afflīctus, hoc testāmentum fēcī.

ego Titum Flāvium Domitiānum, optimum Imperātōrum, hērēdem meum faciō. mandō T. Flāviō Domitiānō rēgnum populumque meum. iubeō omnēs Rēgnēnsēs lēgibus pārēre et 5 vītam quiētam agere. nam prīncipēs Rēgnēnsium mē saepe vexāvērunt. aliī, spē praedae adductī, inter sē pugnāvērunt; aliī, īnsāniā affectī, sēditiōnem contrā Rōmānōs facere temptāvērunt. nunc tamen eōs omnēs oportet discordiam huius modī dēpōnere.

dō lēgō Cn. Iūliō Agricolae statuam meam, ā fabrō Britannicō 10 factam. sīc Agricola mē per tōtam vītam in memoriā habēre potest.

dō lēgō C. Salviō Līberālī, fidēlissimō amīcōrum meōrum, duōs tripodas argenteōs. Salvius vir summae prūdentiae est.

dō lēgō L. Marciō Memorī vīllam meam prope Aquās Sūlis sitam. L. Marcius Memor, ubi aeger ad thermās vēnī, ut auxilium ā 15 deā Sūle peterem, benignē mē excēpit.

dō lēgō Dumnorigī, prīncipī Rēgnēnsium, quem sīcut fīlium dīlēxī, mīlle aureōs aulamque meam. sī forte Dumnorix mortuus est, haec C. Salviō Līberālī lēgō.

dō lēgō Belimicō, prīncipī Cantiacōrum, quīngentōs aureōs et 20 nāvem celerrimam. Belimicus enim mē ab ursā ōlim servāvit, quae per aulam mcam saeviēbat.

mandō C. Salviō Līberālī cūram fūneris meī. volō Salvium corpus meum sepelīre. volō eum mēcum sepelīre gemmās meās, paterās aureās, omnia arma quae ad bellum vēnātiōnemque 25 comparāvī.

mandō C. Salviō Līberālī hoc testāmentum, manū meā scrīptum ānulōque meō signātum. dolus malus ab hōc testāmentō abestō!

lēgibus: lēx	*law*	**sepelīre**	*bury*
praedae: praeda	*booty, plunder, loot*	**dolus ... abestō!**	*may ...*
adductī: addūcere	*lead on, encourage*		*trickery*
affectī: afficere	*affect*		*keep*
discordiam: discordia	*strife*		*away!*
in memoriā habēre	*keep in mind, remember*	**malus**	*evil, bad*
benignē	*kindly*		
excēpit: excipere	*receive*		
mīlle	*a thousand*		
celerrimam: celer	*quick, fast*		

in aulā Salviī

When you have read this story, answer the questions at the end.

Salvius, cum dē morte Cogidubnī audīvisset, ē castrīs discessit. per
prōvinciam iter fēcit ad aulam quam ē testāmentō accēperat. ibi
novem diēs manēbat ut rēs Cogidubnī administrāret. decimō diē,
iterum profectus, pecūniās opēsque ā Britannīs extorquēre incēpit.
nōnnūllī prīncipēs, avāritiā et metū corruptī, Salvium adiuvābant.   5

Belimicus, prīnceps Cantiacōrum, spē praemiī adductus, Salviō
summum auxilium dedit. Britannōs omnia bona trādere coēgit.
aliī, quī potentiam Salviī timēbant, Belimicō statim cessērunt; aliī,
quī eī resistēbant, poenās gravēs dedērunt.

Belimicus autem, quamquam prō hōc auxiliō multa praemia   10
honōrēsque ā Salviō accēpit, haudquāquam contentus erat. rēx
enim Rēgnēnsium esse cupiēbat. hāc spē adductus, cum paucīs
prīncipibus coniūrāre coepit. quī tamen, Belimicō diffīsī, rem
Salviō rettulērunt.

Salvius, audāciā Belimicī incēnsus, eum interficere cōnstituit.   15
amīcōs igitur, quibus maximē cōnfīdēbat, ad sē vocāvit; eōs in
aulam ingressōs rogāvit utrum vim an venēnum adhibēret. amīcī,
ut favōrem Salviī conciliārent, multa et varia cōnsilia
prōposuērunt.

tandem ūnus ex amīcīs, vir callidissimus,   20

"venēnum," inquit, "Belimicō, hostī īnfestō, aptissimum est."

"sed quō modō tālem rem efficere possumus?" inquit Salvius.
"nam Belimicus, vir magnae prūdentiae, nēminī cōnfīdit."

"hunc homunculum dēcipere nōbīs facile est," inquit ille.
"venēnum cibō mixtum multōs virōs callidiōrēs quam Belimicum   25
iam fefellit. ipse sciō venēnum perītē dare."

"euge!" inquit Salvius, cōnsiliō amīcī dēlectātus. "facillimum est mihi illum ad cēnam sūmptuōsam invītāre. mē oportet epistulam blandam eī mittere. verbīs enim mollibus ac blandīs resistere nōn potest."   30

Salvius igitur Belimicum ad aulam sine morā invītāvit. quī, epistulā mendācī dēceptus neque ūllam fraudem suspicātus, ad aulam nōnā hōrā vēnit.

decimō: decimus	tenth	īnfestō: īnfestus	dangerous
profectus	having set out	aptissimum: aptus	suitable
avāritiā: avāritia	greed	mixtum: miscēre	mix
metū: metus	fear	fefellit: fallere	deceive
bona: bona	goods	sūmptuōsam:	expensive,
prō	for, in return for	sūmptuōsus	lavish
haudquāquam	not at all	blandam: blandus	flattering
rettulērunt: referre	tell, report	mollibus: mollis	soft
audāciā: audācia	boldness, audacity	morā: mora	delay
incēnsus	inflamed, angered	neque	and not
utrum ... an	whether ... or	ūllam: ūllus	any
favōrem: favor	favor	fraudem: fraus	trick
conciliārent:		nōnā: nōnus	ninth
conciliāre	win, gain		

Questions

1. Where was Salvius when he heard of Cogidubnus' death? Where did he then travel to (lines 1–2)?
2. How long did Salvius stay there? Why?
3. After setting out again, what did Salvius do next (line 4)?
4. What motivated some chieftains to help him?
5. Why would you have expected Belimicus to be satisfied? Why did he start plotting (lines 11–12)?
6. How did Salvius find out about Belimicus' plot (lines 13–14)?
7. What decision did Salvius take when he heard of Belimicus' treachery? What question did Salvius put to his friends?
8. What did one of the friends suggest? Why was Salvius dubious?
9. The friend gave reasons in support of his suggestion (lines 24–26). Give two of them.
10. What did Salvius say would be very easy to do (lines 27–28)?
11. How did Salvius say he would lure Belimicus into his trap? Why was he certain of success (lines 28–30)?
12. Pick out and translate one group of Latin words in the last sentence to show that Belimicus fell into the trap.

About the Language I: More on the Ablative and Accusative

A In this Stage, you have seen sentences like this:

> Salvius, cum dē **morte** rēgis audīvisset, ē **castrīs** discessit.
> *When Salvius had heard about the **death** of the king, he left the **camp**.*

The words in boldface are in the ablative case. The ablative case is used with a number of prepositions in Latin.

B Study the following sentences:

> mīles, **vulnere** impedītus, tandem cessit.
> *The soldier, hindered **by his wound**, gave in at last.*

> iuvenis, **gladiō** armātus, ad castra contendit.
> *The young man, armed **with a sword**, hurried to the camp.*

> servī, **catēnīs** vīnctī, in fundō labōrābant.
> *The slaves, bound **in chains**, were working on the farm.*

The words in boldface are in the ablative case, but there is no preposition ahead of them in Latin. Notice the various ways of translating these words into English.

C Further examples:
1 Salvius, audāciā Belimicī attonitus, nihil dīxit.
2 mercātor, fūstibus verberātus, in fossā exanimātus iacēbat.
3 mīlitēs, vallō dēfēnsī, barbarīs diū resistēbant.
4 uxor mea ānulum, gemmīs ornātum, ēmit.
5 hospitēs, arte ancillae dēlectātī, plausērunt.

D Study the following examples:

> **nōnā hōrā** ad aulam vēnit.
> *He came to the palace **at the ninth hour**.*

> **decimō diē** discessit.
> *He left **on the tenth day**.*

The words in boldface indicate **when** something happened. To indicate **time when**, Latin uses the ablative case, with no preposition.

E Now study the following:

multōs annōs hīc habitō.
*I have lived here **for many years**.*

duās hōrās labōrābant.
*They worked **for two hours**.*

In these sentences, the words in boldface indicate **how long** something went on. To indicate **duration or extent of time**, Latin uses the accusative case, with no preposition.

F Further examples:
1 hospitēs trēs hōrās cēnābant.
2 quartō diē revēnit rēx.
3 Agricola prōvinciam septem annōs administrābat.
4 secundā hōrā lībertus Memorem excitāre temptāvit.
5 mediā nocte hostēs castra nostra oppugnāvērunt.
6 sex diēs nāvigābāmus; septimō diē ad portum advēnimus.

cēna Salviī

When you have read this story, answer the questions at the end.

Belimicum aulam intrantem Salvius benignē excēpit et in triclīnium addūxit. ibi sōlī sūmptuōsē atque hilare cēnābant. Belimicus, Salvium rīdentem cōnspicātus vīnōque solūtus, audācter dīcere coepit.

"mī Salvī, multa et magna beneficia ā mē accēpistī. postquam   5
effūgērunt Quīntus et Dumnorix, ego sōlus tē adiūvī; multōs continuōs diēs eōs persecūtus Dumnorigem occīdī; multa falsa Agricolae dīxī ut Cogidubnum perfidiae damnārem; post mortem eius, Britannōs pecūniam bonaque sua trādere coēgī. prō hīs tantīs beneficiīs praemium meritum rogō."   10

addūxit: addūcere	*lead*	**solūtus: solvere**	*relax, loosen*
sūmptuōsē	*lavishly*	**persecūtus**	*having pursued*
atque	*and*	**damnārem: damnāre**	*condemn*
hilare	*in high spirits*	**meritum: meritus**	*well-deserved*

Salvius, ubi haec audīvit, arrogantiā Belimicī incēnsus, īram tamen cēlāvit et cōmiter respondit.

"praemium meritum iam tibi parāvī. sed cūr nihil cōnsūmis, mī amīce? volō tē garum exquīsītissimum gustāre quod ex Hispāniā importāvī. puer! fer mihi et Belimicō illud garum!"

cum servus garum ambōbus dedisset, Salvius ad hospitem versus,

"dīc mihi, Belimice," inquit, "quid prō hīs tantīs beneficiīs repetis?"

"iam ex testāmentō Cogidubnī," respondit ille, "quīngentōs aureōs accēpī. id haudquāquam satis est. rēgnum ipsum repetō."

quod cum audīvisset, Salvius "ego," inquit, "nōn Cogidubnus, aureōs tibi dedī. cūr haud satis est?"

"quid dīcis?" exclāmāvit Belimicus. "hoc nōn intellegō."

"illud testāmentum," respondit Salvius, "est falsum. nōn Cogidubnus sed ego scrīpsī."

Hispāniā: Hispānia	*Spain*
repetis: repetere	*claim*
haud	*not*

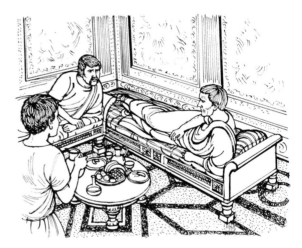

Questions

1 How was Belimicus received and treated when he came to the palace?
2 What made Salvius angry (line 11)? Why do you think he hid his anger?
3 What did Belimicus think Salvius meant by a **praemium meritum** (line 13)? What did Salvius really mean?
4 During the meal, Belimicus changed his tactics: instead of continuing with his plot, he asked Salvius directly for the kingship. What had encouraged him to do this?
5 What had Belimicus already received? How? What did he now learn about the will?

About the Language II: Impersonal Verbs

A In Stage 11, you met the verb **placet**. Notice again how it is used:

mihi **placet** hoc dōnum accipere.
It pleases me to receive this present.
Or, in more natural English:
I am glad to receive this present.

nōbīs **placet**.
It pleases us.
Or, in more natural English:
We like it.

B The following verbs are used in a similar way:

nōs **decet** praemium Modestō dare.
It is proper for us to give a reward to Modestus.
Or, more naturally:
We ought to give a reward to Modestus.

mē **taedet** huius vītae.
It makes me tired of this life.
Or, more naturally:
I am tired of this life.

Rōmānōs numquam **oportet** hostibus crēdere.
It is never right for Romans to trust the enemy.
Or, more naturally:
Romans must never trust the enemy.

C These verbs are known as impersonal verbs. Their literal English equivalent always involves the general idea of "it."

D Further examples:
1 tibi placet?
2 saltātrīcem spectāre volō! mē taedet cibī et vīnī!
3 semper pluit!
4 Britannōs decet extrā aulam manēre.
5 nunc advesperāscit.
6 nōs oportet rēgnum Cogidubnī occupāre.

Belimicus rēx

Belimicus, cum dē testāmentō audīvisset, adeō attonitus erat ut nihil respondēre posset. Salvius autem haec addidit rīdēns:

"mī amīce, cūr tam attonitus es? tū et Cogidubnus semper inimīcī erātis. num quicquam ab illō spērāvistī? nōs autem in amīcitiā sumus. tibi multum dēbeō, ut dīxistī. itaque rēgem tē 5 creāre in animō habeō. sed rēgnum quod tibi dēstinō multō maius est quam Cogidubnī. heus! puer! plūs garī!"

servus, cui Salvius hoc imperāvit, statim exiit. brevī regressus, garum venēnō mixtum intulit atque in Belimicī pateram effūdit. tam laetus erat ille, ubi verba Salviī audīvit, ut garum cōnsūmeret, 10 ignārus perīculī mortis.

"quantum est hoc rēgnum quod mihi prōmīsistī? ubi gentium est?" rogāvit Belimicus.

Salvius cachinnāns "multō maius est," inquit, "quam imperium Rōmānum." 15

Belimicus hīs verbīs perturbātus,

"nimium bibistī, mī amīce," inquit. "nūllum rēgnum nōvī maius quam imperium Rōmānum."

"rēgnum est, quō omnēs tandem abeunt," respondit Salvius. "rēgnum est, unde nēmō redīre potest. Belimice, tē rēgem creō 20 mortuōrum."

Belimicus, metū mortis pallidus, surrēxit. haerēbat lingua in gutture; tintinnābant aurēs; ventrem, quī iam graviter dolēbat, prēnsāvit. metū īrāque commōtus exclāmāvit,

"tū mihi nocēre nōn audēs, quod omnia scelera tua Agricolae 25 dēnūntiāre possum."

"mē dēnūntiāre nōn potes, Belimice, quod nunc tibi imminet mors. nunc tibi abeundum est in rēgnum tuum. avē atque valē, mī Belimice."

Belimicus, venēnō excruciātus, pugiōnem tamen in Salvium 30 coniēcit, spē ultiōnis adductus. deinde magnum gemitum dedit et humī dēcidit mortuus. Salvius, pugiōne leviter vulnerātus, servō imperāvit ut medicum arcesseret. aliī servī corpus Belimicī ē triclīniō extractum quam celerrimē cremāvērunt. flammae, ventō auctae, corpus cōnsūmpsērunt. sīc Belimicus arrogantiae poenās 35 dedit; sīc Salvius cēterīs prīncipibus persuāsit ut in fidē manērent.

spērāvistī: spērāre	*hope for, expect*	scelera: scelus	*crime*
amīcitiā: amīcitia	*friendship*	dēnūntiāre	*denounce, reveal*
creāre	*make, create*	imminet:	
dēstinō: dēstināre	*intend*	imminēre	*hang over*
effūdit: effundere	*pour out*	tibi abeundum est	*you must go away*
ubi gentium?	*where in*	avē atque valē	*hail and farewell*
	the world?	excruciātus:	
		excruciāre	*torture, torment*
perturbātus:		leviter	*slightly*
perturbāre	*disturb, alarm*	cremāvērunt:	
lingua	*tongue*	cremāre	*cremate*
gutture: guttur	*throat*	auctae: augēre	*increase*
tintinnābant:			
tintinnāre	*ring*		
ventrem: venter	*stomach*		
graviter dolēbat:			
graviter dolēre	*be extremely painful*		

Word Patterns: Adjectives and Nouns

A Study the form and meaning of the following adjectives and nouns:

ADJECTIVE		NOUN	
avārus	*greedy, miserly*	avāritia	*greed*
laetus	*happy*	laetitia	*happiness*
īnsānus	*mad*	īnsānia	*madness*

B Now complete the table below:

superbus	*proud*	superbia	.....
trīstis	.....	trīstitia	.....
perītus	.....	perītia	*skill, experience*
prūdēns	*shrewd, sensible*	prūdentia	.....
sapiēns	.....	.....	.....
ēlegāns	.....	ēlegantia	.....

C Give the meaning of the following nouns:

audācia, amīcitia, arrogantia, benevolentia, potentia, perfidia, absentia, neglegentia

Practicing the Language

A Read the story below and complete the phrases by choosing the appropriate words from those in parentheses.

mīles legiōnis secundae, Vorēnus nōmine, ad tabernam Devae (sitam, sitās) commōtus contendit. tabernam (ingressus, ingressī), vīnum poposcit et celerrimē hausit. caupō, quī Vorēnum bene nōverat, rogāvit cūr tam commōtus esset.

"rēs dīra mihi nūper accidit," respondit ille. "hodiē māne in statiōne eram. centuriō mihi imperāverat ut adventum nūntiī exspectārem. itaque campum prō castrīs (iacentem, iacentēs) intentē spectābam. tandem equitem celeriter (venientem, venientēs) procul cōnspexī. ille autem, cum ad mē advenīret, subitō ē cōnspectū discessit. nusquam equitem vidēre poteram. aderat tamen corvus ingēns, quī sinistrā volābat. hīs rēbus (commōtum, commōtus), eventum dīrum exspectō."

simulatque haec dīxit, alium mīlitem tabernam (intrāns, intrantem) vīdit. hunc rogāvit num quid accidisset.

"nōnne scīs?" respondit ille. "nūntius ab Agricolā (missus, missum) ā Britannīs interfectus est. corpus eius nūper (inventum, inventa) in castra portātum est."

campum: campus	*plain*
corvus	*raven*
sinistrā	*on the left*
eventum: eventus	*result*
num quid	*whether anything, if anything*

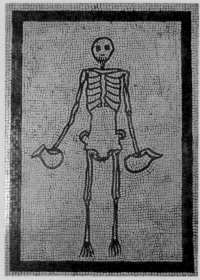

Skeleton mosaic from Pompeii.

B Select the correct subordinate clause to complete the main clauses given below. Then translate each sentence.

a ut vix iter cōnficere posset
b ut Belimicum interficeret
c cum garum exquīsītissimum cōnsūmpsisset
d quot essent armātī, quās urbēs dēlēvissent
e ut nautae nāvem solvere nōllent
f ut dīceret quō Quīntus et Dumnorix effūgissent
g ut testāmentum statim legere vellent
h cum dē Britannīs sub horreō captīs audīvisset
i ut saltātrīcem quaereret

1 Salvius cibum venēnō mixtum parāvit . . . . . .
2 heredēs erant tam avidī . . . . . .
3 Imperātor cognōscere voluit . . . . . .
4 tantus erat ventus . . . . . .
5 Strȳthiō ad vīcum cucurrit . . . . . .
6 Belimicus servō miserō imperāvit . . . . . .
7 Quīntus tam dēfessus erat . . . . . .
8 lēgātus . . . . . Modestum carcerī rūrsus praefēcit.
9 Belimicus, ..., magnum gemitum dedit.

C Complete each sentence with the correct ablative from the box below. Then translate the sentence.

| audāciā | vīnō | gladiō | fūstibus | īrā | catēnīs |

1 nūntius, ... graviter vulnerātus, effugere nōn poterat.
2 Salvius, ... eius attonitus, diū tacēbat.
3 captīvī, ... vīnctī, in longīs ōrdinibus stābant.
4 Britannī, ... armātī, pugnāre volēbant.
5 dominus, ... commōtus, omnēs servōs carnificibus trādidit.
6 hospitēs, ... solūtī, clāmāre et iocōs facere coepērunt.

Interpreting the Evidence: Our Knowledge of Roman Britain

Our knowledge of the Roman occupation of Britain is based on different types of evidence:

1. **literary** evidence: what the Greeks and Romans wrote about Britain;
2. **archaeological** evidence: what archaeologists have discovered from excavations, including:
3. **inscriptional** evidence: inscriptions in Latin (and sometimes Greek) from tombstones, altars, public buildings, and monuments, and from private objects such as writing-tablets, defixiones, etc.

Literary Evidence

A picture of Roman Britain is given in two well-known Latin texts. One is Julius Caesar's account of his brief reconnaissance mission to the southeast coast of Britain in 55 B.C. and his return in greater force the following year when he stormed the fortress of a British king before withdrawing again. The other is Tacitus' biography of his father-in-law, Agricola. Much of this is devoted to Agricola's career in the army in Roman Britain and to his campaigns as governor of the province. The account of Agricola's life in Stage 26 is almost entirely based on Tacitus' description.

Julius Caesar.

Both pieces of writing are to some extent biased. Caesar wrote his account in order to justify his actions to the Senate in Rome and place himself in a favorable light; Tacitus was anxious to honor the memory of his father-in-law and to praise his success as a soldier and a governor. Agricola appears almost too good to be true, in strong contrast to the Emperor Domitian who is portrayed as jealous of Agricola's success and anxious to bring about his downfall.

Archaeological Evidence

The task of archaeologists is to uncover and explain the remains of the past. First they must locate a suitable site to excavate. Some sites are already known but have not been completely excavated; others are found by accident. In 1962 a workman digging a drain came across fragments of a mosaic floor and this chance discovery led to the excavation of the palace at Fishbourne. When sites are needed for road building or other kinds of development, archaeologists may have limited time in which to excavate before the bulldozers move in or the remains are reburied.

Once the site has been located, archaeologists have to plan and carry out a careful scientific survey and excavation of the area. As the earth is removed from a site, they will watch for two things: the existence and position of any building foundations, and the way in which the various levels or layers of earth change color and texture. In this way they build up a picture of the main features on the site.

A rescue excavation of a Roman military bath house discovered during the construction of a new road, seen in the background.

Excavation in the Sacred Spring, Bath.

At the same time they carefully examine the soil for smaller pieces of evidence such as bones, pottery, jewelry, coins, and other small objects. The aim is not simply to find precious objects but to discover as much as possible about the people who used the buildings, what their lives were like, when they lived there, and even perhaps what happened to them. For such work the archaeologist needs some of the same kind of training and skills as a detective.

Certain finds are useful for dating the site. Roman coins can usually be dated accurately because they have emperors' heads and names stamped on them. These in turn can help date the level of soil being excavated. Fairly accurate dates can also be obtained from a study of the styles and patterns of pottery found on a site. Large quantities have survived, as pottery is a durable material which does not rot, and broken pieces (shards) are found in very large numbers on many sites.

Pottery is also one of the clues that can reveal trade and travel patterns. The presence on a British site of pottery which has come from Italy or Gaul shows that, at the time the site was occupied, goods were imported from those areas. In addition, the owner of the villa was wealthy enough to pay for such imported goods.

By painstaking excavation archaeologists have been able to reconstruct a remarkably detailed picture of the Roman occupation of Britain. Layers of ash, charred pottery, and other burned objects indicate a destruction by fire; a mass of broken rubble may suggest that a building was demolished, perhaps to make way for a larger, better one. Many sites in Britain show a gradual development from a simple timber-framed farmhouse building to a larger stone house to a grander, multi-roomed mansion with baths, mosaic pavements, and colonnades. The fact that most of the Romano-British villas were in the southeast, whereas the military fortresses were established in the north and west, suggests that Britain was largely peaceful and prosperous in the southeast but still troubled by the threat of hostile tribes in the northwest. Traces of a vast network of Roman roads have been found, showing just how numerous and effective communications must have been. Parts of many Romano-British towns have been excavated, revealing how advanced urban life was. It is not uncommon to find the remains of an extensive forum,

Finds of coins and pottery are useful in dating levels, but need careful interpretation. This denarius of the Emperor Vespasian, who sent Agricola to govern Britain, was minted in A.D. 73. But coins circulated for many years; this was found with other coins issued a century later.

This small fragment of a pottery bowl can be dated by the style of decoration. It was made in central Gaul about A.D. 240–270. However, it would have been an expensive import and so could have been treasured for generations before it eventually broke and was thrown away.

carefully laid out grids of streets, the foundations of many large buildings including temples with altars and inscriptions, sometimes a theater and an amphitheater, and substantial city walls.

The excavation of military sites, such as forts, marching camps, and legionary fortresses, has shown how important the army was in maintaining peace and protection for the province. It has also shown very clearly the movements of the legions and auxiliaries around the country and told us much about the lives of Roman soldiers.

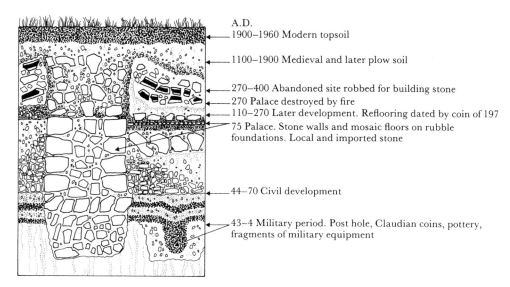

A.D.
1900–1960 Modern topsoil

1100–1900 Medieval and later plow soil

270–400 Abandoned site robbed for building stone
270 Palace destroyed by fire
110–270 Later development. Reflooring dated by coin of 197
75 Palace. Stone walls and mosaic floors on rubble foundations. Local and imported stone

44–70 Civil development

43–4 Military period. Post hole, Claudian coins, pottery, fragments of military equipment

Diagram showing layers of evidence for occupation at Fishbourne.

An amphora that brought garum from Spain to Chester.

Inscriptional Evidence

Some important evidence about the Roman occupation of Britain comes from inscriptions, particularly on the tombstones of soldiers. Here is the inscription on the tombstone of a soldier who was buried at Deva.

```
        D M
    L LICINIUS L F
     TER VALENS
    ARE VETERAN
   LEG XX VV AN VL
        H S E
```

At first sight, this looks difficult to decipher. The task, however, is made easier by the fact that most of these inscriptions follow a standard pattern. The items are usually arranged in the following order:

1 The dedication at the top of the stone – D M – abbreviation for **Dīs Mānibus** (to the spirits of the departed).
2 The praenomen. This is the first of a citizen's three names and is usually abbreviated to a single letter, as here – L for **Lūcius**.
3 The nomen. Always given in full, as here – **Licinius**.
4 The father's name. It is usually only the father's praenomen that is given, and this can be recognized in abbreviated form by the single letter which comes before an F representing **fīlius**. The son often had the same praenomen as his father, as here L F for **Lūciī fīlius**.
5 Tribe. Roman soldiers were Roman citizens and were therefore enrolled in one of the thirty-five Roman tribes which were used for voting purposes. The name of the tribe is abbreviated, as here – TER for **Teretīna**.
6 The cognomen. This is the last of the three names, usually placed after the father's name and the voting tribe in which the soldier was enrolled. It is always given in full, as here – **Valēns**. Three names were a mark of Roman citizenship and therefore an important indication of status.
7 Birthplace. This can usually be identified as a town in the Roman empire, thus ARE for **Arelātē** (modern Arles in the south of France).
8 Rank and legion. They are usually both abbreviated – VETERAN for **veterānus** (a retired soldier or one coming up to retirement); LEG XX VV for **legiōnis XX Valeriae Victrīcis** (20th Legion Valeria Victrix).

9   Age. This is represented by AN or ANN for **annōrum**, followed by a number. This number is often rounded off to a multiple of 5. Sometimes VIX for **vīxit** (lived) is placed before AN.

10   Length of service (not included in the inscription above). This is represented by STIP followed by a number, e.g. STIP X for **stipendia X** (ten years' service).

11   The final statement. This is abbreviated, and usually takes the form of H S E for **hīc situs est** (is buried here) or H F C for **hērēs faciendum cūrāvit** (his heir had this stone set up).

The inscription can therefore be interpreted as follows:

> D(IS) M(ANIBUS)
> L(UCIUS) LICINIUS L(UCII) F(ILIUS)
> TER(ETINA) VALENS
> ARE(LATE) VETERAN(US)
> LEG(IONIS) XX V(ALERIAE) V(ICTRICIS) AN(NORUM)
> V L
> H(IC) S(ITUS) E(ST)

[This stone is dedicated] to the spirits of the departed. Lucius Licinius Valens, son of Lucius, of the Teretine tribe, from Arelate, veteran of the Twentieth Legion Valeria Victrix, aged 45, is buried here.

Here is the inscription on another soldier's tombstone, also found at Chester.

Try to find out from it the following information: the soldier's name, his rank, his legion, his age at death, the length of his service.

In the same way, find as much information as you can from the inscription on page 163.

G·LOVESIVS·PA P R
CA DARVS·EMERTA·M
LEG·XX·V·V·A N·X X·V·S I·IX
FRON I NVS·A QVILO·H·F·C

Word Study

A Match the Latin word to the word which means approximately the same.

1	dīligere	**a**	interficere
2	mandāre	**b**	et
3	metus	**c**	amāre
4	occīdere	**d**	pecūnia
5	opēs	**e**	iubēre
6	atque	**f**	timor

B Give an English derivative from one of the following words to match the definition:

hērēs, īra, lingua, metus, pallidus, praeficere, ventus

1 to supply with fresh air
2 faint in color, wan
3 a person in charge of matters
4 fluent in two languages
5 passed down from predecessors or ancestors
6 anger
7 extremely careful about details

C Complete the following analogies with words from the Stage 28 Vocabulary Checklist:

1 trīstitia : rīsus : : _____ : gaudēre
2 senex : iuvenis : : nihil : _____
3 rēx : rēgnum : : animus : _____
4 cupere : nōlle : : ōdī : _____
5 oculus : vidēre : : _____ : dīcere
6 decem : centum : : centum : _____

Stage 28 Vocabulary Checklist

ac, atque	*and*
arrogantia, arrogantiae, f.	*arrogance, gall*
augeō, augēre, auxī, auctus	*increase*
beneficium, beneficiī, n.	*act of kindness*
cōnstituō, cōnstituere, cōnstituī, cōnstitūtus	*decide*
corpus, corporis, n.	*body*
dīligō, dīligere, dīlēxī, dīlēctus	*be fond of*
doleō, dolēre, doluī	*hurt, be in pain*
gemitus, gemitūs, m.	*groan*
hērēs, hērēdis, m. f.	*heir*
īra, īrae, f.	*anger*
lingua, linguae, f.	*tongue*
malus, mala, malum	*evil, bad*
mandō, mandāre, mandāvī, mandātus	*order, entrust, hand over*
metus, metūs, m.	*fear*
mīlle	*a thousand*
mīlia, mīlium, n. pl.	*thousands*
multō	*much*
occīdō, occīdere, occīdī, occīsus	*kill*
opēs, opum, f. pl.	*money, wealth*
pallidus, pallida, pallidum	*pale*
praeficiō, praeficere, praefēcī, praefectus	*put in charge*
quisquam, quidquam/quicquam	*anyone, anything*
sīc	*thus, in this way*
solvō, solvere, solvī, solūtus	*loosen, untie*
spēs, speī, f.	*hope*
suspicātus, suspicāta, suspicātum	*having suspected*
testāmentum, testāmentī, n.	*will*
ut	*as*
ventus, ventī, m.	*wind*
sexāgintā	*sixty*
septuāgintā	*seventy*
octōgintā	*eighty*
nōnāgintā	*ninety*
centum	*a hundred*
ducentī, ducentae, ducenta	*two hundred*

ROMA

1 in mediā Rōmā est mōns nōtissimus, quī Capitōlium appellātur.
in summō Capitōliō stat templum, ubi deus Iuppiter adōrātur.

2 sub Capitōliō iacet Forum Rōmānum.
forum ab ingentī multitūdine cīvium cotīdiē complētur.
aliī negōtium agunt; aliī in porticibus stant et ab amīcīs salūtantur; aliī
per forum in lectīcīs feruntur. ubīque magnus strepitus audītur.

3 aliquandō pompae splendidae per forum dūcuntur.

4 prope medium forum est templum Vestae, ubi ignis sacer ā Virginibus Vestālibus cūrātur.

Vestae: Vesta *Vesta (Roman goddess of the hearth and the home)*
Virginibus Vestālibus: Virginēs Vestālēs *Vestal Virgins (priestesses of Vesta)*

5 in extrēmō forō stant rostra, ubi contiōnēs apud populum habentur.

6 prope rostra est carcer, ubi captīvī populī Rōmānī custōdiuntur.

nox

nox erat. lūna stēllaeque in caelō serēnō fulgēbant. tempus erat quō hominēs quiēscere solent. Rōmae tamen nūlla erat quiēs, nūllum silentium.

magnīs in domibus, ubi dīvitēs habitābant, cēnae splendidae cōnsūmēbantur. cibus sūmptuōsus ā servīs offerēbātur; vīnum optimum ab ancillīs fundēbātur; carmina ā citharoedīs perītissimīs cantābantur.   5

in altīs autem īnsulīs, nūllae cēnae splendidae cōnsūmēbantur, nūllī citharoedī audiēbantur. ibi pauperēs, famē paene cōnfectī, vītam miserrimam agēbant. aliī ad patrōnōs epistulās scrībēbant ut   10
auxilium eōrum peterent, aliī scelera ac fūrta committere parābant.

prope forum magnus strepitus audiēbātur. nam arcus magnificus in Viā Sacrā exstruēbātur. ingēns polyspaston arcuī imminēbat. fabrī, quī arcum exstruēbant, dīligentissimē labōrābant. aliī figūrās in arcū sculpēbant; aliī titulum in fronte   15
arcūs īnscrībēbant; aliī marmor ad summum arcum tollēbant. omnēs strēnuē labōrābant ut arcum ante lūcem perficerent. nam Imperātor Domitiānus hunc arcum frātrī Titō postrīdiē dēdicāre volēbat. Titum vīvum ōderat; mortuum tamen eum honōrāre cupiēbat. Domitiānus enim favōrem populī Rōmānī, quī Titum   20
maximē dīlēxerat, nunc sibi conciliāre volēbat.

serēnō: serēnus	*calm, clear*	perficerent:	
Rōmae	*in Rome*	perficere	*finish*
altīs: altus	*high*	Titō: Titus	*Titus (Emperor*
īnsulīs: īnsula	*apartment building*		*of Rome,*
famē: famēs	*hunger*		*A.D. 79–81)*
cōnfectī: cōnfectus	*worn out, exhausted*	dēdicāre	*dedicate*
patrōnōs: patrōnus	*patron*		
arcus	*arch*		
Viā Sacrā: Via Sacra	*the Sacred Way*		
	(road running		
	through forum)		
polyspaston	*crane*		
figūrās: figūra	*figure, shape*		
sculpēbant: sculpere	*carve, sculpt*		
titulum: titulus	*inscription*		
fronte: frōns	*front*		
īnscrībēbant: īnscrībere	*write, inscribe*		
marmor	*marble*		
lūcem: lūx	*light, daylight*		

huic operī praeerat Quīntus Haterius Latrōniānus, redēmptor nōtissimus. eā nocte ipse fabrōs furēns incitābat. aderat quoque Gāius Salvius Līberālis, Hateriī patrōnus, quī eum invicem flāgitābat ut opus ante lūcem perficeret. anxius enim erat Salvius   25 quod Imperātōrī persuāserat ut Haterium operī praeficeret. ille igitur fabrīs, quamquam omnīnō dēfessī erant, identidem imperābat nē labōre dēsisterent.

Glitus, magister fabrōrum, Haterium lēnīre temptābat.

"ecce, domine!" inquit. "nōs ā fabrīs adiuvāmur, quī iam arcum   30 paene perfēcērunt. ultimae litterae titulī nunc īnscrībuntur; ultimae figūrae sculpuntur; ultimae marmoris massae ad summum arcum tolluntur."

paulō ante hōram prīmam, fabrī arcum tandem perfēcērunt; abiērunt omnēs ut quiēscerent. paulīsper urbs silēbat.   35

ūnus faber tamen, domum per forum rediēns, subitō trīstēs fēminārum duārum clāmōrēs audīvit. duae enim captīvae, magnō dolōre affectae, in carcere cantābant:

"mī Deus! mī Deus! respice mē! quārē mē dēseruistī?"

operī: opus	*work, construction*
redēmptor	*contractor, builder*
flāgitābat: flāgitāre	*nag at, put pressure on*
dēfessī: dēfessus	*exhausted,*
	tired out
identidem	*repeatedly*
ultimae: ultimus	*last*
litterae: littera	*letter*
massae: massa	*block*
silēbat: silēre	*be silent*
dolōre: dolor	*grief*
affectae: affectus	*overcome*
respice: respicere	*look at,*
	look upon
quārē?	*why?*

About the Language I: Active and Passive Voice

A In Unit 1, you met sentences like these:

> puer clāmōrem **audit**.   *A boy **hears** the shout.*
> ancilla vīnum **fundēbat**.   *A slave-girl **was pouring** wine.*

The words in boldface are active forms of the verb.

B In Stage 29, you have met sentences like these:

> clāmor ā puerō **audītur**.   *The shout **is heard** by a boy.*
> vīnum ab ancillā **fundēbātur**.   *Wine **was being poured** by a slave-girl.*

The words in boldface are passive forms of the verb.

C Compare the following active and passive forms:

PRESENT INDICATIVE

ACTIVE	PASSIVE
portat	portātur
s/he, it carries	*s/he, it is carried, or s/he, it is being carried*
portant	portantur
they carry	*they are carried, or they are being carried*

IMPERFECT INDICATIVE

ACTIVE	PASSIVE
portābat	portābātur
s/he, it was carrying	*s/he, it was being carried*
portābant	portābantur
they were carrying	*they were being carried*

D Further examples:

1. cēna nostra ā coquō nunc parātur.
   (Compare: coquus cēnam nostram nunc parat.)
2. multa scelera in hāc urbe cotīdiē committuntur.
3. laudantur; dūcitur; rogātur; mittuntur.
4. candidātī ab amīcīs salūtābantur.
   (Compare: amīcī candidātōs salūtābant.)
5. fābula ab āctōribus in theātrō agēbātur.
6. audiēbantur; laudābātur; necābantur; tenēbātur

Masada I

When you have read Part I, answer the questions at the end.

ex carcere obscūrō, ubi captīvī custōdiēbantur, trīstēs clāmōrēs tollēbantur. duae enim fēminae Iūdaeae, superstitēs eōrum quī contrā Rōmānōs rebellāverant, fortūnam suam lūgēbant. altera erat anus sexāgintā annōrum, altera mātrōna trīgintā annōs nāta. ūnā cum eīs in carcere erant quīnque līberī, quōrum Simōn nātū 5 maximus sōlācium mātrī et aviae ferre temptābat.

"māter, cūr tū lacrimīs opprimeris? nōlī dolōrī indulgēre! decōrum est Iūdaeīs fortitūdinem in rēbus adversīs praestāre."

māter fīlium amplexa,

"melius erat," inquit, "cum patre vestrō perīre abhinc annōs 10 novem. cūr tum ā morte abhorruī? cūr vōs servāvī?"

Simōn, hīs verbīs commōtus, mātrem rogāvit quō modō periisset pater atque quārē rem prius nōn nārrāvisset. eam ōrāvit ut omnia explicāret. sed tantus erat dolor mātris ut prīmō nihil dīcere posset. mox, cum sē collēgisset, ad fīliōs conversa, 15

"dē morte patris vestrī," inquit, "prius nārrāre nōlēbam nē vōs quoque perīrētis, exemplum eius imitātī. nam tū frātrēsque obstinātiōne iam nimium afficiminī. nunc tamen audeō vōbīs tōtam rem patefacere quod nōs omnēs crās moritūrī sumus.

"nōs Iūdaeī contrā Rōmānōs trēs annōs pugnāre cōgēbāmur. 20 annō quārtō iste Beelzebub, Titus, urbem Ierosolymam expugnāvit. numquam ego spectāculum terribilius vīdī: ubīque

Iūdaeae: Iūdaeus	*Jewish*	**amplexa:**	
superstitēs:		**amplexus**	*having embraced*
superstes	*survivor*	**abhinc**	*ago*
rebellāverant:		**abhorruī:**	
rebellāre	*rebel, revolt*	**abhorrēre**	*shrink (from)*
lūgēbant: lūgēre	*lament, mourn*	**exemplum:**	
altera … altera	*one … the other*	**exemplum**	*example*
… annōs nāta	*… years old*	**imitātī: imitātus**	*having imitated*
ūnā cum	*together with*	**obstinātiōne:**	
nātū maximus	*eldest*	**obstinātiō**	*stubbornness*
aviae: avia	*grandmother*	**afficiminī: afficere**	*affected*
opprimeris:		**crās**	*tomorrow*
opprimere	*overwhelm*	**Beelzebub**	*Beelzebub, devil*
indulgēre	*give way*	**Ierosolymam:**	
rēbus adversīs:		**Ierosolyma**	*Jerusalem*
rēs adversae	*misfortune*	**expugnāvit:**	
		expugnāre	*storm, take by storm*

aedificia flammīs cōnsūmēbantur; ubīque virī, fēminae, līberī occīdēbantur; Templum ipsum ā mīlitibus dīripiēbātur; tōta urbs ēvertēbātur. in illā clāde periērunt multa mīlia Iūdaeōrum; sed 25 nōs, quamquam ā mīlitibus īnfestīs circumveniēbāmur, cum circiter mīlle superstitibus effūgimus. duce Eleazārō, ad rūpem Masadam prōcessimus; quam ascendimus et occupāvimus. tū, Simōn, illō tempore vix quīnque annōs nātus erās.

"rūpēs Masada est alta et undique praerupta, prope lacum 30 Asphaltītēn sita. ibi nōs, mūnītiōnibus validīs dēfēnsī, Rōmānīs diū resistēbāmus. intereā dux hostium, Lūcius Flāvius Silva, rūpem castellīs multīs circumvēnit. tum mīlitēs, iussū Silvae, ingentem aggerem usque ad summam rūpem exstrūxērunt. deinde aggerem ascendērunt, magnamque partem mūnītiōnum 35 ignī dēlēvērunt. tandem cum nox appropinquāret, Silva mīlitēs ad castra redūxit ut proximum diem victōriamque exspectārent."

ubīque	*everywhere*	mūnītiōnibus:	*defense,*
circiter	*about*	mūnītiō	*fortification*
duce: dux	*leader*	validīs: validus	*strong*
rūpem: rūpēs	*rock, crag*	castellīs: castellum	*fort*
undique	*on all sides*	iussū Silvae	*at Silva's order*
lacum Asphaltītēn:	*Lake Asphaltites*	aggerem: agger	*ramp, mound*
lacus Asphaltītēs	*(the Dead Sea)*		*of earth*
		usque ad	*right up to*
		ignī: ignis	*fire*

Questions

1 How old were the two women? How many children were with them in the prison? How were the children related to the two women?
2 How many years previously had the children's father died?
3 What two questions did Simon ask? What was his mother's answer to his second question? Why was she now willing to answer?
4 What disaster had happened to the Jews in the fourth year of their revolt against the Romans?
5 What action was taken by a thousand Jewish survivors? Who was their leader?
6 Judging from lines 30–31, and the picture on page 174, why do you think the Jews at Masada were able to hold out for so long against the Romans?
7 Who was the Roman general at Masada? What method did he use to get his men to the top of the rock?

Artist's impression of the hanging palace of Herod at Masada.

The rock of Masada, showing the Roman siege ramp built on the west side.

Masada II

"illā nocte Eleazārus, dē rērum statū dēspērāns, Iūdaeīs cōnsilium dīrum prōposuit.

"'magnō in discrīmine sumus,' inquit. 'nōs Iūdaeī, Deō cōnfīsī, Rōmānīs adhūc resistimus; nunc illī nōs in servitūtem trahere parant. nūlla spēs salūtis nōbīs ostenditur. nōnne melius est perīre 5 quam Rōmānīs cēdere? ego ipse mortem meā manū īnflīctam accipiō, servitūtem spernō.'

"hīs verbīs Eleazārus Iūdaeīs persuāsit ut mortem sibi cōnscīscerent. tantum ardōrem in eīs excitāvit ut, simulac fīnem ōrātiōnī fēcit, ad exitium statim festīnārent. virī uxōrēs līberōsque 10 amplexī occīdērunt. cum hanc dīram et saevam rem cōnfēcissent, decem eōrum sorte ductī cēterōs interfēcērunt. tum ūnus ex illīs, sorte invicem ductus, postquam novem reliquōs mortī dedit, sē ipsum ferrō trānsfīxit."

"quō modō nōs ipsī effūgimus?" rogāvit Simōn. 15

"ego Eleazārō pārēre nōn potuī," respondit māter. "amōre līberōrum meōrum plūs quam timōre servitūtis afficiēbar. vōbīscum in specū latēbam."

"ignāva!" clāmāvit Simōn. "ego mortem haudquāquam timeō. ego, patris exemplī memor, eandem fortitūdinem praestāre volō." 20

rērum statū: rērum status	*situation, state of affairs*
discrīmine: discrīmen	*crisis*
cōnfīsī: cōnfīsus	*having trusted, having put trust in*
servitūtem: servitūs	*slavery*
īnflīctam: īnflīgere	*inflict*
mortem sibi cōnscīscerent:	
mortem sibi cōnscīscere	*commit suicide*
ardōrem: ardor	*spirit, enthusiasm*
sorte ductī	*chosen by lot*
reliquōs: reliquus	*remaining*
ferrō: ferrum	*sword*
specū: specus	*cave*
memor	*remembering, mindful of*
eandem: īdem	*the same*

The Emperor Titus was enormously popular but reigned less than three years.

About the Language II: More About the Passive Voice

A Study the following examples:

ego dē cōnsiliō dīrō nārrāre **cōgor**.
*I **am forced** to talk about a dreadful plan.*
cūr tū lacrimīs **opprimeris**?
*Why **are you overwhelmed** by tears?*
nōs ā mīlitibus īnfestīs **circumveniēbāmur**.
*We **were being surrounded** by hostile soldiers.*
tū frātrēsque obstinātiōne nimium **afficiminī**.
*You and your brothers **are affected** too much by stubbornness.*

B You have now met all the passive forms for the present and imperfect tenses. Compare them with the active forms.

PRESENT INDICATIVE

ACTIVE		PASSIVE	
portō	*I carry, I am carrying*	portor	*I am (being) carried*
portās	*you carry (are carrying)*	portāris	*you are (being) carried*
portat	*s/he, it carries (is carrying)*	portātur	*s/he, it is (being) carried*
portāmus	*we carry (are carrying)*	portāmur	*we are (being) carried*
portātis	*you carry (are carrying)*	portāminī	*you are (being) carried*
portant	*they carry (are carrying)*	portantur	*they are (being) carried*

IMPERFECT INDICATIVE

ACTIVE		PASSIVE	
portābam	*I was carrying (carried)*	portābar	*I was (being) carried*
portābās	*you were carrying (carried)*	portābāris	*you were (being) carried*
portābat	*s/he, it was carrying (carried)*	portābātur	*s/he, it was (being) carried*
portābāmus	*we were carrying (carried)*	portābāmur	*we were (being) carried*
portābātis	*you were carrying (carried)*	portābāminī	*you were (being) carried*
portābant	*they were carrying (carried)*	portābantur	*they were (being) carried*

C Further examples:
1 cūr ad carcerem redūcimur? ab hostibus circumvenīris.
2 tū et amīcus ā captīvīs dēcipiminī. tacēre iubeor.
3 accūsor; īnstruuntur; docēmur; laediminī; comprehenderis; oppugnātur.
4 ā comitibus deserēbar. in fossās iaciēbāminī.
5 identidem monēbāris ut domī manērēs.
6 ēligēbantur; vītābāris; extrahēbāmur; adiuvābāminī; arcessēbātur; līberābar.

arcus Titī

I

postrīdiē māne ingēns Rōmānōrum multitūdō ad arcum Titī conveniēbat. diēs fēstus ab omnibus cīvibus celebrābātur. Imperātor Domitiānus, quod eō diē frātrī Titō arcum dēdicātūrus erat, pompam magnificam nūntiāverat. clāmōrēs virōrum fēminārumque undique tollēbantur. spectātōrum tanta erat *5* multitūdō ut eī quī tardius advēnērunt nūllum locum prope arcum invenīre possent. eīs cōnsistendum erat procul ab arcū vel in forō vel in viīs. nam iussū Imperātōris pompa tōtam per urbem dūcēbātur.

multae sellae ā servīs prope arcum pōnēbantur. illūc multī *10* senātōrēs, spē favōris Domitiānī, conveniēbant. inter eōs Salvius, dē opere Hateriī glōriātus, locum quaerēbat ubi cōnspicuus esset. inter equitēs, quī post senātōrēs stābant, aderat Haterius ipse. favōrem Imperātōris avidē spērābat et in animō volvēbat quandō ā Salviō praemium prōmissum acceptūrus esset. *15*

āra ingēns, prō arcū exstrūcta, ā servīs flōribus ōrnābātur. circum āram stābant vīgintī sacerdōtēs, togās praetextās gerentēs, ut mōs erat. haruspicēs quoque aderant quī exta victimārum īnspicerent. avium cursus ab auguribus dīligenter notābātur.

dēdicātūrus	*going to dedicate*	quandō	*when*
vel ... vel	*either ... or*	acceptūrus	*going to receive*
glōriātus	*having boasted, boasting*	exta	*entrails*
cōnspicuus	*conspicuous, easily seen*	avium: avis	*bird*
equitēs	*equites (wealthy men ranking below senators)*	cursus	*flight*
		auguribus: augur	*augur*
		notābātur: notāre	*note, observe*

Carving on the arch of Titus, showing the treasures of the Temple at Jerusalem carried in triumph through the streets of Rome.

II

intereā pompa lentē per Viam Sacram dūcēbātur. prīmā in parte incēdēbant tubicinēs tubās īnflantēs. post eōs vēnērunt iuvenēs quī trīgintā taurōs corōnīs ōrnātōs ad sacrificium dūcēbant. tum multī servī, quī gāzam Iūdaeōrum portābant, prīmam pompae partem claudēbant. huius gāzae pars pretiōsissima erat mēnsa sacra, 5 tubae, candēlābrum, quae omnia aurea erant.

septem captīvī Iūdaeī, quī mediā in pompā incēdēbant, ā spectātōribus vehementer dērīdēbantur. quīnque puerī, serēnō vultū incēdentēs, clāmōrēs et contumēliās neglegēbant, sed duae fēminae plūrimīs lacrimīs spectātōrēs ōrābant ut līberīs parcerent. 10

post captīvōs vēnit Domitiānus ipse, currū magnificō vectus. quia Pontifex Maximus erat, togam praetextam gerēbat. post Imperātōrem ambō ībant cōnsulēs, quōrum alter erat L. Flāvius Silva. cōnsulēs et magistrātūs nōbilissimī effigiem Titī in umerīs portābant. ā mīlitibus pompa claudēbātur. 15

ad arcum pompa pervēnit. Domitiānus ē currū ēgressus ut sacrificium faceret, senātōrēs magistrātūsque salūtāvit. tum oculōs in arcum ipsum convertit. admīrātiōne affectus, Imperātor Salvium ad sē arcessītum maximē laudāvit. eī imperāvit ut Hateriō grātiās ageret. inde ad āram prōgressus, cultrum cēpit quō 20 victimam sacrificāret. servus eī iugulum taurī obtulit. deinde Domitiānus, victimam sacrificāns, frātrī Titō precēs adhibuit:

"tibi, dīve Tite, haec victima nunc sacrificātur; tibi hic arcus dēdicātur; tibi precēs populī Rōmānī adhibentur."

subitō, dum Rōmānōrum oculī in sacrificium intentē 25 dēfīguntur, Simōn occāsiōnem nactus prōsiluit. mediōs in sacerdōtēs irrūpit; cultrum rapuit. omnēs spectātōrēs immōtī stābant, audāciā eius attonitī. Domitiānus, pavōre commōtus, pedem rettulit. nōn Imperātōrem tamen, sed mātrem, aviam, frātrēs Simōn petīvit. cultrum in manū tenēns clāmāvit, 30

"nōs, quī superstitēs Iūdaeōrum rebellantium sumus, Rōmānīs servīre nōlumus. mortem obīre mālumus."

haec locūtus, facinus dīrum commīsit. mātrem et aviam amplexus cultrō statim occīdit. tum frātrēs, haudquāquam resistentēs, eōdem modō interfēcit. postrēmō magnā vōce 35 populum Rōmānum dētestātus sē ipsum cultrō trānsfīxit.

gāzam: gāza	*treasure*	**currū: currus**	*chariot*
claudēbant: claudere	*conclude, complete*	**vectus: vehere**	*carry*
vultū: vultus	*expression, face*	**quia**	*because*

Pontifex Maximus	*Chief Priest*	**dum**	*while*
cōnsulēs: cōnsul	*consul*	**dēfīguntur:**	
	(senior magistrate)	**dēfīgere**	*fix*
magistrātūs:	*magistrate (elected*	**nactus**	*having seized*
magistrātus	*official of Roman*	**pedem rettulit:**	
	government)	**pedem referre**	*step back*
admīrātiōne:		**mālumus: mālle**	*prefer*
admīrātiō	*admiration*	**eōdem modō**	*in the same way*
inde	*then*		
cultrum: culter	*knife*		
dīve: dīvus	*divine*		

About the Language III: More on Purpose Clauses

A In Stage 26, you met purpose clauses used with **ut**:

> senex īnsidiās īnstrūxit **ut** fūrēs caperet.
> *The old man set a trap **in order that** he might catch the thieves.*
> Or, in more natural English:
> *The old man set a trap **to** catch the thieves.*

B In Stage 29, you have met purpose clauses used with forms of the relative pronoun **quī**:

> fēmina servum mīsit **quī** cibum emeret.
> *The woman sent a slave **who** was to buy food.*
> Or, in more natural English:
> *The woman sent a slave **to** buy food.*

You have also met purpose clauses used with **ubi**:

> locum quaerēbāmus **ubi** stārēmus.
> *We were looking for a place **where** we might stand.*
> Or, in more natural English:
> *We were looking for a place **to** stand.*

C Further examples:

1. sacerdōs haruspicem arcessīvit quī exta īnspiceret.
2. senātor gemmam pretiōsam quaerēbat quam uxōrī daret.
3. Haterius quīnque fabrōs ēlēgit quī figūrās in arcū sculperent.
4. domum emere volēbam ubi fīlius meus habitāret.

Word Patterns: Compound Verbs I

A Study the way in which the following verbs are formed.

currere	dēcurrere	excurrere	recurrere
to run	*to run down*	*to run out*	*to run back*
iacere	dēicere	ēicere	reicere
to throw	*to throw down*	*to throw out*	*to throw back*

The verbs in the second, third, and fourth columns are known as compound verbs.

B Using Section A as a guide, complete the table below:

trahere	. . . . .	extrahere	. . . .
to pull, drag	. . . . .	. . . . .	. . . . .
cadere	dēcidere	. . . . .	. . . .
to fall	. . . . .	. . . . .	. . . . .
mittere	. . . . .	. . . . .	remittere
to send	. . . .	. . . . .	. . . .

C Give the meanings of the following compound verbs:

exīre, exsilīre, effundere, ēducere, efferre;
dēsilīre, dēspicere, dēscendere, dēpōnere;
respicere, revenīre, revocāre, repōnere, resilīre.

Practicing the Language

A Complete each sentence with the right form of the imperfect subjunctive, using the verb in parentheses, then translate.

For example: equitēs īnsidiās parāvērunt ut ducem hostium (capere).

Answer: equitēs īnsidiās parāvērunt ut ducem hostium caperent.
The cavalry prepared a trap in order to catch the leader of the enemy.

The forms of the imperfect subjunctive are given on page 315 of the Language Information.

1 fabrī strēnuē labōrāvērunt ut arcum (perficere).
2 Domitiānus ad āram prōcessit ut victimam (sacrificāre).
3 ad forum contendēbāmus ut pompam (spectāre).
4 barbarī facēs in manibus tenēbant ut templum (incendere).
5 extrā carcerem stābam ut captīvōs (custōdīre).
6 līberōs redūxērunt quī carmen sacrum (cantāre).
7 decem eōrum sorte dūximus quī cēterōs (interficere).
8 nōnnūllī Iūdaeī rūpem Masadam occupāre cōnstituērunt quae salūtem superstitibus (praebēre).

B Complete each sentence with the most suitable participle from the lists below, using the correct form, and then translate. Do not use any participle more than once.

dūcēns	labōrāns	sedēns	incēdēns	clāmāns
dūcentem	labōrantem	sedentem	incēdentem	clāmantem
dūcentēs	labōrantēs	sedentēs	incēdentēs	clāmantēs

1 videō Salvium prope arcum . . . . . .
2 fabrī, in Viā Sacrā . . . . ., valdē dēfessī erant.
3 nōnne audīs puerōs . . . . .?
4 iuvenis, victimam . . . . ., ad āram prōcessit.
5 spectātōrēs captīvōs, per viās . . . . ., dērīdēbant.

C Complete each sentence with the correct form of the present passive verb, and then translate each sentence.

1 "ab amīcīs meīs (dēseror, dēserimur)," inquit captīvus. "nūlla spēs salūtis mihi ostenditur."

2 "strepitūne fabrōrum (vexāris, vexāminī)?" "vexor. Rōmae nūlla est quiēs."

3 cōnsilium dīrum ā superstitibus prīmō (spernitur, spernuntur).

4 scelestī! nōs omnēs sceleribus vestrīs (dēleor, dēlēmur).

5 magnō in discrīmine estis. ab hostibus (circumvenīris, circumveniminī).

6 līberī miserī ā spectātōribus (dērīdētur, dērīdentur).

D Translate each English sentence into Latin by selecting correctly from the list of Latin words.

1 *The citizens, having been delighted by the show, applauded.*
cīvis   spectāculum   dēlectātus   plaudunt
cīvēs   spectāculō   dēlectātī   plausērunt

2 *I recognized the slave-girl who was pouring the wine.*
ancilla   quī   vīnum   fundēbat   agnōvī
ancillam   quae   vīnō   fundēbant agnōvit

3 *Having returned to the bank of the river, the soldiers halted.*
ad rīpam   flūmine   regressī   mīlitēs   cōnstitērunt
ad rīpās   flūminis regressōs mīlitum   cōnstiterant

4 *The woman, sitting in prison, told a sad story.*
fēmina   in carcerem sedēns   fābulam   trīstis   nārrat
fēminae in carcere   sedentem fābulae   trīstem   nārrāvit

5 *We saw the altar, decorated with flowers.*
āram   flōrī   ōrnāta   vīdī
ārās   flōribus   ōrnātam   vīdimus

6 *They killed the sleeping prisoners with swords.*
captīvī   dormientem gladiōs   occīdērunt
captīvōs   dormientēs gladiīs   occīdit

The Origins of Rome

No one knows the source or the meaning of the name "Rome." However, the Romans themselves claimed that the name of their city came from that of its mythical founder, Romulus, who, according to tradition, drew the sacred city boundary line on the Palatine Hill with his plow in 753 B.C. The discovery of archaic huts confirms the presence of an eighth-century settlement on the Palatine. This settlement, like the rest of the district of Latium at this time, was inhabited by the **Latīnī** who were shepherds and farmers. The geographical position of the Palatine settlement was ideal. It was bounded on the western side by a bend of the Tiber River where the river encircling the Tiber Island was narrow enough to be bridged; there was a ford nearby where sea, river, and land travel and trade converged from Etruria in the north, from Magna Graecia in the south, and from the Tyrrhenian Sea in the west towards the mountains along the Great Salt Way, the **Via Salāria**; and there were seven hills in the area providing strategic defense positions for an expanding population.

From the sixth century onwards a continuous process of expansion transformed the agricultural settlements into one **urbs** extending over all seven hills. The marshy valley-lands were drained by canals, including the great sewer, the **Cloāca Maxima**, into which all the water flowed. There was constant building activity and the city was crowded with temples, public squares, baths, and basilicas.

Even as the city expanded, its form of government also changed. According to legend, Romulus had been followed by six other kings. The last of these, Tarquinius Superbus, was driven out, and the Roman Republic was established in 509 B.C. The kings were replaced by annually elected magistrates. The most senior of these were the two consuls, who presided over the Senate. During the time of Augustus (63 B.C.–A.D. 14), the Roman Republic in effect became an empire, with an emperor at its head.

Archaic cinerary urn in the form of a hut.

Romulus and Remus and the wolf.

The Roman Forum

The Roman Forum seen from the Palatine Hill. Using the diagram below, identify the remains of the various structures.

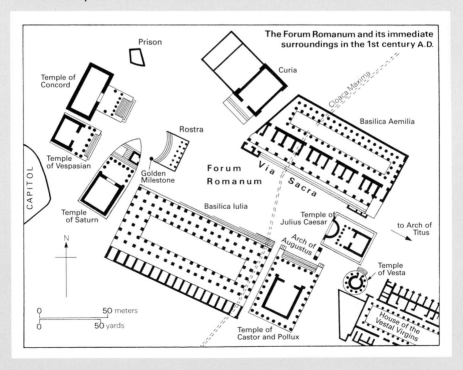

The Forum Romanum and its immediate surroundings in the 1st century A.D.

The Roman Forum

The Palatine may have been the birthplace of Rome but the commercial, cultural, social, and political heart of the city was the **Forum Rōmānum**, which, in turn, was the center of the whole empire. To symbolize this, the Emperor Augustus placed the **mīliārium aureum** (golden milestone) in the Forum Romanum to mark the starting-point of the roads that radiated from the city to all the corners of the empire. The Forum Romanum was not the only forum in the city. By the time of our stories, two other fora had been built by Julius Caesar and Augustus. Then a third in the line of imperial fora was built by Vespasian; it contained the great Temple of Peace. Later, two more fora were added: one by Domitian, completed by Nerva, and one by Trajan. The most splendid of the new fora was Trajan's forum, which contained the famous column commemorating Trajan's victories over the Dacians. But none of these other fora replaced the Forum Romanum as the center of city life.

Ordinary people came in great numbers to the Forum Romanum, to visit its temples and public buildings, to listen to speeches, to watch a procession, and sometimes just to meet their friends and stroll idly about, pausing at times to gossip, listen to an argument, or bargain with a passing street-vendor.

In the basilicas lawyers pleaded their cases in front of large and often noisy audiences, and merchants and bankers negotiated their business deals. Senators made their way to the **cūria** (the senate-house) to conduct the affairs of government under the leadership of the emperor. Sometimes a funeral procession wound its way through the forum, accompanied by noisy lamentations and loud music; sometimes the crowd was forced to make way for a wealthy noble, who was carried through the forum in a sedan-chair by his slaves and escorted by a long line of citizens.

The forum lay on low ground between two of Rome's hills, the Capitoline and the Palatine. On the Capitoline at the western end of the forum stood the Temple of Jupiter Optimus Maximus, the center of the Roman state religion. Here the emperor came to pray for the continued safety of the Roman people, and here the consuls took their solemn vows on January 1st each year at the beginning of their consulship. On the Palatine stood the emperor's residence. In the time of Augustus, this had been a small and simple house; later emperors built palaces of steadily increasing splendor.

Near the foot of the Capitoline stood the **rostra**, a platform from which public speeches were made to the people. It took its name from the **rostra** (ships' prows, which had been captured in a sea battle early in Rome's history) which were used to decorate it. One of the most famous speeches made from the rostra was Mark Antony's speech over the body of Julius Caesar in 44 B.C. The listening crowds, influenced by Antony's words, became so angry at Caesar's murder that they rioted, seized the body, and cremated it in the forum. A temple was later built in Caesar's memory at the eastern end of the forum, on the spot where his body had been burned.

Near the Temple of Julius Caesar was a small round building with a cone-shaped roof. This was the Temple of Vesta, where the Vestal Virgins tended the undying sacred flame which symbolized the endurance of Rome.

The Temple of Vesta.

Through the forum ran the **Via Sacra** (Sacred Way) which provided an avenue for religious or triumphal processions. When the Romans celebrated a victory in war, the triumphal procession passed through the streets of Rome and along the Via Sacra and ended by traveling up to the Capitoline Hill, where the victorious general gave thanks at the Temple of Jupiter. The story on pages 177–178 describes a similar procession to dedicate the Arch of Titus by the Emperor Domitian in A.D. 81. This arch, on the rise of a gentle slope at the eastern end of the Via Sacra, commemorated the victory of Titus, Domitian's brother, over the Jewish people.

Not far from the rostra and the curia was the prison. Prisoners of war, like the seven Jews in the stories of this Stage, were held in this prison before being led in a triumphal procession. Afterwards they would be taken back to the prison and killed.

Rome and Judea

In 65 B.C., Jerusalem was taken by Pompey the Great, and Judea became a client state of Rome. This was simply the latest invasion in a land with a turbulent history of foreign domination. Both Caesar and Augustus had recognized Judaism as a legitimate religion, allowing the construction of synagogues, the celebration of the Sabbath, and the collection of a Temple tax. However, by the time of our stories, imposition of higher taxes had placed a heavy burden on the population. The latest governors were non-Jews who made every effort to exploit their office financially rather than maintain order and security. Lack of unified Jewish leadership resulted in violent clashes among the various Jewish factions.

The piece of pottery with the name ben Ya'ir.

Serious rioting in Jerusalem led to a general revolt against Roman rule in A.D. 66 while Nero was emperor. Vespasian, who was then a commander in the Roman army, was given the job of crushing the rebellion. Civil war in Rome resulted in Vespasian's taking over the throne there. Once he had secured Italy, the Roman army, under the command of his son, Titus, besieged Jerusalem. Jerusalem was conquered and the Temple was destroyed in the spring of A.D. 70. Titus returned to Rome with prisoners and the Temple treasury to celebrate a triumph with his father.

Unwilling to concede defeat, a band of zealots under Eleazar ben Ya'ir occupied Masada, a nearly impregnable fortress built for King Herod on a 1,300-foot (400-meter) butte near the Dead Sea. There they held out against Flavius Silva's X Legion Fretensis until A.D. 73. The Jews' last stand at Masada as described in the story on pages 172–175 is based on the account of the first-century A.D. historian Josephus. The victory over Judea was considered a major military success for the Flavian dynasty (Vespasian, Titus, and Domitian).

The rock of Masada seen from the north.

Word Study

A Complete the following analogies with words from the Stage 29 Vocabulary Checklist:

1 vērus : falsus : : amō : ____
2 nauta : nāvigāre : : mīles : ____
3 meus : noster : : tuus : ____
4 librum : legere : : ____ : cantāre
5 intrāre : exīre : : dīligere : ____
6 crūdēlis : saevus : : gladius : ____
7 suāvis : raucus : : lūcidus : ____
8 domina : ancilla : : imperāre : ____

B Copy the following words. Then put parentheses around the Latin root from this Stage contained inside these derivatives; give the Latin word and its meaning from which the derivative comes.

For example: conservation con(serva)tion servāre – to save

1 assorted
2 coronation
3 depopulate
4 ferrous
5 imperfection
6 revival
7 servile
8 translucent

C Match the definitions to the following words:

1 viviparous   a bold, daring
2 dolorous   b bearing live young
3 farrier   c clarity of thought
4 populous   d to go around
5 audacious   e a person who shoes horses
6 lucidity   f full of people
7 circumvent   g sad, mournful

Stage 29 Vocabulary Checklist

aliquandō — *sometimes*

alius ... alius — *one ... another*
   aliī ... aliī — *some ... others*

amplexus, amplexa, amplexum — *having embraced*

audācia, audāciae, f. — *boldness, audacity*

carmen, carminis, n. — *song*

circumveniō, circumvenīre,
   circumvēnī, circumventus — *surround*

corōna, corōnae, f. — *garland, wreath*

cursus, cursūs, m. — *course, flight*

dēfessus, dēfessa, dēfessum — *exhausted, tired out*

dolor, dolōris, m. — *grief, pain*

ferrum, ferrī, n. — *iron, sword*

incēdō, incēdere, incessī — *march, stride*

līberī, līberōrum, m.pl. — *children*

lūx, lūcis, f. — *light, daylight*

mālō, mālle, māluī — *prefer*

obscūrus, obscūra, obscūrum — *dark, gloomy*

ōdī — *I hate*

perficiō, perficere, perfēcī, perfectus — *finish*

populus, populī, m. — *people*

prius — *earlier*

quiēs, quiētis, f. — *rest*

redūcō, redūcere, redūxī, reductus — *lead back*

salūs, salūtis, f. — *safety, health*

scelus, sceleris, n. — *crime*

serviō, servīre, servīvī — *serve (as a slave)*

sors, sortis, f. — *lot*

spernō, spernere, sprēvī, sprētus — *despise, reject*

undique — *on all sides*

vester, vestra, vestrum — *your (plural)*

vīvus, vīva, vīvum — *alive, living*

A coin of the Emperor Vespasian, issued in
A.D. 71, celebrates the defeat of the Jews.
A victorious Roman stands to the left of the
palm. A Jewish captive sits on the right.

HATERIUS

Stage 30

1 Haterius: quam fēlīx sum!
heri arcus meus ab Imperātōre dēdicātus est.
heri praemium ingēns mihi ā Salviō prōmissum est.
hodiē praemium exspectō …

2 Haterius: anxius sum.
arcus meus nūper ab Imperātōre laudātus est.
nūllum tamen praemium adhūc mihi ā Salviō missum est.
num ego ā Salviō dēceptus sum?
minimē! Salvius vir probus est …

dignitās

When you have read this story, answer the questions on page 195.

cīvēs Rōmānī, postquam arcus ab Imperātōre dēdicātus est, quattuor diēs fēstōs celebrāvērunt. templa vīsitābant ut dīs grātiās agerent; Circum Maximum cotīdiē complēbant ut lūdōs magnificōs ā cōnsulibus ēditōs spectārent; ad arcum ipsum conveniēbant ut figūrās in eō sculptās īnspicerent. plūrimī clientēs   5
domum Salviī veniēbant quī grātulātiōnēs eī facerent. Salvius ipse summō gaudiō affectus est quod Imperātor arcum Hateriī valdē laudāverat.

apud Haterium tamen nūllae grātulantium vōcēs audītae sunt. neque clientēs neque amīcī ab eō admissī sunt. Haterius, īrā   10
commōtus, sōlus domī manēbat. adeō saeviēbat ut dormīre nōn posset. quattuor diēs noctēsque vigilābat. quīntō diē uxor, Vitellia nōmine, quae nesciēbat quārē Haterius adeō īrātus esset, eum mollīre temptābat. ingressa hortum, ubi Haterius hūc illūc ambulābat, eum anxia interrogāvit.   15

dīs = deīs: deus	*god*	**gaudiō: gaudium**	*joy*
Circum Maximum:	*the Circus Maximus*	**grātulantium:**	
Circus Maximus	*(stadium for*	**grātulāns**	*congratulating*
	chariot-racing)	**vigilābat: vigilāre**	*stay awake*
ēditōs: ēdere	*put on, present*	**quīntō: quīntus**	*fifth*
clientēs: cliēns	*client*	**hūc illūc**	*here and there,*
grātulātiōnēs:			*up and down*
grātulātiō	*congratulation*		

Vitellia:	cūr tantā īrā afficeris, mī Haterī? et amīcōs et clientēs, quī vēnērunt ut tē salūtārent, domō abēgistī. neque ūnum verbum mihi hōs quattuor diēs dīcis. sine dubiō, ut istum arcum cōnficerēs, nimis labōrāvistī, neglegēns valētūdinis tuae. nōnne melius est tibi ad vīllam rūsticam mēcum abīre? nam rūrī, cūrārum oblītus, quiēscere potes.	20
Haterius:	quō modō ego, tantam iniūriam passus, quiēscere possum?	
Vitellia:	verba tua nōn intellegō. quis tibi iniūriam intulit?	25
Haterius:	ego ā Salviō, quī mihi favēre solēbat, omnīnō dēceptus sum. prō omnibus meīs labōribus ingēns praemium mihi ā Salviō prōmissum est. nūllum praemium tamen, nē grātiās quidem, accēpī.	
Vitellia:	contentus estō, mī Haterī! redēmptor nōtissimus es, cuius arcus ab Imperātōre ipsō nūper laudātus est. multa aedificia pūblica exstrūxistī, unde magnās dīvitiās comparāvistī.	30
Haterius:	dīvitiās floccī nōn faciō. in hāc urbe sunt plūrimī redēmptōrēs quī opēs maximās comparāvērunt. mihi autem nōn dīvitiae sed dignitās est cūrae.	35
Vitellia:	dignitās tua amplissima est. nam nōn modo dītissimus es sed etiam uxōrem nōbilissimā gente nātam habēs. Rūfilla, soror mea, uxor est Salviī quī tibi semper fāvit et saepe tē Imperātōrī commendāvit. quid aliud ā Salviō accipere cupis?	40
Haterius:	volō ad summōs honōrēs pervenīre, sīcut illī Hateriī quī abhinc multōs annōs cōnsulēs factī sunt. praesertim sacerdōs esse cupiō; multī enim virī, sacerdōtēs ab Imperātōre creātī, posteā ad cōnsulātum pervēnērunt. sed Salvius, quamquam sacerdōtium mihi identidem prōmīsit, fidem nōn servāvit.	45
Vitellia:	nōlī dēspērāre, mī Haterī! melius est tibi ad Salvium īre blandīsque verbīs ab eō hunc honōrem repetere.	
Haterius:	mihi, quī redēmptor optimus sum, nōn decōrum est honōrēs ita quaerere.	50
Vitellia:	cōnsilium optimum habeō. invītā Salvium ad āream tuam! ostentā eī polyspaston tuum! nihil maius nec mīrābilius umquam anteā factum est. deinde Salvium admīrātiōne affectum rogā dē sacerdōtiō.	55

abēgistī: abigere	*drive away*
valētūdinis: valētūdō	*health*
rūrī	*in the country*
oblītus	*having forgotten*
nē ... quidem	*not even*
estō!	*be!*
pūblica: pūblicus	*public*
dīvitiās: dīvitiae	*riches*
est cūrae	*is a matter of concern*
amplissima: amplissimus	*very great*
dītissimus: dīves	*rich*
commendāvit: commendāre	*recommend*
cōnsulātum: cōnsulātus	*consulship (rank of consul)*
sacerdōtium	*priesthood*
fidem ... servāvit: fidem servāre	*keep a promise, keep faith*
āream: ārea	*construction site*
ostentā: ostentāre	*show off, display*
nec	*nor*

Questions

1 How long was the holiday which followed the dedication of the arch? During this holiday, what happened (a) in the temples, (b) at the Circus Maximus, (c) at the arch itself?

2 Why did Salvius' clients come to his house? What happened to the clients of Haterius?

3 What does Vitellia at first think is the matter with Haterius? What action does she suggest?

4 In what way does Haterius consider he has been badly treated?

5 Explain Haterius' reason for saying **dīvitiās floccī nōn faciō** (line 34). How does Vitellia try to answer his objections?

6 What honor does Haterius want to receive in the near future? What does he hope this will lead to?

7 Why does Haterius reject the advice given by Vitellia in lines 48–49? Explain what Haterius means by **ita** (line 51).

8 What suggestion does Vitellia make in lines 52–53? How does she think this will help Haterius to get what he wants?

About the Language I: Perfect Passive Indicative

A In this Stage, you have met the perfect passive indicative. Compare it with the perfect active:

PERFECT ACTIVE INDICATIVE

senex fūrem **accūsāvit**.	*The old man **has accused** the thief.*
	Or, *The old man **accused** the thief.*
Rōmānī hostēs **superāvērunt**.	*The Romans **have overcome** the enemy.*
	Or, *The Romans **overcame** the enemy.*

PERFECT PASSIVE INDICATIVE

fūr ā sene **accūsātus est**.	*The thief **has been accused** by the old man.*
	Or, *The thief **was accused** by the old man.*
hostēs ā Rōmānīs **superātī sunt**.	*The enemy **have been overcome** by the Romans.*
	Or, *The enemy **were overcome** by the Romans.*

B The forms of the perfect passive indicative are as follows:

portātus sum	*I have been carried*, or *I was carried*
portātus es	*you* (s.) *have been carried*, or *you were carried*
portātus est	*he has been carried*, or *he was carried*
portātī sumus	*we have been carried*, or *we were carried*
portātī estis	*you* (pl.) *have been carried*, or *you were carried*
portātī sunt	*they have been carried*, or *they were carried*

Notice that each form is made up of two words:

1 a perfect passive participle (e.g. **portātus**) in either a singular or a plural form,
2 a form of the present tense of **sum**.

C Further examples:

1 arcus ab Imperātōre dēdicātus est.
(Compare: Imperātor arcum dēdicāvit.)
2 vōs ad urbem missī estis.
3 dux hostium ā mīlitibus captus est.
4 audītus est; invītātī sunt; dēceptī sumus; laudātus es; cōnsultus sum.

polyspaston

postrīdiē Haterius Salvium ad āream suam dūxit ut polyspaston eī ostentāret. ibi sedēbat ōtiōsus Glitus magister fabrōrum. quī cum dominum appropinquantem cōnspexisset, celeriter surrēxit fabrōsque dīligentius labōrāre iussit.

tōta ārea strepitū labōrantium plēna erat. columnae ex marmore 5 pretiōsissimō secābantur; laterēs in āream portābantur; ingentēs marmoris massae in plaustra pōnēbantur. Haterius, cum fabrōs labōre occupātōs vīdisset, Salvium ad aliam āreae partem dūxit. ibi stābat ingēns polyspaston quod ā fabrīs parātum erat. in tignō polyspastī sēdēs fīxa erat. tum Haterius ad Salvium versus, 10

"mī Salvī," inquit, "nōnne mīrābile est hoc polyspaston? fabrī meī id exstrūxērunt ut marmor ad summum arcum tollerent. nunc autem tibi tālem urbis prospectum praestāre volō quālem paucī umquam vīdērunt. placetne tibi?"

Salvius, ubi sēdem in tignō fīxam vīdit, palluit. sed, quod fabrī 15 oculōs in eum dēfīxōs habēbant, timōrem dissimulāns in sēdem cōnsēdit. iuxtā eum Haterius quoque cōnsēdit. tum fabrīs imperāvit ut fūnēs, quī ad tignum adligātī erant, summīs vīribus traherent. deinde tignum lentē ad caelum tollēbātur. Salvius pavōre paene cōnfectus clausīs oculīs ad sēdem haerēbat. ubi 20 tandem oculōs aperuit, spectāculō attonitus,

"dī immortālēs!" inquit. "tōtam urbem vidēre possum. ecce templum Iovis! ecce flūmen! ecce Amphitheātrum Flāvium et arcus novus! quam in sōle fulget! Imperātor, simulatque illum arcum vīdit, summā admīrātiōne affectus est. mihi imperāvit ut 25 grātiās suās tibi agerem."

cui respondit Haterius,

"summō gaudiō afficior quod opus meum ab Imperātōre laudātum est. sed praemium illud quod tū mihi prōmīsistī nōndum accēpī." 30

laterēs: later	brick	iuxtā	next to
tignō: tignum	beam	fūnēs: fūnis	rope
sēdēs	seat	adligātī erant: adligāre	tie
fīxa erat: fīgere	fix, fasten	vīribus: vīrēs	strength
tālem ... quālem	such ... us	Iovis	genitive of Iuppiter
prospectum:		Amphitheātrum	Flavian Amphitheater
prospectus	view	Flāvium	(now known as the
timōrem: timor	fear		Colosseum)
dissimulāns:		nōndum	not yet
dissimulāre	conceal, hide		

Salvius tamen vōce blandā,

"dē sacerdōtiō tuō," inquit, "Imperātōrem iam saepe cōnsuluī, et respōnsum eius etiam nunc exspectō. aliquid tamen tibi intereā offerre possum. agellum quendam possideō, quī prope sepulcra Metellōrum et Scīpiōnum situs est. tūne hunc agellum emere velīs?" 35

quae cum audīvisset, Haterius adeō gaudēbat ut dē tignō paene dēcideret.

"ita vērō," inquit, "in illō agellō, prope sepulcra gentium nōbilissimārum, ego quoque sepulcrum splendidum mihi meīsque exstruere velim, figūrīs operum meōrum ōrnātum; ita enim nōmen factaque mea posterīs trādere possum. prō agellō tuō igitur sēstertium vīciēns tibi offerō." 40

Salvius sibi rīsit; agellus enim eī grātīs ab Imperātōre datus erat.

"agellus multō plūris est," inquit, "sed quod patrōnus sum tuus tibi faveō. mē iuvat igitur sēstertium tantum trīciēns ā tē accipere. placetne tibi?" 45

Haterius libenter cōnsēnsit. tum fabrīs imperāvit ut tignum lentē dēmitterent. itaque ambō humum rediērunt, alter spē immortālitātis ēlātus, alter praesentī pecūniā contentus. 50

blandā: blandus	*flattering, charming*
agellum: agellus	*small plot of land*
quendam: quīdam	*one, a certain*
sepulcra: sepulcrum	*tomb*
Metellōrum: Metellī	*the Metelli (famous Roman family)*
Scīpiōnum: Scīpiōnēs	*the Scipiones (famous Roman family)*
meīs: meī	*my family*
facta: factum	*deed, achievement*
posterīs: posterī	*future generations, posterity*
sēstertium vīciēns	*two million sesterces*
multō plūris est	*is worth much more*
mē iuvat	*it pleases me*
sēstertium … trīciēns	*three million sesterces*
humum	*to the ground*
immortālitātis:	
immortālitās	*immortality*
ēlātus	*thrilled, excited*
praesentī: praesēns	*present, ready*

About the Language II: Pluperfect Passive Indicative

A You have now met the pluperfect passive indicative. Compare it with the pluperfect active indicative:

PLUPERFECT ACTIVE INDICATIVE
servus dominum **vulnerāverat**.   *A slave **had wounded** the master.*

PLUPERFECT PASSIVE INDICATIVE
dominus ā servō **vulnerātus erat**.   *The master **had been wounded** by a slave.*

B The forms of the pluperfect passive indicative are as follows:

portātus eram   *I had been carried*
portātus erās   *you (s.) had been carried*
portātus erat   *he had been carried*
portātī erāmus   *we had been carried*
portātī erātis   *you (pl.) had been carried*
portātī erant   *they had been carried*

Each form is made up of a perfect passive participle (e.g. **portātus**) and a form of the imperfect tense of sum (e.g. **erat**). Remember that this participle, as an adjective, agrees with the subject.

C Further examples:
  1 māter ā Simōne vituperāta erat.
    (Compare: Simōn mātrem vituperāverat.)
  2 custōdēs prope arcum positī erant.
  3 tū dīligenter labōrāre iussus erās.
  4 Haterius ā Salviō dēceptus erat.
  5 pūnītī erant; missa erat; audītus eram; reductae erāmus; circumventī erātis.

Word Patterns: Adjectives and Nouns

A Study the forms and meanings of the following adjectives and nouns:

benignus	*kind*	benignitās	*kindness*
celer	*quick*	celeritās	*quickness*
vērus	*true*	vēritās	*truth*

B Using Section A as a guide, complete the table below:

cupidus	*desirous*	.....	*desire*
immortālis	.....	immortālitās	.....
antīquus	.....	.....	.....
.....	.....	gravitās	.....
.....	*generous*	.....	.....

C Give the meaning of the following nouns:

lībertās, cāritās, suāvitās, crūdēlitās, calliditās, sevēritās, probitās, fidēlitās

D What is the gender of each noun above?
To what declension does each belong?

A Roman architect or contractor, holding a measuring stick. On the right (from top) are a chisel, a plumb-line, a set-square, and the capital of a column; on the left, a stonemason's hammer.

Practicing the Language

A Translate each sentence; then, with the help of the table of nouns on pages 296–297 of the Language Information, change the words in boldface from singular to plural, and translate again.

1 mīles perfidus **amīcum** dēseruit.
2 dux virtūtem **legiōnis** laudāvit.
3 Imperātor multōs honōrēs **lībertō** dedit.
4 iūdex epistulam **testī** trādidit.
5 plaustra in **fossā** iacēbant.
6 puella, **flōre** dēlectāta, suāviter rīsit.
7 barbarī **vīllam agricolae** incendērunt.
8 rēx pecūniam **mātrī puerī** reddidit.
9 omnēs **sonitū** avium dēlectātī sunt.
10 sacerdōtēs **effigiem** in umerīs sustulērunt.

B Complete each sentence with the correct word. Then translate.

1 mercātor, ē carcere (līberātus, līberātī), dīs grātiās ēgit.
2 māter, verbīs Eleazārī (territus, territa), cum līberīs in specum fūgit.
3 Salvius epistulam, ab Imperātōre (scrīpta, scrīptam), legēbat.
4 nāvēs, tempestāte paene (dēlētus, dēlēta, dēlētae), tandem ad portum revēnērunt.
5 centuriō septem mīlitēs, gladiīs (armātī, armātōs, armātīs), sēcum dūxit.

C Translate each pair of sentences, then link them together, using **cum** and the pluperfect subjunctive, and translate again.

For example: hospitēs advēnērunt. coquus cēnam intulit.
This becomes: cum hospitēs advēnissent, coquus cēnam intulit.
When the guests had arrived, the cook brought the dinner in.

The forms of the pluperfect subjunctive are given on page 315 of the Language Information.

1 barbarī fugērunt. mīlitēs ad castra revēnērunt.
2 servus iānuam aperuit. senex intrāvit.
3 Imperātor arcum dēdicāvit. senātōrēs populusque plausērunt.

4 fabrī polyspaston parāvērunt. Haterius Salvium ad āream
   dūxit.
5 rem perfēcimus. domum rediimus.

D Complete each sentence with the correct verb and then translate.
1 tignum ad terram lentē (dēmissum est, dēmissa sunt).
2 sepulcra Scīpiōnum prope agellum Salviī (exstrūctum erat,
   exstrūcta erant).
3 opera multa splendidaque Rōmae cotīdiē (creātur, creantur).
4 Haterī! īrā nimis (afficeris, afficiminī)! venī mēcum ad vīllam
   rūsticam.
5 Imperātor palluit. adhūc tamen ipse nōn (petītus erat, petītī
   erant).
6 quamquam dē lūdīs (cōnsulēbar, cōnsulēbāmur), nihil dīcere
   māluimus. quārē? nihil scīvimus!
7 sine dubiō arcus ante lūcem (perfectus est, perfectī sunt).
8 cīvēs! dolōre dēfessī ā senātōribus dīvitibus nihilōminus
   (abigēbāris, abigēbāminī)! ambō cōnsulēs, praetereā, vōs
   neglegēbant!

Busts from the tomb of the Haterii, Rome (possibly of Haterius and Vitellia).

Roman Engineering

The various carvings on the family tomb of the Haterii, especially the crane, suggest that at least one member of the family was a prosperous building contractor. One of his contracts was for a magnificent arch to commemorate the popular Emperor Titus who died after only a short reign (A.D. 79–81). His personal names are unknown but in the stories we have called him Quintus Haterius Latronianus. In Stage 29, Haterius is imagined as anxiously trying to complete the arch during the night before its dedication by the new emperor, Domitian, and in this Stage he is seeking his reward.

Timber frame supporting the stones of an arch. Once the central keystone was in place, the arch could support itself and the wood was removed.

Helped by an architect who provided the design and technical advice, Haterius would have employed sub-contractors to supply the materials and engage the workmen. Most of these were slaves and poor free men working as unskilled, occasional labor, but there were also craftsmen such as carpenters and stonemasons. It was the job of the carpenters to put up a timber framework to give shape and temporary support to the arches as they were being built (see right). They also erected the scaffolding and made the timber molds for shaping concrete. The masons were responsible for the quarrying of the stone and its transport, often by barge up the Tiber River, to the building-site in the city before carving the elaborate decoration and preparing the blocks to be lifted into position. The richly carved panels on Titus' arch show the triumphal procession with prisoners and treasure captured at the sack of Jerusalem in A.D. 70.

Many of our modern hand tools have been inherited almost unchanged from those used by Roman craftsmen (for instance, mallets, chisels, crowbars, trowels, saws, and planes), but with the important difference that the Romans did not have the small electric motor that makes the modern power tool so much quicker and less laborious to use.

Another aid to building was good quality cement. The main ingredients of this versatile and easily produced material were lime

Haterius' Crane

There is a crane carved on the tomb of
Haterius' family. It consisted of two wooden
uprights, forming the jib, fastened together at
the top and splayed apart at the feet. The
hoisting rope ran around two pulleys, one at the
top of the jib, and one at the point where the
load was fastened to the rope. After passing
around the pulleys the rope led down to a
winding drum, which was turned by a treadmill
fixed to the side of the crane and operated by
two or three men inside. Smaller cranes had,
instead of a treadmill, a capstan with projecting
spokes to be turned by hand. This arrangement
of pulleys and ropes multiplied the force
exerted by human muscles so that a small crew
could raise loads weighing up to eight to nine
tons/tonnes. To prevent the crane from toppling
over, stay-ropes were stretched out from the jib,
also with the help of pulleys, and firmly
anchored to the ground. Blocks of dressed stone
were lifted by man-powered cranes like this.
These machines were certainly cumbersome,
slow, and liable to accidents, but with skilled
crews in charge they worked well.

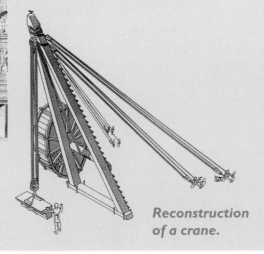

*Reconstruction
of a crane.*

mortar, made by heating pieces of limestone to a high temperature and then crushing them to a powder; fine sand; and clay. These were combined with water to make a smooth paste. In this form the cement mortar was used, as today, for a thin but effective adhesive layer between bricks or stones.

The Romans also mixed cement with rubble, such as stone chips, broken bricks, and pieces of tile, to make **opus caementīcium** (concrete). Concrete became a substitute for stone in the building of arches and vaulted ceilings. The Romans were not the first people to make concrete but they improved its quality and applied it on a grand, revolutionary scale. It made possible bold architectural achievements. For the Romans found that concrete, when shaped into arches, was strong enough to span large spaces without any additional support from pillars, and that it could carry the weight of a heavy superstructure. They used it, for instance, on the aqueducts that supplied Rome with millions of gallons (liters) of fresh water daily, and on the Pantheon, a temple whose domed concrete and brick roof (still in good condition today) has a span of 140 feet (43 meters) and rises to the same height above the floor. They also used it on the huge Flavian Amphitheater (known from medieval times as the Colosseum), which could hold up to 50,000 spectators. This is another building depicted on the tomb of the Haterii.

Concrete could also be sandwiched as a core between two faces of more expensive material, such as good quality stone or brick; these were often then covered with plaster or stucco and painted in bright colors. Marble, too, in thinly cut plates, was used as a facing material where cost was no object.

Not all buildings, of course, were constructed so sturdily. The inhabitants of Rome in the first century A.D. were housed in a vast number of dwellings, many of them apartment buildings (**īnsulae**) which were built much more cheaply, mainly of brick and timber. They had a reputation for being rickety and liable to catch fire. Augustus fixed a limit of 70 feet (21 meters) in height for these insulae. He also organized fire brigades for their protection.

Nevertheless, serious fires did break out from time to time. The great fire of Rome in A.D. 64, when Nero was Emperor, had a lasting effect on the city. As the historian Tacitus writes:

> **The flames, which in full fury fell on the level districts first, then shot up to the hills and sank again to burn the lower parts, kept ahead of all remedial measures, traveling fast, the town being an easy prey owing to the narrow, twisting lanes, and formless streets.**

Concrete

The Romans were not the first people to make concrete – rubble set in mortar – but they improved its quality and applied it on a grand scale. They found that concrete, when shaped into arches, was strong enough to span large spaces without any additional support from pillars, and that it could carry the weight of a heavy superstructure.

The Romans often built walls out of concrete sandwiched between two surfaces of brick or small stones – as we see at the back of a room in the public baths (top left). In the center there is a piece of wall facing us, with the surface stones visible at each side of it. These concrete walls would have been hidden by marble sheets or painted plaster, so that they looked as rich as the colored marble columns and the mosaic floor.

Concrete was used to span large spaces. This is the dome of the Pantheon.

Concrete was used alongside other building materials, as in the Colosseum, above. Top picture: On the outside the amphitheater appears to be all stone. Lower picture: Inside we find a mixture of stone walls (A and B), walls made of brick-faced concrete (C), and concrete vaulting (D).

Only four of the city's fourteen districts remained intact. Another serious fire in A.D. 80 compounded the problem. The program of repair was largely the work of the Flavian Emperors. Domitian completed the restoration of the Temple of Jupiter Optimus Maximus on the Capitoline Hill and the construction of the Flavian Amphitheater (see page 206). He built more temples, a stadium, a concert hall, Titus' Arch (see page 186), and a palace on the Palatine, all no doubt to enhance the influence and majesty of the emperor.

The boast of Augustus, **urbem latericiam accepi, marmoream reliqui** – "I found Rome built of brick and left it made of marble," was certainly an exaggeration. For the spaces between the marble-faced public libraries, baths, and temples were crammed with the homes of ordinary people. Many builders must have spent most of their time working on these dwellings, described by the poet Juvenal as "propped up with sticks." But given the opportunity of a large contract and a technical challenge, Roman builders made adventurous use of concrete, cranes, and arches; and Domitian, who was determined to add to the splendors of his capital city, kept architects and builders very busy throughout most of his reign.

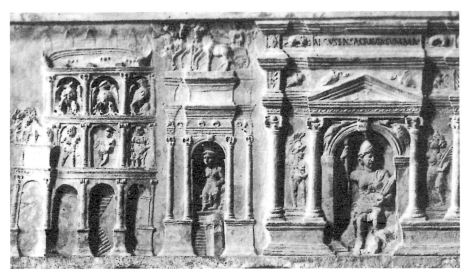

Reliefs of buildings on the tomb of the Haterii. On the left the Flavian Amphitheater, in the center a triumphal arch, on the right the Arch of Titus.

A reconstruction of the Forum looking towards the Palatine Hill. From left to right: Temple of Julius Caesar; Arch of Augustus; Temple of Castor and Pollux; Basilica Iulia. The columns with statues on top were built in the 4th century A.D.

Word Study

A Match the Latin word to the Vocabulary Checklist word which is closest in meaning.

1	creāre	**a**	pavor
2	dīvitiae	**b**	aedificāre
3	exstruere	**c**	cūr
4	quārē	**d**	opēs
5	timor	**e**	facere

B Match the definition to the derivative.

1	ambidextrous	**a**	noisy, boisterous
2	dubious	**b**	afraid, fearful
3	injurious	**c**	causing doubt, vague
4	ludicrous	**d**	merrymaking
5	obstreperous	**e**	harmful, damaging
6	tempestuous	**f**	inventiveness; ability to be productive
7	timorous	**g**	laughably absurd
8	creativity	**h**	birth
9	festivity	**i**	violent, turbulent
10	nativity	**j**	able to use both hands equally

C Using the Latin root in parentheses, give an English derivative to match each of the following definitions:

1 working together (opus)
2 fond feelings (afficere)
3 a short amusing musical play (opus)
4 a glassed-in porch (sōl)
5 to wreathe or garland with flowers (fēstus)
6 simultaneous conflicting feelings toward someone or something (ambō)
7 authoritative; domineering, pompous (magister)
8 the furthest point on the sun's ecliptic [the longest or shortest day of the year] (sōl)

A Roman trowel from Verulamium in Britain.

Stage 30 Vocabulary Checklist

adhūc	*until now*
afficiō, afficere, affēcī, affectus	*affect, overcome*
ambō, ambae, ambō	*both*
cōnsulō, cōnsulere, cōnsuluī, cōnsultus	*consult*
creō, creāre, creāvī, creātus	*make, create*
dēmittō, dēmittere, dēmīsī, dēmissus	*let down, lower*
dīves, dīves, dīves, *gen.* dīvitis	*rich*
dīvitiae, dīvitiārum, f. pl.	*riches*
dubium, dubiī, n.	*doubt*
exstruō, exstruere, exstrūxī, exstrūctus	*build*
fēstus, fēsta, fēstum	*festive, holiday*
iniūria, iniūriae, f.	*injustice, injury*
lūdus, lūdī, m.	*game*
magister, magistrī, m.	*master, foreman*
nātus, nāta, nātum	*born*
nimis	*too*
omnīnō	*completely*
opus, operis, n.	*work, construction*
pallēscō, pallēscere, palluī	*grow pale*
pavor, pavōris, m.	*panic, terror*
praestō, praestāre, praestitī	*show, display*
praetereā	*besides*
quārē?	*why?*
sēdēs, sēdis, f.	*seat*
sepulcrum, sepulcrī, n.	*tomb*
sōl, sōlis, m.	*sun*
soror, sorōris, f.	*sister*
strepitus, strepitūs, m.	*noise, din*
tempestās, tempestātis, f.	*storm*
timor, timōris, m.	*fear*

*Stamp cut from a Roman brick.
Bricks were often stamped with the
date and place of manufacture.*

IN URBE

1 diēs illūcēscēbat.

2 diē illūcēscente, multī saccāriī in rīpā flūminis labōrābant.

3 saccāriīs labōrantibus, advēnit nāvis. nautae nāvem dēligāvērunt.

4 nāve dēligātā, saccāriī frūmentum expōnere coepērunt.

5 frūmentō expositō, magister
nāvis pecūniam saccāriīs
distribuit.

6 pecūniā distribūtā, saccāriī ad
tabernam proximam
festīnāvērunt.

7 tandem sōl occidere coepit.

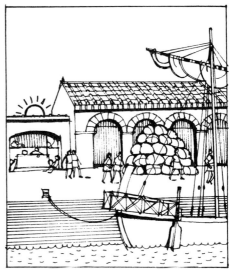

8 sōle occidente, saccāriī ā tabernā
ēbriī discessērunt, omnī pecūniā
cōnsūmptā.

adventus

diē illūcēscente, ingēns Rōmānōrum multitūdō viās urbis
complēbat. pauperēs ex īnsulīs exībant ut aquam ē fontibus
pūblicīs traherent. senātōrēs ad forum lectīcīs vehēbantur. in rīpīs
flūminis Tiberis, ubi multa horrea sita erant, frūmentum ē nāvibus
ā saccāriīs expōnēbātur. servī, quī ā vēnālīciīs ē Britanniā importātī   5
erant, ē nāvibus dūcēbantur, catēnīs gravibus vīnctī.

ex ūnā nāvium, quae modo ā Graeciā advēnerat, puella
pulcherrima exiit. epistulam ad Haterium scrīptam manū tenēbat.
sarcinae eius ā servō portābantur, virō quadrāgintā annōrum. tot
tantaeque erant sarcinae ut servus eās ferre vix posset.   10

sōle ortō, puella ad Subūram advēnit. multitūdine
clāmōribusque hominum valdē obstupefacta est. tanta erat
multitūdō ut puella summā cum difficultāte prōcēderet. mendīcī,
quī ad compita sedēbant, manūs ad praetereuntēs porrigēbant.
ubīque sonitus labōrantium audiēbātur: ā crepidāriīs calceī   15
reficiēbantur; ā ferrāriīs gladiī excūdēbantur; ā fabrīs tigna
secābantur. fabrī, puellā vīsā, clāmāre coepērunt; eam verbīs
procācibus appellāvērunt. quae tamen, clāmōribus fabrōrum
neglēctīs, vultū serēnō celeriter praeteriit. servum iussit festīnāre
nē domum Hateriī tardius pervenīrent.   20

eōdem tempore multī clientēs per viās contendēbant ut
patrōnōs salūtārent. aliī, scissīs togīs ruptīsque calceīs, per lutum
lentē ībant. eīs difficile erat festīnāre quod lutum erat altum, viae
angustae, multitūdō dēnsa. aliī, quī nōbilī gente nātī sunt, celeriter
prōcēdēbant quod servī multitūdinem fūstibus dēmovēbant. hī   25
clientēs, quī sīcut unda per viās ruēbant, puellae prōcēdentī
obstābant.

illūcēscente:		**Subūram: Subūra**	*the Subura*
illūcēscere	*dawn, grow bright*		*(noisy and*
lectīcīs: lectīca	*sedan-chair*		*crowded*
Tiberis: Tiberis	*River Tiber*		*district north*
saccāriīs:			*of the Forum)*
saccārius	*docker,*	obstupefacta est:	
	dock-worker	obstupefacere	*amaze, stun*
expōnēbātur:		mendīcī: mendīcus	*beggar*
expōnere	*unload*	compita: compitum	*crossroads*
catēnīs: catēna	*chain*	porrigēbant: porrigere	*stretch out*
modo	*just*	crepidāriīs:	
sarcinae	*bags, luggage*	crepidārius	*shoemaker*
ortō: ortus	*having risen*	ferrāriīs: ferrārius	*blacksmith*

excūdēbantur:	forge, hammer	appellāvērunt:	
excūdere	out	appellāre	call out to
fabrīs: faber	carpenter,	ruptīs: rumpere	break, split
	workman	lutum	mud
procācibus: procāx	impudent,	dēmovēbant:	
	impolite	dēmovēre	move out of the way

A model of Rome in the fourth century.

Notice these important features from Domitian's time: the Tiber River, the Theater of Marcellus, the Circus Maximus, the Capitol with the Temple of Jupiter, the Palatine Hill, the Forum Romanum, an aqueduct, the Flavian Amphitheater, the Subura.

salūtātiō I

When you have read this story, answer the questions at the end.

prīmā hōrā clientēs ante domum Hateriī conveniēbant. omnēs,
oculīs in iānuam dēfīxīs, patrōnī favōrem exspectābant. aliī
beneficium, aliī sportulam spērābant. puella, servō adstante, in
extrēmā parte multitūdinis cōnstitit; ignāra mōrum Rōmānōrum,
in animō volvēbat cūr tot hominēs illā hōrā ibi stārent.   5

iānuā subitō apertā, in līmine appāruit praecō. corpus eius erat
ingēns et obēsum, vultus superbus, oculī malignī. clientēs,
praecōne vīsō, clāmāre statim coepērunt. eum identidem ōrābant
ut sē ad patrōnum admitteret. ille tamen superbē circumspectāvit
neque quicquam prīmō dīxit.   10

omnibus tandem silentibus, praecō ita coepit:
"dominus noster, Quīntus Haterius Latrōniānus, ratiōnēs suās
subdūcit. iubet igitur trēs cīvēs ratiōnibus testēs subscrībere. cēdite
C. Iūliō Alexandrō, C. Memmiō Prīmō, L. Venūlēiō Aprōniānō."

quī igitur, audītīs nōminibus suīs, alacriter prōgressī domum   15
intrāvērunt. cēterī autem, oculīs in vultum praecōnis dēfīxīs, spē
favōris manēbant.

"ad cēnam," inquit praecō, "Haterius invītat L. Volusium
Maeciānum et M. Licinium Prīvātum. Maeciānus et Prīvātus
decimā hōrā redīre iubentur. nunc autem cēdite aliīs! cēdite   20
architectō C. Rabīriō Maximō! cēdite T. Claudiō Papīriō!"

dum illī per iānuam intrant, cēterīs nūntiāvit praecō:
"vōs omnēs iubēminī Haterium tertiā hōrā ad forum dēdūcere."
hīs verbīs dictīs, paucōs dēnāriōs in turbam sparsit. clientēs, nē
sportulam āmitterent, dēnāriōs rapere temptāvērunt. inter sē   25
vehementer certābant. intereā puella immōta stābat, hōc
spectāculō attonita.

salūtātiō	*the morning visit (paid by clients to patron)*
sportulam: sportula	*handout (gift of food or money)*
extrēmā parte: extrēma pars	*edge*
līmine: līmen	*threshold, doorway*
praecō	*herald*
malignī: malignus	*spiteful*
superbē	*arrogantly*
ratiōnēs ... subdūcit:	
ratiōnēs subdūcere	*draw up accounts, write up accounts*
subscrībere	*sign*
alacriter	*eagerly*
dēdūcere	*escort*

Questions

1 At what time of day did these events take place?
2 Where did the girl stand? What puzzled her?
3 Who was seen on the threshold when the door opened? Describe
   him. What did the clients do when they caught sight of him?
4 Why do you think the herald remained silent at first?
5 How can we tell that all the clients mentioned in line 14 are Roman
   citizens? How can we tell that none of them is a freedman of
   Haterius?
6 What is the effect of the word order in lines 18–19 (**ad cēnam ...
   Haterius invītat ... et M. Licinium Prīvātum**)?
7 In the herald's announcements, find two examples of small tasks
   that clients have to perform for their patrons, and one example of a
   favor granted by patrons to clients.
8 How did the herald distribute the denarii (line 24)? What was the
   clients' reaction? What was the girl's reaction? Suggest why the
   herald distributed the coins in this way.

About the Language I: Ablative Absolute

A Study the following pair of sentences:

> mīlitēs discessērunt.
> *The soldiers departed.*

> **urbe captā**, mīlitēs discessērunt.
> ***With the city having been captured**, the soldiers departed.*

The phrase in boldface is made up of a noun (**urbe**) and participle (**captā**) in the **ablative** case. Phrases of this kind are known as ablative absolute phrases, and are very common in Latin.

B Ablative absolute phrases can be translated in many different ways. For instance, the example in Section A might be translated:

> *When the city had been captured, the soldiers departed.*
> Or, *After the city was captured, the soldiers departed.*

C Further examples:

1. arcū dēdicātō, cīvēs domum rediērunt.
2. pecūniā āmissā, ancilla lacrimāre coepit.
3. victimīs sacrificātīs, haruspex ōmina nūntiāvit.
4. duce interfectō, hostēs dēspērābant.
5. mercātor, clāmōribus audītīs, ē lectō perterritus surrēxit.
6. senātor, hāc sententiā dictā, cōnsēdit.

D In each of the examples above, the participle in the ablative absolute phrase is a perfect passive participle. Ablative absolute phrases can also be formed with present active participles. For example:

> **omnibus tacentibus**, lībertus nōmina recitāvit.
> ***With everyone being quiet**, the freedman read out the names.*
> Or, in more natural English:
> ***When everyone was quiet**, the freedman read out the names.*

Further examples:

1. custōdibus dormientibus, captīvī effūgērunt.
2. pompā per viās prōcēdente, spectātōrēs vehementer plausērunt.
3. Imperātor, sacerdōtibus adstantibus, precēs dīvō Titō obtulit.

Ablative absolute phrases can also be formed with perfect active participles. For example:

dominō ēgressō, servī garrīre coepērunt.
With the master having gone out, the slaves began to chatter.
Or, in more natural English:
After the master had gone out, the slaves began to chatter.

Further examples:

4 mercātōre profectō, rēs dīra accidit.
5 nūntiīs ā Britanniā regressīs, imperātor senātōrēs arcessīvit.
6 cōnsule haec locūtō, omnēs cīvēs attonitī erant.

salūtātiō II

iānuā tandem clausā, abīre clientēs coepērunt. aliī dēnāriīs
collēctīs abiērunt ut cibum sibi suīsque emerent; aliī spē pecūniae
dēiectī invītī discessērunt. Haterium praecōnemque vituperābant.
    deinde servō puella imperāvit ut iānuam pulsāret. praecōnī
regressō servus,   5
    "ecce!" inquit. "domina mea, Euphrosynē, adest."
    "abī, sceleste! nēmō alius hodiē admittitur," respondit praecō
superbā vōce.
    "sed domina mea est philosopha Graeca doctissima," inquit
servus. "hūc missa est ā Quīntō Hateriō Chrȳsogonō ipsō, Haterii   10
lībertō, quī Athēnīs habitat."
    "īnsānīvit igitur Chrȳsogonus," respondit praecō. "odiō sunt
omnēs philosophī Hateriō! redeundum vōbīs est Athēnās unde
missī estis."

suīs: suī	*their families*
spē ... dēiectī	*disappointed in their hope*
Euphrosynē	*Euphrosyne (Her name means "cheerfulness" or "good thoughts.")*
philosopha	*(female) philosopher*
Athēnīs	*in Athens*
odiō sunt: odiō esse	*be hateful*
redeundum vōbīs est	*you must return*

servus arrogantiā praecōnis īrātus, nihilōminus perstitit.   *15*

"sed Eryllus," inquit, "quī est Hateriō arbiter ēlegantiae,
epistulam ad Chrȳsogonum scrīpsit in quā eum rogāvit ut
philosopham hūc mitteret. ergō adsumus!"

hīs verbīs audītīs, praecō, quī Eryllum haudquāquam amābat,
magnā vōce,   *20*

"Eryllus!" inquit. "quis est Eryllus? meus dominus Haterius est,
nōn Eryllus! abī!"

haec locūtus servum in lutum dēpulit, iānuamque clausit.
Euphrosynē, simulatque servum humī iacentem vīdit, eius īram
lēnīre temptāvit.   *25*

"nōlī," inquit, "mentem tuam vexāre. nōs decet rēs adversās
aequō animō ferre. nōbīs crās reveniendum est."

nihilōminus	*nevertheless*
perstitit: perstāre	*persist*
arbiter	*expert, judge*
ēlegantiae: ēlegantia	*good taste*
ergō	*therefore*
dēpulit: dēpellere	*push down*
mentem: mēns	*mind*
aequō animō	*calmly, in a calm spirit*

About the Language II: ut and nē

A In Stage 27, you met examples of indirect commands used with **ut**:

> imperāvit nūntiīs **ut** redīrent.
> *He ordered the messengers **that** they should return.*
> Or, in more natural English:
> *He ordered the messengers **to** return.*

B From Stage 29 onwards, you have met examples of indirect commands used with the word **nē**:

> imperāvit nūntiīs **nē** redīrent.
> *He ordered the messengers **that** they should **not** return.*
> Or, in more natural English:
> *He ordered the messengers **not to** return.*

Further examples:

1 haruspex iuvenem monuit nē nāvigāret.
2 fēminae mīlitēs ōrāvērunt nē līberōs interficerent.
3 mercātor amīcō persuāsit nē gemmās vēnderet.
4 cūr vōbīs imperāvit nē vīllam intrārētis?

C You have also met sentences in which **nē** is used with a purpose clause:

> senex pecūniam cēlāvit **nē** fūrēs eam invenīrent.
> *The old man hid the money **so that** the thieves would **not** find it.*
> Or, *The old man hid the money **in case** the thieves should find it.*

Further examples:

1 per viās celeriter contendēbāmus nē tardī ad arcum advenīrēmus.
2 in fossā latēbam nē hostēs mē cōnspicerent.
3 imperātor multum frūmentum ab Aegyptō importāvit nē cīvēs famē perīrent.
4 servī ē fundō effūgērunt nē poenās darent.

Rome's docklands. A wharf with arched chambers for storing goods in transit.

Word Patterns: Compound Verbs II

A Study the way in which the following verbs are formed:

īre	abīre	circumīre	inīre
go	*go away*	*go around*	*go in*

B Using Section A as a guide, complete the table below:

dūcere	.....	.....	indūcere
.....	*lead away*	.....	.....
.....	auferre	circumferre	.....
carry	.....	.....	.....

C Give the meaning of the following verbs:

abicere, āvertere, abesse, abigere;
circumspectāre, circumstāre, circumpōnere;
irrumpere, īnfundere, inicere, inesse.

Practicing the Language

A Complete each sentence with the correct word. Then translate.

1 multī leōnēs in Āfricā quotannīs (capitur, capiuntur).
2 ecce! ille senex ā latrōnibus (petitur, petuntur).
3 ego ā clientibus nunc (salūtor, salūtāmur).
4 vōs ā praecōne (dīmitteris, dīmittiminī).
5 mīlitēs in ōrdinēs longōs ā centuriōnibus (instruēbātur, instruēbantur).
6 nōs ā barbarīs ferōcibus (oppugnābar, oppugnābāmur).
7 victimae ā sacerdōte (ēligēbātur, ēligēbantur).
8 tū lectīcā per forum (vehēbāris, vehēbāminī).

B Match the active and passive forms of the following verbs and then translate each form.

vectus es, neglēximus, refectum est, dēmīsistis, cōnsultus sum, vexistī, volūtī sunt, exstrūctum est, refēcit, neglēctī sumus, volvērunt, dēmissī estis, cōnsuluī, exstrūxit

C Complete each sentence with the most suitable word from the list below, and then translate.

portābantur, fraude, vītārent, adeptī, morbō, abēgisset

1 puerī in fossam dēsiluērunt ut perīculum . . . . . .
2 Haterius, ... Salviī dēceptus, cōnsēnsit.
3 multae amphorae in triclīnium . . . . . .
4 senex, ... gravī afflīctus, medicum arcessīvit.
5 praecō, cum puellam servumque . . . . ., iānuam clausit.
6 clientēs, sportulam . . . . ., abiērunt.

D Select the correct participle for each blank and then translate each sentence.

neglectīs, temptantibus, admissā, prōgressā, sedentibus, volvente, refectō, vīnctō

1 philosophā nōn . . . . ., servus praecōnem vituperābat.
2 clientibus pecūniam rapere . . . . ., praecō iānuam claudere coepit.
3 mendīcīs ad compita . . . . ., patrōnī in lectīcīs vectī sunt.
4 turbā per viās angustās . . . . ., nōnnūllī līberī celerius prōcēdere poterant.
5 mīlite catēnīs . . . . ., dux ē carcere vultū serēnō discessit.
6 ratiōnibus multōs per annōs . . . . ., ambō dīvitēs palluērunt.
7 opere . . . . ., magister lūdōs spectāre cōnstituerat.
8 fēminā mōrēs Rōmānōs in animō . . . . ., servus in lutō iacēbat.

The Pavilion Convention Center in Virginia Beach,VA. Notice how the building's design echoes the arched chambers of Roman storage buildings.

The City of Rome

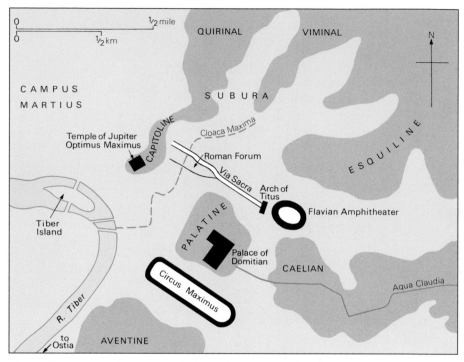

Central features of Rome, including the seven hills.

Rome grew up in a very unplanned and unsystematic way, quite different from the neat grid-pattern of other Roman towns. Huge commercial structures and crowded lower-class neighborhoods lay beside great monumental areas with temples, theaters, circuses, baths, basilicas, and promenades. Rome was also an extremely crowded city, as can be seen by comparing its approximate area and population with those of two modern metropolitan districts in North America. First-century Rome, with an approximate area of 8 square miles (21 square kilometers) and a population of 1,000,000, had a population density of 125,000 people per square mile (48,000 per square kilometer).

city	population density people/sq.mile	people/sq.km.
Rome	125,000	48,000
Los Angeles	8, 000	3,000
Toronto	9,900	3,800
New York City	26, 500	10,600
Calcutta	108,000	41,700

Rome's coastal port was Ostia, at the mouth of the Tiber River, where warships docked and Roman cargo boats brought in merchandise from all over the empire. This hub of commercial and maritime activities boasted a man-made harbor begun by Emperor Claudius and its huge warehouses were indispensable to meet the needs of Rome.

From Ostia, ships brought goods up the Tiber to Rome's river port with its docks, riverside markets (**emporia**) and warehouses (**horrea**). Further upstream, beyond the wharves and warehouses, the river was divided for a short stretch by the Tiber Island (**īnsula Tiberīna**). This elongated island had been built up to look like a ship sailing the river, complete with an ornamental prow (**rostrum**); it contained a Temple of Aesculapius, the god of healing, to which many invalids came in the hope of a cure.

The Tiber, looking north, with the Island, center, and bridges.

In the story on page 214, Euphrosyne and her slave disembark near the Tiber Island and then move off northeastwards. Their route could have taken them around the lower slopes of the Capitoline Hill and through the Forum Romanum (described in Stage 29), passing the Palatine Hill where the Emperor Domitian had his palace.

Euphrosyne and her slave would then have continued through the Subura, a densely populated district north of the Forum, full of stores and large multi-storied, block-long tenement houses or **īnsulae**. Its inhabitants were mostly poor and some very poor indeed; they included barbers, shoemakers, butchers, weavers, blacksmiths, vegetable sellers, prostitutes, and thieves. Several Roman writers refer to the Subura, and

One of the Tiber riverboats, the Isis Giminiana, loading grain at Ostia to be taken to Rome. Her master, Farnaces, superintends the measuring of the grain from his place at the stern.

give a vivid impression of its noise, its dirt, and its crowds. The following passage from Juvenal describes a street which might easily be in the Subura:

> We hurry on, but the way is blocked; there is a tidal wave of people in front, and we're pushed and prodded from behind. One man digs me with his elbow, another with the pole of a sedan-chair; somebody catches me on the head with a plank, and somebody else with a wine-barrel. My legs are plastered with mud, my feet are stepped on by all and sundry, and a soldier is sticking the nail of his boot in my toe.

Many rich and aristocratic Romans settled in the district of the Esquiline Hill, which lay to the east of the Subura. Here they could enjoy peace and seclusion in huge mansions, surrounded by colonnaded gardens and landscaped parks which contrasted very sharply with the Subura's slums and crowded tenement blocks. In our stories Haterius' house, where Euphrosyne's journey ended, is imagined as being on the Esquiline.

Among the well-known landmarks of Rome were the Circus Maximus, where chariot races were held; the Flavian Amphitheater; and the Campus Martius, formerly an army training area, which now provided some much-needed open space for the general population.

Crossing the city in various directions were the aqueducts, which brought water into the city at the rate of 200 million gallons (900 million liters) a day. The houses of the rich citizens were usually connected to this supply by means of pipes which brought water directly into their storage tanks; the poorer people had to collect their fresh water from public fountains on street corners. The city also possessed a very advanced system of drains and sewers: a complicated network of underground channels carried sewage and waste water from the larger private houses, public baths, fountains, and lavatories to the central drain (Cloaca Maxima), which emptied into the Tiber.

Above: *An aqueduct approaching Rome. It carries two water channels, one above the other.*

Left: *Here, remains of the ancient aqueduct system can still be seen, dwarfing the houses. Find the aqueduct on page 215.*

There were many hazards and discomforts for the inhabitants of Rome. As we have seen in Stage 30, fires were frequent and the insulae in the slums were often cheaply built and liable to collapse. The overcrowding and congestion in the streets have already been mentioned above; wheeled traffic was banned from the city center during the hours of daylight, but blockages were still caused by the wagons of builders like Haterius, which were exempt from the ban. Disease was an ever-present danger in the overcrowded poorer quarters;

crime and violence were commonplace in the unlit streets at night. Rome was a city of contrasts, in which splendor and squalor were often found side by side; it could be both an exciting and an unpleasant place to live.

In the Subura, Euphrosyne would have passed a variety of stalls including blacksmiths' shops.

Views of shopping developments in Rome. Left: Tenements on the Via Biberatica.
Right: Inside a shop, looking across the street towards two more. The one
opposite has a window above the shop doorway to light the shop after the
shutters were closed; the shopkeeper would probably live there. Above that is the
support for a balcony belonging to the apartment above – the apartment block is
several stories high. We can see the groove (left) to hold the shutters of the shop
on this side, and also two square holes for the bars that held the shutters in place.

Patronage and Roman Society

The story on pages 216–217 shows an aspect of Roman society known as patronage, in which a patron (**patrōnus**) gave help and protection to others less rich or powerful than himself, who performed various services for him in return. The people waiting outside Haterius' house hoped for various things: money, a meal, a favorable referral for an architect or other craftsman or businessman. In return they might serve as witnesses for documents, pack an audience when the patron gave a recitation of his poems, or swell the importance of their patron by accompanying him through the forum: the more clients, the more important the patron.

The habit of the morning call (**salūtātiō**) had started in Republican times. In a society where the upper classes had the power, clients needed their patrons' favor and advice for any number of financial or legal transactions. In return, the patrons needed their votes in politics and the addition to their prestige that a large number of clients gave. Freedmen would automatically become the clients of their former owner who might help them in setting up a business and then expect part of the profit; soldiers who had served under a particular general would probably become his clients.

EMPEROR nominates SALVIUS to an important priesthood

SALVIUS obtains building contract for HATERIUS

HATERIUS orders distribution of sportula to CLIENTS

The patronage system.

By the time of Domitian, however, a more routine set of formalities had been introduced, and most callers were people down on their luck, ready to dress in the cumbersome (and easily soiled) toga that custom required, and, early each morning, make their way across the city, for as little, sometimes, as the **sportula** handed out to them. The sportula (little basket) might contain food or money – not much money, according to Martial – not even enough to buy a decent dinner. But Martial, as a poet, needed a patron, and so he put up with the inconvenience and sometimes humiliation of being a client. The humiliations might occur not just at the salutatio itself, but later at dinner when the client might be served food and wine inferior to that given to the higher ranking friends and clients of the host. Moreover, being a client gave Martial (or Juvenal) opportunities for satire, and in fact, because much of our information about the salutatio comes from satirists, we really do not know how widespread the practice was.

However, we do know that people of considerably higher rank than the miserable crowd Euphrosyne saw were clients themselves. Haterius depended on the good will of his patron, Salvius. Salvius, in turn, like everyone else, and in particular other senators like himself, looked to the emperor for notice and favors.

The system of patronage shows how society in Rome was organized along clearly defined ranks. By the time of our stories, the emperor was at the head of all other patrons. He would have his lines of callers waiting for the announcement: **Caesarem iam salūtārī** (The emperor is receiving). Lists of callers would be published and it was a bad sign if someone was refused admission.

Below the emperor were the senators, who formerly had been the leaders of the state and society in the Republic. Salvius and Agricola were men of this class. Men could attain the rank of senator because they were the sons of senators, by election to the financial post of quaestor (in the Republic), or by special gift of the emperor. Senators wore togas with broad purple stripes, sat in special reserved places at public ceremonies, and served as high-ranking priests. They would have been required to have a fortune of at least 1,000,000 sesterces. Magistrates called censors periodically checked the lists of people of the senatorial class to see if they could still be financially ranked as senators.

Haterius was a member of the equestrian class or **equitēs**. Members of this class could be very rich indeed, although their fortune needed to be only 400,000 sesterces, but they did not usually attain the same political or military heights that senators could achieve. Whereas a senator was expected to derive his wealth from property, and could not participate in his own name in trade, the equites could and did. Although many equites

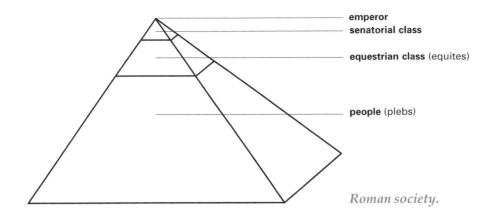

emperor
senatorial class
equestrian class (equites)

people (plebs)

Roman society.

might be primarily businessmen, many were active in politics, too, and only a member of the equestrian class might be governor of Egypt. The equestrians were also allowed to wear a gold ring as a status symbol and a toga with a narrow stripe.

The majority of people in Rome, however, were members of the **plebs**, or plebeian class. These might be small businessmen or craftsmen, with reasonably comfortable lives for themselves and their families, or they could be near destitution, as some of the people outside Haterius' door seemed to be. There had been a distribution of free grain for Roman citizens in the city since Republican times, but even with this help, many lived in extreme poverty as day laborers of one kind or another, and really depended on any help they could get from a patron, if they were lucky enough to have one. In theory they could, by hard work and luck, rise to the equestrian class, but on the whole, power and prestige were beyond their reach.

For the plebs, as for everyone else, the emperor was their patron. Vespasian, Domitian's father, had

The curia or senate house in the Forum Romanum.

Much free grain was distributed to the poor. Here a consignment of grain is being measured.

been approached by an engineer who suggested a labor-saving device to haul some columns up to the Capitol. The emperor did not want to hear about it. He did not want to deprive his "little plebs" (**plebicula**) of the opportunity to earn a living.

Word Study

A Complete the following analogies with words from the Stage 31
   Vocabulary Checklist:
   1 appropinquāre : adīre : : portāre : _____
   2 homō : vir : : ōs : _____
   3 salvē : valē : : solvere : _____
   4 servus : dominus : : cliēns : _____
   5 vērus : falsus : : _____ : privātus
   6 gladius : secāre : : _____ : vincīre
   7 semper : numquam : : omnīnō : _____
   8 poēta : recitāre : : _____ : nūntiāre
   9 laetus : gaudium : : _____ : arrogantia
   10 plausus : laudāre : : _____ : dēcipere

B Copy the following words. Then put parentheses around the Latin
   root from this Stage contained inside these derivatives; give the
   Latin word and its meaning from which the derivative comes.

   For example: conservation con(serva)tion servāre – to save
   1 convoluted
   2 identical
   3 concatenation
   4 extemporaneous
   5 intersection
   6 invective
   7 altimeter

C Match the meaning to the derivative.
   1 fraudulent   a a dining hall in a college or school
   2 vehicle   b a moving forward
   3 preterition   c acting with deceit
   4 refectory   d calmness, tranquility
   5 desperation   e any means of carrying or communicating
   6 serenity   f recklessness resulting from lack of hope
   7 progression   g mentioning something by saying that it is
                         going to be omitted, passed over

Stage 31 Vocabulary Checklist

altus, alta, altum	*high, deep*
angustus, angusta, angustum	*narrow*
ante (+ ACC)	*before, in front of*
catēna, catēnae, f.	*chain*
cliēns, clientis, m.	*client*
dux, ducis, m.	*leader*
favor, favōris, m.	*favor*
fraus, fraudis, f.	*trick*
haudquāquam	*not at all*
īdem, eadem, idem	*the same*
mōs, mōris, m.	*custom*
neglegō, neglegere, neglēxī, neglēctus	*neglect*
ōrō, ōrāre, ōrāvī	*beg*
patrōnus, patrōnī, m.	*patron*
praecō, praecōnis, m.	*herald*
praetereō, praeterīre, praeteriī	*pass by, go past*
prōgressus, prōgressa, prōgressum	*having advanced*
pūblicus, pūblica, pūblicum	*public*
ratiōnēs, ratiōnum, f.pl.	*accounts*
reficiō, reficere, refēcī, refectus	*repair*
secō, secāre, secuī, sectus	*cut*
serēnus, serēna, serēnum	*calm, clear*
spērō, spērāre, spērāvī	*hope, expect*
superbus, superba, superbum	*arrogant, proud*
tempus, temporis, n.	*time*
ubīque	*everywhere*
vehō, vehere, vexī, vectus	*carry*
vinciō, vincīre, vīnxī, vīnctus	*bind, tie up*
volvō, volvere, volvī, volūtus	*turn*
in animō volvere	*wonder, turn over in the mind*
vultus, vultūs, m.	*expression, face*

Originally a Roman sewer cover, this large stone disk is now called the Bocca della Verità, or Mouth of Truth.

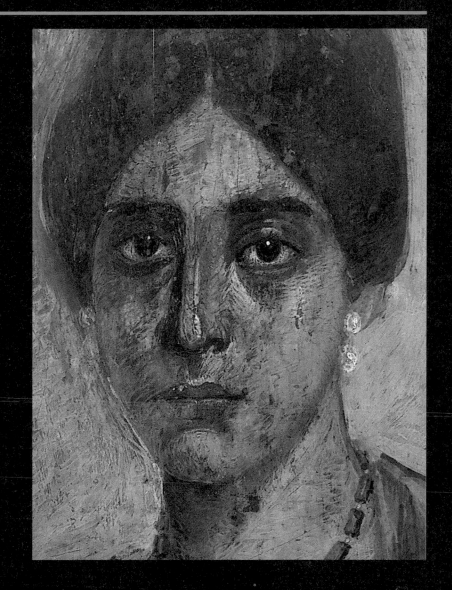

EUPHROSYNE

Stage 32

1 postrīdiē Euphrosynē
domum Hateriī regressa est.
iterum tamen praecō eam
verbīs dūrīs abēgit.

regressa est *returned*

2 servus eam hortātus est ut
praecōnem dōnīs
corrumperet; sed
Euphrosynē ab eiusmodī
factīs abhorruit.

hortātus est *urged*
eiusmodī *of that kind*

3 septem continuōs diēs ā
praecōne abācta,
Euphrosynē dēnique in
Graeciam redīre cōnstituit.
hōc cōnsiliō captō, ad
flūmen Tiberim ut nāvem
cōnscenderet profecta est.

abācta: abigere *drive away*
profecta est *set out*

4 eōdem diē quō Euphrosynē
discēdere cōnstituit,
celebrābat Haterius diem
nātālem. grātulātiōnibus
clientium acceptīs, ōtiōsus
in hortō sedēbat, in umbrā
ingentis laurī. subitō Eryllus
hortum ingressus est.

laurī: laurus *laurel tree*
ingressus est *entered*

Euphrosynē revocāta

Eryllus:	domine! omnia quae mandāvistī parāta sunt. centum amīcī et clientēs ad cēnam invītātī sunt. iussī coquum cibum sūmptuōsum parāre, cellāriumque vīnum Falernum veterrimum dēprōmere. nihil neglēctum est. 5
Haterius:	nōnne petauristāriōs et saltātrīcēs condūxistī? hercle! quam ā petauristāriīs dēlector!
Eryllus:	quid dīcis, domine? hominēs eiusmodī cīvibus urbānīs nōn placent. nunc philosophīs favet optimus quisque. 10
Haterius:	īnsānīs, Erylle! nam philosophī sunt senēs sevērī. neque saltāre neque circulōs trānsilīre possunt.
Eryllus:	at domine, aliquid melius quam philosophum adeptus sum. mē enim auctōre, philosopha quaedam, puella pulcherrima, hūc invītāta est. ā 15 Chrȳsogonō Athēnīs missa est.
Haterius:	philosopham mīsit Chrȳsogonus? optimē fēcistī, Erylle! philosopham nē Imperātor quidem habet. sed ubi est haec philosopha quam adeptus es?
Eryllus:	iamdūdum eam anxius exspectō. fortasse iste 20 praecō, homō summae stultitiae, eam nōn admīsit.
Haterius:	arcesse hūc praecōnem!

exit Eryllus. mox ingreditur praecō.

Haterius:	philosopham pulchram anxius exspectō. num stultus eam abēgistī? 25
praecō:	nūllam philosopham pulchram vīdī, domine.
Haterius:	tibi nōn crēdō. poenās maximās minor nisi vērum loqueris.
praecō:	(*pallēscēns*) domine, ignōsce mihi. nesciēbam quantum tū philosophīs favērēs. illam 30 philosopham, cum hūc vēnisset, nōn rogāvī utrum tū eam invītāvissēs necne. ignārus eam abēgī. māne ad flūmen profecta est ut nāvem cōnscenderet.
Haterius:	abī statim, caudex! festīnā ad Tiberim! nōlī umquam revenīre nisi cum philosophā! 35

domō ēgressus, praecō per viās contendit. ubi ad flūmen advēnit, Euphrosynēn in nāvem cōnscēnsūram cōnspicit. magnā vōce eam appellat. Euphrosynē, nōmine audītō, convertitur.

praecō:	ignōsce mihi, Euphrosynē doctissima! nōlī discēdere! necesse est tibi domum Hateriī mēcum prōcēdere.	*40*
Euphrosynē:	cūr mē revocās? ōdiō sunt omnēs philosophī Hateriō, ut tū ipse dīxistī. Athēnās igitur nunc redeō. valē!	
praecō:	(*effūsīs lacrimīs*) nōlī mē dēserere! sine tē mihi nōn licet domum Hateriī redīre.	*45*

identidem praecō ōrat; identidem philosopha recūsat. dēnique precibus lacrimīsque praecōnis permōta, Euphrosynē domum Hateriī regreditur.

revocāta: revocāre	*recall, call back*
vīnum Falernum	*Falernian wine (a famous wine from Campania)*
veterrimum: vetus	*old*
dēprōmere	*bring out*
petauristāriōs: petauristārius	*acrobat*
optimus quisque	*all the best people*
sevērī: sevērus	*severe, strict*
circulōs: circulus	*hoop*
trānsilīre	*jump through*
at	*but*
adeptus sum	*I have obtained*
mē ... auctōre	*at my suggestion*
quaedam: quīdam	*a certain, a*
iamdūdum	*for a long time*
ingreditur	*enters*
minor	*I am threatening*
nisi	*unless, if ... not*
ignōsce: ignōscere	*forgive*
utrum ... necne	*whether ... or not*
Euphrosynēn	*Greek accusative of* **Euphrosynē**
convertitur	*turns around*
effūsīs lacrimīs	*bursting into tears*
mihi nōn licet	*I am not permitted, I am not allowed*
regreditur	*returns*

About the Language I: Deponent Verbs

A Study the following examples:

> poenās **minor** nisi vērum **loqueris**.
> *I am threatening punishment if you are not telling the truth.*
> Eryllus hortum **ingressus est**.
> *Eryllus entered the garden.*
> aliquid melius quam philosophum **adeptus sum**.
> *I have obtained something better than a philosopher.*

Notice the forms and meanings of the words in boldface. Each verb has a **passive form** but an **active meaning**. Verbs of this kind are known as deponent verbs. (They have "set aside" – **dēpōnere** – their active forms.)

B Further examples:

1 spectātōrēs dē arcū novō loquēbantur.
2 cūr ex urbe subitō ēgressī estis?
3 uxor hortāta est ut tēcum dīcerem.
4 forum Rōmānum nunc ingredimur.
5 prōgressī sunt; precor; regrediminī; suspicātus erat; passus es; convertēbātur.

C In Stage 22, you met perfect active participles. For example:

conspicātus   *having caught sight of*
precātus   *having prayed*

Deponent verbs are the only verbs whose perfect participles are active in meaning. Compare them with the perfect passive participles of regular verbs:

dēceptus   *deceived, having been deceived*
missus   *sent, having been sent*

D Further examples:

DEPONENT VERBS	REGULAR VERBS
adeptus	portātus
secūtus	iussus
profectus	afflictus
locūtus	audītus
ingressus	vulnerātus

cēna Hateriī

nōnā hōrā amīcī clientēsque, quōs Haterius invītāverat ut sēcum
diem nātālem celebrārent, triclīnium ingrediēbantur. inter eōs
aderant fīliī lībertōrum quī humilī locō nātī magnās opēs adeptī
erant. aderant quoque nōnnūllī senātōrēs quī inopiā oppressī
favōrem Hateriī conciliāre cōnābantur.   5

    proximus Haterium recumbēbat T. Flāvius Sabīnus cōnsul, vir
summae auctōritātis. Haterius blandīs et mollibus verbīs Sabīnum
adloquēbātur, ut favōrem eius conciliāret. ipse in prīmō locō
recumbēbat. pulvīnīs Tyriīs innītēbātur; ānulōs gerēbat aureōs quī
gemmīs fulgēbant; dentēs spīnā argenteā perfodiēbat.   10

    intereā duo Aethiopes triclīnium ingrediēbantur. lancem
ingentem ferēbant, in quā positus erat aper tōtus. statim coquus,
quī Aethiopas in triclīnium secūtus erat, ad lancem prōgressus est
ut aprum scinderet. aprō perītē scissō, multae avēs statim

inopiā: inopia	*poverty*	**innītēbātur**	*was leaning,*
cōnābantur	*were trying*		*was resting*
proximus	*next to*	**spīnā: spīna**	*toothpick*
adloquēbātur	*was addressing*	**perfodiēbat: perfodere**	*pick*
pulvīnīs: pulvīnus	*cushion*	**lancem: lānx**	*dish*
Tyriīs: Tyrius	*Tyrian (colored*	**scinderet: scindere**	*carve,*
	with dye from		*cut open*
	the city of Tyre)		

ēvolāvērunt suāviter pīpiantēs. convīvae, cum vīdissent quid *15*
coquus parāvisset, eius artem vehementer laudāvērunt. quā rē
dēlectātus, Haterius servīs imperāvit ut amphorās vīnī Falernī
īnferrent. amphorīs inlātīs, cellārius titulōs quī īnfīxī erant magnā
vōce recitāvit, "Falernum Hateriānum, vīnum centum annōrum!"
tum vīnum in pōcula servī īnfundere coepērunt. *20*

conquer convīvīs laetissimē bibentibus, poposcit Haterius silentium.
spectāculum novum pollicitus est. omnēs convīvae in animō
volvēbant quāle spectāculum Haterius ēditūrus esset. ille rīdēns
digitīs concrepuit. hōc signō datō, Eryllus ē triclīniō ēgressus est.

appāruērunt in līmine duo tubicinēs. tubās vehementer *25*
īnflāvērunt. tum Eryllus Euphrosynēn in triclīnium dūxit.
convīvae, simulatque eam vīdērunt, fōrmam eius valdē admīrātī
sunt.

Haterius rīdēns Euphrosynēn rogāvit ut sēcum in lectō
cōnsīderet. deinde convīvās adlocūtus est. *30*

"haec puella," inquit glōriāns, "est philosopha doctissima,
nōmine Euphrosynē. iussū meō hūc vēnit Athēnīs, ubi habitant
philosophī nōtissimī. illa nōbīs dīligenter audienda est."

tum ad eam versus,

"nōbīs placet, mea Euphrosynē," inquit, "ā tē aliquid *35*
philosophiae discere."

pīpiantēs: pīpiāre	*chirp*
convīvae: convīva	*guest*
titulōs: titulus	*label*
īnfīxī erant: īnfīgere	*fasten onto*
īnfundere	*pour into*
pollicitus est	*promised*
ēditūrus	*going to put on, going to present*
digitīs: digitus	*finger*
concrepuit: concrepāre	*snap*
fōrmam: fōrma	*beauty, appearance*
admīrātī sunt	*admired*
glōriāns	*boasting, boastfully*

Wall painting of fruit in a glass bowl.

About the Language II: Future Active Participle

A Study the following examples:

> nunc ego quoque **moritūrus** sum.
> *Now I, too, am **about to die**.*
> nēmō sciēbat quid Haterius **factūrus** esset.
> *Nobody knew what Haterius was **going to do**.*
> praecō puellam vīdit, nāvem **cōnscēnsūram**.
> *The herald saw the girl **about to go on board** ship.*

The words in boldface are future active participles.

B Further examples:

1 nunc ego vōbīs cēnam splendidam datūrus sum.
2 mīlitēs in animō volvēbant quid centuriō dictūrus esset.
3 convīvae Haterium rogāvērunt num Euphrosynē saltātūra esset.
4 togās vestrās scissūrī sumus.
5 Quīntus nesciēbat num Salvius sē secūtūrus esset.

C Compare the future active participle with the perfect passive participle:

PERFECT PASSIVE PARTICIPLE	FUTURE ACTIVE PARTICIPLE
portātus	portātūrus
(having been) carried	*about to carry*
doctus	doctūrus
(having been) taught	*about to teach*
tractus	tractūrus
(having been) dragged	*about to drag*
audītus	audītūrus
(having been) heard	*about to hear*

philosophia

When you have read this story, answer the questions at the end.

Euphrosynē convīvās, quī avidē spectābant, sīc adlocūta est:
    "prīmum, fābula brevis mihi nārranda est. ōlim fuit homō pauper."
    "quid est pauper?" rogāvit cōnsul Sabīnus, quī mīlle servōs habēbat.   5
    quibus verbīs audītīs, omnēs plausērunt, iocō dēlectātī. Euphrosynē autem, convīvīs tandem silentibus,
    "hic pauper," inquit, "fundum parvum, uxōrem optimam, līberōs cārissimōs habēbat. strēnuē in fundō labōrāre solēbat ut sibi suīsque cibum praebēret."   10
    "scīlicet īnsānus erat," exclāmāvit Apollōnius, quī erat homō ignāvissimus. "nēmō nisi īnsānus labōrat."
    cui respondit Euphrosynē vōce serēnā,
    "omnibus autem labōrandum est. etiam eī quī spē favōris cēnās magistrātibus dant, rē vērā labōrant."   15
    quō audītō, Haterius ērubuit; cēterī, verbīs Euphrosynēs obstupefactī, tacēbant. deinde Euphrosynē,
    "pauper," inquit, "neque dīvitiās neque honōrēs cupiēbat. numquam nimium edēbat nec nimium bibēbat. in omnibus vītae partibus moderātus ac temperāns esse cōnābātur."   20
    L. Baebius Crispus senātor exclāmāvit,
    "scīlicet avārus erat! nōn laudandus est nōbīs sed culpandus. Haterius noster tamen maximē laudandus est quod amīcīs sūmptuōsās cēnās semper praebet."
    huic Baebiī sententiae omnēs plausērunt. Haterius, plausū   25
audītō, oblītus philosophiae servīs imperāvit ut plūs vīnī convīvīs offerrent. Euphrosynē tamen haec addidit,
    "at pauper multōs cāsūs passus est. līberōs enim et uxōrem āmīsit, ubi afflīxit eōs morbus gravissimus; fundum āmīsit, ubi mīlitēs eum dīripuērunt; lībertātem āmīsit, ubi ipse in servitūtem ā   30
mīlitibus vēnditus est. nihilōminus, quia Stōicus erat, rēs adversās semper aequō animō patiēbātur; neque deōs neque hominēs dētestābātur. dēnique senectūte labōribusque cōnfectus, tranquillē mortuus est. ille pauper, quem hominēs miserrimum exīstimābant, rē vērā fēlīx erat."   35
    Haterius cachinnāns "num fēlīcem eum exīstimās," inquit, "quī tot cāsūs passus est?"
    Hateriō hoc rogantī respondit Euphrosynē,

"id quod locūta sum nōn rēctē intellegis. alia igitur fābula mihi
nārranda est. ōlim fuit homō dīves." 40
   sed cōnsul Sabīnus, quem iam taedēbat fābulārum, exclāmāvit,
"satis philosophiae! age, mea Euphrosynē, dā mihi ōsculum,
immō ōscula multa."
   Rabīrius Maximus tamen, quī cum haec audīvisset ēbrius
surrēxit, 45
   "sceleste," inquit, "nōlī eam tangere!"
   haec locūtus, pōculum vīnō plēnum in ōs Sabīnī iniēcit.
   statim rēs ad pugnam vēnit. pōcula iaciēbantur; lectī
ēvertēbantur; togae scindēbantur. aliī Sabīnō, aliī Rabīriō
subveniēbant. Haterius hūc illūc currēbat; discordiam compōnere 50
cōnābātur. eum tamen currentem atque ōrantem nēmō
animadvertit.
   Euphrosynē autem, ad iānuam triclīniī vultū serēnō prōgressa,
convīvās pugnantēs ita adlocūta est:
   "ēn Rōmānī, dominī orbis terrārum, ventris Venerisque servī!" 55
   quibus verbīs dictīs, ad flūmen Tiberim ut nāvem quaereret
profecta est.

philosophia	*philosophy*	patiēbātur	*suffered, endured*
suīs: suī	*his family*	senectūte:	
scīlicet	*obviously*	senectūs	*old age*
rē vērā	*in fact, truly*	tranquillē	*peacefully*
Euphrosynēs	*Greek genitive of*	exīstimābant:	
	Euphrosynē	exīstimāre	*think, consider*
edēbat: edere	*eat*	rēctē	*rightly, properly*
moderātus	*restrained, moderate*	immō	*or rather*
temperāns	*temperate,*	compōnere	*settle*
	self-controlled	animadvertit:	*notice,*
culpandus: culpāre	*blame*	animadvertere	*take notice of*
plausū: plausus	*applause*	orbis terrārum	*world*
cāsūs: cāsus	*misfortune*	Veneris: Venus	*Venus (Roman*
Stōicus	*Stoic (believer in*		*goddess of love)*
	Stoic philosophy)		

Questions

1 Why was Euphrosyne's philosophy lecture a failure?
2 Look again at Euphrosyne's remark **ille pauper ... rē vērā fēlīx erat**
   (lines 34–35). Was Haterius right to suggest that this is a stupid
   remark? Or does it have some point?

About the Language III: More on Gerundives

A In Stage 26, you met the gerundive used in sentences like this:

mihi currendum est.   *I must run.*

B In Stage 32, you have met more sentences containing gerundives. For example:

mihi fābula nārranda est.   *I must tell a story.*

Compare this with another way of expressing the same idea:

necesse est mihi fābulam nārrāre.

C Further examples:

1 mihi epistula scrībenda est.
   (Compare: necesse est mihi epistulam scrībere.)
2 tibi testāmentum faciendum est.
3 nōbīs Haterius vīsitandus est.
4 coquō cēna paranda est.
5 Rōmānīs fidēs servanda est.

Word Patterns: Verbs and Nouns

A As you have already seen in Stage 26, some verbs and nouns are closely connected. Here are further examples:

VERB		NOUN	
lūgēre	*to lament*	lūctus	*grief*
metuere	*to fear*	metus	*fear*
currere	*to run*	cursus	*track, course*

B What do the following nouns mean? Give the associated verbs.

adventus, cantus, cōnsēnsus, cōnspectus, exitus, gemitus, monitus, mōtus, plausus, reditus, rīsus, sonitus

C What is the gender of each noun above?
To what declension does each noun belong?

Practicing the Language

A Make up five Latin sentences using some of the words listed below. Write out each sentence and then translate it. Include at least one sentence which does not contain a nominative.

A genitive usually follows the noun it refers to. For example:

> amīcī rēgis equum invēnērunt.
> *The friends of the king found the horse.*

> amīcī equum rēgis invēnērunt.
> *The friends found the king's horse.*

NOMINATIVES	ACCUSATIVES	GENITIVES	VERBS
soror	opus	avium	invēnit
dux	scelera	mīlitum	invēnērunt
līberī	ratiōnēs	populī Rōmānī	custōdiēbat
clientēs	fraudem	effigiēī	custōdiēbant
lībertus	vultūs	cāsuum	dēlēbat
hostēs	genua	fēminārum	dēlēbant
comitēs	corpora	haruspicis	abstulit
hospes	cursūs	clientium	abstulērunt

B With the help of the Language Information on page 299, complete each sentence by describing the word in boldface with the correct form of the adjective in parentheses, and then translate.

For example: clientēs **patrōnum** (līberālis) laudāvērunt.
Answer: clientēs patrōnum līberālem laudāvērunt.
              The clients praised their generous patron.

1 cōnsul, vir (magnus) **fideī**, ā populō Rōmānō honōrātus est.
2 ēheu! dux relictus est! (nūllus) **spēs** est reditūs eius.
3 Salvius timōrem dissimulāns in (parvus) **sēdem** tignī cōnsēdit.
4 comitēs vestrī **impetū** (ferōx) latrōnum territī sunt.
5 parentēs **vultūs** (laetus) līberōrum spectābant.
6 **saxa** (gravis) ad arcum ā fabrīs trahēbantur.
7 subitō gemitūs **mīlitum** (vulnerātus) audīvimus.
8 Euphrosynē **convīvīs** (īnsolēns) statim respondit.

C In each pair of sentences, translate sentence **a**; then change it from a direct command to an indirect command by completing sentence **b** with an imperfect subjunctive, and translate again.

For example: **a** pontem incende!
　　　　　　b centuriō mīlitī imperāvit ut pontem incender....

Translated and completed, this becomes:

a pontem incende! *Burn the bridge down!*
b centuriō mīlitī imperāvit ut pontem incenderet.
The centurion ordered the soldier to burn the bridge down.

The forms of the imperfect subjunctive are given on page 315 of the Language Information.

1a pecūniam cēlāte!
　b mercātor amīcōs monuit ut pecūniam cēlār....
2a arcum mihi ostende!
　b puer patrem ōrāvit ut arcum sibi ostender....
3a iānuam aperīte!
　b imperātor nōbīs imperāvit ut iānuam aperīr....
4a nōlīte redīre!
　b fēmina barbarīs persuāsit nē redīr....

In sentences **5** and **6**, turn the direct command into an indirect command by adding the necessary words to sentence **b**:

5a cēnam optimam parāte!
　b dominus servīs imperāvit ut . . . .
6a epistulam scrībe!
　b frāter mihi persuāsit . . . .

D Select the correct participle for each blank and then translate the sentence.

passī, precātus, conductum, locūtō, patefacta, adeptus, sprētī, regressa, āmissīs, sublātum

1 Domitiānus frātrem Titum . . . . ., victimam sacrificāvit.
2 alius cliēns sportulam . . . . ., domum laetē rediit; alius cliēns dēnāriīs . . . . ., praecōnem vituperāvit.
3 fraus ā magistrātū . . . . . gravissima est.
4 Iūdaeī multās iniūriās . . . . ., contrā Rōmānōs rebellāvērunt.
5 pauperēs ā patrōnō . . . . . sine pecūniā, sine spē discessērunt.
6 philosopha domum Hateriī . . . . . ā praecōne iterum abācta est.
7 redēmptōrem ā nōbīs . . . . ., opere nōn perfectō, arcessīvimus.
8 marmor ad summum arcum . . . . . figūrīs īnscrīptum est.
9 lībertō verba sapientia . . . . . quam hominī ignāvissimō subvenīre māluimus.

Roman Beliefs

As Euphrosyne and her slave passed through the Roman Forum, they would have been able to see the great Temple to Jupiter Optimus Maximus on the Capitol. If she, as an Athenian, had been told that the temple had been dedicated to the Capitoline triad – Jupiter, Juno, and Minerva – she would have found the deities very similar to the Greek Zeus, Hera, and Athena. She might have been surprised, however, to learn that, in the cella of the temple, was a stone sacred to Terminus, the god of boundaries, whose worship had been established on the Capitoline Hill in the days of the Etruscan kings and did not permit relocation to another site.

The diversity present in the beliefs of the Romans reflected not only the layering of the Greek tradition (gods who looked and behaved like humans) on older agricultural gods and ever-present spirits, such as Terminus, but also their acceptance of a great variety of other deities. Frequently they chose to associate these deities with gods who were familiar to them. In Bath, the local deity, Sulis, was associated with Minerva. The story was the same throughout the Empire.

"Mystery religions" from the east, which offered hope of life after death and required initiation ceremonies known only to believers, also flourished in the Empire. For example, the Temple of Isis at Pompeii had been not only repaired after the earthquake in 62, but also enlarged,

Mithras

Temples of Mithras were constructed to look like caves; the one below left is in Rome. Banqueting couches line the two sides and there is a relief showing the god slaying the bull. Below right is an artist's reconstruction of a ceremony in progress.

whereas the repairs to the temples of Apollo and Jupiter in the forum were still incomplete in 79. Domitian rebuilt the Temple of Isis in Rome as well as the Temple to Jupiter on the Capitol when they had been destroyed by fire.

Roman authorities, however, had not always welcomed religions from elsewhere. Sometimes foreign cults were expelled from Rome. During the Republic, the worship of Bacchus or Liber (Dionysus, god of the vine) had been temporarily banned, and so had the worship of Isis under Augustus.

A religion from the east that found much support in Rome was Mithraism from Persia. Mithras (or Mithra) was the ancient spirit of light (often addressed in Roman dedications as **Sol invictus Mithras**), that became the god of truth and justice, and antagonist of the powers of evil. Mithraism exalted the ideas of loyalty and fraternity, thereby appealing to many soldiers.

Initiates into the rites of Mithras went through seven grades of initiation, involving various tests, in Mithraea that were designed to look like caves or were built partially underground. This was to recall the most famous exploit of Mithras which was the slaying of a bull in a Persian cave, and which was always represented in the shrines. He was depicted doing this in Phrygian (Persian) cap and trousers. The central nave of the Mithraeum was lined with raised benches for the faithful to recline at sacred meals.

There are several Mithraea in Rome, and in many parts of the empire, in cities, in ports in the western Mediterranean, along the frontier provinces of the Rhine and Danube, and at Hadrian's Wall in England. The shrines are usually not large, but some are richly decorated. The religion seems to have appealed to officers in the army and to wealthy businessmen.

Mithras slaying the bull, framed by the zodiac symbols.

Two other religions from the east were Judaism and Christianity. Many Jews in Rome lived across the Tiber from the center of the city. Augustus and other emperors had shown a tolerant attitude towards them. However, Tiberius and Claudius had expelled them from the city, apparently for attempting to convert others to Judaism.

At first the Romans tended to confuse Christianity with Judaism: both came from Judea, and both believed in only one god. There is a reference to followers of Chrestus (sic) as early as the time of Claudius (A.D. 41 – A.D. 54), who expelled them from Rome, classing them as Jews. St. Paul came to Rome to appeal to the emperor in about A.D. 60, and in one of his letters from Rome passed on greetings from Christians living in the city, including some who belonged to "Caesar's house" (the household of the emperor).

This mosaic from Britain shows the letters X and P behind Christ's head. These are the first two letters of "Christ" in Greek, and were often used as a Christian symbol.

Christians at this early period were frequently from the lower classes and could be viewed with suspicion as other foreign religions with secretive rites might be. Nero, casting about for a scapegoat after the great fire in Rome in A.D. 64, accused the Christians and ordered them killed. Other emperors did not follow his example. The Roman government usually preferred to leave Christians alone, although there certainly were sporadic persecutions, the worst of which occurred, ironically, just before Christianity was tolerated in A.D. 313.

Some Romans became interested in philosophy. Euphrosyne had come to Rome to lecture on Stoicism. Despite the behavior of the people at Haterius' dinner party, there were Romans who studied philosophy, particularly Stoicism. Stoics believed, as Euphrosyne tried to explain in the story on page 244, that a man's aim in life should be Virtue, right behavior, rather than Pleasure.

At the time of the stories in Stage 32, the most important Stoic philosopher in Rome was Epictetus, a Greek and a former slave. He had belonged to Epaphroditus, the emperor's freedman. The following are two quotes from his teachings:

> **Men are disturbed not by the things which happen, but by the opinions about the things; for example, death is nothing terrible, for if it were, it would have seemed so to Socrates; for the opinion about death, that it is terrible, is the terrible thing.**

> **Remember that you are an actor in a play of such a kind as the teacher (author) may choose; if short, of a short one; if long, of a long one: if he wishes you to act the part of a poor man, see that you act the part naturally; if the part of a lame man, of a magistrate, of a private person, (do the same). For this is your duty, to act well the part that is given to you; but to select the part belongs to another.**

Stoics tended to disapprove of one-man rule, and to prefer the idea of a republic. They did not think supreme political power should be passed on by inheritance from one ruler to the next, and they thought a ruler should aim to benefit all his subjects, not just a few. As a result of this, at various times during the first century, a number of Roman Stoics challenged the power of the emperor, opposed him in the Senate, or even plotted to kill him. Their efforts were unsuccessful, and they were punished by exile or death.

For the majority of Romans in the first century A.D., however, the numerous temples and their precincts in the city served not just as the site of civic religion, but also as meeting places for the Senate (who had to meet in an inaugurated templum so that the auspices could be taken), offices for important magistrates (e.g., for quaestors in the Temple of Saturn, which was the Roman treasury), or a place for exhibiting significant treaties and works of art or for storing the Sibylline Books. Ceremonies and festivals (**fēriae**) associated with the gods and their temples occurred throughout the year. Such festivals might honor the changing seasons (the dances of the Salii in March, for instance), or deceased family members (the Parentalia in February). Other festivals included the Matronalia in March, when husbands gave presents to their wives, the Vestalia in June, when asses that turned the millstones for grain were garlanded and hung with loaves of bread, and the Saturnalia in December, when Saturn was celebrated in a carnival atmosphere of gift giving and parties. Whether people thought deeply about the religious significance of these festivals we do not know. Sometimes they may not even have remembered why certain very old agricultural ceremonies were being held. Whatever their beliefs, it is clear that religion permeated the life of the Romans.

Our Euphrosyne is fictional. Most philosophers were male, as Haterius said in our stories. Their portraits show rather forbidding characters, like Chrysippos, one of the early Stoics, above.

Word Study

A Match the Latin word to its antonym.

1	aequus	**a**	dīves
2	rēs adversae	**b**	falsus
3	lībertās	**c**	fēlīcitās
4	ōtiōsus	**d**	occupātus
5	pauper	**e**	permōtus
6	vērus	**f**	servitūs

B Match the Latin word or phrase to the word which means approximately the same.

1	cāsus	**a**	iterum atque iterum
2	identidem	**b**	quod
3	ignōscō	**c**	opus
4	labor	**d**	adiuvō
5	quia	**e**	rēs adversae
6	scindō	**f**	dīlaniō
7	subveniō	**g**	veniam dō

C Complete the following analogies with words from the Stage 32 Vocabulary Checklist:

1 ingressus : intrāre :: _____ : temptāre
2 locūtus : dīcere :: _____ : discēdere
3 facere : creāre :: adiuvāre : _____
4 crocodīlus : flūmen :: _____ : caelum
5 cēlāre : patefacere :: _____ : spargere

D Give a derivative of **secūtus, secūta, secūtum** which matches the following definitions:

1 following one another in regular order
2 a person appointed to carry out provisions of another's will
3 to enforce through the process of law
4 to cause to suffer because of religious beliefs

Stage 32 Vocabulary Checklist

addō, addere, addidī, additus — *add*

adversus, adversa, adversum — *hostile, unfavorable*
  rēs adversae, f.pl. — *misfortune*

aequus, aequa, aequum — *fair, calm*
  aequō animō — *calmly, in a calm spirit*

appellō, appellāre, appellāvī, appellātus — *call, call out to*

avis, avis, f. — *bird*

cāsus, cāsūs, m. — *misfortune*

compōnō, compōnere, composuī, compositus — *put together, arrange, settle*

cōnātus, cōnāta, cōnātum — *having tried*

condūcō, condūcere, condūxī, conductus — *hire*

convertō, convertere, convertī, conversus — *turn*

effundō, effundere, effūdī, effūsus — *pour out*

identidem — *repeatedly*

ignōscō, ignōscere, ignōvī (+ DAT) — *forgive*

labor, labōris, m. — *work*

lībertās, lībertātis, f. — *freedom*

nē … quidem — *not even*

nihilōminus — *nevertheless*

opprimō, opprimere, oppressī, oppressus — *crush, overwhelm*

ōtiōsus, ōtiōsa, ōtiōsum — *at leisure, idle, on holiday, on vacation*

pauper, pauper, pauper, *gen.* pauperis — *poor*

permōtus, permōta, permōtum — *alarmed, disturbed*

profectus, profecta, profectum — *having set out*

quia — *because*

quīdam, quaedam, quoddam — *one, a certain*

scindō, scindere, scidī, scissus — *tear, tear up, cut up*

secūtus, secūta, secūtum — *having followed*

strēnuē — *hard, energetically*

subveniō, subvenīre, subvēnī — *help, come to help*

sūmptuōsus, sūmptuōsa, sūmptuōsum — *expensive, lavish, costly*

vērus, vēra, vērum — *true, real*
  rē vērā — *in fact, truly, really*

PANTOMIMUS

Stage 33

1 praecō prīmus: fābula! fābula optima!
Paris, pantomīmus nōtissimus, in theātrō crās
fābulam aget.
Myropnous, tībīcen perītissimus, tībiīs cantābit.

2 praecō secundus: lūdī! lūdī magnificī!
duodecim aurīgae in Circō Maximō crās certābunt.
Imperātor ipse victōrī praemium dabit.

3 praecō tertius: spectāculum! spectāculum splendidum!
quīnquāgintā gladiātōrēs in amphitheātrō Flāviō
crās pugnābunt.
multus sanguis fluet.

Tychicus

in hortō Hateriī, fābula agēbātur. Paris, pantomīmus nōtissimus, mortem rēgīnae Dīdōnis imitābātur. aderant multī spectātōrēs quī ad fābulam ā Vitelliā, uxōre Hateriī, invītātī erant. Haterius ipse nōn aderat. labōribus cōnfectus atque spē sacerdōtiī dēiectus, ad vīllam rūsticam abierat ut quiēsceret. 5

Paris mōtibus ēlegantissimīs aptissimīsque dolōrem rēgīnae morientis imitābātur. cum dēnique quasi mortuus prōcubuisset, omnēs spectātōrēs admīrātiōne affectī identidem plaudēbant. aliī flōrēs iactābant; aliī Paridem deum appellābant. surrēxit Paris ut plausum spectātōrum exciperet. 10

sed priusquam ille plūra ageret, vir quīdam statūrā brevī vultūque sevērō prōgressus magnā vōce silentium poposcit. oculīs in eum statim conversīs, spectātōrēs quis esset et quid vellet rogābant. paucī eum agnōvērunt. Iūdaeus erat, Tychicus nōmine, cliēns T. Flāviī Clēmentis. Paris ipse fābulā interruptā adeō 15 obstupefactus est ut stāret immōtus. omnīnō ignōrābat quid Tychicus factūrus esset.

pantomīmus	*pantomime actor, dancer*	**quasi**	*as if*
Dīdōnis: Dīdō	*Dido (queen of Carthage*	**priusquam**	*before*
	and lover of Aeneas)	**statūrā: statūra**	*height*
imitābātur	*was imitating, was miming*	**interruptā:**	
mōtibus: mōtus	*movement*	**interrumpere**	*interrupt*

"audīte, ō scelestī!" clāmāvit Tychicus. "vōs prāvī hunc hominem tamquam deum adōrātis. sunt tamen nūllī deī praeter ūnum! ūnus Deus sōlus adōrandus est! hunc Deum vērum quem _20_ plērīque vestrum ignōrant, oportet mē nunc vōbīs dēclārāre."

mussitāre coepērunt spectātōrēs. aliī rogāvērunt utrum Tychicus iocōs faceret an īnsānīret; aliī servōs arcessīvērunt quī eum ex hortō ēicerent. Tychicus autem perstitit.

"Deus, ut prophētae nostrī nōbīs praedīxērunt, homō factus est _25_ et inter nōs habitāvit. aegrōs sānāvit; evangelium prōnūntiāvit; vītam aeternam nōbīs pollicitus est. tum in cruce suffīxus, mortuus est et in sepulcrō positus est. sed tertiō diē resurrēxit et vīvus ā discipulīs suīs vīsus est. deinde in caelum ascendit, ubi et nunc rēgnat et in perpetuum rēgnābit." _30_

dum haec Tychicus dēclārat, servī Vitelliae signō datō eum comprehendērunt. domō eum trahēbant magnā vōce clāmantem:

"mox Dominus noster, rēx glōriae, ad nōs reveniet; ē caelō dēscendet cum sonitū tubārum, magnō numerō angelōrum comitante. et vīvōs et mortuōs iūdicābit. nōs Chrīstiānī, sī vītam _35_ pūram vīxerimus et eī crēdiderimus, ad caelum ascendēmus. ibi semper cum Dominō erimus. tū autem, Paris, fīlius diabolī, nisi vitiīs tuīs dēstiteris, poenās dabis. nūlla erit fuga. nam flammae, ē caelō missae, tē et omnēs scelestōs dēvorābunt."

quae cum prōnūntiāvisset, Tychicus multīs verberibus acceptīs _40_ domō ēiectus est. spectātōrum plūrimī eum vehementer dērīdēbant; paucī tamen, praesertim servī ac lībertī, tacēbant, quod Chrīstiānī erant ipsī.

praeter	*except*	**discipulīs:**	
plērīque vestrum	*most of you*	**discipulus**	*disciple,*
dēclārāre	*declare,*		*follower*
	proclaim	**in perpetuum**	*forever*
mussitāre	*murmur*	**glōriae: glōria**	*glory*
prophētae: prophēta	*prophet*	**angelōrum: angelus**	*angel*
praedīxērunt:		**comitante:**	
praedīcere	*foretell, predict*	**comitāns**	*accompanying*
evangelium	*good news, gospel*	**iūdicābit: iūdicāre**	*judge*
prōnūntiāvit:		**pūram: pūrus**	*pure*
prōnūntiāre	*proclaim, preach*	**erimus**	*shall be*
aeternam: aeternus	*eternal*	**diabolī: diabolus**	*devil*
cruce: crux	*cross*	**vitiīs: vitium**	*sin*
suffīxus: suffīgere	*nail, fasten*	**verberibus: verber**	*blow*
resurrēxit: resurgere	*rise again*		

About the Language I: Future Active Indicative

A Study the following examples:

> nōlī dēspērāre! amīcus meus tē **servābit**.
> *Don't give up! My friend **will save** you.*

> servī ad urbem heri iērunt; crās **revenient**.
> *The slaves went to the city yesterday; they **will come back** tomorrow.*

The words in boldface are in the future active indicative.

B The first and second conjugations form their future active indicative in the following way:

FIRST CONJUGATION		SECOND CONJUGATION	
portābō	*I shall/will carry*	docēbō	*I shall/will teach*
portābis	*you will carry*	docēbis	*you will teach*
portābit	*s/he, it will carry*	docēbit	*s/he, it will teach*
portābimus	*we shall/will carry*	docēbimus	*we shall/will teach*
portābitis	*you will carry*	docēbitis	*you will teach*
portābunt	*they will carry*	docēbunt	*they will teach*

C The third and fourth conjugations form their future active indicative in another way:

THIRD CONJUGATION		FOURTH CONJUGATION	
traham	*I shall/will drag*	audiam	*I shall/will hear*
trahēs	*you will drag*	audiēs	*you will hear*
trahet	*s/he, it will drag*	audiet	*s/he, it will hear*
trahēmus	*we shall/will drag*	audiēmus	*we shall/will hear*
trahētis	*you will drag*	audiētis	*you will hear*
trahent	*they will drag*	audient	*they will hear*

D The future tense of **sum** is as follows:

erō	*I shall/will be*	erimus	*we shall/will be*
eris	*you will be*	eritis	*you will be*
erit	*s/he, it will be*	erunt	*they will be*

E Further examples:

1 crās ad Graeciam nāvigābitis; Rōmae erimus.
2 ille mercātor est mendāx; tibi numquam pecūniam reddet.

3   fuge! mīlitēs tē in carcerem conicient!
4   dux noster est vir benignus, quī vōs omnēs līberābit.
5   "quid crās faciēs?" "ad theātrum ībō."
6   laudābō; respondēbit; appropinquābunt; rīdēbitis; redībis;
    erunt.
7   veniēmus; trādent; dīcam; dormiet; ferētis.

in aulā Domitiānī I

When you have read this story, answer the questions at the end.

in scaenā parvā, quae in aulae Domitiānī ātriō exstrūcta erat, Paris
fābulam dē amōre Mārtis et Veneris agēbat. simul pūmiliō,
Myropnous nōmine, tībīcen atque amīcus Paridis, suāviter tībiīs
cantābat. nūllī aderant spectātōrēs nisi Domitia Augusta, uxor
Imperātōris Domitiānī, quae Paridem inter familiārissimōs suōs   5
habēbat. oculīs in eō fīxīs fābulam intentē spectābat. tam mīrābilis,
tam perīta ars eius erat ut lacrimās retinēre Domitia vix posset.

subitō servus, nōmine Olympus, quem Domitia iānuam ātriī
custōdīre iusserat, ingressus est.

"domina," inquit, "ego Epaphrodītum, Augustī lībertum, modo   10
cōnspicātus   sum   trānseuntem   āream,   decem   mīlitibus
comitantibus. mox hūc intrābit."

quibus verbīs audītīs, Paris ad Domitiam versus rīsit.

Paris:	dēliciae meae! quam fortūnāta es! ab Epaphrodītō ipsō, Augustī lībertō, vīsitāris.
Domitia:	*(adventū Epaphrodītī commōta)* mī Pari, tibi perīculōsum est hīc manēre. ōdiō es Epaphrodītō! sī tē apud mē ille invēnerit, poenās certē dabis. iubēbit mīlitēs in carcerem tē conicere. fuge!
Paris:	cūr fugiendum est? illum psittacum Domitiānī floccī nōn faciō.
Domitia:	at ego valdē vereor. nam mihi quoque Epaphrodītus est inimīcus. iussū eius conclāvia mea saepe īnspiciuntur; epistulae meae resignantur; ancillārum meārum fidēs ā ministrīs eius temptātur. potestās eius nōn minor est quam Imperātōris ipsīus.
Paris:	mea columba, dēsine timēre! mē nōn capiet iste homunculus. paulīsper abībō.

15
20
25

haec locūtus, columnam proximam celeriter cōnscendit et per
compluvium ēgressus in tēctō sē cēlāvit. Myropnous quoque sē   *30*
cēlāre cōnstituit. post tapēte quod dē longuriō gravī pendēbat sē
collocāvit. Domitia contrā, quae quamquam perterrita erat in lectō
manēbat vultū compositō, Olympō imperāvit ut aliquōs versūs
recitāret.

simul	*at the same time*	tapēte	*tapestry,*
tībiīs cantābat:			*wall-hanging*
tībiīs cantāre	*play on the pipes*	longuriō:	
familiārissimōs:		longurius	*pole*
familiāris	*close friend*	contrā	*on the other hand*
certē	*certainly*	compositō:	
vereor	*I fear, I am afraid*	compositus	*composed, steady*
conclāvia: conclāve	*room*		
īnspiciuntur:			
īnspicere	*search*		
resignantur:			
resignāre	*open, unseal*		
ministrīs: minister	*servant, agent*		
temptātur: temptāre	*put to the test*		

Questions

1 Where in the palace did Paris' performance take place? What story
   was he performing? Who was supplying the musical
   accompaniment?
2 Who was the only spectator? What effect did Paris' skill have on
   her?
3 What had the slave Olympus been ordered to do? What news did he
   bring? What were Domitia's feelings on hearing this news?
4 Domitia mentions three ways in which Epaphroditus and his men
   are making life unpleasant for her. What are they?
5 Where did (**a**) Paris and (**b**) Myropnous hide?
6 While Paris and Myropnous were hiding, where was Domitia? In
   what ways did she try to pretend that everything was normal?
7 Judging from this story, especially lines 13–28, what impression do
   you have of Paris' personality?

in aulā Domitiānī II

Olympō suāviter recitante, ingressus est Epaphrodītus. decem mīlitēs eum comitābantur.

Epaphrodītus: ubi est iste pantomīmus quem impudēns tū amās?
Domitia: verba tua nōn intellegō. sōla sum, ut vidēs. hic
servus mē versibus dēlectat, nōn Paris. 5
Epaphrodītus: (*conversus ad mīlitēs*) quaerite Paridem! festīnāte!

mīlitēs igitur conclāvia ācriter perscrūtātī sunt, sed frūstrā. Paridem nusquam invenīre poterant.

Epaphrodītus: caudicēs! sī Paris effūgerit, vōs poenās dabitis. cūr
tēctum nōn perscrūtāminī? ferte scālās! 10

quae cum audīvisset Domitia palluit. Myropnous tamen quī per tapēte cautē prōspiciēbat sēcum rīsit; cōnsilium enim callidissimum et audācissimum cēperat. tapēte lēniter manū movēre coepit. mox Epaphrodītus, dum ātrium suspīciōsus circumspectat, mōtum tapētis animadvertit. 15

Epaphrodītus: ecce! movētur tapēte! latebrās Paridis invēnī!
nunc illum capiam.

quibus dictīs, Epaphrodītus ad tapēte cum magnō clāmōre sē praecipitāvit. Myropnous haudquāquam perturbātus, ubi Epaphrodītus appropinquāvit, tapēte magnā vī dētrāxit. dēcidit 20 tapēte, dēcidit longurius. Epaphrodītus, tapētī convolūtus atque simul longuriō percussus, prōcubuit exanimātus. magnopere cachinnāvit Myropnous et exsultāns tībiīs cantāre coepit.

   Domitia, quae sē iam ex pavōre recēperat, ad mīlitēs in ātrium cum scālīs regressōs conversa est. eōs iussit Epaphrodītum 25 extrahere. mīlitibus eum extrahentibus Myropnous assem in labra eius quasi mortuī posuit. dēnique Paris per compluvium dēspexit et Epaphrodītō ita valēdīxit:
   "hīc iacet Tiberius Claudius Epaphrodītus, Augustī lībertus, longuriō gravī strātus." 30

impudēns	*shameless*	dētrāxit: dētrahere	*pull down*
perscrūtātī sunt	*examined*	convolūtus: convolvere	*entangle*
scālās: scālae	*ladders*	assem: as	*as (small coin)*
suspīciōsus	*suspicious*	dēspexit: dēspicere	*look down*
latebrās: latebrae	*hiding-place*	strātus: sternere	*lay low*
sē praecipitāvit:			
sē praecipitāre	*hurl oneself*		

About the Language II: Future Perfect Active Indicative

A Study the following examples:

> sī epistulam tuam **accēperō**, statim respondēbō.
> *If **I receive** your letter, I shall reply at once.*

> sī tē hīc **invēnerint**, poenās dabis.
> *If **they find** you here, you will be punished.*

> sī id **aedificāveris**, venient.
> *If **you build** it, they will come.*

The verbs in boldface are future perfect active indicative. The future perfect tense is used in Latin to indicate an action completed (**perfectum**) in the future before another action in the future. For example, in the last sentence the building takes place in the future, but before the coming.

B The forms of the future perfect active indicative are as follows:

portāverō	portāverimus
portāveris	portāveritis
portāverit	portāverint

C The literal translation for the future perfect is not very common in English:

> *I shall/will have carried*
> *you will have carried* etc.

Instead, English usually uses a present tense (as in the examples above).

D Further examples:

1 sī Epaphrodītus nōs cōnspexerit, mē interficiet.
2 sī dīligenter quaesīveris, pecūniam inveniēs.
3 sī servī bene labōrāverint, eīs praemium dabō.
4 sī mīlitēs vīderō, fugiam.

Word Patterns: Diminutives

A Study the form and meaning of the following nouns:

homō	*man*	homunculus	*little man*
servus	*slave*	servulus	*little slave*
corpus	*body*	corpusculum	*little body*
ager	*field*	agellus	*small plot of land*

B Using Section A as a guide, complete the table below:

lapis	*rock*	lapillus	. . . . .
fīlia	. . . . .	fīliōla	. . . . .
versus	. . . . .	versiculus	. . . . .
liber	. . . . .	. . . . .	*booklet*

C The nouns in the right hand columns above are known as diminutives. Suggest a meaning for each of the following diminutives:

cēnula, fābella, gladiōlus, mēnsula, nāvicula, ponticulus, vīllula

D Study the following nouns and their diminutives:

calx	*stone*
calculus	*pebble (used as a piece in board games, as a voting "ballot," and as a counter for making calculations)*
capsa	*box (for books)*
capsula	*small container*
cōdex (often spelled caudex)	*a piece of wood; someone with no more sense than a block of wood, i.e. a blockhead*
cōdicillī	*wooden writing tablets; codicil (written instructions added to a will)*
grānum	*grain, seed*
grānulum	*small grain or granule*
mūs	*mouse*
musculus	*little mouse; muscle*
sporta	*basket*
sportula	*little basket; gift for clients from a patron (named after its original container)*

Practicing the Language

A Complete each sentence with the right word and then translate.

1 hīs verbīs (audītīs, portātīs), Paris aequō animō respondit.
2 signō (victō, datō), servī Tychicum ēiēcērunt.
3 cēnā (cōnsūmptā, parātā), Haterius amīcōs in triclīnium dūxit.
4 nāve (āmissā, refectā), mercātor dēspērābat.
5 clientibus (dīmissīs, dēpositīs), praecō iānuam clausit.
6 tergīs (īnstrūctīs, conversīs), hostēs fūgērunt.

B In each pair of sentences, translate sentence **a**; then, with the help of page 312 of the Language Information, express the same idea in a different way by completing sentence **b** with a passive form, and translate again.

For example: **a** tabernāriī cibum vēndēbant.
              b cibus ā tabernāriīs . . . . . .
Translated and completed, this becomes:
              a tabernāriī cibum vēndēbant.
                    The storekeepers were selling food.
              b cibus ā tabernāriīs vēndēbātur.
                    Food was being sold by the storekeepers.

In sentences **1–3**, the verbs are in the imperfect tense; in sentences **4–6**, they are in the present tense:

1a servī amphorās portābant.
 b amphorae ā servīs . . . . . .
2a Salvius Haterium dēcipiēbat.
 b Haterius ā Salviō . . . . . .
3a barbarī horreum oppugnābant.
 b horreum ā barbarīs . . . . . .
4a rhētor puerōs docet.
 b puerī ā rhētore . . . . . .
5a aliquis iānuam aperit.
 b iānua ab aliquō . . . . . .
6a centuriō mīlitēs cōnsistere iubet.
 b mīlitēs ā centuriōne cōnsistere . . . . . .

C Read lines 33–39 on page 258 again. Make two lists, one future tense, and one future perfect tense. You will find eight verbs in the future tense, and three verbs in the future perfect tense.

D Select the correct form of the verb and translate each sentence.

1 crās ācriter nōs (certābō, certābimus) quod multa praemia, quae rēgīna praebuit, capere (volam, volēmus).
2 sī togās scideritis, hospes vōs nōn (excipiet, excipient).
3 sī quīdam rē vērā pauperēs identidem oppresserint, nūllōs bonōs dēnique amīcōs (inveniet, invenient).
4 eī quī patriam prōdidērunt semper ōdiō nōbīs (erit, erunt).
5 dux fraude fugāque magistrātūs obstupefactus populō facinora eius crās (patefaciet, patefacient).
6 nisi tapēte lēniter mōveris, longurium (frangēs, frangētis).
7 philosophus Stoicus convīvīs philosophiae oblītīs vultū sevērō sententiās (aperiet, aperient).
8 crās amphitheātrum Flāvium praeteriēns dē gladiātōribus, quī in arēnā pugnābunt, (exīstimābō, exīstimābimus).

Roman Entertainment

The Roman year was punctuated by days dedicated to the gods as official **lūdī** (games), which usually began with a series of **lūdī scaenicī** (theatrical shows), and followed with some days devoted to **lūdī circensēs** (chariot races). At the end of the Republic, ludi were celebrated on over fifty days each year, and during the empire this number increased. The **Lūdī Rōmānī**, the oldest, had started under the kings. Other games followed: e.g., they might be held after the invasion of Hannibal, or to propitiate various gods, for instance Apollo and the Magna Mater, or to honor military victories. These public celebrations affirmed the conservative Roman ideas on class distinction. The senators and equestrians had seats in the front and sometimes the poor stood at the top. Women sat with men in the Circus but sat separately at other performances. Because everyone attended, even ordinary citizens could voice approval and disapproval of both people and performers.

By the time of Domitian, formal plays, both tragedy and comedy, were no longer very popular, although when they had been produced it might have been with more lavishness than good taste. For instance, in one revival of a play during the Republic, 600 mules were brought on stage. Pantomimes and mimes had taken the place of drama. Paris was a famous pantomime actor in this period and is described on page 257 performing the tragedy of Dido, and then a famous story from myth

*The Circus Maximus, with Domitian's palace on the Palatine overlooking it on the left. You can see the central **spīna** of the circus around which the chariots raced – it has a tree planted at the nearer end.*

The interior of the Flavian Ampitheater. The animal cages and machinery below were originally hidden by a wooden floor covered with sand.

about Mars and Venus. He would have danced and acted all the parts of the story, without speaking, and would have had a musical accompaniment, whether an orchestra and chorus, or just a single performer, like Myropnous. Mimes, on the other hand, were slapstick farces on themes from everyday life and usually involved several actors.

The final days of the ludi were devoted to the ludi circenses in the Circus Maximus. This could hold 250,000 spectators, an indication of how popular chariot races were in Rome (and in other cities of the empire, too). Fans bet on their favorite teams and also tried to harm their opponents by means of the defixiones described on page 41. Four teams (**factiōnēs**) competed: the whites, reds, blues, and greens. Domitian added purple and gold, which do not seem to have continued after his death. After a procession into the Circus, the presiding magistrate signaled the start of the race by dropping a napkin (**mappa**).

A day's program normally consisted of twenty-four races, each lasting seven laps (about 5 miles or 8 kilometers) and taking about a quarter of an hour to run. Seven huge eggs of marble or wood were hoisted high above the central platform (**spīna**), and every time the lead chariot completed a lap, one egg was lowered. The charioteer had to race at full speed down the length of the circus and then display his greatest skill at the turning-point (**mēta**); if he took the bend too slowly he would be overtaken, and if he took it too fast he might crash. He raced with the reins tied tightly around his body, and in his belt he carried a knife: if he crashed, his life might depend on how quickly he could cut himself free from the wreckage.

In addition to the ludi, upper-class Romans in the pre-imperial period sometimes paid for **mūnera** or gladiatorial shows. These munera were originally part of the rites owed to the dead. They became examples, though, of conspicuous consumption when people like Pompey or Julius Caesar staged not only many gladiatorial duels, but also **vēnātiōnēs** using exotic animals. In 55 B.C. when Pompey dedicated his theater, the first stone theater in Rome, he exhibited hundreds of lions and leopards in the Circus Maximus, but the last day ended anticlimactically when eighteen elephants were brought out to be hunted. The Roman audience pitied them, and the elephants also nearly stampeded into the seats. Later, when Caesar staged his games in his triumph in 46 B.C., he used the elephants displayed as transport, not as targets!

In the empire, only the emperor put on these munera, which continued to involve not just animals and professional gladiators, but

A picture made from pieces of colored marbles, showing the procession at the start of the chariot races. The patron of the games, perhaps an emperor, drives a two-horse chariot. Behind him are riders in the colors of the four teams, red, blue, green, and white.

also condemned criminals. Augustus sponsored numerous venationes in the Circus and in the Forum. In addition, on the bank of the Tiber, he constructed special areas for **naumachiae** (naval battles). Domitian's father, Vespasian, started the **Amphitheātrum Flāvium** (the Colosseum), which was opened by his brother, Titus, in A.D. 80. Rome now had a permanent arena for the gladiatorial combats, one which could hold 50,000 people.

Not least among the entertainments offered free to all Romans were the numerous processions and ceremonies throughout the city, held at the beginning of most events, including the ludi. But the parade of all parades was the triumphal procession after a military victory. In the Republic, the highest

An ivory carving showing a pantomime performer with the masks and props of three characters.

honor the state could bestow was the right to march through the city as a **triumphātor**. In the empire, only the emperor could enjoy such an honor, and Josephus, the historian of *The Jewish War*, has left an account of the joint triumph of Vespasian and Titus, commemorated on the Arch of Titus in the Forum. The day began in the Campus Martius. Vespasian and Titus, dressed in triumphal robes, offered prayers to the gods and entered the city through the **Porta Triumphālis**. In front of the parade came all the splendors of the spoils of war; then huge traveling stages, some three and four stories high, exhibiting scenes from the conquest; groups of captives elaborately dressed; more spoils carried by more soldiers; and then Vespasian and Titus in chariots, with Domitian on a horse alongside. The procession finished at the Temple of Jupiter on the Capitol, where they waited until the announcement came that the leader of the enemy had just been killed, before beginning the concluding sacrifices and prayers.

Such parades, along with the spectacles of the ludi and munera and the numerous festivals throughout the year, offered everyone the chance to see and be seen with the political and social leaders of the day. However dubiously we may view some of these occasions, as bloodthirsty, garish, or simply puzzling, they permitted all people in the city, Romans and non-Romans, rich and poor, a share in the splendor of the city's gods, its history, and its power.

Two Scenes at the Circus Maximus

In the terracotta plaque below:

1 The charioteer on the left has fallen from his chariot. Why might this accident have happened?
2 What urgent action must he take now?
3 What is the purpose of the rows of dolphins in the background?

In another plaque below:

4 It has been suggested that the charioteer on the left is reining in the inside horse. Why would he do this?
5 The horseman on the right seems to be whipping his horse. What might be his purpose in the race?

Word Study

A Complete the following analogies with words from the Stage 33 Vocabulary Checklist:

1 ante : post : : heri : _____
2 uxor : marītus : : _____ : rēx
3 caput : pēs : : _____ : pavīmentum
4 et : ac : : sed : _____
5 falsus : probus : : longus : _____
6 trīstis : laetus : : lēniter : _____
7 anteā : posteā : : ibi : _____
8 quiēs : labor : : prō : _____

B Copy the following words. Then put parentheses around the Latin root from this Stage contained inside these derivatives; give the Latin word and its meaning from which the derivative comes.

For example: conservation con(serva)tion servāre – to save

1 abbreviation
2 acrimonious
3 persevere
4 centrifugal
5 concerted
6 conjecture
7 ejection
8 incontrovertible
9 procrastinate
10 protection

C Fill in the blanks with derivatives based on the ordinal numbers in the Stage 33 Vocabulary Checklist.

1 Finding a job is a matter of . . . . . importance for a graduate.
2 The singer's range was nearly three . . . . . .
3 Metric measurements are based on the . . . . . system.
4 In the nineteenth century, many children in rural areas were unable to attend . . . . . school to further their elementary education.
5 Two violins, a viola, and a cello comprise a string . . . . . .
6 The stock's value increased from $20 to $100 per share in a month; delighted investors . . . . . their investment.
7 A nine-sided figure is called a . . . . . .

Stage 33 Vocabulary Checklist

ācriter	keenly, fiercely
at	but
brevis, brevis, breve	short, brief
certō, certāre, certāvī	compete
coniciō, conicere, coniēcī, coniectus	hurl, throw
contrā (+ ACC)	against, on the other hand
crās	tomorrow
ēiciō, ēicere, ēiēcī, ēiectus	throw out
et ... et	both ... and
excipiō, excipere, excēpī, exceptus	receive
fuga, fugae, f.	escape
hīc	here
lēniter	gently
moveō, movēre, mōvī, mōtus	move
nisi	except, unless
obstupefaciō, obstupefacere, obstupefēcī, obstupefactus	amaze, stun
odiō sum, odiō esse	be hateful
potestās, potestātis, f.	power
rēgīna, rēgīnae, f.	queen
sevērus, sevēra, sevērum	severe, strict
tēctum, tēctī, n.	ceiling, roof
utrum	whether

ORDINAL NUMBERS

prīmus, prīma, prīmum	first
secundus, secunda, secundum	second
tertius, tertia, tertium	third
quārtus, quārta, quārtum	fourth
quīntus, quīnta, quīntum	fifth
sextus, sexta, sextum	sixth
septimus, septima, septimum	seventh
octāvus, octāva, octāvum	eighth
nōnus, nōna, nōnum	ninth
decimus, decima, decimum	tenth

Coin of the Emperor Titus, celebrating the opening of the Flavian Amphitheater.

EPAPHROD
MVIATORITRIBVN
ORONISAVREISDO

LIBERTUS

Stage 34

ultiō Epaphrodītī

Epaphrodītus, ā Paride atque Domitiā ēlūsus, eōs ulcīscī vehementissimē cupiēbat. Imperātor quoque, īrā et suspīciōne commōtus, Epaphrodītum saepe hortābātur ut Paridem Domitiamque pūnīret. Epaphrodītō tamen difficile erat Domitiam, uxōrem Imperātōris, et Paridem, pantomīmum nōtissimum, 5 apertē accūsāre. auxilium igitur ab amīcō C. Salviō Līberāle petīvit.

Epaphrodītus "nōn modo ego," inquit, "sed etiam Imperātor poenās Paridis Domitiaeque cupit. sī mē in hāc rē adiūveris, magnum praemium tibi dabitur."

Salvius, rē paulīsper cōgitātā, tranquillē respondit: 10
"cōnfīde mihi, amīce; ego tibi rem tōtam administrābō. īnsidiae parābuntur; Domitia et Paris in īnsidiās ēlicientur; ambō capientur et pūnientur."

"quid Domitiae accidet?" rogāvit Epaphrodītus.

"Domitia accūsābitur; damnābitur; fortasse relēgābitur." 15
"et Paris?"

Salvius rīsit.
"ēmovēbitur."

ēlūsus: ēlūdere	*trick, outwit*	**ēlicientur: ēlicere**	*lure, entice*
ulcīscī	*to take revenge on*	**relēgābitur: relēgāre**	*exile*
suspīciōne: suspīciō	*suspicion*		

Epaphroditus

Epaphroditus was a former slave of the Emperor Nero. Under Domitian, Epaphroditus' official title was a secretary, **ā libellīs** (in charge of petitions – the word **ā** has a special meaning in this phrase), which means that he helped the emperor to deal with the various petitions or requests submitted to him by groups and individuals. The opportunities for bribery are obvious, and imperial freedmen like him were widely unpopular.

The large block of marble below is part of an inscription honoring him. The top line tells us he is the emperor's freedman: [A]VGL stands for **Augustī lībertus**. The bottom line boasts of gold crowns (**corōnīs aureīs**) he has been awarded, possibly as a reward for the part he played in unmasking a conspiracy against Nero.

When he eventually fell out of favor with Domitian, he was executed on the grounds that he helped Nero commit suicide twenty-seven years before.

Epaphroditus wearing the toga, the mark of a citizen. When he was freed he gained the right to wear it. On the table is his pilleus, the cap of liberty he was given to mark his manumission.

īnsidiae

When you have read this story, answer the questions at the end.

paucīs post diēbus Domitia ancillam, nōmine Chionēn, ad sē
vocāvit.

"epistulam," inquit, "ā Vitelliā, uxōre Hateriī, missam modo
accēpī. ēheu! Vitellia in morbum gravem incidit. statim mihi
vīsitanda est. tē volō omnia parāre." 5

tum Chionē, ē cubiculō dominae ēgressa, iussit lectīcam parārī
et lectīcāriōs arcessī. medicum quoque nōmine Asclēpiadēn
quaesīvit quī medicāmenta quaedam Vitelliae parāret. inde
Domitia lectīcā vecta, comitantibus servīs, domum Hateriī
profecta est. difficile erat eīs per viās prōgredī, quod nox obscūra 10
erat multumque pluēbat.

cum domum Hateriī pervēnissent, iānuam apertam invēnērunt.
servīs extrā iānuam relictīs, Domitia cum Chionē ingressa est.
spectāculum inopīnātum eīs ingredientibus obiectum est. ātrium
magnificē ōrnātum erat: ubīque lūcēbant lucernae, corōnae 15
rosārum dē omnibus columnīs pendēbant. sed omnīnō dēsertum
erat ātrium. inde fēminae, triclīnium ingressae, id quoque
dēsertum vīdērunt. in mediō tamen cēna sūmptuōsa posita erat:
mēnsae epulīs exquīsītissimīs cumulātae erant, pōcula vīnō
optimō plēna erant. quibus vīsīs, ancilla timidā vōce, 20

"cavendum est nōbīs," inquit. "aliquid mīrī hīc agitur."

"fortasse Vitellia morbō affecta est cum cēnāret. sine dubiō iam
in cubiculō convalēscit," respondit Domitia, ignāra īnsidiārum
quās Salvius parāverat.

itaque per domum dēsertam, ancillā timidē sequente, Domitia 25
prōgredī coepit. cum ad cubiculum ubi Vitellia dormīre solēbat
pervēnisset, in līmine cōnstitit. cubiculum erat obscūrum. Chionēn
ad triclīnium remīsit quae lucernam ferret. in silentiō noctis diū
exspectābat dum redīret ancilla. haec tamen nōn rediit. tandem
Domitia morae impatiēns in cubiculum irrūpit. vacuum erat. tum 30
dēmum pavōre magnō perturbāta est. tenebrae, silentium, ancillae
absentia, haec omnia perīculī indicia esse vidēbantur. scīlicet falsa
fuerat epistula, mendāx nūntius morbī!

Domitia ad aulam quam celerrimē regredī cōnstituit priusquam
aliquid malī sibi accideret. dum per vacua conclāvia fugit, vōce 35
hominis subitō perterrita est.

"dēliciae meae, salvē! tūne quoque ad cēnam invītāta es?"

tum vōcem agnōvit.

"mī Parī," inquit, "īnsidiae, nōn cēna, nōbīs parātae sunt. effugiendum nōbīs est, dum possumus."   *40*

Chionēn	*Greek accusative of* **Chionē**
parārī	*to be prepared*
lectīcāriōs: lectīcārius	*chair-carrier, sedan-chair carrier*
arcessī	*to be summoned, to be sent for*
Asclēpiadēn	*Greek accusative of* **Asclēpiadēs**
medicāmenta: medicāmentum	*medicine, drug*
inopīnātum: inopīnātus	*unexpected*
obiectum est	*met, was presented*
epulīs: epulae	*dishes*
cumulātae erant: cumulāre	*heap*
cavendum est: cavēre	*beware*
mīrī: mīrus	*extraordinary, strange*
remīsit: remittere	*send back*
dum	*until, while*
vacuum: vacuus	*empty*
tum dēmum	*then at last, only then*
absentia	*absence*
vidēbantur: vidērī	*seem*
nūntius	*message, news*

Questions

1 What message about Vitellia did Domitia receive? What did she decide to do immediately?
2 What preparations did Chione make?
3 Why was the journey difficult?
4 What did Domitia and Chione discover (**a**) at the entrance to the house, (**b**) in the atrium, (**c**) in the triclinium?
5 What explanation of the situation did Domitia give Chione in lines 22–23?
6 Where did Domitia and Chione go next? Why did Domitia send Chione back?
7 **haec tamen nōn rediit** (line 29). Suggest an explanation for this.
8 What did Domitia at last realize? What made her realize this?
9 Who is the speaker in line 37? How had he been lured to the house? What do you suppose will be the next step in Salvius' plan?

About the Language I: Present Passive Infinitive

A In Stage 13, you met sentences containing infinitives:

currere volō.   *I want **to run**.*
servī **labōrāre** nōn possunt.   *The slaves are not able **to work**.*

This infinitive is known in full as the present active infinitive.

B In Stage 34, you have met another kind of infinitive:

volō epistulam **recitārī**.   *I want the letter **to be read out**.*
Paris **cōnspicī** nōluit.   *Paris did not want **to be seen**.*

This infinitive is known as the present passive infinitive.

C Compare the following examples of present active and present passive infinitives:

CONJUGATION	PRESENT ACTIVE		PRESENT PASSIVE	
First	portāre	*to carry*	portārī	*to be carried*
Second	docēre	*to teach*	docērī	*to be taught*
Third	trahere	*to drag*	trahī	*to be dragged*
Fourth	audīre	*to hear*	audīrī	*to be heard*

D Further examples of the present passive infinitive:

1 volō iānuam aperīrī.
2 neque Vitellia neque ancilla vidērī poterant.
3 fūr capī nōlēbat.
4 dux iussit captīvum līberārī.

E Notice how deponent verbs form their infinitive:

First Conjugation	cōnārī	*to try*
Second Conjugation	pollicērī	*to promise*
Third Conjugation	ingredī	*to enter*
Fourth Conjugation	orīrī	*to rise*

Further examples:

1 lībertus iussit mīlitēs pantomīmum sequī.
2 aegrōtī deam precārī volēbant.
3 nūntius tandem proficīscī cōnstituit.
4 puerī tam perterritī erant ut loquī nōn possent.

exitium

I

Domitiā Paridem monente, Myropnous, quī dominum comitābātur, ad iānuam contendit. cautē prōspexit. ecce! via tōta mīlitibus praetōriānīs plēna erat. neque lectīca, neque medicus, neque servī usquam vidērī poterant.

ad ātrium reversus Myropnous "āctum est dē nōbīs!" 5
exclāmāvit. "appropinquant praetōriānī! mox hūc ingredientur!"

hōc tamen cognitō, Paris "nōlī dēspērāre," inquit. "cōnsilium habeō. Myropnū, tibi iānua custōdienda est. prohibē mīlitēs ingredī. sī mē vel Domitiam hōc locō cēperint, certē nōs interficient. cōnābimur per postīcum ēlābī." 10

Myropnous igitur iānuam claudere contendit. quō factō ad triclīnium reversus lectōs mēnsāsque raptim in faucēs trahere coepit. sellās quoque ex ātriō, lectōs ē cubiculīs proximīs collēctōs in cumulum imposuit. brevī ingēns pyra in faucibus exstrūcta est.

mīlitēs praetōriānī, cum iānuam clausam cōnspexissent, 15
haesitantēs cōnstitērunt. sed tribūnus, nē Paris et Domitia effugerent, iānuam effringī iussit.

"iānuam secūribus pulsāte!" inquit. "sī prōditōrēs effūgerint, vōs omnēs pūniēminī."

Myropnous ubi strepitum pulsantium audīvit pyram incendit. 20
amphoram oleī ē culīnā portāvit quā flammās augēret. tum pyrā flagrante, amīcōs sequī contendit.

praetōriānīs:	*praetorian (member of*	**imposuit: impōnere**	*put onto*
praetōriānus	*emperor's bodyguard)*	**pyra**	*pyre*
usquam	*anywhere*	**effringī: effringere**	*break down*
reversus: revertī	*return*	**secūribus: secūris**	*axe*
āctum est		**prōditōrēs: prōditor**	*traitor*
dē nōbīs	*it's all over for us*	**flagrante: flagrāre**	*blaze*
postīcum	*back gate*		
ēlābī	*escape*		
faucēs	*passage, entrance-way*		

II

Paris et Domitia, ubi ad postīcum pervēnērunt, duōs mīlitēs ibi positōs invēnērunt. quōs cum vīdissent, quamquam Domitia omnīnō dē salūte dēspērābat, Paris in hōc discrīmine audācissimum atque callidissimum sē praestitit. nam cēlātā haud procul Domitiā, ipse per postīcum audācter prōgressus sē mīlitibus ostendit. tum quasi fugiēns, retrō in hortum cucurrit. 5

statim clāmāvērunt mīlitēs: "ecce Paris! Paris effugere cōnātur!"

mīlitibus sequentibus, Paris per hortum modo hūc modo illūc ruēbat. post statuās sē cēlābat mīlitēsque vōce blandā dērīdēbat. illī incertī ubi esset pantomīmus, vōcem Paridis circā hortum sequēbantur. 10

tandem audīvit Paris strepitum cēterōrum mīlitum domum irrumpentium. brevī tōta domus mīlitibus plēna erat. tribūnus aliōs iussit aquam ferre ut flammās exstinguerent, aliōs gladiīs dēstrictīs omnēs domūs partēs perscrūtārī ut Paridem invenīrent. 15 hic bene intellēxit quantō in perīculō esset sed etiam tum haudquāquam dēspērāvit.

mediō in hortō stābat laurus veterrima, quae tēctō domūs imminēbat. simulatque intrāvērunt mīlitēs hortum, laurum Paris cōnscendit. hinc prōsilīre in tēctum cōnātus est. prōsiluit, sed 20 tēgulae tēctī lūbricae erant. paulīsper in margine tēctī stetit; deinde praeceps humum lāpsus est.

intereā Domitia, quae per postīcum nūllō vidente ēgressa erat, haud procul exspectābat dum Paris ad sē venīret. lāpsō tamen corpore eius, tantus erat fragor ut etiam ad aurēs Domitiae 25 advenīret. quae metū āmēns vītaeque suae neglegēns in hortum reversa est. ubi corpus Paridis humī iacēns vīdit, dolōre cōnfecta sē in eum coniēcit eīque ōscula multa dedit.

"valē, dēliciae meae, valē!"

adiit tribūnus. Domitiam ad aulam dēdūcī iussit. ipse caput 30 pantomīmī amputātum ad Epaphrodītum rettulit.

retrō	*back*	**cōnfecta: cōnfectus**	*overcome*
modo … modo	*now … now*	**amputātum: amputāre**	*cut off*
circā	*around*		
exstinguerent: exstinguere	*put out*		
dēstrictīs: dēstringere	*draw, unsheathe*		
prōsilīre	*jump*		
tēgulae: tēgula	*tile*		
lūbricae: lūbricus	*slippery*		
margine: margō	*edge*		
nūllō (*used as ablative*			
of **nēmō**)	*no one*		
fragor	*crash*		
āmēns	*out of her mind, in a frenzy*		

About the Language II: Future Passive Indicative

A Study the following examples:

cēna sūmptuōsa **parābitur.**
An expensive dinner will be prepared.

ab Imperātōre **honōrābor.**
I shall be honored by the Emperor.

crās nūntiī ad rēgem **mittentur.**
Tomorrow messengers will be sent to the king.

vōs omnēs **pūniēminī.**
You will all be punished.

The verbs in boldface are future passive indicative.

B First and second conjugation verbs form their future passive indicative in the following way:

FIRST CONJUGATION		SECOND CONJUGATION	
portābor	*I shall/will be carried*	docēbor	*I shall/will be taught*
portāberis	*you will be carried*	docēberis	*you will be taught*
portābitur	*s/he, it will be carried*	docēbitur	*s/he, it will be taught*
portābimur	*we shall/will be carried*	docēbimur	*we shall/will be taught*
portābiminī	*you will be carried*	docēbiminī	*you will be taught*
portābuntur	*they will be carried*	docēbuntur	*they will be taught*

C Third and fourth conjugation verbs form their future passive indicative in the following way:

THIRD CONJUGATION		FOURTH CONJUGATION	
trahar	*I shall/will be dragged*	audiar	*I shall/will be heard*
trahēris	*you will be dragged*	audiēris	*you will be heard*
trahētur	*s/he, it will be dragged*	audiētur	*s/he, it will be heard*
trahēmur	*we shall/will be dragged*	audiēmur	*we shall/will be heard*
trahēminī	*you will be dragged*	audiēminī	*you will be heard*
trahentur	*they will be dragged*	audientur	*they will be heard*

D Further examples:

1 ingēns praemium victōrī dabitur. omnēs vīllae dēlēbuntur.
2 nisi effūgerimus, capiēmur. in carcerem iaciēris.
3 damnābiminī; condūcentur; ēiciētur; cogēris; accūsābor.

E Notice how the future indicative of deponent verbs is formed:

cōnābor	*I shall/will try*	loquar	*I shall/will speak*
cōnāberis	*you will try*	loquēris	*you will speak*
cōnābitur	*s/he, it will try*	loquētur	*s/he, it will speak*
cōnābimur	*we shall/will try*	loquēmur	*we shall/will speak*
cōnābiminī	*you will try*	loquēminī	*you will speak*
cōnābuntur	*they will try*	loquentur	*they will speak*

F Further examples:

1 mīlitēs crās proficīscentur. dux hostium nihil suspicābitur.
2 sī hoc venēnum cōnsūmpseris, moriēris.
3 revertentur; prōgrediar; ēgrediēminī; amplectāberis; hortābitur.

honōrēs

Salviō aulam intrantī obviam iit Epaphrodītus. cōmiter excēpit.

Epaphrodītus: mī Salvī, quālis artifex es! tuā arte iste pantomīmus occīsus est. tuā arte Domitia ex Ītaliā relēgāta est. Imperātor, summō gaudiō affectus, spectāculum splendidissimum in amphitheātrō 5 Flāviō darī iussit. crās diēs fēstus ab omnibus cīvibus celebrābitur; puerī puellaeque deōrum effigiēs corōnīs flōrum ōrnābunt; sacerdōtēs sacrificia offerent; ingēns cīvium multitūdō Imperātōrem ad templum Iovis comitābitur, ubi 10 ille dīs immortālibus grātiās aget. mox senātōrēs ad cūriam fēstīs vestīmentīs prōgredientur et Domitiānō grātulābuntur. venī mēcum! nōn morandum est nōbīs. Imperātor enim nōs exspectat. mihi ōrnāmenta praetōria, tibi 15 cōnsulātum prōmīsit.
Salvius: cōnsulātum adipīscar? quam fortūnātus sum!
Epaphrodītus: venī! oportet nōs Imperātōrī grātiās agere.

Epaphrodītō et Salviō ēgressīs ut Domitiānum salūtārent, ē latebrīs rēpsit Myropnous. manifesta nunc omnia erant. nunc 20 dēnique intellēxit quis esset auctor exitiī Paridis. lacrimīs effūsīs,

indignam amīcī mortem lūgēbat. tum manibus ad caelum sublātīs
nōmen Salviī dētestātus est. tībiās āmēns frēgit. ultiōnem sibi hīs
verbīs prōmīsit:
    "ego numquam iterum tībiīs cantābō priusquam perierit   25
Salvius."

artifex	*artist*	**auctor**	*person*
cūriam: cūria	*senate-house*		*responsible,*
morandum est: morārī	*delay*		*originator*
ōrnāmenta praetōria	*honorary praetorship,*	**indignam:**	*unworthy,*
	honorary rank of	**indignus**	*undeserved*
	praetor (judicial	**sublātīs: tollere**	*raise, lift up*
	magistrate)	**priusquam**	*until, before*
manifesta: manifestus	*clear*		

Word Patterns: Verbs and Nouns

A Study the form and meaning of the following verbs and nouns:

VERB		NOUN	
haesitāre	*to hesitate*	haesitātiō	*hesitation*
nāvigāre	*to sail*	nāvigātiō	*voyage*
mūtāre	*to change, alter*	mūtātiō	*change, alteration*

B Using Section A as a guide, complete the table below:

VERB		NOUN	
coniūrāre	*to conspire*	coniūrātiō	.....
salūtāre	.....	.....	*greeting*
cōgitāre	.....	cōgitātiō	.....

C Match the correct translation to the following nouns:

1	dubitātiō	a	encouragement
2	festīnātiō	b	refusal
3	hortātiō	c	public reading
4	recitātiō	d	uncertainty
5	recūsātiō	e	haste
6	rogātiō	f	request

D What is the gender of each noun above?
To what declension does each noun belong?

Practicing the Language

A Select the correct form of the verb and then translate each sentence.

1 vōbīs rem tōtam (nārrābit, nārrābitur).
2 cibus vestīmentaque nōbīs ab amīcīs nostrīs (praebēbunt, praebēbuntur).
3 spectāculum splendidum in amphitheātrō ab Imperātōre (dabit, dabitur).
4 fortiōrēs estis quam illī barbarī; eōs facile (superābitis, superābiminī).
5 caudex! ā custōdibus statim (capiēs, capiēris).
6 ego sum probus; tibi pecūniam (reddam, reddar).
7 fugite! mox (damnābitis, damnābiminī) et in carcerem (coniciētis, coniciēminī).
8 lectī ē cubiculīs collēctī in cumulum (impōnent, impōnentur); brevī ingēns pyra (exstruet, exstruētur).

B Select the correct infinitive form and then translate each sentence.

1 necesse est senātōribus sacerdōtēs ad templum Iovis (salūtārī, comitārī).
2 dux nōs statim (proficīscī, conicī) iussit ut barbarīs resisterēmus.
3 marmor tam grave erat ut ā fabrīs vix (prōgredī, movērī) posset.
4 Paris post statuās cēlātus mīlitēs (cōnspicārī, dērīdērī) poterat.
5 Domitia Chionēn (incitārī, hortārī) cōnstituit nē tenebrās aliaque indicia perīculī timēret.
6 Myropnous, postquam tribūnus corpus Paridis ex hortō (trahī, adipīscī) iussit, magnum dolōrem passus est.

C Translate each English sentence into Latin by selecting correctly from the list of Latin words.

1 *Many flowers were being thrown by the spectators.*

multa	flōris	ā spectātōribus	iactābant
multī	flōrēs	inter spectātōrēs	iactābantur

2 *They warned my friend not to cross the bridge.*

amīcum	meīs	monuerant	nē	pōns	trānsīret
amīcōs	meum	monuērunt	ut	pontem	trānsībat

3 *Having been ordered by the leader, we carried out the body.*
   ad ducem   iussus   corpus   extulī
   ā duce   iussī   corporum   extulimus
4 *We saw the man whose brother you (s.) had arrested.*
   hominem   quī   frāter   comprehenderātis   vidēmus
   hominum   cuius frātrem comprehenderās   vīdimus
5 *When the soldiers had been drawn up (two Latin words only), I gave the centurion a sign.*
   mīlitibus   īnstrūctīs   centuriōnem   signum   dedī
   mīlitēs   īnstrūctōs   centuriōnī   signō   dedit

D In each pair of sentences, translate sentence **a**; then, with the help of page 313 of the Language Information, express the same idea in a different way by completing sentence **b** with a passive form, and translate again.

For example: **a** centuriō fūrēs vulnerāverat.
              b fūrēs ā centuriōne ......
Translated and completed, this becomes:
              a centuriō fūrēs vulnerāverat.
                 The centurion had wounded the thieves.
              b fūrēs ā centuriōne vulnerātī erant.
                 The thieves had been wounded by the centurion.

1a coquus cibum parāverat.
  b cibus ā coquō ......
2a mercātor latrōnēs superāverat.
  b latrōnēs ā mercātōre ......
3a dominī servōs laudāvērunt.
  b servī ā dominīs ......
4a clientēs patrōnum salūtāvērunt.
  b patrōnus ā clientibus ......
5a rēx mē ipsum accūsāvit.
  b ego ipse ā rēge ......
6a custōs magnum clāmōrem audīvit.
  b magnus clāmor ā custōde ......

Freedmen and Freedwomen

As you learned from earlier readings, the legal status granted to ex-slaves was noticeably more generous in ancient Rome than in other slave-owning societies. When slaves were manumitted, they ceased to be the property of their masters and became **libertī** or **libertae**. The freedmen of a Roman citizen became Roman citizens themselves. This practice seems to have been unique to Rome.

As a Roman citizen, the freedman now had three names, of which the first two came from the name of his ex-master. For example, Tiro, the freedman of Marcus Tullius Cicero, became Marcus Tullius Tiro, and, in our stories, we have imagined that Clemens became Quintus Caecilius Clemens. As a citizen, the libertus now had the right to vote in elections and to make a will or business agreements which would be valid in the eyes of the law. He could also get married. If he had been living in an unofficial marriage with a slave-woman, one of his first acts after manumission might have been to save up enough money to buy her out of slavery and marry her legally.

Augustales

To be chosen as an Augustalis, or priest of the emperor, was the greatest honor open to many freedmen. Top: The hall in Herculaneum where the Augustales would meet for worship and for ceremonial dinners. Below: Part of the inscription from a tomb at Pompeii, put up by a freedman for himself and his patroness, Vesonia. Notice how he must have been made an Augustalis after he had had the tomb built, because the word has been awkwardly squeezed in by a different letter-cutter. The honor, when it came, was too important to leave out of Vesonius Phileros' tomb inscription.

There were, however, some limits to the rights and privileges of ex-slaves, compared with other Roman citizens. A libertus could not become a senator or an eques, except by special favor of the emperor, and a liberta could not become a senator's wife. A libertus could not serve in the legions or stand as a candidate in elections. But the limitations were relatively few, and any children were wholly exempt from them.

A freedman retained legal obligations to his former master, becoming a cliens of his ex-master while his former owner was now his patronus. A freedman was supposed to leave money to his patron in his will, although ex-masters did not often insist on this; he was forbidden to do anything that would bring harm to his patron; and he had to do a certain number of days' work for his patron every year or pay him a sum of money instead. A freedman was bound to show deference and respect to his patron, attend him on public occasions, and assist him in misfortune.

In return, a patron would help a needy client with the sportula distributed at the salutatio. If a freedman died first, his patron paid for a decent funeral and had the ashes buried near the place where his own ashes would rest. He was also the guardian of the freedman's children. The patron often helped his freedman with funds to make a start in his new life, just as, in our stories, Quintus established Clemens in a glass shop; or a patron might introduce and recommend his client to potential customers. Sometimes the freedman even continued to live in his ex-master's household, doing the same work that he had done as a slave. One such man was Pliny's talented freedman, Zosimus, who was equally skilled at reciting, lyre-playing, and comedy-acting. Pliny treated Zosimus with kindness and affection, and when Zosimus fell ill with tuberculosis, Pliny arranged a holiday abroad for him. In short, the patron-client relationship tended to be one of mutual helpfulness.

Further evidence of friendly relationships between ex-masters and freedmen comes from the large number of inscriptions, particularly on tombstones, that refer to freedmen and freedwomen. Sometimes, for example, freedmen set up tombstones in honor of their ex-masters:

D M T. FLAVIO HOMERO T. FLAVIVS HYACINTHVS PATRONO BENE MERENTI	**DM = dīs manibus** *to the spirits of the departed* **bene merentī: bene merēns** *well deserving, deserving kindness*

Sometimes ex-masters set up tombstones to their favorite freedmen:

> D M
> IVLIO VITALI
> PATRONVS LIBERTO
> BENE MERENTI

Some ex-masters allowed freedmen and freedwomen to be buried with them in their tombs:

> D M
> TITVS FLAVIVS EV
> MOLPVS ET FLAVIA
> QVINTA SIBI FECE
> RVNT ET LIBERTIS LI
> BERTABVSQVE POS
> TERISQVE EORVM

lībertābus: līberta *freedwoman*
posterīs: posterī *future generations*

An ex-master might marry his freedwoman:

> D M
> T. FLAVIVS CERIALIS
> FLAVIAE PHILAENIDI
> LIBERTAE IDEM
> ET COIVGI
> B M F

idem here = *also*
coiugī = coniugī: coniūnx *wife*
BMF = bene merentī fēcit

Some slaves might be manumitted as a reward for long service or for some exceptional action, such as Felix's rescue of baby Quintus in our stories. But it is clear from the legal obligations of a client that it would often be financially worthwhile for a master to manumit a slave; the patron would still be able to make some use of the ex-slave's services, but would no longer have to provide for his food, clothing, and shelter.

Many highly skilled or educated freedmen were quickly able to earn a good living because they already possessed some special ability or experience; for example, a freedman might already be a skilled craftsman, teacher, musician, or secretary, or be experienced in accountancy, trade, or banking. Freedmen who had previously used these skills in their masters' service could now use them for their own benefit. The most competent freedmen found lucrative careers, even important managerial posts in small businesses and industry. There was plenty of demand for such services and not much competition from freeborn Romans, who often lacked the necessary skills or regarded such work as beneath their dignity.

It is not surprising, therefore, that many freedmen became rich and successful, and a few freedmen became very rich indeed. The Vettii brothers, who set up their own business in Pompeii and eventually owned one of the most splendid houses in the town, are good examples of such successful freedmen. But perhaps the most famous example of a wealthy freedman is a fictitious one: Trimalchio, the vulgar and ostentatious millionaire in Petronius' novel *Satyrica*. The story **cēna Hateriī** in Stage 32 is partly based on Petronius' account of Trimalchio's dinner party.

After manumission, a freedman had to put up with a certain amount of prejudice from those who despised him for having been a slave. Even the next generation, although having full privileges of citizenship, continued to be viewed by the citizens of freeborn ancestry as social inferiors. The poet Juvenal writes that at a banquet the patron gets "a delicate loaf white as snow, kneaded of the finest flour" while his clients are served "a bit of hard bread that you can scarce break in two or bits of solid dough that have turned moldy." This custom of having different food for different guests was disapproved of by the more discerning Romans. Pliny wrote, "I invite my guests to dine and not to be humiliated." The poet Horace was the object of suspicion and envy because of his friendship with Maecenas, a famous patron of the arts. Horace's father was a freedman whom Horace proudly praised for giving him the intellectual and moral training which won him a place in Maecenas' circle. Horace also praised Maecenas for his social fairness: "You, Maecenas, do not, like most of the world, curl up your nose at men of unknown birth, men like myself, a freedman's son."

One privilege, however, was available to freedmen and to no one else. A freedman could become one of the six priests (**sevirī Augustālēs**) who were appointed in many Italian towns and some provincial ones to oversee the cult of Rome and the worship of the deified Emperor Augustus. Like all priesthoods, the priesthood of Augustus was a position of honor and prestige, but this one was open to freedmen only.

A small but very important group of freedmen worked as personal assistants to the emperor. As slaves, they had been known as **servī Caesaris** and as freedmen they were known as **lībertī Augustī**. (**Caesar** and **Augustus** were both used as titles of the emperor.) One of these men was Epaphroditus (full name Tiberius Claudius Neronis Augusti libertus Epaphroditus), Domitian's secretary **ā libellīs** (see page 275).

Other freedmen of the emperor were in charge of correspondence (**ab epistulīs**) and accounts (**ā ratiōnibus**). They all worked closely with the emperor in the day-to-day running of government business.

Under some emperors, especially Claudius and Nero, these freedmen became immensely rich and powerful. They were often bitterly resented by the Roman nobles and senators. This resentment can be seen very plainly in two letters which Pliny wrote about Pallas, the secretary a rationibus of the Emperor Claudius. Pallas had been awarded the **ōrnāmenta praetōria** (honorary praetorship), like Epaphroditus in our stories. This means he was given the various privileges normally possessed by a praetor – special dress, special seat at public ceremonies, special funeral after death, and so on – without having any of the responsibilities. Pliny, when he came across the inscription commemorating these honors, was indignant and furious, even though the whole incident had happened fifty years previously. He described Pallas as a "furcifer," and much else besides. He was particularly angry that the inscription praised Pallas for refusing a further gift of 15 million sesterces. In Pliny's opinion, Pallas was insulting the praetorian rank by refusing the money as excessive while accepting the privileges as if they meant less; besides, he already had 300 million sesterces of his own. Pliny's outburst shows very clearly how much ill feeling could be caused by an emperor's use of ex-slaves as important and powerful assistants in running the empire.

Tombstone of a dwarf pipe player called Myropnous.

Word Study

A Match the Latin word or phrase to the word which means approximately the same.

1	exstinguere	**a**	redīre
2	comitārī	**b**	dēlēre
3	conārī	**c**	discēdere
4	ēgredī	**d**	mortem obīre
5	ingredī	**e**	exīre
6	loquī	**f**	intrāre
7	morī	**g**	temptāre
8	proficīscī	**h**	dēdūcere
9	revertī	**i**	dīcere

B Match the definition to the English derivative.

1	circumlocution	**a**	inactive, but acted upon
2	consecutive	**b**	being reborn; showing new life
3	eloquent	**c**	illogical; trivial
4	inconsequential	**d**	an entrance
5	ingredient	**e**	enduring trouble without complaining
6	ingress	**f**	inborn, not acquired
7	innate	**g**	a roundabout way of expressing something
8	passive	**h**	any of the elements which form a mixture
9	patient	**i**	forceful and persuasive
10	renascent	**j**	following in order; successive

C Match the Latin word to its antonym.

1	sequī	**a**	vīvere
2	damnāre	**b**	postquam
3	priusquam	**c**	dūcere
4	morī	**d**	prope
5	procul	**e**	ignōscere

Stage 34 Vocabulary Checklist

auctor, auctōris, m.	*creator, originator*
mē auctōre	*at my suggestion*
damnō, damnāre, damnāvī, damnātus	*condemn*
dum	*while, until*
exstinguō, exstinguere, exstīnxī,	*extinguish, put out,*
exstīnctus	*destroy*
gaudium, gaudiī, n.	*joy*
haud	*not*
immineō, imminēre, imminuī (+ DAT)	*hang over*
indicium, indiciī, n.	*sign, evidence*
modo	*just*
obviam eō, obviam īre, obviam iī (+ DAT)	*meet, go to meet*
pendeō, pendēre, pependī	*hang*
priusquam	*before, until*
procul	*far*
quasi	*as if*
tenebrae, tenebrārum, f. pl.	*darkness*
ultiō, ultiōnis, f.	*revenge*
vel	*or*
vestīmenta, vestīmentōrum, n. pl.	*clothes*

DEPONENT VERBS

adipīscor, adipīscī, adeptus sum	*obtain*
amplector, amplectī, amplexus sum	*embrace*
comitor, comitārī, comitātus sum	*accompany*
cōnor, cōnārī, cōnātus sum	*try*
cōnspicor, cōnspicārī, cōnspicātus sum	*catch sight of*
ēgredior, ēgredī, ēgressus sum	*go out*
hortor, hortārī, hortātus sum	*encourage, urge*
ingredior, ingredī, ingressus sum	*enter*
loquor, loquī, locūtus sum	*speak*
morior, morī, mortuus sum	*die*
nāscor, nāscī, nātus sum	*be born*
patior, patī, passus sum	*suffer*
precor, precārī, precātus sum	*pray (to)*
proficīscor, proficīscī, profectus sum	*set out*
regredior, regredī, regressus sum	*go back, return*
revertor, revertī, reversus sum	*turn back, return*
sequor, sequī, secūtus sum	*follow*

LANGUAGE INFORMATION

Contents

About the Language   296

Nouns   296

Adjectives   299

Comparison of Adjectives   301

Adverbs   303

Pronouns   305

Regular Verbs   311

Deponent Verbs   318

Irregular Verbs   321

Uses of the Cases   324

Uses of the Participle   328

Uses of the Subjunctive   333

Word Order   337

Longer Sentences   338

Complete Vocabulary   340

Part One: About the Language
Nouns

A You have now met examples of all the declensions and all the cases. For the ways in which the different cases are used, see pages 324–327.

	first declension	*second declension*		
	f.	m.	m.	n.
SINGULAR				
nominative and *vocative*	puella	servus (*voc.* serve)	faber	templum
genitive	puellae	servī	fabrī	templī
dative	puellae	servō	fabrō	templō
accusative	puellam	servum	fabrum	templum
ablative	puellā	servō	fabrō	templō
PLURAL				
nominative and *vocative*	puellae	servī	fabrī	templa
genitive	puellārum	servōrum	fabrōrum	templōrum
dative	puellīs	servīs	fabrīs	templīs
accusative	puellās	servōs	fabrōs	templa
ablative	puellīs	servīs	fabrīs	templīs

	fourth declension		*fifth declension*	
	m.	n.	m.	f.
SINGULAR				
nominative and *vocative*	portus	genū	diēs	rēs
genitive	portūs	genūs	diēī	reī
dative	portuī	genū	diēī	reī
accusative	portum	genū	diem	rem
ablative	portū	genū	diē	rē
PLURAL				
nominative and *vocative*	portūs	genua	diēs	rēs
genitive	portuum	genuum	diērum	rērum
dative	portibus	genibus	diēbus	rēbus
accusative	portūs	genua	diēs	rēs
ablative	portibus	genibus	diēbus	rēbus

third declension

m.	f.	m. f.	n.	n.	
					SINGULAR
leō	vōx	cīvis	nōmen	mare	*nominative* and *vocative*
leōnis	vōcis	cīvis	nōminis	maris	*genitive*
leōnī	vōcī	cīvī	nōminī	marī	*dative*
leōnem	vōcem	cīvem	nōmen	mare	*accusative*
leōne	vōce	cīve	nōmine	marī	*ablative*
					PLURAL
leōnēs	vōcēs	cīvēs	nōmina	maria	*nominative* and *vocative*
leōnum	vōcum	cīvium	nōminum	marium	*genitive*
leōnibus	vōcibus	cīvibus	nōminibus	maribus	*dative*
leōnēs	vōcēs	cīvēs	nōmina	maria	*accusative*
leōnibus	vōcibus	cīvibus	nōminibus	maribus	*ablative*

B For all declensions except the 2nd, the vocative singular is the same as the nominative singular. This is also true for 2nd declension neuter nouns (e.g. **templum**) and 2nd declension nouns ending in **-r** (e.g. **puer, vir**). 2nd declension nouns ending in **-us** form their vocative like **servus** (e.g. **domine, Marce**). 2nd declension nouns ending in **-ius** drop the ending completely in the vocative (e.g. **fīlī, Salvī**).

C 1st declension nouns like **puella** and **via** are usually feminine.
2nd declension nouns are usually either masculine like **servus**, or neuter like **templum**.
3rd declension nouns may be either masculine like **leō**, feminine like **vōx**, or neuter like **nōmen**.
4th declension nouns like **portus** are usually masculine.
5th declension nouns like **rēs** are usually feminine.

D Translate each sentence, then change the words in boldface from singular to plural, and translate again.

1 ancilla **cīvī** aquam obtulit.
2 dominus **amīcō** cibum praebuit.
3 hostēs **nūntium rēgis** interfēcērunt.
4 amīcus noster **nāvem mercātōris** vīdit.
5 māter **pompam deae** laudāvit.
6 nūntius in **urbe** multōs mīlitēs invēnit.
7 agricola, **gladiō** vulnerātus, **gemitum** dedit.
8 sacerdōtēs **effigiēī** appropinquāvērunt.

E Translate each sentence, then change the words in boldface from plural to singular, and translate again.

1 senex **puellīs** sellam reddidit.
2 rēgīna **uxōrēs cīvium** ad aulam vocāvit.
3 medicus **oculōs mīlitum** īnspexit.
4 rhētor **nōmina puerōrum** recitāvit.
5 ancilla **manūs fēminārum** lāvit.
6 fabrī **effigiēs** cōnfēcērunt.
7 sacerdōtēs in **templīs** deōs adōrant.
8 bēstiāriī ā **leōnibus** necātī sunt.

F Notice again the way in which the cases of third-declension nouns are formed. In particular, compare the nominative singular of **leō**, **vox**, and **nōmen** with the genitive singular and other cases. Use the Complete Vocabulary to find the genitive singular of the following nouns, and then use the table in Section A to find their ablative singular and plural:

dux; homō; pēs; difficultās; nox; iter.

G With the help of Section A, find the Latin for the words in boldface italics in the following sentences:

1 Eight *days* had now passed.
2 The ships departed from the *harbor*.
3 The injured man's *knees* were very painful.
4 The senators praised the province's *harbors*.
5 It was the sixth hour of the *day*.
6 On his *knees* he begged for mercy.
7 The messenger set out on the third *day*.

Adjectives

A The following adjectives belong to the 1st and 2nd declension:

	masculine (2nd)	feminine (1st)	neuter (2nd)	masculine (2nd)	feminine (1st)	neuter (2nd)
SINGULAR						
nominative and *vocative*	bonus (voc. bone)	bona	bonum	pulcher	pulchra	pulchrum
genitive	bonī	bonae	bonī	pulchrī	pulchrae	pulchrī
dative	bonō	bonae	bonō	pulchrō	pulchrae	pulchrō
accusative	bonum	bonam	bonum	pulchrum	pulchram	pulchrum
ablative	bonō	bonā	bonō	pulchrō	pulchrā	pulchrō
PLURAL						
nominative and *vocative*	bonī	bonae	bona	pulchrī	pulchrae	pulchra
genitive	bonōrum	bonārum	bonōrum	pulchrōrum	pulchrārum	pulchrōrum
dative	bonīs	bonīs	bonīs	pulchrīs	pulchrīs	pulchrīs
accusative	bonōs	bonās	bona	pulchrōs	pulchrās	pulchra
ablative	bonīs	bonīs	bonīs	pulchrīs	pulchrīs	pulchrīs

B The following adjectives belong to the 3rd declension:

	masc.	fem.	neut.	masc. and fem.	neut.
SINGULAR					
nominative and *vocative*	celer	celeris	celere	ingēns	ingēns
genitive	celeris	celeris	celeris	ingentis	ingentis
dative	celerī	celerī	celerī	ingentī	ingentī
accusative	celerem	celerem	celer	ingentem	ingēns
ablative	celerī	celerī	celerī	ingent-ī/-e	ingent-ī/-e
PLURAL					
nominative and *vocative*	celerēs	celerēs	celeria	ingentēs	ingentia
genitive	celerium	celerium	celerium	ingentium	ingentium
dative	celeribus	celeribus	celeribus	ingentibus	ingentibus
accusative	celerēs	celerēs	celeria	ingentēs	ingentia
ablative	celeribus	celeribus	celeribus	ingentibus	ingentibus

C Compare the third-declension adjectives in Section B with the third-declension nouns on page 297. Notice in particular the possible different endings of the ablative singular. The **-ī** ending is generally used when the adjective modifies a stated noun, e.g. **ā servō ingentī** (*by the huge slave*). The **-e** ending is generally used when the adjective describes a noun not stated, but understood, e.g. **ab ingente** (*by the huge (person)*).

D Adjectives agree with the noun they describe in case, number, and gender.

> **urbem pulchram** vīsitābāmus.
> fabrī **templa ingentia** aedificāvērunt.

E Translate each sentence, then change the words in boldface from singular to plural, and translate again.

1 **barbarus ferōx** līberōs **terrēbat**.
2 **carmen suāve** audīvimus.
3 sacerdōs **manū sublātā** deam precātus est.
4 hostēs fortitūdinem **mīlitis Rōmānī** laudāvērunt.
5 servus **amphoram gravem** in plaustrum posuit.
6 quis **captīvō mendācī** crēdidit?
7 senātor occāsiōnem **cōnsulātūs clārī** cupiēbat.
8 **tālem rem** facere nōn ausim.

F Translate each sentence, then change the words in boldface from plural to singular, and translate again.

1 **gemitūs magnī** captīvī custōdem **perturbāvērunt**.
2 **quālia praemia** exspectās?
3 dē **dominīs crūdēlibus** audīre nōlō.
4 pater fidem **fīliōrum fortium** laudāvit.
5 centuriō **mīlitibus ignāvīs** in viā occurrit.
6 amīcus meus **cāsūs gravēs** passus est.
7 **comitibus dēsertīs**, iuvenis ad urbem rediit.
8 solācium **fēminīs trīstibus** obtulimus.

Comparison of Adjectives

A Regular forms:

Positive	Comparative	Superlative
longus	longior	longissimus
long	*longer*	*longest, very long*
pulcher	pulchrior	pulcherrimus
beautiful	*more beautiful*	*most beautiful, very beautiful*
fortis	fortior	fortissimus
brave	*braver*	*bravest, very brave*
fēlīx	fēlīcior	fēlīcissimus
lucky	*luckier*	*luckiest, very lucky*
prūdēns	prūdentior	prūdentissimus
shrewd	*shrewder*	*shrewdest, very shrewd*
facilis	facilior	facillimus
easy	*easier*	*easiest, very easy*

B Irregular forms:

bonus	melior	optimus
good	*better*	*best, very good*
malus	peior	pessimus
bad	*worse*	*worst, very bad*
magnus	maior	maximus
big	*bigger*	*biggest, very big*
parvus	minor	minimus
small	*smaller*	*smallest, very small*
multus	plūs	plūrimus
much	*more*	*most, very much*
multī	plūrēs	plūrimī
many	*more*	*most, very many*

Note: **plūs**, the comparative form of **multus** above, is a neuter noun, e.g. **plūs pecūniae** *more (of) money.*

C Study the forms of the comparative adjective **longior** (*longer*) and the superlative adjective **longissimus** (*longest, very long*):

	masc. and fem.	neuter	masculine	feminine	neuter
SINGULAR					
nominative and *vocative*	longior	longius	longissimus (*voc.* longissime)	longissima	longissimum
genitive	longiōris	longiōris	longissimī	longissimae	longissimī
dative	longiōrī	longiōrī	longissimō	longissimae	longissimō
accusative	longiōrem	longius	longissimum	longissimam	longissimum
ablative	longiōre	longiōre	longissimō	longissimā	longissimō
PLURAL					
nominative and *vocative*	longiōrēs	longiōra	longissimī	longissimae	longissima
genitive	longiōrum	longiōrum	longissimōrum	longissimārum	longissimōrum
dative	longiōribus	longiōribus	longissimīs	longissimīs	longissimīs
accusative	longiōrēs	longiōra	longissimōs	longissimās	longissima
ablative	longiōribus	longiōribus	longissimīs	longissimīs	longissimīs

D Translate the following examples:

1 "nēmō fortior est quam Modestus," inquit Vilbia.
2 longissima erat pompa, pulcherrima quoque.
3 peior es quam fūr!
4 Salviī vīlla erat minor quam aula Cogidubnī.
5 facillimum erat nōbīs urbem capere.
6 numquam tabernam meliōrem quam tuam vīsitāvī.
7 Memor ad maiōrēs honōrēs ascendere volēbat.
8 in mediō oppidō labōrābant plūrimī fabrī, quī templum maximum exstruēbant.

E You have also met another way of translating the superlative:

Rūfe, prūdentissimus es omnium amīcōrum quōs habeō.
Rufus, you are the shrewdest of all the friends that I have.

The following examples can be translated in the same way:

1 Bregāns erat īnsolentissimus omnium servōrum quōs Salvius habēbat.
2 omnēs mīlitēs meī sunt fortēs; tū tamen fortissimus es.
3 postrēmō Athēnās vīsitāvimus, pulcherrimam omnium urbium.

Adverbs

A Adverbs ending in **-ē** are connected with first- and second-declension adjectives.

ADVERB	ADJECTIVE
laetē *happily*	laetus, laeta, laetum *happy*
pulchrē *beautifully*	pulcher, pulchra, pulchrum *beautiful*

B Adverbs ending **-ter** are connected with third-declension adjectives.

ADVERB	ADJECTIVE
fortiter *bravely*	fortis, fortis, forte *brave*
audācter *boldly*	audāx, audāx, audāx *bold*

C The comparative form of adverbs is the same as the neuter nominative singular of comparative adjectives.

ADVERB	ADJECTIVE
laetius *more happily*	laetior, laetior, laetius *happier*
fortius *more bravely*	fortior, fortior, fortius *braver*

D The superlative form of adverbs ends in **-ē**, since superlative adjectives are all first and second declension.

ADVERB	ADJECTIVE
laetissimē *very happily*	laetissimus, laetissima, laetissimum *very happy*
fortissimē *very bravely*	fortissimus, fortissima, fortissimum *very brave*

E Irregular forms. Compare these adverbial forms with the adjectives on page 301.

bene	melius	optimē
well	*better*	*best, very well*
male	peius	pessimē
badly	*worse*	*worst, very badly*
magnopere	magis	maximē
greatly	*more*	*most, very greatly*
paulum	minus	minimē
little	*less*	*least, very little*
multum	plūs	plūrimum
much	*more*	*most, very much*

F Comparative forms (of both adjectives and adverbs) are sometimes used with the meaning "too."

> medicus **tardius** advēnit.
> *The doctor arrived **too late**. (i.e. "later than he should have")*

G Superlative forms (of both adjectives and adverbs) are sometimes used with quam, meaning *"as ... as possible."*

> **quam celerrimē** advēnit.
> *He arrived **as quickly as possible**.*

H Translate the following examples.

1 nēmō rēs meās prūdentius cūrat quam tū.
2 servus dominō breviter respondit.
3 rēx tōtam īnsulam occupāre perfidē cupit.
4 Belimicus maiōra praemia audācius postulābat.
5 quis hanc prōvinciam administrāre melius scit quam Imperātor?
6 captīvī ad carcerem reductī sunt, custōdem maxime vituperantēs.
7 hīs iuvenibus quam minimē crēdere dēbēmus.
8 fūrēs in cubiculum tacitē intrāvērunt, ē cubiculō timidē fūgērunt.

Pronouns

A ego, tū, nōs, and vōs (*I, you (sg.), we, you (pl.)*)

	singular		*plural*	
nominative	ego	tū	nōs	vōs
genitive	meī	tuī	nostrum	vestrum
dative	mihi	tibi	nōbīs	vōbīs
accusative	mē	tē	nōs	vōs
ablative	mē	tē	nōbīs	vōbīs

mēcum, **tēcum** = *with me, with you* (singular)
nōbīscum, **vōbīscum** = *with us, with you* (plural)

B sē (*herself, himself, itself, themselves, etc.*)

	singular	*plural*
nominative (*no forms*)		
genitive	suī	suī
dative	sibi	sibi
accusative	sē	sē
ablative	sē	sē

sēcum (*with himself, with herself, etc.*) is formed like **mēcum**, **tēcum**, etc.

Notice some of the ways it can be translated:

> tribūnus multōs comitēs **sēcum** habēbat.
> *The tribune had many companions **with him**.*
> Rūfilla ancillās **sēcum** habēbat.
> *Rufilla kept the slave-girls **with her**.*
> vēnātōrēs canēs ferōcēs **sēcum** habēbant.
> *The hunters had ferocious dogs **with them**.*
> Agricola **sēcum** cōgitābat.
> *Agricola thought **with himself**.*
> Or, in more natural English: *Agricola thought to himself.*

C is (*he, she, it*, etc.)

	singular			plural		
	masculine	feminine	neuter	masculine	feminine	neuter
nominative	is	ea	id	eī	eae	ea
genitive	eius	eius	eius	eōrum	eārum	eōrum
dative	eī	eī	eī	eīs	eīs	eīs
accusative	eum	eam	id	eōs	eās	ea
ablative	eō	eā	eō	eīs	eīs	eīs

The forms of **is** can also be used to mean *that, those*, etc.:

eā nocte rediit dominus.   *That night, the master returned.*

D hic (*this, these*, etc.)

	singular			plural		
	masculine	feminine	neuter	masculine	feminine	neuter
nominative	hic	haec	hoc	hī	hae	haec
genitive	huius	huius	huius	hōrum	hārum	hōrum
dative	huic	huic	huic	hīs	hīs	hīs
accusative	hunc	hanc	hoc	hōs	hās	haec
ablative	hōc	hāc	hōc	hīs	hīs	hīs

The various forms of **hic** can also be used to mean *he, she, they*, etc.:

hic tamen nihil dīcere poterat.
He, however, could say nothing.
hī tamen nihil dīcere poterant.
They, however, could say nothing.

E ille (*that, those,* etc.; sometimes used with the meaning *he, she, it,* etc.)

	singular			plural		
	masculine	feminine	neuter	masculine	feminine	neuter
nominative	ille	illa	illud	illī	illae	illa
genitive	illīus	illīus	illīus	illōrum	illārum	illōrum
dative	illī	illī	illī	illīs	illīs	illīs
accusative	illum	illam	illud	illōs	illās	illa
ablative	illō	illā	illō	illīs	illīs	illīs

F **ipse** (*myself, yourself, himself,* etc.)

	singular			plural		
	masculine	*feminine*	*neuter*	*masculine*	*feminine*	*neuter*
nominative	ipse	ipsa	ipsum	ipsī	ipsae	ipsa
genitive	ipsīus	ipsīus	ipsīus	ipsōrum	ipsārum	ipsōrum
dative	ipsī	ipsī	ipsī	ipsīs	ipsīs	ipsīs
accusative	ipsum	ipsam	ipsum	ipsōs	ipsās	ipsa
ablative	ipsō	ipsā	ipsō	ipsīs	ipsīs	ipsīs

> sacerdōs **ipse** lacrimābat.
> *The priest **himself** was weeping.*
> dominus mē **ipsum** līberāvit, sed nōn līberōs meōs.
> *The master freed me **myself**, but not my children.*

Further examples:

1 ego ipse servum pūnīvī.
2 ego ipsa marītum vocāvī.
3 nōs ipsī in templō aderāmus.
4 subitō ursam ipsam vīdimus.
5 templum ipsum nōn erat magnum.
6 Cogidubnum ipsum audīvimus.
7 dea ipsa mihi appāruit.

G From Stage 23 onwards, you have met various forms of the word **īdem**, meaning *the same (person)*:

	singular			plural		
	masculine	*feminine*	*neuter*	*masculine*	*feminine*	*neuter*
nominative	īdem	eadem	idem	eīdem	eaedem	eadem
genitive	eiusdem	eiusdem	eiusdem	eōrundem	eārundem	eōrundem
dative	eīdem	eīdem	eīdem	eīsdem	eīsdem	eīsdem
accusative	eundem	eandem	idem	eōsdem	eāsdem	eadem
ablative	eōdem	eādem	eōdem	eīsdem	eīsdem	eīsdem

Compare the forms of **īdem** with **is** in Section C.

With the help of the table above, find the Latin for the words in boldface italics in the following sentences:

1 I heard *the same* boy again.
2 *The same* women were there.
3 This is *the same* man's house.
4 He saw *the same* girl.

H With the help of Sections A–G and (if necessary) the gender information in the table of nouns on pages 296–297, find the Latin for the words in boldface italics in the following sentences.

1 I have never seen *that* girl before.
2 Guard *those* slaves!
3 *These* lions are dangerous.
4 Do you know the name of *this* citizen?
5 We soon found *him*.
6 Those voices are too harsh. I do not want to listen to *them*.
7 Where are the temples? I want to see *them*.
8 I hurried to *his* house.
9 We described the bear to *him*.
10 You *yourself* (f.) were called by the Emperor's wife.
11 He is always talking to *himself*.
12 This is not the *same thing*.

I **quī** (*who, which,* etc.)

	singular			plural		
	masculine	feminine	neuter	masculine	feminine	neuter
nominative	quī	quae	quod	quī	quae	quae
genitive	cuius	cuius	cuius	quōrum	quārum	quōrum
dative	cui	cui	cui	quibus	quibus	quibus
accusative	quem	quam	quod	quōs	quās	quae
ablative	quō	quā	quō	quibus	quibus	quibus

Examples of sentences with forms of the relative pronoun **quī**:

senex **cuius** vīlla ardēbat magnōs clāmōrēs tollēbat.
*The old man **whose** house was on fire was raising great shouts.*
duōs servōs ēmī, **quōrum** alter Graecus, alter Aegyptius erat.
*I bought two slaves, one **of whom** was a Greek, the other an Egyptian.*
mercātor **cui** sellās mēnsāsque herī vēndidī hodiē revēnit.
*The merchant **to whom** I sold chairs and tables yesterday came back today.*
nūntiī **quibus** mandāta dedimus herī discessērunt.
*The messengers **to whom** we gave the instructions departed yesterday.*

Further examples of the various forms of **quī**:

1 mīlitēs quōs Salvius ēmīserat tandem rediērunt.
2 iuvenis, cuius nōmen erat Narcissus, sē in aquā vīdit.
3 centuriō custōdēs quī dormīverant sevērissimē pūnīvit.
4 servus, cui sacerdōs signum dederat, victimās ad āram dūxit.
5 templum, quod in mediō oppidō stābat, saepe vīsitābam.
6 hic est gladius quō centum hostēs occīdī.
7 agricolae, quōrum plaustrum servī Salviī frēgerant, in fossam cucurrērunt.
8 amīcī dē quibus dīcēbāmus subitō advēnērunt.

J Sometimes the relative pronoun is used at the *beginning* of a sentence. Study the different ways of translating it:

> Salviī amīcī īnsidiās Belimicō parāvērunt. **quī**, nihil suspicātus, ad aulam libenter vēnit.
> *Salvius' friends prepared a trap for Belimicus. Having suspected nothing,* **he** *came willingly to the palace.*
> mīles pecūniam custōdiēbat. **quem** cum cōnspexissent, fūrēs fūgērunt.
> *A soldier was guarding the money. When the thieves had caught sight of* **him***, they ran away.*
> centuriō "ad carnificēs dūcite!" inquit. **quibus** verbīs perterritī, captīvī clāmāre ac lacrimāre coepērunt.
> *"Take them to the executioners!" said the centurion. Terrified by* **these** *words, the prisoners began to shout and weep.*

Further examples:

1 "cūr mihi nihil dās?" rogāvit Belimicus. quod cum audīvisset, Salvius īrātissimus erat.
2 domina ancillīs pecūniam trādidit. quae, postquam cibum vīnumque ēmērunt, ad vīllam revēnērunt.
3 Memor īrātus clāmāre coepit. cui Cephalus nihil respondēre audēbat.
4 multī mīlitēs iam aulam complēbant. quōs cum vīdissent, sacerdōtēs surrēxērunt.
5 cum fūr dormīret, centuriōnēs thermās intrāvērunt. quōrum vōcibus excitātus, fūr post columnam sē cēlāvit.

K From Stage 26 you have met the relative pronoun used with forms of the pronoun **is**:

> fēcī **id quod** iussistī.
> *I have done **that which** you ordered.*
> Or, in more natural English, use the word *what* to translate both Latin words:
> *I have done **what** you ordered.*

Further examples:

1 id quod Salvius in epistulā scrīpsit falsum est.
2 nūntius ea patefēcit quae apud Britannōs audīverat.
3 id quod mihi dīxistī vix intellegere possum.
4 servus tamen, homō ignāvissimus, id quod dominus iusserat omnīnō neglēxit.

Regular Verbs

Indicative

A Active

first conjugation	second conjugation	third conjugation	third "-iō" conjugation	fourth conjugation
PRESENT *(I carry, etc.)*				
portō	doceō	trahō	capiō	audiō
portās	docēs	trahis	capis	audīs
portat	docet	trahit	capit	audit
portāmus	docēmus	trahimus	capimus	audīmus
portātis	docētis	trahitis	capitis	audītis
portant	docent	trahunt	capiunt	audiunt
IMPERFECT *(I was carrying, etc.)*				
portābam	docēbam	trahēbam	capiēbam	audiēbam
portābās	docēbās	trahēbās	capiēbās	audiēbās
portābat	docēbat	trahēbat	capiēbat	audiēbat
portābāmus	docēbāmus	trahēbāmus	capiēbāmus	audiēbāmus
portābātis	docēbātis	trahēbātis	capiēbātis	audiēbātis
portābant	docēbant	trahēbant	capiēbant	audiēbant
FUTURE *(I shall/will carry, etc.)*				
portābō	docēbō	traham	capiam	audiam
portābis	docēbis	trahēs	capiēs	audiēs
portābit	docēbit	trahet	capiet	audiet
portābimus	docēbimus	trahēmus	capiēmus	audiēmus
portābitis	docēbitis	trahētis	capiētis	audiētis
portābunt	docēbunt	trahent	capient	audient
PERFECT *(I have carried, I carried, etc.)*				
portāvī	docuī	trāxī	cēpī	audīvī
portāvistī	docuistī	trāxistī	cēpistī	audīvistī
portāvit	docuit	trāxit	cēpit	audīvit
portāvimus	docuimus	trāximus	cēpimus	audīvimus
portāvistis	docuistis	trāxistis	cēpistis	audīvistis
portāvērunt	docuērunt	trāxērunt	cēpērunt	audīvērunt

portāveram	docueram	trāxeram	cēperam	audīveram
portāverās	docuerās	trāxerās	cēperās	audīverās
portāverat	docuerat	trāxerat	cēperat	audīverat
portāverāmus	docuerāmus	trāxerāmus	cēperāmus	audīverāmus
portāverātis	docuerātis	trāxerātis	cēperātis	audīverātis
portāverant	docuerant	trāxerant	cēperant	audīverant

FUTURE PERFECT *(I shall/will have carried, etc.)*

portāvero	docuerō	trāxerō	cēperō	audīverō
portāveris	docueris	trāxeris	cēperis	audīveris
portāverit	docuerit	trāxerit	cēperit	audīverit
portāverimus	docuerimus	trāxerimus	cēperimus	audīverimus
portāveritis	docueritis	trāxeritis	cēperitis	audīveritis
portāverint	docuerint	trāxerint	cēperint	audīverint

B *Passive*

PRESENT *(I am carried, I am being carried, etc.)*

portor	doceor	trahor	capior	audior
portāris	docēris	traheris	caperis	audīris
portātur	docētur	trahitur	capitur	audītur
portāmur	docēmur	trahimur	capimur	audīmur
portāminī	docēminī	trahiminī	capiminī	audīminī
portantur	docentur	trahuntur	capiuntur	audiuntur

IMPERFECT *(I was being carried, etc.)*

portābar	docēbar	trahēbar	capiēbar	audiēbar
portābāris	docēbāris	trahēbāris	capiēbāris	audiēbāris
portābātur	docēbātur	trahēbātur	capiēbātur	audiēbātur
portābāmur	docēbāmur	trahēbāmur	capiēbāmur	audiēbāmur
portābāminī	docēbāminī	trahēbāminī	capiēbāminī	audiēbāminī
portābantur	docēbantur	trahēbantur	capiēbantur	audiēbantur

FUTURE *(I shall/will be carried, etc.)*

portābor	docēbor	trahar	capiar	audiar
portāberis	docēberis	trahēris	capiēris	audiēris
portābitur	docēbitur	trahētur	capiētur	audiētur
portābimur	docēbimur	trahēmur	capiēmur	audiēmur
portābiminī	docēbiminī	trahēminī	capiēminī	audiēminī
portābuntur	docēbuntur	trahentur	capientur	audientur

PERFECT *(I have been carried, I was carried, etc.)*

portātus sum	doctus sum	tractus sum	captus sum	audītus sum
portātus es	doctus es	tractus es	captus es	audītus es
portātus est	doctus est	tractus est	captus est	audītus est
portātī sumus	doctī sumus	tractī sumus	captī sumus	audītī sumus
portātī estis	doctī estis	tractī estis	captī estis	audītī estis
portātī sunt	doctī sunt	tractī sunt	captī sunt	audītī sunt

PLUPERFECT *(I had been carried, etc.)*

portātus eram	doctus eram	tractus eram	captus eram	audītus eram
portātus erās	doctus erās	tractus erās	captus erās	audītus erās
portātus erat	doctus erat	tractus erat	captus erat	audītus erat
portātī erāmus	doctī erāmus	tractī erāmus	captī erāmus	audītī erāmus
portātī erātis	doctī erātis	tractī erātis	captī erātis	audītī erātis
portātī erant	doctī erant	tractī erant	captī erant	audītī erant

FUTURE PERFECT *(I shall/will have been carried, etc.)*

portātus erō	doctus erō	tractus erō	captus erō	audītus erō
portātus eris	doctus eris	tractus eris	captus eris	audītus eris
portātus erit	doctus erit	tractus erit	captus erit	audītus erit
portātī erimus	doctī erimus	tractī erimus	captī erimus	audītī erimus
portātī eritis	doctī eritis	tractī eritis	captī eritis	audītī eritis
portātī erunt	doctī erunt	tractī erunt	captī erunt	audītī erunt

C In Section A, find the Latin for:

they will carry; I was dragging; we had captured; s/he will have taught; you (sg.) are listening; you (pl.) will drag; I shall have listened; they have taught.

D In Section B, find the Latin for:

we are being carried; you (pl.) had been captured; they will be heard; you (sg.) were being dragged; I shall have been taught; he has been captured; you (pl.) will be carried; she is being dragged.

E Notice again that the perfect, pluperfect, and future perfect passive indicative are formed with perfect passive participles, which change their endings to indicate *number* (singular or plural) and *gender* (masculine, feminine, or neuter). For example:

masculine singular:	puer ā mīlitibus **captus** est.
neuter singular:	templum ā mīlitibus **captum** est.
feminine singular:	urbs ā mīlitibus **capta** est.
feminine plural:	multae urbēs ā mīlitibus **captae** sunt.

What would be the Latin for the following?

she has been taught; it had been dragged; they [= the girls] were heard; it has been taken.

F Translate each word. Then, with the help of Section A, change it to the future tense, keeping the same person and number (e.g. 1st person plural) and translate again. For example, **portāmus** (*we carry*) would become **portābimus** (*we shall/will carry*):

portātis, docēbam, capiēbāmus; trahō; audīs; capit, audiēbat.

G Translate each verb form. Then, with the help of Section B, change it from singular to plural, keeping the same person (e.g. 1st person) and translate again. For example, **portor** (*I am being carried*) would become **portāmur** (*we are being carried*):

audior; capiētur; iussus es; circumveniēbātur; oppugnāberis; laesus eram; spernar; līberātus erit; dērīdēbāris; accūsābor.

H Translate each word. Then, with the help of Sections A and B, change it to the passive voice, keeping the same person and number (e.g. 1st person plural) and translate again. For example, **portāmus** (*we carry*) would become **portāmur** (*we are being carried*):

trahit; capiēmus; audīveram; portāverint; docēbās; cēpistis; portābō; trāxerat; capis; docueritis.

Subjunctive

A Active

first conjugation	second conjugation	third conjugation	third "-iō" conjugation	fourth conjugation
IMPERFECT SUBJUNCTIVE				
portārem	docērem	traherem	caperem	audīrem
portārēs	docērēs	traherēs	caperēs	audīrēs
portāret	docēret	traheret	caperet	audīret
portārēmus	docērēmus	traherēmus	caperēmus	audīrēmus
portārētis	docērētis	traherētis	caperētis	audīrētis
portārent	docērent	traherent	caperent	audīrent
PLUPERFECT SUBJUNCTIVE				
portāvissem	docuissem	trāxissem	cēpissem	audīvissem
portāvissēs	docuissēs	trāxissēs	cēpissēs	audīvissēs
portāvisset	docuisset	trāxisset	cēpisset	audīvisset
portāvissēmus	docuissēmus	trāxissēmus	cēpissēmus	audīvissēmus
portāvissētis	docuissētis	trāxissētis	cēpissētis	audīvissētis
portāvissent	docuissent	trāxissent	cēpissent	audīvissent

There are various ways of translating the subjunctive, depending on the way it is being used in a particular sentence (see pages 333–336, Uses of the Subjunctive).

B Complete each sentence with the correct word and then translate.

1 intellegere nōn poteram cūr tū portum (peterēs, peterētis).
2 optiō in fossam dēsiluit ut hastās hostium (vītāret, vītārent).
3 senātor scīre voluit num pater meus (superfuisset, superfuissent).
4 cum senex tergum (vertisset, vertissent), fūrēs per fenestram tacitē intrāvērunt.
5 frātrēs meī nōbīs tandem persuāsērunt ut ānulum aureum (redderem, redderēmus).
6 tanta erat nūbēs ut ego sōlem vidēre nōn (possem, possēmus).
7 Imperātor, cum vōs aulam (intrāvissēs, intrāvissētis), statim effūgit.
8 intellēxī quō modō tū custōdēs (superāvissēs, superāvissētis).
9 Haterius fabrōs hortātus est ut arcum quam celerrimē (cōnficeret, cōnficerent).
10 māter rogāvit ubi nōs īnfantem (invēnissem, invēnissēmus).

Other Forms

A

PRESENT ACTIVE INFINITIVE

portāre	docēre	trahere	capere	audīre
to carry	*to teach*	*to drag*	*to take*	*to hear*

PRESENT PASSIVE INFINITIVE

portārī	docērī	trahī	capī	audīrī
to be carried	*to be taught*	*to be dragged*	*to be taken*	*to be heard*

B

IMPERATIVE

(sg.) portā	docē	trahe	cape	audī
(pl.) portāte	docēte	trahite	capite	audīte
carry!	*teach!*	*drag!*	*take!*	*hear!*

NEGATIVE IMPERATIVE

(sg.)

nōlī portāre	nōlī docēre	nōlī trahere	nōlī capere	nōlī audīre

(pl.)

nōlīte portāre	nōlīte docēre	nōlīte trahere	nōlīte capere	nōlīte audīre
do not carry!	*do not teach!*	*do not drag!*	*do not take!*	*do not listen!*

C

PRESENT ACTIVE PARTICIPLE

portāns	docēns	trahēns	capiēns	audiēns
carrying	*teaching*	*dragging*	*taking*	*hearing*

For the declension of the present participle, see page 329.

D

PERFECT PASSIVE PARTICIPLE

first conjugation	*second conjugation*	*third conjugation*	*third "-iō" conjugation*	*fourth conjugation*
portātus	doctus	tractus	captus	audītus
having been carried	*having been taught*	*having been dragged*	*having been taken*	*having been heard*

Perfect passive participles change their endings in the same way as **bonus**. See also page 299.

E

FUTURE ACTIVE PARTICIPLE

portātūrus	doctūrus	tractūrus	captūrus	audītūrus
about to carry,	*about to teach,*	*about to drag,*	*about to take,*	*about to hear,*
going to carry	*going to teach*	*going to drag*	*going to take*	*going to hear*

Future participles change their endings in the same way as **bonus**. See also page 299.

For examples of ways in which participles are used, see pages 328– 332.

F

GERUNDIVE (sometimes called the Future Passive Participle)

portandus	docendus	trahendus	capiendus	audiendus

Gerundives change their endings in the same way as **bonus**.

Notice again the way in which the gerundive is used:

nōbīs audiendum est.   mihi amphora portanda est.
We must listen.   *I must carry the wine-jar.*

Deponent Verbs

A Indicative

first conjugation	second conjugation	third conjugation	third "-iō" conjugation	fourth conjugation

PRESENT ("I try," etc.)

cōnor	vereor	loquor	ingredior	orior
cōnāris	verēris	loqueris	ingrederis	orīris
cōnātur	verētur	loquitur	ingreditur	orītur
cōnāmur	verēmur	loquimur	ingredimur	orīmur
cōnāminī	verēminī	loquiminī	ingrediminī	orīminī
cōnantur	verentur	loquuntur	ingrediuntur	oriuntur

IMPERFECT ("I was trying," etc.)

cōnābar	verēbar	loquēbar	ingrediēbar	oriēbar
cōnābāris	verēbāris	loquēbāris	ingrediēbāris	oriēbāris
cōnābātur	verēbātur	loquēbātur	ingrediēbātur	oriēbātur
cōnābāmur	verēbāmur	loquēbāmur	ingrediēbāmur	oriēbāmur
cōnābāminī	verēbāminī	loquēbāminī	ingrediēbāminī	oriēbāminī
cōnābantur	verēbantur	loquēbantur	ingrediēbantur	oriēbantur

FUTURE ("I will try," etc.)

cōnābor	verēbor	loquar	ingrediar	oriar
cōnāberis	verēberis	loquēris	ingrediēris	oriēris
cōnābitur	verēbitur	loquētur	ingrediētur	oriētur
cōnābimur	verēbimur	loquēmur	ingrediēmur	oriēmur
cōnābiminī	verēbiminī	loquēminī	ingrediēminī	oriēminī
cōnābuntur	verēbuntur	loquentur	ingredientur	orientur

PERFECT ("I have tried," "I tried," etc.)

cōnātus sum	veritus sum	locūtus sum	ingressus sum	ortus sum
cōnātus es	veritus es	locūtus es	ingressus es	ortus es
cōnātus est	veritus est	locūtus est	ingressus est	ortus est
cōnātī sumus	veritī sumus	locūtī sumus	ingressī sumus	ortī sumus
cōnātī estis	veritī estis	locūtī estis	ingressī estis	ortī estis
cōnātī sunt	veritī sunt	locūtī sunt	ingressī sunt	ortī sunt

PLUPERFECT *("I had tried," etc.)*

cōnātus eram	veritus eram	locūtus eram	ingressus eram	ortus eram
cōnātus erās	veritus erās	locūtus erās	ingressus erās	ortus erās
cōnātus erat	veritus erat	locūtus erat	ingressus erat	ortus erat
cōnātī erāmus	veritī erāmus	locūtī erāmus	ingressī erāmus	ortī erāmus
cōnātī erātis	veritī erātis	locūtī erātis	ingressī erātis	ortī erātis
cōnātī erant	veritī erant	locūtī erant	ingressī erant	ortī erant

FUTURE PERFECT *("I shall/will have tried," etc.)*

cōnātus erō	veritus erō	locūtus erō	ingressus erō	ortus erō
cōnātus eris	veritus eris	locūtus eris	ingressus eris	ortus eris
cōnātus erit	veritus erit	locūtus erit	ingressus erit	ortus erit
cōnātī erimus	veritī erimus	locūtī erimus	ingressī erimus	ortī erimus
cōnātī eritis	veritī eritis	locūtī eritis	ingressī eritis	ortī eritis
cōnātī erunt	veritī erunt	locūtī erunt	ingressī erunt	ortī erunt

Other Forms

B

PRESENT INFINITIVE

cōnārī	verērī	loquī	ingredī	orīrī
to try	*to fear*	*to speak*	*to enter*	*to rise*

C

PRESENT (ACTIVE) PARTICIPLE

cōnāns	verēns	loquēns	ingrediēns	oriēns
trying	*fearing*	*speaking*	*entering*	*rising*

For the forms of the present active participle, see Section C on page 316.

D

PERFECT (ACTIVE) PARTICIPLE

cōnātus	veritus	locūtus	ingressus	ortus
having tried	*having feared*	*having spoken*	*having entered*	*having risen*

Perfect active participles change their endings in the same way as **bonus**. See also page 299.

E

FUTURE (ACTIVE) PARTICIPLE

cōnātūrus	veritūrus	locutūrus	ingressūrus	oritūrus
about to try,	*about to fear,*	*about to speak,*	*about to enter,*	*about to rise,*
going to try	*going to fear*	*going to speak*	*going to enter*	*going to rise*

Future active participles change their endings in the same way as **bonus**. See also page 299.

F

Gerundives change their endings in the same way as **bonus**. For the use of gerundives, see Section F on page 317.

G Give the meaning of:

cōnātus eram; ingrediēbāris; oriuntur; loquēmur; veritī estis; cōnābiminī; vereor; locūtus erit.

H Translate each verb. Then change it from singular to plural, keeping the same person (e.g. 1st person) and translate again. For example, **cōnor** (*"I am trying"*) would become **cōnāmur** (*"we are trying"*):

profectus es; suspicābor; regreditur; precātus erās; ēgressus erit; sequēbar; revertar; nactus est; hortāris; passus eram.

I For further practice with deponent verbs, see Sections H to I on page 341.

Irregular Verbs

A

PRESENT ACTIVE INFINITIVE

esse	posse	īre	velle	ferre
to be	*to be able*	*to go*	*to want*	*to bring*

PRESENT INDICATIVE *(I am, etc.)*

sum	possum	eō	volō	ferō
es	potes	īs	vīs	fers
est	potest	it	vult	fert
sumus	possumus	īmus	volumus	ferimus
estis	potestis	ītis	vultis	fertis
sunt	possunt	eunt	volunt	ferunt

IMPERFECT INDICATIVE *(I was, etc.)*

eram	poteram	ībam	volēbam	ferēbam
erās	poterās	ībās	volēbās	ferēbās
erat	poterat	ībat	volēbat	ferēbat
erāmus	poterāmus	ībāmus	volēbāmus	ferēbāmus
erātis	poterātis	ībātis	volēbātis	ferēbātis
erant	poterant	ībant	volēbant	ferēbant

FUTURE INDICATIVE *(I shall/will be, etc.)*

erō	poterō	ībō	volam	feram
eris	poteris	ībis	volēs	ferēs
erit	poterit	ībit	volet	feret
erimus	poterimus	ībimus	volēmus	ferēmus
eritis	poteritis	ībitis	volētis	ferētis
erunt	poterunt	ībunt	volent	ferent

PERFECT INDICATIVE *(I have been, I was, etc.)*

fuī	potuī	iī	voluī	tulī
fuistī etc.	potuistī etc.	iistī etc.	voluistī etc.	tulistī etc.

PLUPERFECT INDICATIVE *(I had been, etc.)*

fueram	potueram	ieram	volueram	tuleram
fuerās etc.	potuerās etc.	ierās etc.	voluerās etc.	tulerās etc.

FUTURE PERFECT INDICATIVE *(I shall/will have been, etc.)*

fuerō	potuerō	ierō	voluerō	tulerō
fueris etc.	potueris etc.	ieris etc.	volueris etc.	tuleris etc.

B The verbs **nōlle** (*to be unwilling*) and **mālle** (*to prefer*) are compounds of the verb **velle**. Their present indicative forms are somewhat irregular:

nōlō	mālō
nōn vīs	māvīs
nōn vult	māvult
nōlumus	mālumus
nōn vultis	māvultis
nōlunt	mālunt

Other tenses (**nōlēbam**, **mālam**, **nōluī**, etc.) are formed regularly.

C The verb **ferre** also has passive forms:

PRESENT PASSIVE INDICATIVE (*I am carried, I am being carried, etc.*)
feror
ferris
fertur
ferimur
feriminī
feruntur

IMPERFECT PASSIVE INDICATIVE (*I was being carried, etc.*)
ferēbar
ferēbāris etc.

FUTURE PASSIVE INDICATIVE (*I shall/will be carried, etc.*)
ferar
ferēris etc.

PERFECT PASSIVE INDICATIVE (*I have been carried, etc.*)
lātus sum
lātus es etc.

PLUPERFECT PASSIVE INDICATIVE (*I had been carried, etc.*)
lātus eram
lātus erās etc.

FUTURE PERFECT PASSIVE INDICATIVE (*I shall/will have been carried, etc.*)
lātus erō
lātus eris etc.

D The subjunctive forms of irregular verbs follow the usual pattern:

IMPERFECT SUBJUNCTIVE

essem	possem	īrem	vellem	ferrem
essēs etc.	possēs etc.	īrēs etc.	vellēs etc.	ferrēs etc.

PLUPERFECT SUBJUNCTIVE

fuissem	potuissem	iissem	voluissem	tulissem
fuissēs etc.	potuissēs etc.	iissēs etc.	voluissēs etc.	tulissēs etc.

E The following forms also exist:

PRESENT ACTIVE INFINITIVE

esse	posse	īre	velle	ferre

PRESENT PASSIVE INFINITIVE

				ferrī

IMPERATIVE

		ī, īte	(nōlī, nōlīte)	fer, ferte

PRESENT ACTIVE PARTICIPLE

		iēns, euntis	volēns, volentis	ferēns, ferentis

PERFECT PASSIVE PARTICIPLE

				lātus

FUTURE ACTIVE PARTICIPLE

futūrus		itūrus		lātūrus

GERUNDIVE

		eundus		ferendus

F Translate each verb. Then change it from singular to plural, keeping the same person (e.g. 1st person) and translate again. For example, **sum** (*"I am"*) would become **sumus** (*"we are"*):

est; ībō; vīs; ferris; potuit; nōlō; lātus eram; tulerit; mālēs; poteram.

G Translate each verb. Then change it from plural to singular, keeping the same person (e.g. 1st person) and translate again. For example, **sumus** (*"we are"*) would become **sum** (*"I am"*):

ferunt; ībāmus; eritis; māvultis; tulerant; ferēbāminī; potuerāmus; nōlunt; lātī eritis; poterunt.

Uses of the Cases

A *Nominative*

  1 The *nominative case* indicates the subject of a verb:

    captīvus clāmābat.   *The **prisoner** was shouting.*

  2 The *nominative case* also indicates the *subjective completion* of a copulative or linking verb like **esse**. This use is sometimes called a *predicate nominative* or a *subjective complement*:

    Valerius erat **centuriō**.   *Valerius was **a centurion**.*
    līberī erant **laetī**.   *The children were **happy**.*

B *Vocative*

  The *vocative case* indicates a person or thing which is being addressed:

    cūr tacēs, **Cephale**?   *Why are you silent, **Cephalus**?*
    mē audīte, **amīcī**!   *Listen to me, **friends**!*

C *Genitive*

  1 The *genitive case* indicates possession:

    māter **puerōrum** nōbīs dīxit.   *The **boys'** mother spoke to us.*
    templum **deae** intrāvimus.   *We entered the temple **of the goddess**.*

  2 The *partitive genitive* or *genitive of quantity* indicates the whole from which a part is taken:

    Rūfus est optimus **tribūnōrum meōrum**.   *Rufus is the best **of my tribunes**.*
    plūs **pecūniae** volō.   *I want more **money**.*

  3 The *genitive of description* usually refers to non-physical qualities of a person:

    tū es vir **summae prūdentiae**.   *You are a man **of very great common sense**. (You are a **very sensible** man.)*

  4 Another use is the *genitive of indefinite price or value*:

    id **minimī momentī** est.   *That is **of very little importance**.*

D *Dative*

1 The *dative case* indicates the indirect object of a verb:

fēminae togam trādidit.   *He handed **the woman** a toga.*

2 Certain verbs in Latin are completed by a noun in the *dative case*, when the English equivalent uses a direct object:

Imperātōrī semper pārēmus.   *We always obey **the Emperor**.*

3 The *dative of interest* or *reference* indicates a person or thing benefited or harmed:

tibi dōnum habeō.   *I have a gift **for you**.*
mihi tripodas abstulit.   *He stole the tripods **from me**.*

4 The *dative of interest* or *reference* is often combined with a *dative of purpose* in a *double dative* to complete the verb **esse**:

dignitās **mihi** est **cūrae**.   *Prestige is **of concern to me**.*
ōdiō sunt **Hateriō** philosophī.   *Philosophers are **hateful to Haterius**. (**Haterius hates** philosophers.)*

5 The *dative of agent* is used with the *gerundive* + **esse** (*passive periphrastic*) to indicate who must do the action:

mihi festīnandum est.   *I must hurry.*

E *Accusative*

1 The *accusative case* indicates the direct object of a verb:

pontem trānsiimus.   *We crossed **the bridge**.*

2 The *accusative case* is used with certain prepositions:

per **agrōs** ad **vīllam** contendērunt.   *They hurried through **the fields** to **the house**.*

3 The *accusative case* indicates *duration* or *extent of time*:

trēs hōrās labōrābam.   *I worked **for three hours**.*

4 With certain nouns and place names, the *accusative case* without a preposition indicates *place to which*:

domum rediērunt.   *They returned **home**.*
Rōmam pervēnī.   *I arrived **in Rome**.*

F *Ablative*

1 The *ablative case* is used with certain prepositions:

cum **amīcīs** ē **tabernā** discessit.   *He left **the inn** with **friends**.*

2 The *ablative of agent* is used with the preposition **ā/ab** to indicate the doer of an action:

Dumnorix ab **equitibus** interfectus est.   *Dumnorix was killed by **the horsemen**.*

3 The *ablative of means* answers the question, "by what means?":

Salvius **pugiōne** vulnerātus est.   *Salvius was wounded **by a dagger**.*

4 The *ablative of manner* answers the question, "in what manner?":

Simōn **summā (cum) celeritāte** incēdēbat.
*Simon was marching **with the greatest quickness**.*

5 The *ablative of description* usually refers to the physical qualities of a person:

praecō erat homō **malignīs oculīs**.   *The herald was a man **with spiteful eyes**.*

6 The *ablative of source* indicates the origin of someone or something:

hī iuvenēs, **humilī locō** nātī, magnās opēs adeptī erant.
*These young men, born **of lowly stature**, had obtained great riches.*

7 The *ablative of time when* indicates the time at which or within which something happens:

quārtō diē revēnit.   *He came back **on the fourth day**.*

8 The *ablative of measure/degree of difference* indicates by how much someone or something is different from another:

hoc **multō** difficilius est.   *This is **much** more difficult.*

9 The *ablative of respect* indicates in what respect something is true:

architectus **nōmine** Haterius id exstrūxit.   *An architect **named** Haterius built it.*

10 With certain nouns and place names, the *ablative case* without a preposition indicates *place from which*.

domō exiit.　*He left* **home**.
Pompēiīs effūgimus.　*We escaped* **from Pompeii**.

11 *Ablative absolute* phrases are made up of a noun or pronoun plus a participle, adjective, or second noun grammatically disconnected (**absolūtus**) from the rest of the sentence:

Euphrosynē **nōmine audītō** cōnstitit.　*Euphrosyne stopped after* **hearing her name**.
mē auctōre philosopha hūc missa est.　**At my suggestion** *a female philosopher has been sent here*.

G *Locative*

Those nouns and place names which omit the preposition for *place to which* and *place from which* use a form called the *locative* to express *place in which*. For first and second declension singular nouns, the *locative* resembles the *genitive case*. For most third declension nouns and all plural nouns, the *locative* resembles the *ablative case*.

domī manēbās.　*You were staying* **at home**.
Athēnīs habitat.　*He is living* **in Athens**.

H Translate the following sentences:

1 Vitellia, uxor Hateriī, erat fēmina summae patientiae.
2 sextā hōrā Rōmam profectī sumus.
3 rēge mortuō, Salvius multōs mēnsēs per prōvinciam prōcēdēbat, pecūniam opēsque Britannōrum extorquēns.
4 Belimicus, verbīs blandīs dēceptus, in animō volvēbat quod rēgnum multō maius esset imperiō Rōmānō.
5 cōnsilium quod prōposuistī, līberte, nūllō auxiliō mihi erat.
6 dominō meō crēdere nōn possum, quod nimium vīnī rūrsus bibit.
7 multae amīcārum meārum Londiniī per hiemem manent.
8 sī Epaphrodītus aulam cum mīlitibus intrāverit, nōbīs effugiendum erit.

Uses of the Participle

A In Stage 20 you met the *present active participle*:

canis dominum **intrantem** vīdit.
*The dog saw his master **entering**.*

B In Stage 21, you met the *perfect passive participle*:

servus, graviter **vulnerātus**, sub plaustrō iacēbat.
*The slave, (**having been**) seriously **wounded**, was lying under the
cart.*

C In Stage 22, you met the *perfect active participle* of a *deponent verb*:

aegrōtī, deam **precātī**, remedium mīrābile spērābant.
*The invalids, **having prayed** to the goddess, were hoping for a
remarkable cure.*

D Translate the following examples. Find the participle in each
sentence and say whether it is present, perfect passive, or perfect
active/deponent:

1 Latrō, prope iānuam tabernae stāns, pugnam spectābat.
2 Vilbia, ē tabernā ēgressa, sorōrem statim quaesīvit.
3 fūrēs, ad iūdicem ductī, veniam petīvērunt.
4 centuriō, amphoram vīnī optimī adeptus, ad amīcōs celeriter
rediit.
5 subitō equōs appropinquantēs audīvimus.
6 iuvenis callidus pecūniam, in terrā cēlātam, invēnit.

A participle is used to describe a noun. For example, in sentence **1**
above, **stāns** (*standing*) describes **Latrō**. Find the nouns described
by the participles in sentences **2–6**.

E A participle agrees with the noun it describes in three ways: in
case, number, and gender. For example:

nominative:	**rēx**, in mediā turbā **sedēns**, dōna accipiēbat.
accusative:	Quīntus **rēgem**, in mediā turbā **sedentem**, agnōvit.
singular:	**lēgātus**, ad carcerem **regressus**, nēminem ibi invēnit.
plural:	**custōdēs**, ad carcerem **regressī**, nēminem ibi invēnērunt.

masculine:	**nūntius**, statim **profectus**, ad fundum contendit.
feminine:	**uxor**, statim **profecta**, ad fundum contendit.

F Note the forms of the *present participle*:

	singular		plural	
	masc. and fem.	*neuter*	*masc. and fem.*	*neuter*
nominative and vocative	portāns	portāns	portantēs	portantia
genitive	portantis	portantis	portantium	portantium
dative	portantī	portantī	portantibus	portantibus
accusative	portantem	portāns	portantēs	portantia
ablative	portant-ī/-e	portant-ī/-e	portantibus	portantibus

Compare the endings of **portāns** with the endings of the adjective **ingēns** (*huge*), on page 299.

G Note the forms of the *perfect passive participle*:

	singular			plural		
	masculine	*feminine*	*neuter*	*masculine*	*feminine*	*neuter*
nominative and vocative	portātus (portāte)	portāta	portātum	portātī	portātae	portāta
genitive	portātī	portātae	portātī	portātōrum	portātārum	portātōrum
dative	portātō	portātae	portātō	portātīs	portātīs	portātīs
accusative	portātum	portātam	portātum	portātōs	portātās	portāta
ablative	portātō	portātā	portātō	portātīs	portātīs	portātīs

Note the forms of the *perfect active participle*:

	singular			plural		
	masculine	*feminine*	*neuter*	*masculine*	*feminine*	*neuter*
nominative and vocative	cōnātus (cōnāte)	cōnāta	cōnātum	cōnātī	cōnātae	cōnāta
genitive	cōnātī	cōnātae	cōnātī	cōnātōrum	cōnātārum	cōnātōrum
dative	cōnātō	cōnātae	cōnātō	cōnātīs	cōnātīs	cōnātīs
accusative	cōnātum	cōnātam	cōnātum	cōnātōs	cōnātās	cōnāta
ablative	cōnātō	cōnātā	cōnātō	cōnātīs	cōnātīs	cōnātīs

Compare the endings of **portātus** and **cōnātus** with the endings of the adjective **bonus** (*good*), on page 299.

H With the help of Sections F and G above, find the Latin words for the participles in the following sentences:

1 I saw the soldiers **dragging** the slave to prison.
2 The goddess, **having been carried** in procession, watched her sacred boat.
3 The king, **having tried** to escape, faced the bear.

I Notice that a Latin participle can be translated in various ways. For example:

nūntius, aulam ingressus, rēgem quaesīvit.
The messenger, having entered the palace, looked for the king.
After the messenger had entered the palace, he looked for the king.
On entering the palace, the messenger looked for the king.
The messenger entered the palace and looked for the king.

J Translate the following examples and pick out the participle in each sentence:

1 ingēns multitūdō lūdōs, ab imperātōre ēditōs, spectābat.
2 custōdēs captīvō dormientī appropinquāvērunt.
3 mīlitēs, ā centuriōnibus instrūctī, in longīs ōrdinibus stābant.
4 mercātor amīcum, ā Graeciā regressum, ad cēnam sūmptuōsam invītāvit.

Find the nouns described by the participles in the sentences above, and say whether each noun-and-participle pair is nominative, dative, or accusative.

K In Stage 32 you met the *future active participle*:

nōs omnēs **moritūrī** sumus.
We are all going to die.

L Note the forms of the *future active participle*:

	singular			plural		
	masculine	feminine	neuter	masculine	feminine	neuter
nominative and *vocative*	portātūrus (portātūre)	portātūra	portātūrum	portātūrī	portātūrae	portātūra
genitive	portātūrī	portātūrae	portātūrī	portātūrōrum	portātūrārum	portātūrōrum
dative	portātūrō	portātūrae	portātūrō	portātūrīs	portātūrīs	portātūrīs
accusative	portātūrum	portātūram	portātūrum	portātūrōs	portātūrās	portātūra
ablative	portātūrō	portātūrā	portātūrō	portātūrīs	portātūrīs	portātūrīs

Compare the endings of **portātūrus** with the endings of the adjective **bonus** (*good*) on page 299.

M Notice the various translations for the *future active participle*:

senātor rēgem vīsitātūrus erat.
The senator was going to visit the king.
The senator was about to visit the king.
The senator was intending to visit the king.

N Translate the following examples:
1 vōbīs aliam fābulam nārrātūra sum.
2 lēgātus mīlitēs crās adlocūtūrus est.
3 Modestus scīre volēbat quod cōnsilium lībertus datūrus esset.
4 senātor rogāvit quandō iuvenēs plaustrum refectūrī essent.
5 Rōmam quam celerrimē regressūrī sumus.
6 Domitia in animō volvēbat num Epaphrodītus Paridem inventūrus esset.

O Since Stage 30 we have met examples of participles used as nouns:

tōta ārea strepitū **labōrantium** plēna erat.
*The whole construction site was filled with the sound **of workers** (of working ones).*

Further examples:
1 multitūdō adōrantium templō appropinquāvit.
2 senex manūs ad praetereuntēs porrigēbat.
3 decōrum est victōribus victīs parcere.
4 corpus ā dolentibus circumventum est.

P In Stage 31, you met examples of the *ablative absolute*, consisting of a noun and participle in the ablative case:

bellō cōnfectō, Agricola ad Ītaliam rediit.
With the war having been finished, Agricola returned to Italy.
Or, in more natural English:
When the war had been finished, Agricola returned to Italy, or
After finishing the war, Agricola returned to Italy.

Further examples:

1 ponte dēlētō, nēmō flūmen trānsīre poterat.
2 hīs verbīs audītīs, cīvēs plausērunt.
3 nāve refectā, mercātor ā Britanniā discessit.
4 iuvenēs, togīs dēpositīs, balneum intrāvērunt.
5 cōnsule ingrediente, omnēs senātōrēs surrēxērunt.
6 fēle absente, mūrēs semper lūdunt.

Q From Stage 31 onwards, you have met examples in which a noun and participle in the *dative* case are placed at the beginning of the sentence:

amīcō auxilium petentī multam pecūniam obtulī.
To a friend asking for help I offered a lot of money.
Or, in more natural English:
When my friend asked for help I offered him a lot of money.

Further examples:

1 servō haesitantī Vitellia "intrā!" inquit.
2 Hateriō haec rogantī Salvius nihil respondit.
3 praecōnī regressō senex epistulam trādidit.
4 puellae prōcēdentī obstābat ingēns multitūdō clientium.

Uses of the Subjunctive

A *With* **cum** (meaning *when*)

Iūdaeī, cum cōnsilium Eleazārī audīvissent, libenter cōnsēnsērunt.
When the Jews had heard Eleazar's plan, they willingly agreed.

Further examples:

1 Agricola, cum legiōnem īnspēxisset, mīlitēs centuriōnēsque
   laudāvit.
2 cum haruspex in templō cēnāret, rēx ipse appropinquābat.
3 fabrī, cum pecūniam accēpissent, abiērunt.
4 fūr, cum amulētum ē fonte extrāxisset, attonitus erat.
5 iuvenis, cum omnēs Imperātōrem spectārent, cultrum rapuit.
6 ego, cum captīvōs custōdīrēs, cēnam magnificam
   cōnsūmēbam.

B *Indirect Question*

cōnsul nesciēbat quis arcum novum aedificāvisset.
The consul did not know who had built the new arch.
mē rogāvērunt num satis pecūniae habērem.
They asked me whether I had enough money.

From Stage 28 onwards, you have met the words **utrum** and **an** in
indirect questions:

incertī erant utrum dux mortuus an vīvus esset.
They were unsure whether their leader was dead or alive.

Further examples:

1 incertus eram quam longum esset flūmen. (Compare this with
   the direct question: "quam longum est flūmen?")
2 cognōscere voluimus cūr multitūdō convēnisset. (Compare
   this with the direct question: "cūr multitūdō convēnit?")
3 equitēs fēminās rogāvērunt num fugitīvōs vīdissent.
   (Compare this with the direct question: "fugitīvōsne
   vīdistis?")
4 nēmō sciēbat num Memor lībertō venēnum praebuisset.
5 Rōmānī nesciēbant quot hostēs in castrīs manērent.
6 mē rogāvit utrum māter mea vīveret an Pompēiīs periisset.

C *Purpose Clause*

ad urbem iter fēcimus ut amphitheātrum vīsitārēmus.
We traveled to the city in order to visit the amphitheater.

Further examples:

1 amīcī ad urbem festīnāvērunt ut auxilium cīvibus ferrent.
2 epistulam scrīpsī ut lēgātum dē perīculō monērem.
3 senātor mē arcessīvit ut rem hospitibus nārrārem.

In Stage 29, you met purpose clauses used with the relative pronoun **quī**:

nūntiōs ēmīsit quī prīncipēs ad aulam arcesserent.
He sent out messengers who were to summon the chieftains to the palace.
   Or, in more natural English:
He sent out messengers to summon the chieftains to the palace.

This use of the subjunctive also involves the adverbs **ubi**, **quō**, and **unde**.

Salvius locum quaerēbat ubi cōnspicuus esset.
Salvius was looking for a place where he might be conspicuous.

Since Stage 29, you have met purpose clauses used with **nē**:

centuriō omnēs portās clausit nē captīvī effugerent.
The centurion shut all the gates so that the prisoners would not escape.

Since Stage 33, you have met the subjunctive used with **priusquam** (*before*) and **dum** (*until*):

Myropnous iānuam clausit priusquam mīlitēs intrārent.
Myropnous shut the door before the soldiers could enter.
exspectābam dum amīcus advenīret.
I was waiting until my friend should arrive.
   Or, in more natural English:
I was waiting for my friend to arrive.

Further examples:

4 duās cohortēs ēlēgit quae Quīntum quaererent.
5 captīvōs dīligenter numerāvimus nē errārēmus.
6 ad castra celeriter regressus es priusquam lēgātus tē
   vituperāret.
7 imperātor Salvium ad Britanniam mīsit unde dīvitiās
   remitteret.

D *Indirect Command*

Domitiānus Salviō imperāverat ut rēgnum Cogidubnī occupāret.
Domitian had ordered Salvius to seize Cogidubnus' kingdom.

Further examples:

1 nūntius Britannīs persuāsit ut dōna ad aulam ferrent.
  (Compare the direct command: "dōna ad aulam ferte!")
2 dominus nōbīs imperāvit ut sellās lectōsque emerēmus.
  (Compare this with the direct command: "sellās lectōsque
  emite!")
3 senex deam Sūlem ōrāvit ut morbum sānāret.

In Stage 29, you met indirect commands introduced by **nē**:

puer agricolam ōrāvit nē equum occīderet.
The boy begged the farmer not to kill the horse.
Haterius ab amīcīs monitus est nē Salviō cōnfīderet.
Haterius was warned by friends not to trust Salvius.

Further examples:

4 magister fabrōs hortābātur nē opus dēsineret.
5 fēminae ōrābant nē līberīs nocērēmus.
6 nōnne rogātī estis nē comitēs dēsererētis?

E *Result Clause*

tam perītus erat tībīcen ut omnēs eum laudārent.
The pipe player was so skillful that everyone praised him.

Further examples:

1 tam dīligenter carcerem custōdīvī ut lēgātus ipse mē laudāret.
2 mercātor tot vīllās habēbat ut eās numerāre nōn posset.
3 tantus erat timor iuvenum ut astrologō crēderent.
4 Haterius adeō cupiēbat agellum accipere ut pretium
  rīdiculum offerret.
5 tantus erat clāmor ut nēmō verba mea audīret.
6 tam celerēs erant nāvēs ut ad īnsulam ante noctem
  pervenīrēmus.

F If you want to understand why a subjunctive is being used in a particular sentence, you must look at the whole sentence, not just the subjunctive by itself.

For example, study these two sentences; one contains a *purpose* clause, and the other contains a *result* clause:

1 tam īrātus erat Agricola ut dormīre nōn posset.
   Agricola was so angry that he could not sleep.
2 Belimicus per silvās quaerēbat ut Quīntum invenīret.
   Belimicus was searching through the woods to find Quintus.

Sentence **1** clearly contains the result clause; Agricola's failure to sleep was the *result* of his anger. The word **tam** (*so*) is a further clue; it is often followed by a result clause later in the sentence. Other words like **tam** are **tantus** (*so great*), **tot** (*so many*), and **adeō** (*so* or *so much*).

Sentence **2** clearly contains the purpose clause; finding Quintus was Belimicus' *purpose* in searching the crowds.

G Translate the following examples:

1 lībertus, cum venēnum bibisset, mortuus prōcubuit.
2 tot hostēs castra nostra oppugnābant ut dē vītā dēspērārēmus.
3 prīncipēs mē rogāvērunt cūr pontem trānsīre vellem.
4 Gutta sub mēnsā sē cēlāvit ut perīculum vītāret.
5 centuriōnēs mīlitibus imperāvērunt ut plaustra reficerent.
6 cum ancillae pōcula lavārent, quattuor equitēs ad tabernam advēnērunt.
7 adeō attonitus erat fīlius meus ut diū immōtus stāret.
8 portās cellārum aperuimus ut amīcōs nostrōs līberārēmus.
9 amīcus mē monuit ut latērem.
10 Modestus explicāre nōn poterat quō modō captīvī effūgissent.
11 cum servī vīnum intulissent, Haterius silentium poposcit.
12 tanta erat fortitūdō Iūdaeōrum ut perīre potius quam cēdere māllent.
13 nēmō sciēbat utrum Haterius an Salvius rem administrāvisset.
14 uxor mihi persuāsit nē hoc susciperem.
15 extrā carcerem stābant decem mīlitēs quī captīvōs custōdīrent.

For each sentence, give the reason why a subjunctive is being used.

Word Order

A In Unit 1, you met the following word order:

dēspērābat senex. *The old man was in despair.*

Further examples:

1 fugit Modestus.   2 revēnērunt mercātōrēs.

B Since Stage 21, you have met the following word order:

dedit signum haruspex. *The soothsayer gave the signal.*

Further examples:

1 rapuērunt pecūniam fūrēs.   2 īnspiciēbat mīlitēs Agricola.

C Since Stage 23, you have met the following word order:

ēmīsit Salvius equitēs. *Salvius sent out horsemen.*

Further examples:

1 tenēbat Cephalus pōculum.   2 posuērunt cīvēs statuam.

D Further examples of all three types of word order:

1 discessit nūntius.   4 poposcit captīvus lībertātem.
2 fēcērunt hostēs impetum.   5 vexābant mē puerī.
3 reficiēbat mūrum faber.   6 periērunt īnfantēs.

E Study the word order in the following examples:

in hāc prōvinciā   ad nostrum patrem
in this province   *to our father*

You have also met a different word order:

mediīs in undīs   hanc ad tabernam
in the middle of the waves   *to this shop*

Further examples:

1 hāc in urbe   4 omnibus cum legiōnibus
2 multīs cum mīlitibus   5 tōtam per noctem
3 parvum ad oppidum   6 mediō in flūmine

Longer Sentences

A Study the following groups of sentences:

  1 puerī timēbant.
    The boys were afraid.
    puerī timēbant quod prope iānuam iacēbat ingēns canis.
    The boys were afraid because near the door was lying a huge dog.
    puerī timēbant quod prope iānuam iacēbat ingēns canis,
    vehementer latrāns.
    The boys were afraid because near the door was lying a huge dog,
    barking loudly.

  2 Strȳthiōnem cōnspexit.
    He caught sight of Strythio.
    ubi ā culīnā redībat, Strȳthiōnem cōnspexit.
    When he was returning from the kitchen, he caught sight of
Strythio.
    ubi ā culīnā in quā cēnāverat redībat, Strȳthiōnem cōnspexit.
    When he was returning from the kitchen in which he had been
    dining, he caught sight of Strythio.

B Further examples:

  3 Salvius incertus erat.
    Salvius incertus erat quō fūgisset Dumnorix.
    Salvius incertus erat quō fūgisset Dumnorix, cūr abesset
    Quīntus.

  4 centuriō immōtus manēbat.
    centuriō immōtus manēbat, quamquam appropinquābant
    hostēs.
    centuriō immōtus manēbat, quamquam appropinquābant
    hostēs, quī hastās vibrābant.

  5 omnēs cīvēs plausērunt.
    ubi puellae cantāre coepērunt, omnēs cīvēs plausērunt.
    ubi puellae quae prō pompā ambulābant cantāre coepērunt,
    omnēs cīvēs plausērunt.

  6 nūntius prīncipia petīvit.
    nūntius quī epistulam ferēbat prīncipia petīvit.
    nūntius quī epistulam ferēbat, simulac ad castra advēnit,
    prīncipia petīvit.

C Further examples of the longer type of sentences:

1 tantae erant flammae ut vīllam magnam dēlērent, quam architectus clārus aedificāverat.
2 lībertus cubiculum intrāre nōlēbat quod Memor, quī multum vīnum biberat, graviter iam dormiēbat.
3 Agricola, Belimicō diffīsus, tribūnum arcessīvit ut vērum cognōsceret.
4 postquam ad forum vēnimus, ubi mercātōrēs negōtium agere solēbant, rem mīrābilem vīdimus.
5 pater, cum fīliōs pōcula haurientēs cōnspexisset, vehementer saeviēbat.
6 explōrātōrēs mox cognōvērunt ubi hostēs castra posuissent, quot mīlitēs in castrīs essent, quis mīlitibus praeesset.

D Study each sentence and answer the questions that follow it:

1 postquam Haterius fabrōs, quī labōrābant in āreā, dīmīsit, Salvius negōtium agere coepit.
Where were the craftsmen working? What did Haterius do to them? What did Salvius then do? Translate the sentence.
2 spectātōrēs, cum candēlābrum aureum ē templō Iūdaeōrum raptum cōnspexissent, iterum iterumque plaudēbant.
What did the spectators catch sight of? Where had it been seized? What was the reaction of the spectators? Translate the sentence.
3 fūr, cum verba centuriōnis audīvisset, tantō metū poenārum affectus est ut pecūniam quam ē tabernā abstulerat, statim abicere cōnstitueret.
What did the thief hear? What were his feelings? What did he decide to do? Where had the money come from? Translate the sentence.

E Further examples for study and translation:

1 ancillae, quod dominam vehementer clāmantem audīvērunt, cubiculum eius quam celerrimē petīvērunt.
2 equitēs adeō pugnāre cupiēbant ut, simulac dux signum dedit, ē portīs castrōrum ērumperent.
3 postquam cōnsul hanc sententiam dīxit, Domitiānus servō adstantī imperāvit ut epistulam ab Agricolā nūper missam recitāret.

Part Two: Complete Vocabulary

A Nouns are listed in the following way:

> nominative, genitive, and gender

B Adjectives are listed in the following way:

> the masculine, feminine, and neuter nominative singular
> the genitive singular, if necessary to show the stem

C Prepositions used with the ablative, such as **ex**, are marked (+ ABL); those used with the accusative, such as **per**, are marked (+ ACC).

D Verbs are usually listed in the following way:

- the 1st person singular of the present active indicative, e.g. **pōnō** (*I place*);
- the present active infinitive, e.g. **pōnere** (*to place*);
- the 1st person singular of the perfect active indicative, e.g. **posuī** (*I placed*);
- the perfect passive participle, e.g. **positus** (*having been placed*);
- any special information, such as (+ DAT);
- the meaning, e.g. *place*.

Dictionaries often list the fourth part of the verb in **-um**. This is called the *supine*, a form that will be explained in Unit 4. Some verbs which have a supine may not have a perfect passive participle. If so, we have not given the fourth principal part in this vocabulary.

E Study the following examples of verbs. They are listed in the way described in Section D. Notice particularly the patterns in which the different conjugations form their principal parts:

1st conjugation
amō, amāre, amāvī, amātus *love, like*
laudō, laudāre, laudāvī, laudātus *praise*

2nd conjugation
moneō, monēre, monuī, monitus *warn*
praebeō, praebēre, praebuī, praebitus *provide*

3rd conjugation
Verbs of the 3rd conjugation form their perfect active indicative and perfect passive participle in several different ways that are not always predictable. Here are some of the ways:

claudō, claudere, clausī, clausus *shut, close*
dūcō, dūcere, dūxī, ductus *lead*
frangō, frangere, frēgī, frāctus *break*

3rd conjugation ("-iō")
faciō, facere, fēcī, factus *do, make*
rapiō, rapere, rapuī, raptus *seize*

4th conjugation
custōdiō, custōdīre, custōdīvī, custōdītus *guard*
impediō, impedīre, impedīvī, impedītus *hinder*

F Use Section E to find the meaning of:

amāvī; laudātus; monēre; praebitus; dūxī; frēgī; frāctus; facere; rapiō; custōdīre; impedītus.

G Deponent verbs (met and explained in Stage 32) are listed in the following way:

- the 1st person singular of the present indicative. This always ends in **-or**, e.g. **cōnor** (*I try*).
- the present infinitive. This always ends in **-ī**, e.g. **cōnārī** (*to try*);
- the 1st person singular of the perfect indicative, e.g. **cōnātus sum** (*I tried*);
- the meaning, e.g. *try*.

So, if the following principal parts are given:

loquor, loquī, locūtus sum *speak*
loquor means *I speak*, **loquī** means *to speak*, **locūtus sum** means *I spoke*.

H Study the following deponent verbs, listed in the way described in Section G:

cōnspicor, cōnspicārī, cōnspicātus sum *catch sight of*
ingredior, ingredī, ingressus sum *enter*
lābor, lābī, lāpsus sum *fall*

Give the meaning of:

cōnspicor, ingredī, lāpsus sum, ingredior, cōnspicātus sum, lābī.

I Use pages 342–369 to find the meaning of:

ēgredior, hortātus sum, pollicērī, sequor, minārī, adeptus sum.

J All words which are given in the **Vocabulary Checklists** for Stages 1–34 are marked with an asterisk (*).

a

* ā, ab (+ ABL) *from; by*
   ab epistulīs *in charge of correspondence*
   ā libellīs *in charge of petitions*
   ā ratiōnibus *in charge of accounts*
   abdūcō, abdūcere, abdūxī, abductus
      lead away
*abeō, abīre, abiī *go away*
   abhinc *ago*
   abhorreō, abhorrēre, abhorruī *shrink
      (from)*
   abigō, abigere, abēgī, abāctus *drive
      away*
   absēns, absēns, absēns, *gen.* absentis
      absent
   absentia, absentiae, f. *absence*
* abstulī SEE auferō
* absum, abesse, āfuī *be out, be absent, be
      away*
   absurdus, absurda, absurdum *absurd*
* ac *and*
* accidō, accidere, accidī *happen*
* accipiō, accipere, accēpī, acceptus
      accept, take in, receive
   accurrō, accurrere, accurrī *run up*
* accūsō, accūsāre, accūsāvī, accūsātus
      accuse
* ācriter *keenly, eagerly, fiercely*
* āctus SEE agō
* ad (+ ACC) *to, at*
* addō, addere, addidī, additus *add*
   addūcō, addūcere, addūxī, adductus
      lead, lead on, encourage
* adeō, adīre, adiī *approach, go up to*
* adeō *so much, so greatly*
* adeptus, adepta, adeptum *having
      obtained, having received*
* adest SEE adsum
   adhibeō, adhibēre, adhibuī, adhibitus
      use, apply
      precēs adhibēre *offer prayers to*
* adhūc *until now*
* adipīscor, adipīscī, adeptus sum *receive,
      obtain*
   aditus, aditūs, m. *entrance*
* adiuvō, adiuvāre, adiūvī *help*
   adligō, adligāre, adligāvī, adligātus *tie*
   adloquor, adloquī, adlocūtus sum *speak
      to, address*

* administrō, administrāre, administrāvī,
      administrātus *look after, manage*
   rem administrāre *manage the task*
   admīrātiō, admīrātiōnis, f. *admiration*
   admīror, admīrārī, admīrātus sum
      admire
   admittō, admittere, admīsī, admissus
      admit, let in
   adōrō, adōrāre, adōrāvī, adōrātus
      worship
   adstō, adstāre, adstitī *stand by*
* adsum, adesse, adfuī *be here, be present*
* adveniō, advenīre, advēnī *arrive*
* adventus, adventūs, m. *arrival*
* adversus, adversa, adversum *hostile,
      unfavorable*
*   rēs adversae *misfortune*
   advesperāscit, advesperāscere,
      advesperāvit *get dark, become dark*
* aedificium, aedificiī, n. *building*
* aedificō, aedificāre, aedificāvī,
      aedificātus *build*
* aeger, aegra, aegrum *sick, ill*
   aegrōtus, aegrōtī, m. *invalid*
   Aegyptius, Aegyptia, Aegyptium
      Egyptian
   Aegyptus, Aegyptī, f. *Egypt*
* aequus, aequa, aequum *fair, calm*
*   aequō animō *calmly, in a calm spirit*
   aeternus, aeterna, aeternum *eternal*
   Aethiopes, Aethiopum, m.pl.
      Ethiopians
   afferō, afferre, attulī, adlātus *bring*
* afficiō, afficere, affēcī, affectus *affect*
      affectus, affecta, affectum *overcome,
         struck*
   afflīgō, afflīgere, afflīxī, afflīctus *afflict,
      hurt*
   agellus, agellī, m. *small plot of land*
   ager, agrī, m. *field*
   agger, aggeris, m. *ramp, mound of earth*
   aggressus, aggressa, aggressum *having
      attacked*
* agitō, agitāre, agitāvī, agitātus *chase,
      hunt*
* agmen, agminis, n. *column (of people),
      procession*
   agna, agnae, f. *lamb*
* agnōscō, agnōscere, agnōvī, agnitus
      recognize

* agō, agere, ēgī, āctus   *do, act*
   āctum est dē nōbīs   *it's all over for us*
   age!   *come on!*
*   fābulam agere   *act in a play*
*   grātiās agere   *thank, give thanks*
*   negōtium agere   *do business, work*
   officium agere   *do one's duty*
   persōnam agere   *play a part*
   vītam agere   *lead a life*
* agricola, agricolae, m.   *farmer*
  alacriter   *eagerly*
  ālea, āleae, f.   *dice*
* aliquandō   *sometimes*
  aliquī, aliquae, aliqua   *some*
* aliquis, aliquid   *someone, something*
  aliquid mīrī   *something extraordinary*
* alius, alia, aliud   *other, another, else*
*   alius … alius   *one … another*
*   aliī … aliī   *some … others*
* alter, altera, alterum   *the other, another,*
    a second, the second
   alter … alter   *one … the other*
* altus, alta, altum   *high, deep*
  amārus, amāra, amārum   *bitter*
* ambō, ambae, ambō   *both*
* ambulō, ambulāre, ambulāvī   *walk*
  āmēns, āmēns, āmēns, *gen.* āmentis   *out*
   of one's mind, in a frenzy
  amīcitia, amīcitiae, f.   *friendship*
* amīcus, amīcī, m.   *friend*
* āmittō, āmittere, āmīsī, āmissus   *lose*
* amō, amāre, amāvī, amātus   *love, like*
* amor, amōris, m.   *love*
  amphitheātrum, amphitheātrī, n.
   amphitheater
  Amphitheātrum Flāvium   *Flavian*
   Amphitheater
  amphora, amphorae, f.   *wine-jar*
* amplector, amplectī, amplexus sum
   embrace
* amplexus, amplexa, amplexum   *having*
   embraced
  amplissimus, amplissima, amplissimum
   very great
  amputō, amputāre, amputāvī, amputātus
   cut off
  amulētum, amulētī, n.   *amulet, lucky*
   charm
  an   *or*
   utrum … an   *whether … or*

* ancilla, ancillae, f.   *slave-girl, slave-*
  woman
  angelus, angelī, m.   *angel*
  angulus, angulī, m.   *corner*
* angustus, angusta, angustum   *narrow*
  animadvertō, animadvertere,
   animadvertī, animadversus   *notice,*
   take notice of
* animus, animī, m.   *spirit, soul, mind*
*   aequō animō   *calmly, in a calm spirit*
   in animō habēre   *have in mind, intend*
*   in animō volvere   *wonder, turn over in*
   the mind
* annus, annī, m.   *year*
* ante (+ ACC)   *before, in front of*
* anteā   *before*
  antīquus, antīqua, antīquum   *old, ancient*
* ānulus, ānulī, m.   *ring*
  anus, anūs, f.   *old woman*
  anxius, anxia, anxium   *anxious*
  aper, aprī, m.   *boar*
* aperiō, aperīre, aperuī, apertus   *open*
  apertē   *openly*
  apodytērium, apodytēriī, n.   *changing-*
   room
* appāreō, appārēre, appāruī   *appear*
* appellō, appellāre, appellāvī, appellātus
   call, call out to
* appropinquō, appropinquāre,
   appropinquāvī (+ DAT)   *approach,*
   come near to
  aptus, apta, aptum   *suitable*
* apud (+ ACC)   *among, at the house of*
* aqua, aquae, f.   *water*
  Aquae Sūlis, Aquārum Sūlis, f.pl.   *Aquae*
   Sulis (modern Bath)
  aquila, aquilae, f.   *eagle; standard (of a*
   legion)
  aquilifer, aquiliferī, m.   *standard-bearer*
   (of a legion)
* āra, ārae, f.   *altar*
  arānea, arāneae, f.   *spider, spider's web*
  arbiter, arbitrī, m.   *expert, judge*
  arca, arcae, f.   *strong-box, chest*
* arcessō, arcessere, arcessīvī, arcessītus
   summon, send for
  architectus, architectī, m.   *builder,*
   architect
  arcus, arcūs, m.   *arch*
* ardeō, ardēre, arsī   *burn, be on fire*

ardor, ardōris, m.   *spirit, enthusiasm*
ārea, āreae, f.   *courtyard, construction site*
argenteus, argentea, argenteum   *made of silver*
arma, armōrum, n.pl.   *arms, weapons*
armārium, armāriī, n.   *chest, cupboard*
armātus, armāta, armātum   *armed*
* arrogantia, arrogantiae, f.   *arrogance, gall*
* ars, artis, f.   *art, skill*
artifex, artificis, m.   *artist, craftsman*
as, assis, m.   *as (small coin)*
* ascendō, ascendere, ascendī   *climb, rise*
asinus, asinī, m.   *ass, donkey*
aspiciō, aspicere, aspexī   *look towards*
astrologus, astrologī, m.   *astrologer*
* at   *but*
Athēnae, Athēnārum, f.pl.   *Athens*
    Athēnīs   *at Athens*
* atque   *and*
* ātrium, ātriī, n.   *atrium, reception hall*
* attonitus, attonita, attonitum   *astonished*
* auctor, auctōris, m.   *creator, originator, person responsible*
*   mē auctōre   *at my suggestion*
* auctōritās, auctōritātis, f.   *authority*
* auctus SEE augeō
* audācia, audāciae, f.   *boldness, audacity*
audācter   *boldly*
* audāx, audāx, audāx, gen. audācis   *bold, daring*
* audeō, audēre   *dare*
ausim   *I would dare*
* audiō, audīre, audīvī, audītus   *hear, listen to*
* auferō, auferre, abstulī, ablātus   *take away, steal*
* augeō, augēre, auxī, auctus   *increase*
augur, auguris, m.   *augur*
* aula, aulae, f.   *palace*
* aureus, aurea, aureum   *golden, made of gold*
aurīga, aurīgae, m.   *charioteer*
* auris, auris, f.   *ear*
ausim SEE audeō
* autem   *but*
* auxilium, auxiliī, n.   *help*
avāritia, avāritiae, f.   *greed*
* avārus, avārī, m.   *miser*
avē atque valē   *hail and farewell*
avia, aviae, f.   *grandmother*

* avidē   *eagerly*
avidus, avida, avidum   *eager*
* avis, avis, f.   *bird*

b

balneum, balneī, n.   *bath*
barba, barbae, f.   *beard*
barbarus, barbara, barbarum   *barbarian*
* barbarus, barbarī, m.   *barbarian*
basilica, basilicae, f.   *lawcourt, commercial exchange; great hall (of a military camp)*
Beelzebub, m.   *Beelzebub, the Devil*
* bellum, bellī, n.   *war*
*   bellum gerere   *wage war, campaign*
* bene   *well*
bene merēns   *well deserving, deserving kindness*
*   optimē   *very well*
* beneficium, beneficiī, n.   *act of kindness, favor*
benignē   *kindly*
* benignus, benigna, benignum   *kind*
bēstia, bēstiae, f.   *wild animal, beast*
* bibō, bibere, bibī   *drink*
blanditiae, blanditiārum, f.pl.   *flatteries*
blandus, blanda, blandum   *flattering, charming, enticing*
* bonus, bona, bonum   *good*
bona, bonōrum, n.pl.   *goods*
*   melior, melius   *better*
melius est   *it would be better*
*   optimus, optima, optimum   *very good, excellent, best*
optimus quisque   *all the best people*
bracchium, bracchiī, n.   *arm*
brevī   *in a short time*
* brevis, brevis, breve   *short, brief*
Britannī, Britannōrum, m.pl.   *Britons*
Britannia, Britanniae, f.   *Britain*
Britannicus, Britannica, Britannicum   *British*

c

C. = Gāius
caballus, caballī, m.   *nag, horse*
cachinnō, cachinnāre, cachinnāvī   *laugh, cackle*

cadō, cadere, cecidī *fall*
caecus, caeca, caecum *blind*
* caedō, caedere, cecīdī, caesus *kill*
* caelum, caelī, n. *sky, heaven*
calceus, calceī, m. *shoe*
Calēdonia, Calēdoniae, f. *Scotland*
caligae, caligārum, f.pl. *military sandals*
calliditās, calliditātis, f. *cleverness,
    shrewdness*
* callidus, callida, callidum *clever,
    smart*
campus, campī, m. *plain, field*
candēlābrum, candēlābrī, n. *lampstand,
    candelabrum*
candidātus, candidātī, m. *candidate*
* canis, canis, m. *dog; the lowest throw at
    dice*
* cantō, cantāre, cantāvī *sing, chant*
    tībiīs cantāre *play on the pipes*
capillī, capillōrum, m.pl. *hair*
* capiō, capere, cēpī, captus *take, catch,
    capture*
    cōnsilium capere *make a plan, have an
    idea*
Capitōlium, Capitōliī, n. *Capitol*
captīva, captīvae, f. *(female) prisoner,
    captive*
* captīvus, captīvī, m. *prisoner, captive*
* caput, capitis, n. *head*
* carcer, carceris, m. *prison*
* carmen, carminis, n. *song*
carnifex, carnificis, m. *executioner*
* cārus, cāra, cārum *dear*
casa, casae, f. *small house, cottage*
castellum, castellī, n. *fort*
* castīgō, castīgāre, castīgāvī, castīgātus
    scold, nag
* castra, castrōrum, n.pl. *military camp*
    praefectus castrōrum *commander of
    the camp*
* cāsus, cāsūs, m. *misfortune*
* catēna, catēnae, f. *chain*
caudex, caudicis, m. *blockhead, idiot*
caupō, caupōnis, m. *innkeeper*
causa, causae, f. *reason, cause*
cautē *cautiously*
caveo, cavēre, cāvī *beware*
cecidī SEE cadō
cecīdī SEE caedō
* cēdō, cēdere, cessī *give in, yield*

* celebrō, celebrāre, celebrāvī, celebrātus
    celebrate
celer, celeris, celere *quick, fast*
    celerrimus, celerrima, celerrimum
    very fast
* celeriter *quickly, fast*
    celerrimē *very quickly, very fast*
    quam celerrimē *as quickly as possible*
cella, cellae, f. *cell, sanctuary*
cellārius, cellāriī, m. *(house) steward*
* cēlō, cēlāre, cēlāvī, cēlātus *hide*
* cēna, cēnae, f. *dinner*
* cēnō, cēnāre, cēnāvī *eat dinner, dine*
* centum *a hundred*
* centuriō, centuriōnis, m. *centurion*
* cēpī SEE capiō
* cēra, cērae, f. *wax, wax tablet*
* certāmen, certāminis, n. *struggle,
    contest, fight*
certē *certainly*
* certo, certāre, certāvī *compete*
certus, certa, certum *certain, infallible*
    prō certō habēre *know for certain*
* cessī SEE cēdō
* cēterī, cēterae, cētera *the others, the rest*
Chrīstiānī, Chrīstiānōrum, m.pl.
    Christians
* cibus, cibī, m. *food*
cingulum, cingulī, n. *military belt*
* cinis, cineris, m. *ash*
circā (+ ACC) *around*
circiter (+ ACC) *about*
circulus, circulī, m. *hoop*
* circum (+ ACC) *around*
* circumspectō, circumspectāre,
    circumspectāvī *look around*
* circumveniō, circumvenīre, circumvēnī,
    circumventus *surround*
circus, circī, m. *circus, stadium*
Circus Maximus *Circus Maximus*
citharoedus, citharoedī, m. *cithara
    player*
* cīvis, cīvis, m.f. *citizen*
clādēs, clādis, f. *disaster*
clām *secretly, in private*
* clāmō, clāmāre, clāmavī *shout*
* clāmor, clāmōris, m. *shout, uproar,
    racket*
* clārus, clāra, clārum *famous,
    distinguished*

* claudō, claudere, clausī, clausus *shut,*
    close, block, conclude, complete
clēmēns, clēmēns, clēmēns, *gen.*
    clēmentis *merciful*
* cliens, clientis, m. *client*
cloāca, cloācae, f. *drain*
    Cloāca Maxima *Cloaca Maxima (the*
    great sewer in Rome)
Cn. = Gnaeus
* coepī *I began*
* cōgitō, cōgitāre, cōgitāvī *think, consider*
    rem cōgitāre *consider the problem*
    sēcum cōgitāre *consider to oneself*
* cognōscō, cognōscere, cognōvī, cognitus
    find out, get to know
* cōgō, cōgere, coēgī, coāctus *force,*
    compel
* cohors, cohortis, f. *cohort*
* colligō, colligere, collēgī, collēctus
    gather, collect, assemble
* collocō, collocāre, collocāvī, collocātus
    place, put
* colloquium, colloquiī, n. *talk, chat*
colō, colere, coluī, cultus *seek favor of,*
    make friends with
columba, columbae, f. *dove, pigeon*
columna, columnae, f. *pillar*
* comes, comitis, m.f. *comrade, companion*
cōmiter *politely, courteously*
* comitor, comitārī, comitātus sum
    accompany
    comitāns, comitāns, comitāns, *gen.*
    comitantis *accompanying*
commeātus, commeātūs, m. *(military)*
    leave
* commemorō, commemorāre,
    commemorāvī, commemorātus
    talk about, mention, recall
commendō, commendāre, commendāvī,
    commendātus *recommend*
committō, committere, commīsī,
    commissus *commit, begin*
* commodus, commoda, commodum
    convenient
* commōtus, commōta, commōtum
    moved, upset, affected, alarmed, excited,
    distressed, overcome
* comparō, comparāre, comparāvī,
    comparātus *obtain*
compitum, compitī, n. *crossroads*

* compleō, complēre, complēvī, complētus
    fill
compluvium, compluviī, n. *compluvium*
    (opening in roof of atrium)
* compōnō, compōnere, composuī,
    compositus *put together, arrange,*
    settle, mix, make up
    compositus, composita, compositum
    composed, steady
* comprehendō, comprehendere,
    comprehendī, comprehēnsus
    arrest, seize
* cōnātus, cōnāta, cōnātum *having tried*
conciliō, conciliāre, conciliāvī, conciliātus
    win over, gain
conclāve, conclāvis, n. *room*
concrepō, concrepāre, concrepuī *snap*
* condūcō, condūcere, condūxī, conductus
    hire
* cōnficiō, cōnficere, cōnfēcī, cōnfectus
    finish
    cōnfectus, cōnfecta, cōnfectum *worn*
    out, exhausted, overcome
    rem cōnficere *finish the job*
* cōnfīdō, cōnfīdere (+ DAT) *trust, put*
    trust in
    cōnfīsus, cōnfīsa, cōnfīsum (+ DAT)
    having trusted, having put trust in
* coniciō, conicere, coniēcī, coniectus
    hurl, throw
coniunx, coniugis, m. or f. *spouse*
* coniūrātiō, coniūrātiōnis, f. *plot,*
    conspiracy
coniūrō, coniūrāre, coniūrāvī *plot,*
    conspire
* cōnor, cōnārī, cōnātus sum *try*
* cōnscendō, cōnscendere, cōnscendī
    climb on, embark on, go on board,
    mount
cōnscīscō, cōnscīscere, cōnscīvī *inflict*
    mortem sibi cōnscīscere *commit*
    suicide
* cōnsentiō, cōnsentīre, cōnsēnsī *agree*
cōnsīdō, cōnsīdere, cōnsēdī *sit down*
* cōnsilium, cōnsiliī, n. *plan, idea, advice*
    cōnsilium capere *make a plan, have an*
    idea
* cōnsistō, cōnsistere, cōnstitī *stand one's*
    ground, stand firm, halt, stop
cōnspectus, cōnspectūs, m. *sight*

* cōnspicātus, cōnspicāta, cōnspicātum
    having caught sight of
* cōnspiciō, cōnspicere, cōnspexī,
    cōnspectus *catch sight of*
* cōnspicor, cōnspicārī, cōnspicātus sum
    catch sight of
  cōnspicuus, cōnspicua, cōnspicuum
    conspicuous, easily seen
* cōnstituō, cōnstituere, cōnstituī,
    cōnstitūtus *decide*
  cōnsul, cōnsulis, m. *consul (highest
    elected official of Roman government)*
  cōnsulātus, cōnsulātūs, m. *the office of
    consul, consulship*
* cōnsulō, cōnsulere, cōnsuluī, cōnsultus
    consult
* cōnsūmō, cōnsūmere, cōnsūmpsī,
    cōnsūmptus *eat*
  contemnō, contemnere, contempsī,
    contemptus *reject, despise*
* contendō, contendere, contendī *hurry*
  contentiō, contentiōnis, f. *argument*
* contentus, contenta, contentum *satisfied*
  contineō, continēre, continuī *contain*
  continuus, continua, continuum
    continuous, on end
  contiō, contiōnis, f. *speech*
* contrā (1) (+ ACC) *against*
        (2) *on the other hand*
  contrārius, contrāria, contrārium
    opposite
    rēs contrāria *the opposite*
  contubernium, contuberniī, n.
    *contubernium (eight-man section of a
    Roman army)*
  contumēlia, contumēliae, f. *insult, abuse*
  convalēscō, convalēscere, convaluī *get
    better, recover*
* conveniō, convenīre, convēnī *come
    together, gather, meet*
  conversus SEE convertor
* convertō, convertere, convertī, conversus
    turn
  convertor, convertī, conversus sum
    turn
  convīva, convīvae, m. *guest*
  convolvō, convolvere, convolvī,
    convolūtus *entangle*
* coquō, coquere, coxī, coctus *cook*
* coquus, coquī, m. *cook*

* corōna, corōnae, f. *garland, wreath*
* corpus, corporis, n. *body*
  corrumpō, corrumpere, corrūpī,
    corruptus *corrupt*
    dōnīs corrumpere *bribe*
  corvus, corvī, m. *raven*
* cotīdiē *every day*
* crās *tomorrow*
* crēdō, crēdere, crēdidī (+ DAT) *trust,
    believe, have faith in*
  cremō, cremāre, cremāvī, cremātus
    cremate
* creō, creāre, creāvī, creātus *make, create*
  crepidārius, crepidāriī, m. *shoemaker*
  crīmen, crīminis, n. *charge*
* crūdēlis, crūdēlis, crūdēle *cruel*
  cruentus, cruenta, cruentum *bloody,
    blood-stained*
  crux, crucis, f. *cross*
* cubiculum, cubiculī, n. *bedroom*
* cucurrī SEE currō
* cui, cuius SEE quī
* culīna, culīnae, f. *kitchen*
  culpō, culpāre, culpāvī *blame*
  culter, cultrī, m. *knife*
* cum (1) *when*
* cum (2) (+ ABL) *with*
  cumulō, cumulāre, cumulāvī, cumulātus
    heap
  cumulus, cumulī, m. *pile, heap*
* cupiō, cupere, cupīvī *want*
* cūr? *why?*
* cūra, cūrae, f. *care*
    cūrae esse *be a matter of concern*
  cūria, cūriae, f. *senate-house*
* cūrō, cūrāre, cūrāvī *take care of,
    supervise*
* currō, currere, cucurrī *run*
  currus, currūs, m. *chariot*
* cursus, cursūs, m. *course, flight*
    cursus pūblicus, cursūs pūblicī
    Imperial Post
* custōdiō, custōdīre, custōdīvī, custōdītus
    guard
* custōs, custōdis, m. *guard*

d

* damnō, damnāre, damnāvī, damnātus
    condemn

* dare SEE dō
* dē (+ ABL)   *from, down from; about*
* dea, deae, f.   *goddess*
* dēbeō, dēbēre, dēbuī, dēbitus   *owe;*
      ought, should, must
  Deceanglī, Deceanglōrum, m.pl.
      Deceangli (a British tribe)
* decem   *ten*
* decet, decēre, decuit   *be proper*
      nōs decet   *we ought*
* dēcidō, dēcidere, dēcidī   *fall down*
* decimus, decima, decimum   *tenth*
* dēcipiō, dēcipere, dēcēpī, dēceptus
      deceive, trick
  dēclārō, dēclārāre, dēclārāvī, dēclārātus
      declare, proclaim
* decōrus, decōra, decōrum   *right, proper*
* dedī SEE dō
  dēdicō, dēdicāre, dēdicāvī, dēdicātus
      dedicate
  dēdūcō, dēdūcere, dēdūxī, dēductus
      escort
  dēfendō, dēfendere, dēfendī, dēfēnsus
      defend
* dēfessus, dēfessa, dēfessum   *exhausted,*
      tired out
  dēfīgō, dēfīgere, dēfīxī, dēfīxus   *fix*
  dēfīxiō, dēfīxiōnis, f.   *curse*
* dēiciō, dēicere, dēiēcī, dēiectus   *throw*
      down, throw
  dēiectus, dēiecta, dēiectum
      disappointed, downcast
* deinde   *then*
* dēlectō, dēlectāre, dēlectāvī, dēlectātus
      delight, please
* dēleō, dēlēre, dēlēvī, dēlētus   *destroy*
  dēliciae, dēliciārum, f.pl.   *darling*
  dēligō, dēligāre, dēligāvī, dēligātus
      bind, tie, tie up, moor
* dēmittō, dēmittere, dēmīsī, dēmissus
      let down, lower
* dēmōnstrō, dēmōnstrāre, dēmōnstrāvī,
      dēmōnstrātus   *point out, show*
  dēmoveō, dēmovēre, dēmōvī, dēmōtus
      dismiss, move out of
  dēmum   *at last*
      tum dēmum   *then at last, only then*
  dēnārius, dēnāriī, m.   *denarius (a small*
      coin worth four sesterces)
* dēnique   *at last, finally*

  dēns, dentis, m.   *tooth, tusk*
* dēnsus, dēnsa, dēnsum   *thick*
  dēnūntiō, dēnūntiāre, dēnūntiāvī,
      dēnūntiātus   *denounce, reveal*
  dēpellō, dēpellere, dēpulī, dēpulsus
      drive off, push down
* dēpōnō, dēpōnere, dēposuī, dēpositus
      put down, take off
  dēprōmō, dēprōmere, dēprōmpsī,
      dēprōmptus   *bring out*
* dērīdeō, dērīdēre, dērīsī, dērīsus   *mock,*
      make fun of
* dēscendō, dēscendere, dēscendī   *go*
      down, come down
* dēserō, dēserere, dēseruī, dēsertus
      desert
  dēsiliō, dēsilīre, dēsiluī   *jump down*
* dēsinō, dēsinere   *end, cease*
  dēsistō, dēsistere, dēstitī   *stop*
* dēspērō, dēspērāre, dēspērāvī   *despair,*
      give up
  dēspiciō, dēspicere, dēspexī   *look down*
  dēstinō, dēstināre, dēstināvī, dēstinātus
      intend
  dēstringō, dēstringere, dēstrīnxī,
      dēstrictus   *draw out, draw (a sword),*
      pull out
  dētestātus SEE dētestor
  dētestor, dētestārī, dētestātus sum
      curse
  dētrahō, dētrahere, dētrāxī, dētractus
      pull down
* deus, deī, m.   *god*
*   dī immortālēs!   *heavens above!*
      dīs mānibus (DM)   *to the spirits of the*
      departed
  Deva, Devae, f.   *Deva (modern Chester)*
      Devae   *at Deva*
      Devam   *to Deva*
  dēvorō, dēvorāre, dēvorāvī, dēvorātus
      devour, eat up
* dī SEE deus
  diabolus, diabolī, m.   *devil*
* dīcō, dīcere, dīxī, dictus   *say*
      salūtem plūrimam dīcere   *send best*
      wishes
  dictō, dictāre, dictāvī, dictātus   *dictate*
* diēs, diēī, m.   *day*
      diēs fēstus, diēī fēstī, m.   *festival,*
      holiday

*   diēs nātālis, diēī nātālis, m. *birthday*
* difficilis, difficilis, difficile *difficult*
   difficillimus, difficillima, difficillimum
      very difficult
  difficultās, difficultātis, f. *difficulty*
  diffīsus, diffīsa, diffīsum (+ DAT) *having*
      distrusted
  digitus, digitī, m. *finger*
* dignitās, dignitātis, f. *dignity,*
      importance, honor, prestige
  dignus, digna, dignum *worthy,*
      appropriate
  dīlaniō, dīlaniāre, dīlaniāvī, dīlaniātus
      tear to pieces
* dīligenter *carefully*
* dīligentia, dīligentiae, f. *industry, hard*
      work
* dīligō, dīligere, dīlēxī *be fond of*
* dīmittō, dīmittere, dīmīsī, dīmissus
      send away, dismiss
  diplōma, diplōmatis, n. *government*
      warrant, travel pass
  dīrigō, dīrigere, dīrēxī, dīrēctus *steer*
  dīripiō, dīripere, dīripuī, dīreptus *tear*
      apart, ransack
* dīrus, dīra, dīrum *dreadful, awful*
* dīs SEE deus
* discēdō, discēdere, discessī *depart,*
      leave
  disciplīna, disciplīnae, f. *discipline,*
      orderliness
  discipulus, discipulī, m. *disciple,*
      follower
  discō, discere, didicī *learn*
  discordia, discordiae, f. *strife*
  discrīmen, discrīminis, n. *crisis*
* dissentiō, dissentīre, dissēnsī *disagree,*
      argue
  dissimulō, dissimulāre, dissimulāvī,
      dissimulātus *conceal, hide*
  distribuō, distribuere, distribuī,
      distribūtus *distribute*
* diū *for a long time*
  diūtius *for a longer time*
* dīves, dīves, dīves, gen. dīvitis *rich*
  dītissimus, dītissima, dītissimum
      very rich
* dīvitiae, dīvitiārum, f.pl. *riches*
  dīvus, dīva, dīvum *divine*
* dīxī SEE dīcō

DM SEE deus
* dō, dare, dedī, datus *give*
*   poenās dare *pay the penalty, be*
      punished
* doceō, docēre, docuī, doctus *teach*
*   doctus, docta, doctum *educated,*
      learned, skillful
* doleō, dolēre, doluī *hurt, be in pain*
      graviter dolēre *be extremely painful*
* dolor, dolōris, m. *pain, grief*
  dolus, dolī, m. *trickery*
* domina, dominae, f. *lady (of the house),*
      mistress
* dominus, dominī, m. *master (of the*
      house)
* domus, domūs, f. *home*
    domī *at home*
    domum redīre *return home*
    domus urbāna *(luxurious) city house*
* dōnum, dōnī, n. *present, gift*
    dōnīs corrumpere *bribe*
* dormiō, dormīre, dormīvī *sleep*
* dubium, dubiī, n. *doubt*
* ducentī, ducentae, ducenta *two hundred*
* dūcō, dūcere, dūxī, ductus *lead*
    sorte ductus *chosen by lot*
* dulcis, dulcis, dulce *sweet*
* dum *while, until*
* duo, duae, duo *two*
  duodecim *twelve*
* dūrus, dūra, dūrum *harsh, hard*
* dux, ducis, m. *leader*
* dūxī SEE dūcō

e

* ē, ex (+ ABL) *from, out of*
* ea, eā, eam SEE is
* eādem, eandem SEE īdem
* eās SEE is
  ēbrius, ēbria, ēbrium *drunk*
* ecce! *see! look!*
  edō, edere, ēdī, ēsus *eat*
  ēdō, ēdere, ēdidī, ēditus *put on, present*
  efferō, efferre, extulī, ēlātus *bring out,*
      carry out
    ēlātus, ēlāta, ēlātum *thrilled, excited*
* efficiō, efficere, effēcī, effectus *carry out,*
      accomplish
* effigiēs, effigiēī, f. *image, statue*

effringō, effringere, effrēgī, effrāctus
  break down
* effugiō, effugere, effūgī escape
* effundō, effundere, effūdī, effūsus pour
  out
  effūsīs lacrimīs bursting into tears
* ēgī SEE agō
* ego, meī I, me
  mēcum with me
* ēgredior, ēgredī, ēgressus sum go out
* ēgressus, ēgressa, ēgressum having left
* ēheu! alas! oh dear!
* eī SEE is
* ēiciō, ēicere, ēiēcī, ēiectus throw out
* eīs, eius SEE is
  eiusmodī of that kind
  ēlābor, ēlābī, ēlāpsus sum escape
  ēlāpsus, ēlāpsa, ēlāpsum having escaped
  ēlātus SEE efferō
  ēlegāns, ēlegāns, ēlegāns, gen. ēlegantis
    tasteful, elegant
  ēlegantia, ēlegantiae, f. good taste,
    elegance
  ēliciō, ēlicere, ēlicuī, ēlicitus lure, entice
* ēligō, ēligere, ēlēgī, ēlēctus choose
  ēlūdō, ēlūdere, ēlūdī, ēlūsus slip past,
    trick, outwit
* ēmittō, ēmittere, ēmīsī, ēmissus throw,
    send out
* emō, emere, ēmī, ēmptus buy
  ēmoveō, ēmovēre, ēmōvī, ēmōtus move,
    clear away, remove
  emporium, emporiī, n. market
  ēn! look!
    ēn iūstitia! so this is justice!
    ēn Rōmānī! so these are the Romans!
* enim for
* eō, īre, iī, go
  obviam īre (+ DAT) meet, go to meet
* eō SEE is
* eōdem SEE īdem
* eōrum, eōs SEE is
* epistula, epistulae, f. letter
  ab epistulīs in charge of correspondence
  epulae, epulārum, f.pl. dishes, banquet
* eques, equitis, m. horseman; man of
    equestrian rank
  equitō, equitāre, equitāvī ride a horse
* equus, equī, m. horse
* eram SEE sum

ergō therefore
ēripiō, ēripere, ēripuī, ēreptus snatch,
  tear
* errō, errāre, errāvī make a mistake
  longē errāre make a big mistake
  ērubēscō, ērubēscere, ērubuī blush
  ērumpō, ērumpere, ērūpī break away,
    break out
* est, estō SEE sum
  ēsuriō, ēsurīre be hungry
* et and
* et ... et both ... and
* etiam even, also
    nōn modo ... sed etiam not only ...
      but also
* euge! hurrah!, hurray!
* eum SEE is
  evangelium, evangeliī, n. good news,
    gospel
  ēventus, ēventūs, m. outcome
  ēvertō, ēvertere, ēvertī, ēversus
    overturn
  ēvolō, ēvolāre, ēvolāvī fly out
* ex, ē (+ ABL) from, out of
* exanimātus, exanimāta, exanimātum
    unconscious
* excipiō, excipere, excēpī, exceptus
    receive
* excitō, excitāre, excitāvī, excitātus
    arouse, wake up, awaken
* exclāmō, exclāmāre, exclāmāvī exclaim,
    shout
  excruciō, excruciāre, excruciāvī,
    excruciātus torture, torment
  excūdō, excūdere, excūdī, excūsus
    forge, hammer out
  exemplum, exemplī, n. example
* exeō, exīre, exiī go out
* exerceō, exercēre, exercuī, exercitus
    exercise
  exercitus, exercitūs, m. army
  exilium, exiliī, n. exile
  exīstimō, exīstimāre, exīstimāvī,
    exīstimātus think, consider
* exitium, exitiī, n. ruin, destruction
  expellō, expellere, expulī, expulsus
    drive out
* explicō, explicāre, explicāvī, explicātus
    explain
  explōrātor, explōrātōris, m. scout, spy

expōnō, expōnere, exposuī, expositus *unload*

expugnō, expugnāre, expugnāvī, expugnātus *storm, take by storm*

exquīsītus, exquīsīta, exquīsītum *special*

* exspectō, exspectāre, exspectāvī, exspectātus *wait for*

* extinguō, extinguere, extīnxī, extīnctus *extinguish, put out, destroy*

* exstruō, exstruere, exstrūxī, exstrūctus *build*

exsultō, exsultāre, exsultāvī *exult, be triumphant*

exta, extōrum, n.pl. *entrails*

extorqueō, extorquēre, extorsī, extortus *take by force, extort*

* extrā (+ ACC) *outside*

* extrahō, extrahere, extrāxī, extractus *drag out, pull out, take out*

extrēmus, extrēma, extrēmum *furthest*
extrēma pars *edge*

extulī SEE efferō

exuō, exuere, exuī, exūtus *take off*

f

* faber, fabrī, m. *craftsman, carpenter, workman*

* fābula, fābulae, f. *play, story*

* fābulam agere *act in a play*

* facēs SEE fax

* facile *easily*

* facilis, facilis, facile *easy*

* facinus, facinoris, n. *crime*

* faciō, facere, fēcī, factus *make, do*
floccī nōn faciō *I don't give a hoot about*
impetum facere *charge, make an attack*
sēditiōnem facere *revolt*

factiō, factiōnis, f. *(racing) team*

factum, factī, n. *deed, achievement*

factus SEE fīō, faciō

Falernus, Falerna, Falernum *Falernian*

fallō, fallere, fefellī, falsus *deceive*

falsum, falsī, n. *lie*

* falsus, falsa, falsum *false, untrue, dishonest*

famēs, famis, f. *hunger*

* familiāris, familiāris, m. *relative, relation, close friend*

faucēs, faucium, f.pl. *passage, entranceway*

* faveō, favēre, fāvī *favor, support*

* favor, favōris, m. *favor*

* fax, facis, f. *torch*

* fēcī SEE faciō

fefellī SEE fallō

fēlēs, fēlis, f. *cat*

fēlīx, fēlīx, fēlīx, gen. fēlīcis *lucky, happy*

* fēmina, fēminae, f. *woman*

femur, femoris, n. *thigh*

fenestra, fenestrae, f. *window*

fēriae, fēriārum, f.pl. *festival*

* ferō, ferre, tulī, lātus *bring, carry*
graviter ferre *take badly*

* ferōciter *fiercely*

* ferōx, ferōx, ferōx, gen. ferōcis *fierce, ferocious*

ferrārius, ferrāriī, m. *blacksmith*

* ferrum, ferrī, n. *iron, sword*

* fessus, fessa, fessum *tired*

* festīnō, festīnāre, festīnāvī *hurry*

* fēstus, fēsta, fēstum *festive, holiday*
diēs fēstus, diēī fēstī, m. *holiday*

fībula, fībulae, f. *brooch*

* fidēlis, fidēlis, fidēle *faithful, loyal*

* fidēs, fideī, f. *loyalty, trustworthiness*
fidem servāre *keep a promise, keep faith*

fīdus, fīda, fīdum *loyal, trustworthy*

fīgō, fīgere, fīxī, fīxus *fix, fasten*

figūra, figūrae, f. *figure, shape*

* fīlia, fīliae, f. *daughter*

* fīlius, fīliī, m. *son*

fingō, fingere, fīnxī, fictus *invent, pretend*

fīnis, fīnis, m. *end*

fīō, fierī, factus sum *become*
factus sum *I became*

fīxus SEE fīgō

flāgitō, flāgitāre, flāgitāvī *nag at, put pressure on*

flagrō, flagrāre, flagrāvī *blaze*

* flamma, flammae, f. *flame*

floccī nōn faciō *I don't give a hoot about*

* flōs, flōris, m. *flower*

* flūmen, flūminis, n. *river*

* fluō, fluere, flūxī *flow*

* fōns, fontis, m. *fountain, spring*

fōrma, fōrmae, f.   *beauty, shape*
* fortasse   *perhaps*
* forte   *by chance*
* fortis, fortis, forte   *brave, strong*
* fortiter   *bravely*
fortitūdō, fortitūdinis, f.   *courage*
fortūna, fortūnae, f.   *fortune, luck*
fortūnātus, fortūnāta, fortūnātum   *lucky*
* forum, forī, n.   *forum, business center*
    Forum Rōmānum   *the Roman Forum*
fossa, fossae, f.   *ditch*
* frāctus, frācta, frāctum   *broken*
fragor, fragōris, m.   *crash*
* frangō, frangere, frēgī, frāctus   *break*
* frāter, frātris, m.   *brother*
* fraus, fraudis, f.   *trick*
frōns, frontis, f.   *front*
frūmentum, frūmentī, n.   *grain*
* frūstrā   *in vain*
* fuga, fugae, f.   *escape*
* fugiō, fugere, fūgī   *run away, flee (from)*
fugitīvus, fugitīvī, m.   *fugitive, runaway*
* fuī SEE sum
fulgeō, fulgēre, fulsī   *shine, glitter*
* fundō, fundere, fūdī, fūsus   *pour*
* fundus, fundī, m.   *farm*
fūnis, fūnis, m.   *rope*
fūnus, fūneris, n.   *funeral*
* fūr, fūris, m.   *thief*
furcifer, furciferī, m.   *scoundrel, crook*
* furēns, furēns, furēns, gen. furentis
    furious, in a rage
fūrtum, fūrtī, n.   *theft, robbery*
fūstis, fūstis, m.   *club, stick*

g

garriō, garrīre, garrīvī   *chatter, gossip*
garum, garī, n.   *sauce*
* gaudeō, gaudēre   *be pleased, rejoice*
* gaudium, gaudiī, n.   *joy*
gāza, gāzae, f.   *treasure*
geminī, geminōrum, m.pl.   *twins*
* gemitus, gemitūs, m.   *groan*
gemma, gemmae, f.   *jewel, gem*
genius, geniī, m.   *guardian spirit*
* gēns, gentis, f.   *family, tribe*
    ubi gentium?   *where in the world?*
genū, genūs, n.   *knee*
* gerō, gerere, gessī, gestus   *wear*

* bellum gerere   *wage war, campaign*
gladiātor, gladiātōris, m.   *gladiator*
* gladius, gladiī, m.   *sword*
glōria, glōriae, f.   *glory*
glōriāns, glōriāns, glōriāns, gen.
    glōriantis   *boasting, boastfully*
glōriātus, glōriāta, glōriātum   *having
    boasted, boasting*
glōrior, glōriārī, glōriātus sum   *boast*
Graecia, Graeciae, f.   *Greece*
Graecus, Graeca, Graecum   *Greek*
grānum, grānī, n.   *grain*
grātiae, grātiārum, f.pl.   *thanks*
*   grātiās agere   *thank, give thanks*
grātīs   *free*
grātulāns, grātulāns, grātulāns, gen.
    grātulantis   *congratulating*
grātulātiō, grātulātiōnis, f.
    congratulation
grātulor, grātulārī, grātulātus sum
    congratulate
* gravis, gravis, grave   *heavy, serious*
* graviter   *heavily, soundly, seriously*
    graviter dolēre   *be extremely painful*
    graviter ferre   *take badly*
grōma, grōmae, f.   *groma (a surveyor's
    instrument)*
gubernātor, gubernātōris, m.   *helmsman*
* gustō, gustāre, gustāvī, gustātus   *taste*
guttur, gutturis, n.   *throat*

h

* habeō, habēre, habuī, habitus   *have*
    in animō habēre   *have in mind, intend*
    in memoriā habēre   *keep in mind,
        remember*
    minōris pretiī habēre   *care less about*
    prō certō habēre   *know for certain*
    prō hostibus habēre   *consider as
        enemies*
    sermōnem habēre   *have a conversation,
        talk*
* habitō, habitāre, habitāvī   *live*
* hāc, hae, haec SEE hic
* haereō, haerēre, haesī   *stick, cling*
* haesitō, haesitāre, haesitāvī   *hesitate*
* hanc SEE hic
* haruspex, haruspicis, m.   *diviner,
    soothsayer*

* hās SEE hic
* hasta, hastae, f.   *spear*
* haud   *not*
* haudquāquam   *not at all*
  hauriō, haurīre, hausī, haustus   *drain, drink up*
  hercle!   *by Hercules!*
* hērēs, hērēdis, m.f.   *heir*
* heri   *yesterday*
  heus!   *hey!*
* hic, haec, hoc   *this*
* hīc   *here, in this place*
  hiems, hiemis, f.   *winter*
  hilare   *cheerfully*
  hinc   *from here*
  Hispānia, Hispāniae, f.   *Spain*
* hoc, hōc SEE hic
* hodiē   *today*
* homō, hominis, m.   *person, man*
  homunculus, homunculī, m.   *little man, pip-squeak*
* honor, honōris, m.   *honor, official position*
  honōrō, honōrāre, honōrāvī, honōrātus   *honor*
* hōra, hōrae, f.   *hour*
  hōroscopos, hōroscopī, m.   *horoscope*
* horreum, horreī, n.   *barn, granary, warehouse*
  hortātus SEE hortor
* hortor, hortārī, hortātus sum   *encourage, urge*
* hortus, hortī, m.   *garden*
* hōrum SEE hic
* hospes, hospitis, m.   *guest, host*
* hostis, hostis, m.f.   *enemy*
    prō hostibus habēre   *consider as enemies*
* hūc   *here, to this place*
    hūc illūc   *here and there, up and down*
* huic, huius SEE hic
  humilis, humilis, humile   *low-born, of low class*
  humus, humī, f.   *ground*
*   humī   *on the ground*
    humum   *to the ground*
* hunc SEE hic

i

* iaceō, iacēre, iacuī   *lie, rest*

* iaciō, iacere, iēcī, iactus   *throw*
* iactō, iactāre, iactāvī, iactātus   *throw*
* iam   *now, already*
  iamdūdum   *for a long time*
* iānua, iānuae, f.   *door*
* ībam SEE eō
* ibi   *there*
* id SEE is
* īdem, eadem, idem   *the same*
* identidem   *repeatedly*
  iecur, iecoris, n.   *liver*
  Ierosolyma, Ierosolymae, f.   *Jerusalem*
* igitur   *therefore, and so*
* ignārus, ignāra, ignārum   *not knowing, unaware*
* ignāvus, ignāva, ignāvum   *cowardly, lazy*
  ignis, ignis, m.   *fire*
  ignōrō, ignōrāre, ignōrāvī   *not know about*
* ignōscō, ignōscere, ignōvī (+ DAT)   *forgive*
  ignōtus, ignōta, ignōtum   *unknown*
* iī SEE eō
* ille, illa, illud   *that, he, she*
* illūc   *there, to that place*
    hūc illūc   *here and there, up and down*
  illūcēscō, illūcēscere, illūxī   *dawn, grow bright*
  imitātus, imitāta, imitātum   *having imitated*
  imitor, imitārī, imitātus sum   *imitate, mime*
* immemor, immemor, immemor, gen.
    immemoris   *forgetful*
* immineō, imminēre, imminuī (+ DAT)   *hang over*
  immō   *or rather*
* immortālis, immortālis, immortāle   *immortal*
*   dī immortālēs!   *heavens above!*
  immortālitās, immortālitātis, f.   *immortality*
* immōtus, immōta, immōtum   *still, motionless*
  impatiēns, impatiēns, impatiēns, gen.
    impatientis   *impatient*
* impediō, impedīre, impedīvī, impedītus   *delay, hinder*
  impellō, impellere, impulī, impulsus   *push, force*

* imperātor, imperātōris, m. *emperor*
* imperium, imperiī, n. *empire*
* imperō, imperāre, imperāvī (+ DAT)
    order, command
* impetus, impetūs, m. *attack*
    impetum facere *charge, make an attack*
  impōnō, impōnere, imposuī, impositus
    impose, put into, put onto
  importō, importāre, importāvī,
    importātus *import*
  imprecātiō, imprecātiōnis, f. *curse*
  impudēns, impudēns, impudēns, *gen.*
    impudentis *shameless*
  impulī SEE impellō
* in (1) (+ ACC) *into, onto*
    (2) (+ ABL) *in, on*
  inānis, inānis, ināne *empty, meaningless*
* incēdō, incēdere, incessī *march, stride*
* incendō, incendere, incendī, incēnsus
    burn, set fire to
  incēnsus, incēnsa, incēnsum *inflamed,*
    angered
  incertus, incerta, incertum *uncertain*
* incidō, incidere, incidī *fall*
* incipiō, incipere, incēpī, inceptus *begin*
* incitō, incitāre, incitāvī, incitātus *urge*
    on, encourage
  inclūsus, inclūsa, inclūsum *shut up,*
    imprisoned, trapped
  incurrō, incurrere, incurrī *run onto,*
    collide with, bump into
  inde *then*
* indicium, indiciī, n. *sign, evidence*
  indignus, indigna, indignum *unworthy,*
    undeserved
  indulgeō, indulgēre, indulsī *give way*
  induō, induere, induī, indūtus *put on*
  inest SEE īnsum
* īnfāns, īnfantis, m. *baby, child*
* īnfēlīx, īnfēlīx, īnfēlīx, *gen.* īnfēlīcis
    unlucky
* īnferō, īnferre, intulī, inlātus *bring in,*
    bring on, bring against
    iniūriam īnferre *do an injustice, bring*
    injury
* īnfestus, īnfesta, īnfestum *hostile,*
    dangerous
  īnfīgō, īnfīgere, īnfīxī, īnfīxus *fasten onto*
  īnflīgō, īnflīgere, īnflīxī, īnflīctus *inflict*
  īnflō, īnflāre, īnflāvī *blow*

  īnfundō, īnfundere, īnfūdī, īnfūsus *pour*
    into
* ingenium, ingeniī, n. *character*
* ingēns, ingēns, ingēns, *gen.* ingentis
    huge
  ingravēscō, ingravēscere *grow worse*
* ingredior, ingredī, ingressus sum *enter*
* ingressus, ingressa, ingressum *having*
    entered
* iniciō, inicere, iniēcī, iniectus *throw in*
  inimīcitia, inimīcitiae, f. *feud, dispute*
* inimīcus, inimīcī, m. *enemy*
* iniūria, iniūriae, f. *injustice, injury*
    iniūriam īnferre *do an injustice, bring*
    injury
* inlātus SEE īnferō
  innītor, innītī, innīxus sum *lean, rest*
  innīxus, innīxa, innīxum *leaning*
  innocēns, innocēns, innocēns, *gen.*
    innocentis *innocent*
  inopia, inopiae, f. *poverty*
  inopīnātus, inopīnāta, inopīnātum
    unexpected
  inquīsītiō, inquīsītiōnis, f. *board of*
    investigation
* inquit *says, said*
    inquam *I said*
  īnsānia, īnsāniae, f. *insanity*
  īnsāniō, īnsānīre, īnsānīvī *be crazy, be*
    insane
* īnsānus, īnsāna, īnsānum *crazy, insane*
  īnscrībō, īnscrībere, īnscrīpsī, īnscrīptus
    write, inscribe
* īnsidiae, īnsidiārum, f.pl. *trap, ambush*
  īnsolēns, īnsolēns, īnsolēns, *gen.*
    īnsolentis *rude, insolent*
  īnsolenter *rudely, insolently*
* īnspiciō, īnspicere, īnspexī, īnspectus
    look at, inspect, examine, search
* īnstruō, īnstruere, īnstrūxī, īnstrūctus
    draw up, set up
* īnsula, īnsulae, f. *island; apartment*
    building
  īnsula Tiberīna *Tiber Island*
  īnsum, inesse, īnfuī *be inside*
* intellegō, intellegere, intellēxī, intellēctus
    understand
    rem intellegere *understand the truth*
* intentē *intently*
* inter (+ ACC) *among, between*

inter sē *among themselves, with each other*

* intereā *meanwhile*
* interficiō, interficere, interfēcī, interfectus *kill*

interrogō, interrogāre, interrogāvī, interrogātus *question*

interrumpō, interrumpere, interrūpī, interruptus *interrupt*
* intrō, intrāre, intrāvī *enter*
* intulī SEE īnferō

intus *inside*

inultus, inulta, inultum *unavenged*
* inveniō, invenīre, invēnī, inventus *find*

invicem *in turn*
* invītō, invītāre, invītāvī, invītātus *invite*
* invītus, invīta, invītum *unwilling, reluctant*

iō! *hurrah!*
* iocus, iocī, m. *joke*

Iovis SEE Iuppiter
* ipse, ipsa, ipsum *himself, herself, itself*
* īra, īrae, f. *anger*
* īrātus, īrāta, īrātum *angry*
* īre SEE eō
* irrumpō, irrumpere, irrūpī *burst in, burst into*
* is, ea, id *he, she, it*
* iste, ista, istud *that*
* ita *in this way*
*   ita vērō *yes*

Ītalia, Ītaliae, f. *Italy*
* itaque *and so*
* iter, itineris, n. *journey, trip, progress*
* iterum *again*

itinerārium, itinerāriī, n. *guide map (for travelers)*
* iubeō, iubēre, iussī, iussus *order*

iussū Silvae *at Silva's order*

Iūdaeī, Iūdaeōrum, m.pl. *Jews*

Iūdaeus, Iūdaea, Iūdaeum *Jewish*
* iūdex, iūdicis, m. *judge*

iūdicō, iūdicāre, iūdicāvī, iūdicātus *judge*

iugulum, iugulī, n. *throat*

Iuppiter, Iovis, m. *Jupiter (god of the sky, greatest of Roman gods)*
* iussī SEE iubeō
* iussum, iussī, n. *order, instruction*

iūstitia, iūstitiae, f. *justice*

ēn iūstitia! *so this is justice!*

iuvat, iuvāre *please*

mē iuvat *it pleases me*
* iuvenis, iuvenis, m. *young man*

iuxtā (+ ACC) *next to*

l

L. = Lūcius

labefaciō, labefacere, labefēcī, labefactus *weaken*

lābor, lābī, lāpsus sum *fall*
* labor, labōris, m. *work*
* labōrō, labōrāre, labōrāvī *work*

labrum, labrī, n. *lip*

lacertus, lacertī, m. *muscle*
* lacrima, lacrimae, f. *tear*

lacrimīs effūsīs *bursting into tears*
* lacrimō, lacrimāre, lacrimāvī *cry, weep*

lacus, lacūs, m. *lake*

lacus Asphaltītēs, lacūs Asphaltītae *the Dead Sea*
* laedō, laedere, laesī, laesus *harm*

laetē *happily*
* laetus, laeta, laetum *happy*

lānx, lancis, f. *dish*

lāpsus SEE lābor

lar, laris, m. *household god*

latebrae, latebrārum, f.pl. *hiding-place*
* lateō, latēre, latuī *lie hidden*

later, lateris, m. *brick*

Latīnī, Latīnōrum, m.pl. *the Latini (early tribe in Italy)*

latrō, latrōnis, m. *robber*
* lātus, lāta, lātum *wide*
* laudō, laudāre, laudāvī, laudātus *praise*

laurus, laurī, f. *laurel tree*
* lavō, lavāre, lāvī, lautus *wash*

lectīca, lectīcae, f. *sedan-chair, carrying-chair*

lectīcārius, lectīcāriī, m. *chair-carrier, sedan-chair carrier*
* lectus, lectī, m. *couch, bed*
* lēgātus, lēgātī, m. *commander (of a legion)*

lēgibus SEE lēx
* legiō, legiōnis, f. *legion*

lēgō, lēgāre, lēgāvī, lēgātus *bequeath*

* legō, legere, lēgī, lēctus *read*
lēniō, lēnīre, lēnīvī, lēnītus *soothe, calm down*
* lēniter *gently*
* lentē *slowly*
* leō, leōnis, m. *lion*
leviter *lightly, slightly*
lēx, lēgis, f. *law*
libellus, libellī, m. *little book*
  ā libellīs *in charge of petitions*
* libenter *gladly*
* liber, librī, m. *book*
* līberālis, līberālis, līberāle *generous*
* līberī, līberōrum, m.pl. *children*
* līberō, līberāre, līberāvī, līberātus *free, set free*
līberta, lībertae, f. *freedwoman*
* lībertās, lībertātis, f. *freedom*
* lībertus, lībertī, m. *freedman, ex-slave*
* librōs SEE liber
* librum SEE liber
licet, licēre, licuit *be permitted*
  mihi licet *I am allowed, I may*
līmen, līminis, n. *threshold, doorway*
* lingua, linguae, f. *tongue*
littera, litterae, f. *letter*
* lītus, lītoris, n. *seashore, shore*
līvidus, līvida, līvidum *lead-colored*
* locus, locī, m. *place*
* locūtus, locūta, locūtum *having spoken*
longē *far*
  longē errāre *make a big mistake*
longurius, longuriī, m. *pole*
longus, longa, longum *long*
loquāx, loquāx, loquāx, gen. loquācis *talkative*
* loquor, loquī, locūtus sum *speak*
lōrīca segmentāta, lōrīcae segmentātae, f. *segmented breastplate*
lūbricus, lūbrica, lūbricum *slippery*
* lūcem SEE lūx
lūceō, lūcēre, lūxī *shine*
lucerna, lucernae, f. *lamp*
lūdō, lūdere, lūsī *play*
* lūdus, lūdī, m. *game*
  lūdī circensēs *chariot races*
  lūdī scaenicī *theatrical shows*
lūgeō, lūgēre, lūxī *lament, mourn*
* lūna, lūnae, f. *moon*
lutum, lutī, n. *mud*

* lūx, lūcis, f. *light, daylight*

m

M. = Marcus
madidus, madida, madidum *soaked through, drenched*
magicus, magica, magicum *magic*
* magis SEE magnopere
* magister, magistrī, m. *master, foreman*
magistrātus, magistrātūs, m. *public official*
magnificē *splendidly, magnificently*
magnificus, magnifica, magnificum *splendid, magnificent*
* magnopere *greatly*
*   magis *more, rather*
*   maximē *very greatly, very much, most of all*
* magnus, magna, magnum *big, large, great*
    maior, maior, maius, gen. maiōris *bigger, larger, greater*
*   maximus, maxima, maximum *very big, very large, very great, greatest*
    Pontifex Maximus *Chief Priest*
maiestās, maiestātis, f. *treason*
malignus, maligna, malignum *spiteful*
* mālō, mālle, māluī *prefer*
mālim *I would prefer*
* malus, mala, malum *evil, bad*
    peior, peior, peius, gen. peiōris *worse*
*   pessimus, pessima, pessimum *very bad, worst*
* mandātum, mandātī, n. *instruction, order*
* mandō, mandāre, mandāvī, mandātus *order, entrust, hand over*
* māne *in the morning*
* maneō, manēre, mānsī *remain, stay*
manifestus, manifesta, manifestum *clear*
mansiō, mansiōnis, f. *resthouse (for travelers)*
* manus, manūs, f. *hand; band*
mappa, mappae, f. *napkin, handkerchief*
* mare, maris, n. *sea*
margō, marginis, m. *edge*
* marītus, marītī, m. *husband*

marmor, marmoris, n. *marble*
Mārs, Mārtis, m. *Mars (god of war)*
Masada, Masadae, f. *Masada (a fortress in Judea)*
massa, massae, f. *block*
* māter, mātris, f. *mother*
mātrimōnium, mātrimōniī, n. *marriage*
mātrōna, mātrōnae, f. *lady, married woman*
* maximē SEE magnopere
* maximus SEE magnus
* mē SEE ego
medicāmentum, medicāmentī, n. *ointment, medicine, drug*
medicus, medicī, m. *doctor*
* medius, media, medium *middle*
* melior SEE bonus
melius est SEE bonus
memor, memor, memor, *gen.* memoris *remembering, mindful of*
memoria, memoriae, f. *memory*
  in memoriā habēre *keep in mind, remember*
* mendāx, mendācis, m. *liar*
mendāx, mendāx, mendāx, *gen.* mendācis *lying, deceitful*
mendīcus, mendīcī, m. *beggar*
mēns, mentis, f. *mind*
* mēnsa, mēnsae, f. *table*
mēnsis, mēnsis, m. *month*
* mercātor, mercātōris, m. *merchant*
merēns, merēns, merēns, *gen.* merentis *deserving*
  bene merēns *well deserving, deserving kindness*
meritus, merita, meritum *well-deserved*
mēta, mētae, f. *turning-point*
* metus, metūs, m. *fear*
* meus, mea, meum *my, mine*
  meī, meōrum, m.pl. *my family*
  mī Haterī *my dear Haterius*
  mī Quīnte *my dear Quintus*
* mihi SEE ego
* mīles, mīlitis, m. *soldier*
mīliārium aureum, mīliāriī aureī, n. *golden milestone*
mīlitō, mīlitāre, mīlitāvī *be a soldier*
* mīlle *a thousand*
*   mīlia *thousands*
* minimē *no, least, very little*
* minimus SEE parvus
minister, ministrī, m. *servant, agent*
* minor SEE parvus
minor, minārī, minātus sum *threaten*
* mīrābilis, mīrābilis, mīrābile *marvelous, strange, wonderful*
mīrus, mīra, mīrum *extraordinary*
  aliquid mīrī *something extraordinary*
misceō, miscēre, miscuī, mixtus *mix*
* miser, misera, miserum *miserable, wretched, sad*
  ō mē miserum! *oh wretched me!*
* mittō, mittere, mīsī, missus *send*
moderātus, moderāta, moderātum *restrained, moderate*
* modo *just, now, only*
  modo ... modo *now ... now*
  nōn modo ... sed etiam *not only ... but also*
* modus, modī, m. *manner, way, kind*
*   quō modō? *how? in what way?*
*   rēs huius modī *a thing of this kind*
* molestus, molesta, molestum *troublesome*
molliō, mollīre, mollīvī, mollītus *soothe*
mollis, mollis, molle *soft, gentle*
mōmentum, mōmentī, n. *importance*
* moneō, monēre, monuī, monitus *warn, advise*
* mōns, montis, m. *mountain*
mora, morae, f. *delay*
* morbus, morbī, m. *illness*
* morior, morī, mortuus sum *die*
  (eī) moriendum est *(he) must die*
  moriēns, moriēns, moriēns, *gen.* morientis *dying*
  moritūrus, moritūra, moritūrum *going to die*
*   mortuus, mortua, mortuum *dead*
moror, morārī, morātus sum *delay*
* mors, mortis, f. *death*
  mortem sibi cōnscīscere *commit suicide*
* mortuus SEE morior
* mōs, mōris, m. *custom*
mōtus, mōtūs, m. *movement*
* moveō, movēre, mōvī, mōtus *move*
* mox *soon*
* multitūdō, multitūdinis, f. *crowd*
* multō *much*

multum   *much*

* multus, multa, multum   *much*
*   multī   *many*
*   plūrimī, plūrimae, plūrima   *very many*
*   plūrimus, plūrima, plūrimum   *very much, most*
    plūris est   *is worth more*
*   plūs, plūris, n.   *more*
    plūs vīnī   *more wine*
    salūtem plūrimam dīcere   *send best wishes*
    mūnera, mūnerum, n.pl.   *gladiatorial shows*
    mūnītiō, mūnītiōnis, f.   *defense, fortification*
* mūrus, mūrī, m.   *wall*
    mūs, mūris, m.f.   *mouse*
    mussitō, mussitāre, mussitāvī   *murmur*
    mūtātiō, mūtātiōnis, f.   *posting station, way station*

n

    nactus, nacta, nactum   *having seized*
* nam   *for*
* nārrō, nārrāre, nārrāvī, nārrātus   *tell, relate*
    rem nārrāre   *tell the story*
* nāscor, nāscī, nātus sum   *be born*
    nātū maximus   *eldest*
    trīgintā annōs nātus   *thirty years old*
    nāsus, nāsī, m.   *nose*
    nātālis, nātālis, nātāle   *natal*
*   diēs nātālis, diēī nātālis, m.   *birthday*
* nātus, nāta, nātum   *born*
    naumachia, naumachiae, f.   *(site for a) naval battle*
* nauta, nautae, m.   *sailor*
* nāvigō, nāvigāre, nāvigāvī   *sail*
* nāvis, nāvis, f.   *ship*
    nē   *that ... not, so that ... not*
*   nē ... quidem   *not even*
    nec   *and not, nor*
    utrum ... necne   *whether ... or not*
* necesse   *necessary*
* necō, necāre, necāvī, necātus   *kill*
* neglegēns, neglegēns, neglegēns, *gen.* neglegentis   *careless*

* neglegō, neglegere, neglēxī, neglēctus   *neglect*
* negōtium, negōtiī, n.   *business*
*   negōtium agere   *do business, work*
* nēmō (acc. nēminem)   *no one, nobody*
    neque   *and not, nor*
*   neque ... neque   *neither ... nor*
* nescio, nescīre, nescīvī   *not know*
    niger, nigra, nigrum   *black*
* nihil   *nothing*
* nihilōminus   *nevertheless*
* nimis   *too*
* nimium, nimiī, n.   *too much*
* nisi   *except, unless*
* nōbilis, nōbilis, nōbile   *noble, of noble birth*
* nōbīs SEE nōs
    nocēns, nocēns, nocēns, *gen.* nocentis   *guilty*
* noceō, nocēre, nocuī (+ DAT)   *hurt*
* noctis SEE nox
    noctū SEE nox
* nōlō, nōlle, nōluī   *not want, refuse*
    nōlī, nōlīte   *do not, don't*
* nōmen, nōminis, n.   *name*
* nōn   *not*
* nōnāgintā   *ninety*
    nōndum   *not yet*
* nōnne?   *surely?*
* nōnnūllī, nōnnūllae, nōnnūlla   *some, several*
* nōnus, nōna, nōnum   *ninth*
* nōs   *we, us*
* noster, nostra, nostrum   *our*
    notō, notāre, notāvī, notātus   *note, observe, jot down*
* nōtus, nōta, nōtum   *known, well-known, famous*
* novem   *nine*
* nōvī   *I know*
* novus, nova, novum   *new*
* nox, noctis, f.   *night*
    noctū   *by night*
* nūbēs, nūbis, f.   *cloud*
* nūllus, nūlla, nūllum   *not any, no*
* num? (1)   *surely ... not?*
* num (2)   *whether*
    num quid   *whether anything, if anything*
    nūmen, nūminis, n.   *power, divinity*

* numerō, numerāre, numerāvī,
      numerātus *count*
  numerus, numerī, m. *number*
* numquam *never*
* nunc *now*
* nūntiō, nūntiāre, nūntiāvī, nūntiātus
      announce
* nūntius, nūntiī, m. *messenger, message,
      news*
* nūper *recently*
* nusquam *nowhere*

o

  obdormiō, obdormīre, obdormīvī *fall
      asleep*
  obeō, obīre, obiī (+ DAT) *meet, go to meet*
  obēsus, obēsa, obēsum *fat*
  obiciō, obicere, obiēcī, obiectus *present*
  oblītus, oblīta, oblītum *having forgotten*
* obscūrus, obscūra, obscūrum *dark,
      gloomy*
  obstinātiō, obstinātiōnis, f. *stubbornness,
      obstinacy*
  obstinātus, obstināta, obstinātum
      stubborn
* obstō, obstāre, obstitī (+ DAT) *obstruct,
      block the way*
* obstupefaciō, obstupefacere, obstupefēcī,
      obstupefactus *amaze, stun*
* obtulī SEE offerō
* obviam eō, obviam īre, obviam iī (+ DAT)
      meet, go to meet
  occāsiō, occāsiōnis, f. *opportunity*
* occīdō, occīdere, occīdī, occīsus *kill*
  occidō, occidere, occidī *set*
* occupātus, occupāta, occupātum *busy*
* occupō, occupāre, occupāvī, occupātus
      seize, take over
* occurrō, occurrere, occurrī (+ DAT) *meet*
* octāvus, octāva, octāvum *eighth*
* octō *eight*
* octōgintā *eighty*
* oculus, oculī, m. *eye*
* ōdī *I hate*
* odiō sum, odiō esse *be hateful*
* offerō, offerre, obtulī, oblātus *offer*
  officium, officiī, n. *duty*
      officium agere *do one's duty*
  oleum, oleī, n. *oil*

* ōlim *once, some time ago*
  ōmen, ōminis, n. *omen*
  omittō, omittere, omīsī, omissus *drop,
      leave out, omit*
* omnīnō *completely*
* omnis, omnis, omne *all*
      omnia *all, everything*
* opēs, opum, f.pl. *money, wealth*
* oportet, oportēre, oportuit *be right*
*   mē oportet *I must*
* oppidum, oppidī, n. *town*
* opprimō, opprimere, oppressī,
      oppressus *crush, overwhelm*
* oppugnō, oppugnāre, oppugnāvī,
      oppugnātus *attack*
* optimē SEE bene
* optimus SEE bonus
  optiō, optiōnis, m. *optio*
* opus, operis, n. *work, construction*
      opus caementīcium *concrete*
  ōrātiō, ōrātiōnis, f. *speech*
  orbis, orbis, m. *globe*
      orbis terrārum *world*
* ōrdō, ōrdinis, m. *row, line*
      prīmī ōrdinēs *first rank (senior
      centurions)*
  orior, orīrī, ortus sum *rise*
  ōrnāmentum, ōrnāmentī, n. *ornament,
      decoration*
      ōrnāmenta praetōria *the honorary
      rank and privileges of a praetor*
  ōrnātus, ōrnāta, ōrnātum *decorated,
      elaborately furnished*
* ōrnō, ōrnāre, ōrnāvī, ōrnātus *decorate*
* ōrō, ōrāre, ōrāvī *beg*
  ortus SEE orior
* ōs, ōris, n. *face*
* ōsculum, ōsculī, n. *kiss*
* ostendō, ostendere, ostendī, ostentus
      show
  ostentō, ostentāre, ostentāvī, ostentātus
      show off, display
* ōtiōsus, ōtiōsa, ōtiōsum *at leisure, with
      time off, idle, on vacation*

p

* paene *nearly, almost*
* pallēscō, pallēscere, palluī *grow pale*
* pallidus, pallida, pallidum *pale*

pallium, palliī, n. *cloak*
pālus, pālī, m. *stake, post*
pantomīmus, pantomīmī, m. *pantomime actor, dancer*
* parātus, parāta, parātum *ready, prepared*
* parcō, parcere, pepercī (+ DAT) *spare*
parēns, parentis, m.f. *parent*
* pāreō, pārēre, pāruī (+ DAT) *obey*
* parō, parāre, parāvī, parātus *prepare*
* pars, partis, f. *part*
  extrēma pars *edge*
  in prīmā parte *in the forefront*
* parvus, parva, parvum *small*
*   minor, minor, minus, *gen.* minōris *less, smaller*
*   minimus, minima, minimum *very little, least*
* passus, passa, passum *having suffered*
pāstor, pāstōris, m. *shepherd*
* patefaciō, patefacere, patefēcī, patefactus *reveal*
* pater, patris, m. *father*
patera, paterae, f. *bowl*
patientia, patientiae, f. *patience*
* patior, patī, passus sum *suffer, endure*
* patrōnus, patrōnī, m. *patron*
* paucī, paucae, pauca *few, a few*
* paulīsper *for a short time*
paulō/paulum *a little*
* pauper, pauper, pauper, *gen.* pauperis *poor*
pavīmentum, pavīmentī, n. *pavement, floor*
* pavor, pavōris, m. *panic*
* pāx, pācis, f. *peace*
* pecūnia, pecūniae, f. *money*
* pedem SEE pēs
* peior SEE malus
penātēs, penātium, m. pl. *household gods*
* pendeō, pendēre, pependī *hang*
* per (+ ACC) *through, along*
percutiō, percutere, percussī, percussus *strike*
perdomitus, perdomita, perdomitum *conquered*
* pereō, perīre, periī *die, perish*
* perficiō, perficere, perfēcī, perfectus *finish*
  rem perficere *finish the job*

* perfidia, perfidiae, f. *treachery*
* perfidus, perfida, perfidum *treacherous, untrustworthy*
perfodiō, perfodere, perfōdī, perfossus *pick (teeth)*
perfuga, perfugae, m. *deserter*
perīculōsus, perīculōsa, perīculōsum *dangerous*
* perīculum, perīculī, n. *danger*
* periī SEE pereō
perītē *skillfully*
* perītus, perīta, perītum *skillful*
* permōtus, permōta, permōtum *alarmed, disturbed*
perpetuus, perpetua, perpetuum *perpetual*
  in perpetuum *forever*
perrumpō, perrumpere, perrūpī, perruptus *burst through, burst in*
perscrūtor, perscrūtārī, perscrūtātus sum *examine*
persecūtus, persecūta, persecūtum *having pursued*
persōna, persōnae, f. *character*
  persōnam agere *play a part*
perstō, perstāre, perstitī *persist*
* persuādeō, persuādēre, persuāsī (+ DAT) *persuade*
perterreō, perterrēre, perterruī, perterritus *terrify*
* perterritus, perterrita, perterritum *terrified*
perturbō, perturbāre, perturbāvī, perturbātus *disturb, alarm*
* perveniō, pervenīre, pervēnī *reach, arrive at*
* pēs, pedis, m. *foot, paw*
  pedem referre *step back*
pessimē *very badly*
* pessimus SEE malus
* pestis, pestis, f. *pest, rascal*
petauristārius, petauristāriī, m. *acrobat*
* petō, petere, petīvī, petītus *head for, attack; seek, beg for, ask for*
philosopha, philosophae, f. *(female) philosopher*
philosophia, philosophiae, f. *philosophy*
philosophus, philosophī, m. *philosopher*
pīlum, pīlī, n. *javelin*
pīpiō, pīpiāre, pīpiāvī *chirp, peep*

* placet, placēre, placuit   *please, suit*
* plaudō, plaudere, plausī, plausus
    applaud, clap
* plaustrum, plaustrī, n.   *wagon, cart*
  plausus, plausūs, m.   *applause*
  plebicula, plebiculae, f.   *the little plebs*
  plebs, plebis, f.   *the plebs, the common
    people*
* plēnus, plēna, plēnum   *full*
  plērīque, plēraeque, plēraque   *most*
  pluit, pluere, pluit   *rain*
* plūrimus *SEE* multus
* plūs, plūris, n.   *more*
* pōculum, pōculī, n.   *cup (often for wine)*
* poena, poenae, f.   *punishment*
*   poenās dare   *pay the penalty, be
    punished*
* poēta, poētae, m.   *poet*
  poliō, polīre, polīvī, polītus   *polish*
  polliceor, pollicērī, pollicitus sum
    promise
  polyspaston, polyspastī, n.   *crane*
  pompa, pompae, f.   *procession*
  Pompēiānus, Pompēiāna, Pompēiānum
    Pompeian
* pōnō, pōnere, posuī, positus   *put, place,
    put up*
* pōns, pontis, m.   *bridge*
  pontifex, pontificis, m.   *priest*
    Pontifex Maximus   *Chief Priest*
* poposcī *SEE* poscō
* populus, populī, m.   *people*
  porrigō, porrigere, porrēxī, porrēctus
    stretch out
  porrō   *what's more, furthermore*
* porta, portae, f.   *gate*
  porticus, porticūs, f.   *colonnade*
* portō, portāre, portāvī, portātus   *carry*
* portus, portūs, m.   *harbor*
* poscō, poscere, poposcī   *demand,
    ask for*
* positus *SEE* pōnō
  possideō, possidēre, possēdī, possessus
    possess
* possum, posse, potuī   *can, be able*
* post (+ ACC)   *after, behind*
* posteā   *afterwards*
  posterī, posterōrum, m.pl.   *future
    generations, posterity*
  postīcum, postīcī, n.   *back gate*

* postquam   *after, when*
* postrēmō   *finally, lastly*
* postrīdiē   *(on) the next day*
* postulō, postulāre, postulāvī, postulātus
    demand
* posuī *SEE* pōnō
* potēns, potēns, potēns, *gen.* potentis
    powerful
  potentia, potentiae, f.   *power*
* potes *SEE* possum
* potestās, potestātis, f.   *power*
  potius   *rather*
* potuī *SEE* possum
* praebeō, praebēre, praebuī, praebitus
    provide
* praeceps, praeceps, praeceps, *gen.*
    praecipitis   *headlong, rash*
  praecipitō, praecipitāre, praecipitāvī
    hurl
* praecō, praecōnis, m.   *herald,
    announcer*
  praeda, praedae, f.   *booty, plunder,
    loot*
  praedīcō, praedīcere, praedīxī,
    praedictus   *foretell, predict*
  praefectus, praefectī, m.   *commander*
    praefectus castrōrum   *commander of
    the camp*
* praeficiō, praeficere, praefēcī, praefectus
    put in charge
* praemium, praemiī, n.   *prize, reward,
    profit*
  praeruptus, praerupta, praeruptum
    sheer, steep
  praesēns, praesēns, praesēns, *gen.*
    praesentis   *present, ready*
  praesertim   *especially*
* praesidium, praesidiī, n.   *protection*
* praestō, praestāre, praestitī   *show,
    display*
* praesum, praeesse, praefuī (+ DAT)   *be in
    charge of*
  praeter (+ ACC)   *except*
* praetereā   *besides*
* praetereō, praeterīre, praeteriī   *pass by,
    go past*
  praetextus, praetexta, praetextum   *with
    a purple border*
  praetōriānus, praetōriānī, m.   *praetorian
    (member of emperor's bodyguard)*

praetōrium, praetōriī, n.   *praetorium*
(*commander's living quarters*)
praetōrius, praetōria, praetōrium
praetorian
  ōrnāmenta praetōria   *honorary*
  praetorship, honorary rank of praetor
* prāvus, prāva, prāvum   *evil*
* precātus, precāta, precātum   *having*
prayed (to)
* precēs, precum, f.pl.   *prayers*
* precor, precārī, precātus sum   *pray (to)*
prēnsō, prēnsāre, prēnsāvī, prēnsātus
take hold of, clutch
pretiōsus, pretiōsa, pretiōsum
expensive, precious
* pretium, pretiī, n.   *price*
  minōris pretiī habēre   *care less about*
prīmō   *at first*
prīmum   *first*
* prīmus, prīma, prīmum   *first*
  in prīmā parte   *in the forefront*
  in prīmīs   *in particular*
  prīmī ōrdinēs   *first rank (senior
  centurions)*
  prīmus pīlus   *senior centurion*
* prīnceps, prīncipis, m.   *chief,
  chieftain*
* prīncipia, prīncipiōrum, n.pl.
headquarters
prior, prior, prius   *first, in front*
* prius   *earlier*
* priusquam   *before, until*
prō (+ ABL)   *in front of, for, in return for*
  prō certō habēre   *know for certain*
  prō hostibus habēre   *reckon as
  enemies*
probus, proba, probum   *honest*
procāx, procāx, procāx, *gen.* procācis
impudent, impolite
* prōcēdō, prōcēdere, prōcessī   *advance,
  proceed, step forward*
* procul   *far off*
prōcumbō, prōcumbere, prōcubuī   *fall
  down*
prōcūrātor, prōcūrātōris, m.   *manager*
prōditor, prōditōris, m.f.   *traitor*
prōdō, prōdere, prōdidī, prōditus
betray
* profectus, profecta, profectum   *having
  set out*

* proficīscor, proficīscī, profectus sum
set out
prōgredior, prōgredī, prōgressus sum
advance, step forward
* prōgressus, prōgressa, prōgressum
*having advanced, having stepped
forward*
prohibeō, prohibēre, prohibuī, prohibitus
prevent
* prōmittō, prōmittere, prōmīsī, prōmissus
promise
prōmoveō, prōmovēre, prōmōvī,
prōmōtus   *promote*
prōnūntiō, prōnūntiāre, prōnūntiāvī,
prōnūntiātus   *proclaim, preach*
* prope (+ ACC)   *near*
prophēta, prophētae, m.   *prophet*
prōpōnō, prōpōnere, prōposuī,
prōpositus   *propose, put forward*
prōpraetor, prōpraetōris, m.   *governor*
prōsiliō, prōsilīre, prōsiluī   *leap forward,
jump*
prospectus, prospectūs, m.   *view*
prospiciō, prospicere, prospexī   *look out*
* prōvincia, prōvinciae, f.   *province*
* proximus, proxima, proximum   *nearest,
next to*
prūdēns, prūdēns, prūdēns, *gen.*
prūdentis   *shrewd, intelligent,
sensible*
* prūdentia, prūdentiae, f.   *prudence, good
sense, shrewdness*
psittacus, psittacī, m.   *parrot*
* pūblicus, pūblica, pūblicum   *public*
* puella, puellae, f.   *girl*
* puer, puerī, m.   *boy*
pugiō, pugiōnis, m.   *dagger*
* pugna, pugnae, f.   *fight*
* pugnō, pugnāre, pugnāvī   *fight*
* pulcher, pulchra, pulchrum   *beautiful*
* pulsō, pulsāre, pulsāvī, pulsātus   *hit,
knock on, whack, punch*
pulvīnus, pulvīnī, m.   *cushion*
pūmiliō, pūmiliōnis, m.   *dwarf*
* pūniō, pūnīre, pūnīvī, pūnītus   *punish*
pūrgō, pūrgāre, pūrgāvī, pūrgātus
clean
pūrus, pūra, pūrum   *pure, clean,
spotless*
pyra, pyrae, f.   *pyre*

q

* quā SEE quī
* quadrāgintā   *forty*
* quae SEE quī
* quaedam SEE quīdam
* quaerō, quaerere, quaesīvī, quaesītus
      search for, look for, inquire
* quālis, quālis, quāle   *what sort of*
      tālis … quālis   *such … as*
* quam (1)   *how*
      quam celerrimē   *as quickly as possible*
* quam (2)   *than*
* quam (3) SEE quī
* quamquam   *although*
      quandō   *when*
* quantus, quanta, quantum   *how big*
* quārē?   *why?*
* quārtus, quārta, quārtum   *fourth*
* quasi   *as if*
* quattuor   *four*
* -que   *and*
* quendam SEE quīdam
* quī, quae, quod   *who, which, what*
* quia   *because*
* quicquam SEE quisquam
* quid? SEE quis?
      quid vīs SEE quis?
* quīdam, quaedam, quoddam   *one, a*
      certain
      quidem   *indeed*
      nē … quidem   *not even*
* quiēs, quiētis, f.   *rest*
      quiēscō, quiēscere, quiēvī   *rest*
      quiētus, quiēta, quiētum   *quiet*
      quīngentī, quīngentae, quīngenta   *five*
      hundred
* quīnquāgintā   *fifty*
* quīnque   *five*
* quīntus, quīnta, quīntum   *fifth*
* quis? quid?   *who? what?*
      num quid   *whether anything*
      quid vīs?   *what do you want?*
* quisquam, quicquam / quidquam
      anyone, anything
      quisque, quaeque, quidque   *each one*
      optimus quisque   *all the best people*
* quō? (1)   *where? where to?*
* quō (2) SEE quī
* quō modō?   *how? in what way?*

* quod (1)   *because*
* quod (2) SEE quī
* quondam   *one day, once*
* quoque   *also, too*
* quōs SEE quī
* quot?   *how many?*
      quotannīs   *every year*
      quotiēns   *whenever*

r

      rādō, rādere, rāsī, rāsus   *scratch, scrape*
* rapiō, rapere, rapuī, raptus   *seize, grab*
      raptim   *hastily, quickly*
      ratiō, ratiōnis, f.   *sum, addition*
      ā ratiōnibus   *in charge of accounts*
*   ratiōnēs, ratiōnum, f.pl.   *accounts*
      ratiōnēs subdūcere   *write up accounts*
      raucus, rauca, raucum   *harsh*
* rē SEE rēs
      rebellō, rebellāre, rebellāvī   *rebel, revolt*
* rēbus SEE rēs
* recipiō, recipere, recēpī, receptus
      recover, take back
      sē recipere   *recover*
      recitō, recitāre, recitāvī, recitātus   *recite,*
      read out
      rēctē   *rightly, properly, correctly*
* recumbō, recumbere, recubuī   *lie down,*
      recline
* recūsō, recusāre, recūsāvī, recūsātus
      refuse
* reddō, reddere, reddidī, redditus   *give*
      back, make
      redēmptor, redēmptōris, m.   *contractor,*
      builder
* redeō, redīre, rediī   *return, go back, come*
      back
      redeundum est vōbīs   *you must*
      return
      reditus, reditūs, m.   *return*
* redūcō, redūcere, redūxī, reductus   *lead*
      back
* referō, referre, rettulī, relātus   *bring back,*
      carry, deliver, tell, report
      pedem referre   *step back*
* reficiō, reficere, refēcī, refectus   *repair*
* rēgīna, rēgīnae, f.   *queen*
      Regnēnsēs, Regnēnsium, m.pl.
      Regnenses (a British tribe)

rēgnō, rēgnāre, rēgnāvī   *reign*
* rēgnum, rēgnī, n.   *kingdom*
* regredior, regredī, regressus sum   *go back, return*
* regressus, regressa, regressum   *having returned*
  relēgō, relēgāre, relēgāvī, relēgātus   *exile*
* relinquō, relinquere, relīquī, relictus *leave*
  reliquus, reliqua, reliquum   *remaining*
* rem SEE rēs
* remedium, remediī, n.   *cure*
  remittō, remittere, remīsī, remissus *send back*
  renovō, renovāre, renovāvī, renovātus *restore, renew, repeat*
  repetō, repetere, repetīvī, repetītus *claim*
  rēpō, rēpere, rēpsī   *crawl*
* rēs, reī, f.   *thing, business, affair*
*   rē vērā   *in fact, truly, really*
     rem administrāre   *manage the task*
     rem cōgitāre   *consider the problem*
     rem cōnficere   *finish the job*
     rem intellegere   *understand the truth*
     rem nārrāre   *tell the story*
     rem perficere   *finish the job*
     rem suscipere   *undertake the task*
     rērum status   *situation, state of affairs*
*   rēs adversae   *misfortune*
     rēs contrāria   *the opposite*
     rēs huius modī   *a matter of this kind*
  resignō, resignāre, resignāvī, resignātus *open, unseal*
* resistō, resistere, restitī (+ DAT)   *resist*
  respiciō, respicere, respexī   *look at, look upon*
* respondeō, respondēre, respondī   *reply*
  respōnsum, respōnsī, n.   *answer*
  resurgō, resurgere, resurrēxī   *rise again*
* retineō, retinēre, retinuī, retentus   *keep, hold back*
  retrō   *back*
* rettulī SEE referō
* reveniō, revenīre, revēnī   *come back, return*
* revertor, revertī, reversus sum   *turn back, return*
  revocō, revocāre, revocāvī, revocātus *recall, call back*

* rēx, rēgis, m.   *king*
  rhētor, rhētoris, m.   *teacher*
* rīdeō, rīdēre, rīsī   *laugh, smile*
  rīdiculus, rīdicula, rīdiculum   *ridiculous, silly*
  rīma, rīmae, f.   *crack, chink*
* rīpa, rīpae, f.   *river bank*
  rīsus, rīsūs, m.   *smile*
* rogō, rogāre, rogāvī, rogātus   *ask*
  Rōma, Rōmae, f.   *Rome*
     Rōmae   *at Rome*
  Rōmānī, Rōmānōrum, m.pl.   *Romans*
     ēn Rōmānī!   *so these are the Romans!*
  Rōmānus, Rōmāna, Rōmānum   *Roman*
  rosa, rosae, f.   *rose*
  rostrum, rostrī, n.   *beak; ship's ram*
     rostra, rostrōrum, n.pl.   *speaker's platform*
  rumpō, rumpere, rūpī, ruptus   *break, split*
* ruō, ruere, ruī   *rush*
  rūpēs, rūpis, f.   *rock, crag*
  rūrī   *in the country*
* rūrsus   *again*
  rūsticus, rūstica, rūsticum   *country, in the country*
     vīlla rūstica   *house in the country*

s

  saccārius, saccāriī, m.   *stevedore, dock-worker*
  saccus, saccī, m.   *bag, purse*
  sacellum, sacellī, n.   *chapel*
* sacer, sacra, sacrum   *sacred*
* sacerdōs, sacerdōtis, m.   *priest*
  sacerdōtium, sacerdōtiī, n.   *priesthood*
  sacrificium, sacrificiī, n.   *offering, sacrifice*
  sacrificō, sacrificāre, sacrificāvī, sacrificātus   *sacrifice*
* saepe   *often*
* saeviō, saevīre, saeviī   *be in a rage*
* saevus, saeva, saevum   *savage, cruel*
  saltātrīx, saltātrīcis, f.   *dancing-girl*
  saltō, saltāre, saltāvī   *dance*
* salūs, salūtis, f.   *safety, health*
     salūtem plūrimam dīcere   *send best wishes*

salūtātiō, salūtātiōnis, f.   *the morning visit*

* salūtō, salūtāre, salūtāvī, salūtātus   *greet*
* salvē!   *hello!*
* sānē   *obviously*
* sanguis, sanguinis, m.   *blood*
sānō, sānāre, sānāvī, sānātus   *heal, cure, treat*
sānus, sāna, sānum   *well, healthy*
* sapiēns, sapiēns, sapiēns, *gen.* sapientis   *wise*
sarcinae, sarcinārum, f.pl.   *bags, luggage*
* satis   *enough*
* saxum, saxī, n.   *rock*
scaena, scaenae, f.   *stage, scene*
scālae, scālārum, f.pl.   *ladders*
* scelestus, scelesta, scelestum   *wicked*
* scelus, sceleris, n.   *crime*
scīlicet   *obviously*
* scindō, scindere, scidī, scissus   *tear, tear up, cut up, cut open, carve*
* scio, scīre, scīvī   *know*
scrība, scrībae, m.   *secretary*
* scrībō, scrībere, scrīpsī, scrīptus   *write*
sculpō, sculpere, sculpsī, sculptus   *sculpt, carve*
scurrīlis, scurrīlis, scurrīle   *obscene, dirty*
scūtum, scūtī, n.   *shield*
* sē   *himself, herself, themselves*
inter sē   *among themselves, with each other*
sēcum   *with him, with her, with them*
sēcum cōgitāre   *consider to oneself*
* secō, secāre, secuī, sectus   *cut*
sēcrētus, sēcrēta, sēcrētum   *secret*
* secundus, secunda, secundum   *second*
secūris, secūris, f.   *axe*
* secūtus, secūta, secūtum   *having followed*
* sed   *but*
* sedeō, sedēre, sēdī   *sit*
* sēdēs, sēdis, f.   *seat*
sēditiō, sēditiōnis, f.   *rebellion*
sēditiōnem facere   *revolt*
sella, sellae, f.   *chair*
* semper   *always*
* senātor, senātōris, m.   *senator*
senectūs, senectūtis, f.   *old age*
* senex, senis, m.   *old man*
* sententia, sententiae, f.   *opinion*
* sentiō, sentīre, sēnsī, sēnsus   *feel, notice*

sepeliō, sepelīre, sepelīvī, sepultus   *bury*
* septem   *seven*
* septimus, septima, septimum   *seventh*
* septuāgintā   *seventy*
* sepulcrum, sepulcrī, n.   *tomb*
* sequor, sequī, secūtus sum   *follow*
sequēns, sequēns, sequēns, *gen.* sequentis   *following*
* serēnus, serēna, serēnum   *calm, clear*
* sermō, sermōnis, m.   *conversation*
sermōnem habēre   *have a conversation, talk*
* serviō, servīre, servīvī   *serve (as a slave)*
servitūs, servitūtis, f.   *slavery*
* servō, servāre, servāvī, servātus   *save, protect*
fidem servāre   *keep a promise, keep faith*
* servus, servī, m.   *slave*
sēstertius, sēstertiī, m.   *sesterce (coin)*
sēstertium vīciēns   *two million sesterces*
sevērē   *severely*
* sevērus, sevēra, sevērum   *severe, strict*
sevirī Augustālēs, sevirōrum Augustālium, m.   *priests of the cult of the deified Augustus*
* sex   *six*
* sexāgintā   *sixty*
* sextus, sexta, sextum   *sixth*
* sī   *if*
* sibi SEE sē
* sīc   *thus, in this way*
siccō, siccāre, siccāvī, siccātus   *dry*
* sīcut   *like, as*
signifer, signiferī, m.   *standard-bearer*
significō, significāre, significāvī, significātus   *mean, indicate*
signō, signāre, signāvī, signātus   *sign, seal*
* signum, signī, n.   *seal, signal*
* silentium, silentiī, n.   *silence*
sileō, silēre, siluī   *be silent*
* silva, silvae, f.   *woods, forest*
simul   *at the same time*
* simulac, simulatque   *as soon as*
* sine (+ ABL)   *without*
sinistrā   *on the left*
situs, sita, situm   *situated*
* sōl, sōlis, m.   *sun*
sōlācium, sōlāciī, n.   *comfort*

* soleō, solēre *be accustomed*
  sollemniter *solemnly*
* sollicitus, sollicita, sollicitum *worried,*
    anxious
  sōlum *only*
    nōn sōlum ... sed etiam *not only ...*
      but also
* sōlus, sōla, sōlum *alone, lonely, only, on*
    one's own
  solūtus, solūta, solūtum *relaxed*
* solvō, solvere, solvī, solūtus *loosen,*
    untie, cast off
* sonitus, sonitūs, m. *sound*
  sordidus, sordida, sordidum *dirty*
* soror, sorōris, f. *sister*
* sors, sortis, f. *lot*
    sorte ductus *chosen by lot*
  spargō, spargere, sparsī, sparsus *scatter*
* spectāculum, spectāculī, n. *show,*
    spectacle
  spectātor, spectātōris, m. *spectator*
* spectō, spectāre, spectāvī, spectātus
    look at, watch
  specus, specūs, m. *cave*
* spernō, spernere, sprēvī, sprētus
    despise, reject
* spērō, spērāre, spērāvī *hope, expect*
* spēs, speī, f. *hope*
  spīna, spīnae, f. *thorn, toothpick; central*
    platform of a race course
  splendidus, splendida, splendidum
    splendid, impressive
  sportula, sportulae, f. *handout*
  squālidus, squālida, squālidum *covered*
    with dirt, filthy
* stābam SEE stō
* statim *at once*
* statiō, statiōnis, f. *post*
  statua, statuae, f. *statue*
  statūra, statūrae, f. *height*
  status, statūs, m. *state*
    rērum status *situation, state of affairs*
  stella, stellae, f. *star*
  sternō, sternere, strāvī, strātus *lay low*
  stilus, stilī, m. *pen, stick*
* stō, stāre, stetī *stand, lie at anchor*
  Stōicus, Stōicī, m. *Stoic*
  stola, stolae, f. *(long) dress*
* strēnuē *hard, energetically*
* strepitus, strepitūs, m. *noise, din*

  studium, studiī, n. *enthusiasm, zeal*
  stultitia, stultitiae, f. *stupidity,*
    foolishness
* stultus, stulta, stultum *stupid, foolish*
* suāvis, suāvis, suāve *sweet*
  suāviter *sweetly*
* sub (+ ABL or ACC) *under, beneath*
  subdūcō, subdūcere, subdūxī, subductus
    draw up
    ratiōnēs subdūcere *draw up accounts,*
      write up accounts
* subitō *suddenly*
* sublātus SEE tollō
  subscrībō, subscrībere, subscrīpsī,
    subscrīptus *sign*
* subveniō, subvenīre, subvēnī (+ DAT)
    help, come to help
  sūdō, sūdāre, sūdāvī *sweat*
  suffīgō, suffīgere, suffīxī, suffīxus *nail,*
    fasten
  Sūlis, Sūlis, f. *Sulis*
* sum, esse, fuī *be*
    estō! *be!*
  summa, summae, f. *sum, total*
* summus, summa, summum *highest,*
    greatest, top
  sūmptuōsē *lavishly*
* sūmptuōsus, sūmptuōsa, sūmptuōsum
    expensive, lavish, costly
  superbē *arrogantly*
  superbia, superbiae, f. *arrogance*
* superbus, superba, superbum *arrogant,*
    proud
* superō, superāre, superāvī, superātus
    overcome, overpower
  superstes, superstitis, m. *survivor*
* supersum, superesse, superfuī
    survive
* surgō, surgere, surrēxī *get up, stand up,*
    rise
* suscipiō, suscipere, suscēpī, susceptus
    undertake, take on
    rem suscipere *undertake the task*
* suspicātus, suspicāta, suspicātum
    having suspected
  suspiciō, suspīciōnis, f. *suspicion*
  suspīciōsus, suspīciōsa, suspīciōsum
    suspicious
  suspicor, suspicārī, suspicātus sum
    suspect

suspīrium, suspīriī, n. *heart-throb*
* sustulī SEE tollō
susurrō, susurrāre, susurrāvī *whisper,*
    mumble
* suus, sua, suum *his, her, their, his own*
    suī, suōrum, m.pl. *his men, his family,*
    their families

t

T. = Titus
* taberna, tabernae, f. *store, shop, inn*
tabernārius, tabernāriī, m. *store-owner,*
    storekeeper
* tablīnum, tablīnī, n. *study*
tabula, tabulae, f. *tablet, writing-tablet*
* taceō, tacēre, tacuī *be silent, be quiet*
    tacē! *shut up! be quiet!*
* tacitē *quietly, silently*
* tacitus, tacita, tacitum *quiet, silent, in*
    silence
* taedet, taedēre, taeduit *be tiring*
*   mē taedet *I am tired, I am bored*
* tālis, tālis, tāle *such*
    tālis … quālis *such … as*
* tam *so*
* tamen *however*
* tamquam *as, like*
* tandem *at last*
tangō, tangere, tetigī, tāctus *touch*
* tantum *only*
* tantus, tanta, tantum *so great, such a*
    great
tapēte, tapētis, n. *tapestry, wall-*
    hanging
tardē *late*
    tardius *too late*
* tardus, tarda, tardum *late*
taurus, taurī, m. *bull*
* tē SEE tū
* tēctum, tēctī, n. *ceiling, roof*
tēgula, tēgulae, f. *tile*
temperāns, temperāns, temperāns, *gen.*
    temperantis *temperate, self-*
    controlled
* tempestās, tempestātis, f. *storm*
* templum, templī, n. *temple*
* temptō, temptāre, temptāvī, temptātus
    try, put to the test
* tempus, temporis, n. *time*

* tenebrae, tenebrārum, f.pl. *darkness*
* teneō, tenēre, tenuī, tentus *hold, own*
tergum, tergī, n. *back*
terō, terere, trīvī, trītus *waste (time)*
* terra, terrae, f. *ground, land*
    orbis terrārum *world*
* terreō, terrēre, terruī, territus *frighten*
terribilis, terribilis, terribile *terrible*
* tertius, tertia, tertium *third*
tesserārius, tesserāriī, m. *tesserarius*
    (officer in charge of guards and
    passwords)
* testāmentum, testāmentī, n. *will*
* testis, testis, m.f. *witness*
theātrum, theātrī, n. *theater*
thermae, thermārum, f.pl. *baths*
Tiberis, Tiberis, m. *Tiber River*
* tibi SEE tū
tībia, tībiae, f. *pipe*
    tībiīs cantāre *play on the pipes*
tībīcen, tībīcinis, m. *pipe player*
tignum, tignī, n. *beam*
* timeō, timēre, timuī *be afraid, fear*
timidē *fearfully*
timidus, timida, timidum *fearful,*
    frightened
* timor, timōris, m. *fear*
tintinnō, tintinnāre, tintinnāvī *ring*
titulus, titulī, m. *advertisement, slogan,*
    inscription, label
* toga, togae, f. *toga*
* tollō, tollere, sustulī, sublātus *raise, lift*
    up, hold up
tormentum, tormentī, n. *torture*
torqueō, torquēre, torsī, tortus *torture,*
    twist
* tot *so many*
* tōtus, tōta, tōtum *whole*
* trādō, trādere, trādidī, trāditus *hand*
    over
* trahō, trahere, trāxī, tractus *drag*
tranquillē *peacefully*
trāns (+ ACC) *across*
trānscendō, trānscendere, trānscendī
    climb over
* trānseō, trānsīre, trānsiī *cross*
trānsfīgō, trānsfīgere, trānsfīxī, trānsfīxus
    pierce, stab
trānsiliō, trānsilīre, trānsiluī *jump*
    through

tremō, tremere, tremuī *tremble, shake*
* trēs, trēs, tria *three*
tribūnal, tribūnālis, n. *platform*
* tribūnus, tribūnī, m. *tribune*
    tribūnus angusticlāvius *junior tribune*
    tribūnus lāticlāvius *senior tribune*
trīciēns sēstertium *three million sesterces*
* triclīnium, triclīniī, n. *dining-room*
* trīgintā *thirty*
tripodes, tripodum, m.pl. *tripods*
* trīstis, trīstis, trīste *sad*
triumphātor, triumphātōris, m. *triumphator (central figure in a "triumph" parade)*
* tū, tuī *you (singular)*
    tēcum *with you (singular)*
* tuba, tubae, f. *trumpet*
tubicen, tubicinis, m. *trumpeter*
* tum *then*
    tum dēmum *then at last, only then*
* tunica, tunicae, f. *tunic*
* turba, turbae, f. *crowd*
* tūtus, tūta, tūtum *safe*
    tūtius est *it would be safer*
* tuus, tua, tuum *your (singular), yours*
Tyrius, Tyria, Tyrium *Tyrian (colored with dye from city of Tyre)*

u

* ubi *where, when*
    ubi gentium *where in the world*
* ubīque *everywhere*
ulcīscor, ulcīscī, ultus sum *take revenge on*
* ūllus, ūlla, ūllum *any*
* ultimus, ultima, ultimum *furthest, last*
* ultiō, ultiōnis, f. *revenge*
ululō, ululāre, ululāvī *howl*
* umbra, umbrae, f. *shadow, ghost*
* umerus, umerī, m. *shoulder*
* umquam *ever*
ūnā cum (+ ABL) *together with*
* unda, undae, f. *wave*
* unde *from where*
* undique *on all sides*
unguō, unguere, ūnxī, ūnctus *anoint, smear*

* ūnus, ūna, ūnum *one*
urbānus, urbāna, urbānum *fashionable, sophisticated*
* urbs, urbis, f. *city*
    Urbs, Urbis, f. *Rome*
ursa, ursae, f. *bear*
usquam *anywhere*
usque ad (+ ACC) *right up to*
* ut (+ INDIC) *as*
* ut (+ SUBJUNCT) *that, so that, in order that*
* ūtilis, ūtilis, ūtile *useful*
* utrum *whether*
    utrum ... an *whether ... or*
    utrum ... necne *whether ... or not*
* uxor, uxōris, f. *wife*

v

vacuus, vacua, vacuum *empty*
vah! *ugh!*
* valdē *very much, very*
* valē *good-bye, farewell*
valedīcō, valedīcere, valedīxī *say good-bye*
valētūdinārium, valētūdināriī, n. *hospital*
valētūdō, valētūdinis, f. *health*
validus, valida, validum *strong*
vallum, vallī, n. *embankment of earth, rampart*
varius, varia, varium *different*
* vehementer *violently, loudly*
* vehō, vehere, vexī, vectus *carry*
* vel *or*
    vel ... vel *either ... or*
* velim, vellem SEE volō
vēnālīcius, vēnālīciī, m. *slave-dealer*
* vēnātiō, vēnātiōnis, f. *hunt*
* vēndō, vēndere, vēndidī, vēnditus *sell*
venēnātus, venēnāta, venēnātum *poisoned*
* venēnum, venēnī, n. *poison*
* venia, veniae, f. *mercy*
* veniō, venīre, vēnī *come*
venter, ventris, m. *stomach*
* ventus, ventī, m. *wind*
Venus, Veneris, f. *Venus (goddess of love); the highest throw at dice*
vēr, vēris, n. *spring*
verber, verberis, n. *blow*

* verberō, verberāre, verberāvī, verberātus
    strike, beat
* verbum, verbī, n. *word*
  vereor, verērī, veritus sum *fear, be afraid*
  versus, versa, versum *having turned*
  versus, versūs, m. *verse, line of poetry*
* vertō, vertere, vertī, versus *turn*
    sē vertere *turn around*
* vērum, vērī, n. *truth*
* vērus, vēra, vērum *true, real*
*   rē vērā *in fact, truly, really*
* vester, vestra, vestrum *your (plural)*
* vestīmenta, vestīmentōrum, n.pl.
    clothes
* vestrum SEE vōs
  vetus, vetus, vetus, *gen.* veteris *old*
* vexō, vexāre, vexāvī, vexātus *annoy*
  vī SEE vīs
* via, viae, f. *street, way*
  vibrō, vibrāre, vibrāvī, vibrātus *wave,*
    brandish
  vīciēns sēstertium *two million sesterces*
* victī SEE vincō
  victī, victōrum, m.pl. *the conquered*
  victima, victimae, f. *victim*
  victor, victōris, m. *victor, winner*
  victōria, victōriae, f. *victory*
* victus SEE vincō
  vīcus, vīcī, m. *town, village, settlement*
→* videō, vidēre, vīdī, vīsus *see*
  videor, vidērī, vīsus sum *seem*
  vigilō, vigilāre, vigilāvī *stay awake*
* vīgintī *twenty*
* vīlla, vīllae, f. *villa, (large) house*
  vīlla rūstica *house in the country*
* vinciō, vincīre, vīnxī, vīnctus *bind,*
    tie up
→ vincō, vincere, vīcī, victus *conquer, win,*
    be victorious

* vīnum, vīnī, n. *wine*
* vir, virī, m. *man*
  vīrēs, vīrium, f.pl. *strength*
  virgō, virginis, f. *virgin*
    Virginēs Vestālēs *Vestal Virgins*
* virtūs, virtūtis, f. *courage*
  vīs, f. (acc. vim) *force, violence*
* vīs SEE volō
  vīsitō, vīsitāre, vīsitāvī, vīsitātus *visit*
* vīsus SEE videō
* vīta, vītae, f. *life*
    vītam agere *lead a life*
  vītis, vītis, f. *centurion's cane/staff*
  vitium, vitiī, n. *sin*
* vītō, vītāre, vītāvī, vītātus *avoid*
* vituperō, vituperāre, vituperāvī,
    vituperātus *find fault with, tell off,*
    curse
* vīvō, vīvere, vīxī *live, be alive*
* vīvus, vīva, vīvum *alive, living*
* vix *hardly, scarcely, with difficulty*
* vōbīs SEE vōs
* vōcem SEE vōx
* vocō, vocāre, vocāvī, vocātus *call*
* volō, velle, voluī *want*
    quid vīs? *what do you want?*
    velim *I would like*
* volvō, volvere, volvī, volūtus *turn*
*   in animō volvere *wonder, turn over in*
    the mind
* vōs *you (plural)*
    vōbīscum *with you (plural)*
  vōtum, vōtī, n. *vow, votive offering*
* vōx, vōcis, f. *voice*
* vulnerō, vulnerāre, vulnerāvī, vulnerātus
    wound, injure
* vulnus, vulneris, n. *wound*
* vult SEE volō
* vultus, vultūs, m. *expression, face*

Index of Cultural Topics

The page references are for illustrations and for the Cultural Background sections at the ends of the Stages.

ā libellīs   275, 289
ā ratiōnibus   290
ab epistulīs   290
Aesculapius   225
agger   78
Agricola   118–120, 122, 156, 159, 230
Agrippa   78
amphitheater   135, 137, 160
Antony   186
Apollo   59, 250, 266
Appian Way   77, 81
Aquae Sulis   1, 2, 18–24, 37, 41, 47, 61, 158, 249
aqueducts   205, 215, 226, 227
aquila   136, 140
aquilifer   98, 116, 136
Aquitania   119
Arch of Titus   165, 177, 184, 186, 191, 203, 207, 224, 269
archaeology   19, 157–163
archers   102
arches   203, 205, 206, 207, 221, 223
architecture (see engineering)
Arval Brotherhood   60
astrology   62
augurēs   59
Augustus   61, 78, 183, 184, 185, 187, 205, 207, 208, 250, 269, 289
auxiliaries   97, 100, 102, 117

Bacchus   250
barges   81, 203
basilica   135, 184, 185, 208
Bath (see Aquae Sulis)

baths   22, 135, 136, 137, 159, 206
Boudica   61, 119
Brundisium   81
building contractor   200, 203, 207, 229

Caesar   156, 185, 186, 187, 268, 289
caligae   99
Caligula   119
Campus Martius   224, 226, 269
Camulodunum   2, 61
Capitoline Hill   185, 186, 207, 215, 224, 225, 249
castra (see military fortress)
caupōnēs   81
cavalry   100, 102, 117, 120
cella   23, 249
Celtic religion   18, 60, 61
cement   203, 205
censors   230
centurion   98, 102, 116–117, 119, 137
century (military unit)   116–117, 137
Ceres   59
chariot-racing   226, 266–268, 270
Charon   42
Chester (see Deva)
Christianity   250–251
Cicero   286
cingulum   99
circumnavigation of Britain   120
Circus Maximus   215, 224, 226, 266, 267–268, 269, 270
Claudius   61, 225, 250, 251, 290
clients   229–232, 287–289
Cloaca Maxima   183, 184, 224, 227
Cogidubnus   24, 57
cohorts   116–117, 135, 136
Colchester (see Camulodunum)

Colosseum (*see* Flavian
    Amphitheater)
communication   77–82, 159
concrete   77, 78, 203, 205, 206, 207
cōnsul   119, 183, 185
contubernium   137
cranes   191, 204, 207
cūria   184, 185, 186, 231
cursus pūblicus   78

Dacians   185
Dead Sea   187
dēfīxiōnēs   27, 41–42, 44, 156, 267
Deva   2, 22, 72, 120, 124, 135, 160,
    161–162
Diana   59
Dido   266
diplōma   78
divination   58–59
domes   205, 206
Domitian   101, 118, 120,156, 185,
    186, 187, 203, 207, 215, 224,
    225, 230, 231, 250, 266, 267,
    269, 275, 289
domus urbāna   136
duty roster   100

Eboracum   2, 137
Eleazar ben Ya'ir   187
emporia   225
engineering   19–21, 77, 97, 200,
    203–207, 232
Epaphroditus   251, 273, 275, 289,
    290
Epictetus   251
equitēs   117, 230–231, 266, 287
Esquiline Hill   224, 226
Etruria   183
Etruscans   249
exercitus   97

factiōnēs   267
fēriae   252
Fishbourne   2, 157, 160

Flavian Amphitheater   205, 206,
    207, 215, 224, 226, 267, 269, 272
Flavians   187, 207
fora   185
Forum Romanum   184–186, 208,
    215, 224, 225, 231, 269
freedmen   229, 275, 286–290
freedwomen   286–288

genius   61
gladius   99
Great Fire   251
grōma   77

Hannibal   266
haruspex   23, 45, 58–59
Haterii   202, 203, 204, 205, 207
Horace   81, 289
hōroscopos   62
horreum   127, 134, 135, 136, 137,
    139, 225

inquīsītiō   97
inscriptions   100, 118, 161–163,
    275, 286, 287–288
īnsulae   205, 226, 227, 228
Isis   249–250
itinerāria   78

Jerusalem   177, 187, 203
Jews   186, 187, 190, 250–251
Josephus   187, 269
Judaism   187, 250
Judea   187–188, 250
Juno   59, 249
Jupiter   59, 136, 185, 186, 207, 249,
    250
Juvenal   207, 226, 230, 289

larēs and penātēs   57
Latini   183
Latium   183
lēgātus   116, 117, 118, 136
legionary fortress   121, 134–139

legionary soldier 85, 90, 97–102, 229
legions 97, 105, 116–117, 119, 287
lībertī Augustī 275, 289
lōrīca segmentāta 99
lūdī 266–268
lūdī circensēs 266–268
Lūdī Rōmānī 266
lūdī scaenicī 266–267

Maecenas 289
Magna Graecia 183
Magna Mater 266
mansiōnēs 78
manumission 275, 286, 288, 289
mappa 267
Mars 41, 58, 59, 60, 267
Marseille (*see* Massilia)
Martial 230
Masada 174, 187–188
Massilia 119
Matronalia 252
Memor, L. Marcius 12, 23, 47, 58
mēta 268
mīles 97
mīliārium aureum 184, 185
mime 266–267
Minerva 23, 58, 59, 60, 61, 249
Mithraea 249, 250
Mithras 249–250
Mons Graupius 2, 120
mūnera 268–269
mūtātiōnēs 78
mystery religion 249–250

naumachia 269
Nero 187, 205, 251, 275, 290
Nerva 185
nūmina 57

ōmina 42, 59
optiō 116, 117, 137
opus caementīcium 205
ōrnāmenta praetōria 290

Ostia 224, 225

Palatine Hill 183, 184, 185, 207, 208, 215
Pallas 290
Pantheon 205, 206
pantomīmus 266–267, 269
Parentalia 252
Paris 266–267
patrons 229–232, 287–289
patrōnus 229, 287
pavīmentum 77
Petronius 289
pilleus 275
pīlum 99
plebs 231–232
Pliny 81, 287, 289, 290
Pompey 187, 268
Pontifex Maximus 57, 60, 61
Porta Triumphalis 269
praefectus castrōrum 116, 117, 135
praetōrium 134, 135, 136
prīmī ōrdinēs 117
prīmus pīlus 116, 117
prīncipia 121, 134, 135, 136
prison 135, 184, 186
prōpraetor 120
pugiō 99, 104

quaestor 230, 252

religion 19, 42, 57–62, 64, 249–252
roads 72, 76, 77–78, 84, 159, 185
Roma 61
Roman state religion 59–62, 185
Romanization 23, 61–62, 120
Romulus 183
rostra 184, 185, 186, 225

sacellum 135, 136
sacrifices 45, 47, 57–59, 269
Salii 252
salūtātiō 229, 287

Salvius   59, 60, 229, 230
Saturnalia   252
Scotland   120
scūtum   99
Senate   117, 156, 183, 252
senatorial class   117, 230, 231, 266,
    287
servī Caesaris   289
sevirī Augustālēs   286, 289
ships   82
Sibylline Books   252
signifer   116, 117
Silva, Flavius   187
Silvanus   58
slingers   102
spīna   267, 268
sportula   229, 230, 287
St. Paul   251
Stoicism   251–252
Styx   42
Subura   215, 224, 225–226, 228
Sulis Minerva   12, 18, 23, 57, 60, 61,
    249
surveyors (*see* engineering)

Tabula Peutingeriana   67, 80–81
Tacitus   61, 118–120, 156, 205
Temples   184, 204, 252
    Aesculapius   225
    Claudius   61
    in Jerusalem   177, 187
    Isis   249–250
    Julius Caesar   184, 186, 208
    Jupiter Optimus Maximus   185,
        186, 207, 215, 224, 249, 250, 269
    Peace   185
    Saturn   184, 252
    Sulis Minerva   22–23, 60, 61
    Vesta   184, 186
Terminus   249
tesserārius   116, 117
Tiber   183, 203, 215, 224, 225, 226,
    227, 250, 269
Tiberius   119, 250

Tiro   286
Titus   118, 175, 186, 187, 203, 269,
    272
toga   230–231, 275
tombstones   161–163, 286, 287–288
trade   158, 183, 230
Trajan   185
travel   77–82
tribūnus   116, 117, 119, 135
Trimalchio   289
triumphātor   269
Tyrrhenian Sea   183

Underworld   42

valētūdinārium   134, 135, 136
vallum   134, 135
Vegetius   97–98
vēnātiōnēs   268
Venus   59, 267
Vespasian   118, 159, 184, 185, 187,
    190, 231–232, 269
Vesta   57, 184, 186
Vestal Virgins   184, 186
Vestalia   252
Vettii   289
via praetōria   134, 135
via prīncipālis   134, 135
via quīntāna   134, 135
Via Sacra   184, 186, 224
Via Salaria   183
vīcī   137
Vindolanda   100–101
Viroconium   2, 119
vītis   102, 117
Vitruvius   77
vōta   57
Verulamium   2, 118, 209

Wales   120

York (*see* Eboracum)

Zosimus   287

Index of Grammatical Topics

ablative absolute   218–219, 327, 332

ablative case   148, 300, 326–327

accusative case   149, 325

active verbs   171, 176, 311–312

adjectives   15, 39, 132, 153, 200, 299–300

   see also comparison of adjectives

adverbs   15, 39, 303–304

   see also comparison of adverbs

antonyms   74

case   324–327

   see also ablative case, accusative case, dative case, genitive case, locative case, nominative case, vocative case

commands   128, 335

   direct   128, 316

   indirect   128, 335

   negative   316

comparative *see* comparison of adjectives, adverbs

comparison of adjectives   51, 301–302

comparison of adverbs   51–52, 303–304

compound verbs   180, 222

conjugations *see* verbs

cum clauses   70, 73, 333

dative case   325, 332

decet *see* impersonal verbs

declensions *see* nouns

demonstrative pronouns (**hic, ille,** etc.)   306

deponent verbs *see* verbs, deponent

determinative pronouns (**is, ea, id,** etc.)   306, 310

diminutives   264

dum clauses   334

eō (īre) *see* verbs, irregular

ferō (ferre) *see* verbs, irregular

future perfect tense   263, 311, 312, 313, 321, 322

future tense   259, 281, 282, 321

gender   95, 297

genitive case   38, 324

   expressing amount or quantity 38

   genitive of description   38

gerundive   113, 246, 317, 320, 323

īdem, eadem, idem (pronoun) 307

imperative   316, 323

impersonal verbs   151

indicative   196, 199, 311–314, 318–319, 321–322

indirect commands   128, 335

   negative   221, 335

indirect questions   91, 333

infinitive   55, 316, 319, 323

   present active   278, 316, 321, 323

   present deponent   278, 319

   present passive   278, 316, 323

intensive pronouns (**ipse, ipsa, ipsum,** etc.)   307

locative case   327
longer sentences   338–339

nē *see* indirect commands,
    negative; purpose clauses,
    negative
nōlō (**nōlle**) *see* verbs, irregular
nominative case   324
nouns   55, 114, 132, 153, 200, 246,
    283, 296–298

oportet *see* impersonal verbs

participles   316–317, 319–320,
    323, 328–332
    future (active)   243, 317,
        319–320, 323, 331
    gerundive *see* gerundive
    perfect active (deponent)   33,
        49, 219, 240, 319, 329
    perfect passive   11–12, 33, 49,
        55, 196, 199, 218, 240, 243, 313,
        316, 323, 329
    present active   11, 49, 218, 316,
        319, 323, 329
passive verbs   171, 176, 196, 199,
    281, 312–313, 322
personal pronouns (**ego**, **tū**, etc.)
    305
placet *see* impersonal verbs
possum *see* verbs, irregular
prepositions   148
priusquam   334
pronouns   305–310
    see also demonstrative
        pronouns; determinative
        pronouns; **īdem**, **eadem**,
        idem; intensive pronouns;
        personal pronouns; reflexive
        pronouns; relative pronouns
purpose clauses   110, 179, 334
    negative   221, 334

with relative pronoun   179,
    334
with **ubi**   179, 334

questions
    direct   91
    indirect   91, 333

reflexive pronouns   305
relative pronouns   308–310
result clauses   130, 335

sī   263
subjunctive   315, 323, 333–336,
    338–339
    imperfect   73, 94, 315, 323
    pluperfect   70, 94, 315, 323
subordinate clauses   333–336,
    338–339
sum (**esse**) *see* verbs, irregular
superlative *see* comparison of
    adjectives, adverbs

taedet *see* impersonal verbs
tenses *see* verbs
time, expressions of   148–149

ut *see* indirect commands; purpose
    clauses; result clauses

verbs   114, 246, 283, 311–323
    regular   311–317
    deponent   240, 318–320
    irregular   321–323
vocative case   297, 324
voice   171, 176
volō *see* verbs, irregular

word order   337

Time Chart

Date	Britain	Rome and Italy
B.C. *c.* 2500	Salisbury Plain inhabited	
c. 2200–1300	Stonehenge built	
c. 1900	Tin first used in Britain	
c. 1450	Wessex invaded from Europe	
c. 900	Celts move into Britain	
c. 750	Plow introduced into Britain	Rome founded (traditional date) 753
post 500	Maiden Castle, Iron Age fort in Britain	Kings expelled and Republic begins, 509
		Duodecim Tabulae, 450
4th C	Hill forts used by Celts	Gauls capture Rome, 390
c. 330–320	Pytheas, Greek, circumnavigates Britain	Rome controls Italy/Punic Wars, 300–200
c. 300	Druid lore increases in Britain	Hannibal crosses the Alps, 218
		Rome expands outside Italy, 200–100
c. 125	Gallo-Belgic coins introduced	Gracchi and agrarian reforms, 133–123
		Cicero, Roman orator (106–43)
55–54	Julius Caesar invades Britain	
		Julius Caesar assassinated, 44
		Augustus becomes emperor, 27
		Vergil, author of the *Aeneid*, 70–19
A.D. 30–41	Cunobelinas, ruler in S.E. (Roman ally)	Tiberius becomes emperor, 14
c. 51	Cartimandua, client queen of Brigantes	Nero emperor, 54–68
60	Boudica leads Iceni revolt	Great Fire at Rome/Christians blamed, 64
		Vespasian emperor, 69–79
c. 75	Fishbourne Palace begun	Colosseum begun, *c.* 72
78–84	Agricola governor in Britain	Titus emperor, 79–81
c. 80	Salvius arrives in Britain	Vesuvius erupts, 79
		Tacitus, historian, *c.* 56–117
		Domitian emperor, 81–96
		Trajan emperor, 98–117
		Hadrian emperor, 117–138
143–163	Antonine Wall in Scotland	Septimius Severus dies in Britain, 211
c. 208	St. Alban martyred at Verulamium	Constantine tolerates Christianity, 313
from 367	Picts, Scots, Saxons raid	Bible translated into Latin, *c.* 385
410	Rome refuses Britain help against Saxons	Alaric the Goth sacks Rome, 410
		Last Roman Emperor deposed, 476

World History	World Culture	Date
Babylonian/Sumerian Civilizations		B.C. *c.* 3000
Pharaohs in Egypt		*c.* 3000–332
Indo-European migrations, *c.* 2100	Maize cultivation, American SW	*c.* 2000
Hammurabi's Legal Code, *c.* 1750	Epic of Gilgamesh	post 2000
Minoan Civilization at its height, *c.* 1500	Rig-Veda verses (Hinduism) collected	*c.* 1500
Israelite exodus from Egypt, *c.* 1250	Development of Hinduism	*c.* 1450
Israel and Judah split, *c.* 922	Phoenician alphabet adapted by Greeks	*c.* 1000–800
Kush/Meroe Kingdom expands	*Iliad* and *Odyssey*	*c.* 800
	First Olympic Games	776
Solon, Athenian lawgiver, 594	Buddha	*c.* 563–483
	Confucius	551–479
Persia invades Egypt and Greece, *c.* 525–400	Golden Age of Greece	500–400
	Death of Socrates	399
Conquests of Alexander the Great		335–323
	Museum founded in Alexandria	290
Great Wall of China built		*c.* 221
Judas Maccabaeus regains Jerusalem	Feast of Hanukkah inaugurated	165
	Adena Serpent Mound, Ohio	2nd C
Julius Caesar in Gaul, 58–49	Canal locks exist in China	50
	Glass blowing begins in Sidon	post 50
Cleopatra commits suicide		30
Herod rebuilds the Temple, Jerusalem		*c.* 20
Roman boundary at Danube, 15	Birth of Jesus	*c.* 4
	Crucifixion of Jesus	A.D. *c.* 29
Britain becomes a Roman province, 43	St. Peter in Rome	42–67
	St. Paul's missionary journeys	45–67
	Camel introduced into the Sahara	1st C
Sack of Jerusalem and the Temple		70
Roman control extends to Scotland		77–85
	Paper invented in China	*c.* 100
		c. 56–117
	Construction at Teotihuacán begins	*c.* 100
Roman Empire at its greatest extent		98–117
Hadrian's Wall in Britain		122–127
"High Kings" of Ireland		*c.* 200–1022
Byzantium renamed Constantinople, 330	Golden Age of Guptan Civilization, India	*c.* 320–540
	Last ancient Olympic Games	393
Mayan Civilization		*c.* 300–1200
Byzantine Empire expands		518

Date	Britain	Rome and Italy
? 537	Death of King Arthur	Gregory the Great, Pope, 590–604
9th–10th C	Saxon forts against the Vikings	Period of turmoil in Italy, 800–1100
c. 900	Alfred drives Danes from England	Republic of St. Mark, Venice, 850
1189–1199	Richard the Lionheart	
12th C	Robin Hood legends circulated	
		Independent government in Rome, 1143–1455
1258	Salisbury Cathedral finished	Marco Polo travels to the East, 1271–1295
1346	Battle of Crécy, cannon first used	Dante, poet, 1265–1321
1348	Black Death begins	Renaissance begins in Italy, c. 1400
1485	Henry VII, first Tudor king	Botticelli, painter, 1445–1510
1509–1547	Henry VIII	Leonardo da Vinci, 1452–1519
		Titian, painter, 1489–1576
		Rebuilding of St. Peter's begins, 1506
1518	Royal College of Physicians founded	Michelangelo starts Sistine Chapel ceiling, 1508
1536–1540	Dissolution of Monasteries	Rome sacked by German/Spanish troops, 1527
1558–1603	Elizabeth I	Spain controls much of Italy, 1530–1796
1577–1580	Drake circumnavigates the globe	
1588	Defeat of Spanish Armada	Fontana rediscovers Pompeii, 1594
1603	James I, first Stuart king	Galileo invents the telescope, 1610
1649	Charles I executed	Bernini, architect and sculptor, 1598–1680
1649–1659	Cromwellian Protectorate	
1660	Restoration of Charles II	
1675	Wren begins St. Paul's Cathedral	
1760–1820	George III	
1789	Wilberforce moves to end slave trade	
1795–1821	John Keats, poet	Napoleon enters Italy, 1796
1796	Smallpox vaccination in England	
1798	Nelson defeats French at the Nile	Verdi, composer, 1813–1901
1833	Factory Act limits child labor in Britain	G. Leopardi, poet, dies, 1837
1837–1901	Victoria, queen	Mazzini, Garibaldi, Cavour, active 1846–1861
1844	Railways begin in Britain	Victor Emmanuel II, United Italy, 1861
1846–1849	Irish potato famine	Rome, Italy's capital, 1870
1859	Dickens' *Tale of Two Cities*	Marconi uses wireless telegraphy, 1896
1876	School attendance compulsory	
1903	Emily Pankhurst leads suffragettes	Mussolini controls Italy, 1922–1945
1940	Churchill Prime Minister	Italy a Republic, 1946
1946	National Health Act	

World History	World Culture	Date
	Birth of Mohammed	570
Charlemagne crowned, 800	Arabs adopt Indian numerals	*c.* 771
	1001 Nights collected in Iraq	ante 942
Vikings reach America, c. 1000	*Tale of Genji*, Japan	1010
Norman invasion of England, 1066	Ife-Benin art, Nigeria	1100–1600
First Crusade, 1096	Classic Pueblo Cliff dwellings	1050–1300
	Al-Idrisi, Arab geographer	1100–1166
Magna Carta, 1215	Arabs use black (gun) powder in a gun	1304
Genghis Khan, 1162–1227	Chaucer's *Canterbury Tales*	ante 1400
Mali Empire expands, 1235		
Joan of Arc dies, 1431	Gutenberg Bible printed	1456
Inca Empire expands, 1438	Building at Zimbabwe	c. 15th C–c. 1750
Turks capture Constantinople, 1453	Vasco da Gama sails to India	1497–1498
Moors driven from Spain, 1492		
Columbus arrives in America, 1492		
	Martin Luther writes 95 Theses	1517
Cortez conquers Mexico		1519–1522
Mogul Dynasty established	Magellan names Pacific Ocean	1520
French settlements in Canada, 1534	Copernicus publishes heliocentric theory	1543
Turks defeated, Battle of Lepanto, 1571	Shakespeare	1564–1616
Burmese Empire at a peak	Muskets first used in Japan	*c.* 1580
Continuing Dutch activity in the East	Cervantes publishes *Don Quixote*	1605
Pilgrims land at Plymouth Rock, 1620	Taj Mahal begun	1632
Manchu Dynasty, China, 1644–1912	Palace of Versailles begun	1661
Peter the Great rules Russia, 1682–1725	Newton discovers the Law of Gravity	1682
	J. S. Bach, composer	1685–1750
Industrial Revolution begins, *c.* 1760	Mozart, composer	1756–1791
US Declaration of Independence	Quakers refuse to own slaves	1776
French Revolution begins	Washington, US President	1789
Napoleon defeated at Waterloo	Bolivar continues struggle, S. America	1815
Mexico becomes a Republic, 1824	S. B. Anthony, women's rights advocate	1820–1906
American Civil War, 1861–1865	Communist manifesto	1848
Lincoln's *Emancipation Proclamation*		1863
Canada becomes a Dominion	French Impressionism begins	1867
Serfdom abolished in Russia, 1861	Mahatma Gandhi	1869–1948
Cetewayo, King of the Zulus, 1872	Edison invents phonograph	1877
	First modern Olympic Games	1896
First World War, 1914–1918	Model T Ford constructed	1909
Bolshevik Revolution in Russia, 1918	Bohr theory of the atom	1913
	US Constitution gives women the vote	1920
Second World War		1939–1945
United Nations Charter		1945

Acknowledgments

Thanks are due to the following for permission to reproduce photographs:
p. 1, p. 24, Pitkin Unichrome; p. 19, Bath Archaeological Trust Ltd.; p. 20 *r*, p. 27, HAB White; p. 26, p. 60 *l*, Roman Baths Museum, Bath; p. 35 *r*, p. 60 *t*, p. 90, p. 101, p. 251, p. 270 *b*, p. 272, p. 293, © Copyright The British Museum; p. 44, p. 158, Institute of Archaeology, Oxford; p. 45, © Photo RMN – H. Lewandowski; p. 58, p. 82 *l*, p. 100, p. 154, p. 183 *l*, p. 191, p. 202 *l*, p. 202 *r*, p. 204, p. 228 *t*, Photo Scala, Florence; p. 62, Museo Archeologico Nazionale, Naples; p. 64, Amey Roadstone Corporation; p. 65, Musée du Bardo, Tunis; p. 67, Österreichische NationalBibliothek, Vienna; p. 72, Cambridge University Committee for Aerial Photography; p. 79 *b*, Villa Romana del Casale, Sicily/Bridgeman Art Library; p. 80 *t*, Rheinisches Landes Museum, Trier; p. 80 *b*, p. 81, Museum of Classical Archaeology, Cambridge; p. 82 *r*, p. 165, p. 232, p. 242, CSCP; p. 118, p. 121, p. 136, Grosvenor Museum, Chester; p. 120, National Museums of Scotland; p. 122, Colchester Castle Museum; p. 123, Rex Features Ltd.; p. 124 *t*, D. Swarbrick c/o Grosvenor Museum, Chester; p. 124 *b*, Airviews; p. 127, Coventry Arts and Heritage; p. 141, Michael Holford; p. 157, English Heritage; p. 159 *t*, Ancient Art and Architecture Collection; p. 159 *b*, Whitby Museum; p. 174 *t*, AKG London/Peter Connolly; p. 174 *b*, Nathan Meron; p. 188, Baron Wolman; p. 190, Fitzwilliam Museum, Cambridge; p. 207, Mansell Collection; p. 208, Alberto Carpececi *Rome 2000 Years Ago* pub. Bonechi; p. 209, St. Albans Museums; p. 223, Convention and Visitor Development, Virginia Beach; p. 235, Manchester Museum; p. 250, Courtesy of the Museum of London; p. 269, Visual Publications; p. 270 *t*, Kunsthistorisches Museum, Vienna; p. 273 *b*, Musée royal du Mariemont, Morlanwelz, Belgium; p. 290, German Archaeological Institute, Rome.

Other photography by Roger Dalladay.

Every effort has been made to reach copyright holders. The publishers would be glad to hear from anyone whose rights they have unknowingly infringed.